D1117007

THE COLLAPSE OF FREEDOM OF EXPRESSION

CATHOLIC IDEAS FOR A SECULAR WORLD

O. Carter Snead, series editor

Under the sponsorship of the de Nicola Center for Ethics and Culture at the University of Notre Dame, the purpose of this interdisciplinary series is to feature authors from around the world who will expand the influence of Catholic thought on the most important conversations in academia and the public square. The series is "Catholic" in the sense that the books will emphasize and engage the enduring themes of human dignity and flourishing, the common good, truth, beauty, justice, and freedom in ways that reflect and deepen principles affirmed by the Catholic Church for millennia. It is not limited to Catholic authors or even works that explicitly take Catholic principles as a point of departure. Its books are intended to demonstrate the diversity and enhance the relevance of these enduring themes and principles in numerous subjects, ranging from the arts and humanities to the sciences.

THE COLLAPSE OF
FREEDOM OF
EXPRESSION

*Reconstructing the Ancient
Roots of Modern Liberty*

JORDI PUJOL

Foreword by
John Durham Peters

University of Notre Dame Press
Notre Dame, Indiana

University of Notre Dame Press
Notre Dame, Indiana 46556
undpress.nd.edu

All Rights Reserved

Copyright © 2023 by University of Notre Dame

Published in the United States of America

Library of Congress Control Number: 2022947715

ISBN: 978-0-268-20396-2 (Hardback)
ISBN: 978-0-268-20398-6 (WebPDF)
ISBN: 978-0-268-20395-5 (Epub)

Dedicated to Norberto González Gaitano
and the School of Church Communications
(Pontifical University of Santa Croce)

CONTENTS

FOREWORD

We Must Not Be Enemies

This book comes from a thinker immersed in the tradition of Christian humanism who faces the Anglo-American liberal tradition with judiciousness, erudition, and occasional—but highly productive—puzzlement. The result is an orchestration, rapprochement, or encounter of two rich (and by no means always internally homogenous) sources for thinking about free speech. The book is both classical and contemporary. It offers a traditional answer—in the best sense—for nontraditional times. It is a mansion of many chambers and draws on many disciplines: the history of ideas, law, philosophy, theology, ethics, politics, and media studies. Its case studies are highly informative, and if you want to learn about how chain reactions of news and outrage work in real time, for instance, this is the place. Fr. Jordi Pujol's account of the sources and ends of free speech assesses the confusions and commotions of our digital moment and is at once informative, compelling, and wise. The world would be a better place if we all heeded its teachings!

In its critical appreciation and reconstruction of the Anglo-American tradition of thinking about free speech, the book celebrates what the liberal tradition offers at its best: a vision of free speech as a human good. And yet the book checks the liberal tradition's tendency to become hollow and rootless, especially in the past century. Transgressive, offensive speech is not an end in itself. It is a means, a catalyst, a spice of liberty, a goad to education and reflection. Pujol has a genuine admiration for, along with a healthy skepticism toward, the Anglo-American tradition. He is no scold, spoilsport, or killjoy. He recognizes that satire can advance public debate and even afford public pleasure and amusement. Free speech can be fun!

Pujol's mode of thinking is to be consistently humane, open, reflective, and questioning, dialectically balancing, repeatedly steering us into paradoxes. In this he practices what he preaches. His analysis models the norms and attitudes it advances. Thus, though Pujol firmly supports free speech as a legal, political, and ethical principle, he also thinks those newspaper editors were wise who refused to reprint the *Charlie Hebdo* pictures that were designed to insult Islam. He prefers the Australian policy of recognizing the public realm as consisting of plural neutralities to the French policy of embracing a single, all-bulldozing *laïcité* (secularism). His account of free speech does not ban subtlety and prudence: it calls for them. For him, free speech is not what he colorfully calls a "perpetual carnival" of suspended rules! A philosophy of free speech should not disable our discernment about what is good and bad in the public realm. It should enhance it.

The book is thus also a diagnosis of modernity and of the hazards of burning up the finite fossil fuels of the European tradition. It is striking that early modern thinkers about free speech insisted on thick moral foundations. In his treatise *Areopagitica* (1644), for instance, John Milton stated that his purpose was "to advance the public good." Tunis Wortman, an early American lawyer influenced by Thomas Jefferson, wrote in his fascinating *Treatise, Concerning Political Inquiry, and the Freedom of the Press* (1800): "The freedom of speech and opinion, is not only necessary to the happiness of Man, considered as a Moral and Intellectual Being, but indispensably requisite to the perpetuation of Civil Liberty." Here he treats free speech as a question of moral and political philosophy and does so within a clear vision of human flourishing. Interestingly, Wortman's twin poles of danger—the extremes to which societies can lean or lurch in either direction—are "licentiousness" and "despotism," which he also sometimes calls "anarchy" and "tyranny." These worries, found among a variety of modern political thinkers concerned with the fate of democracy (such as Montesquieu, Madison, and Mill, to stick to the letter M), have a certain similarity to Pujol's extremes of relativism and fundamentalism. Chaos or confusion (as license) and compulsion or closure (as overreaction to the effects of license) have long been the dangers that haunt liberty in all of its forms.

Pujol deplores the separation of speech from morality and a purely formalist approach to the public realm (i.e., the principled indifference to the content, media, and effects of speech). In part, the thinkers of the Enlightenment saw the horrid effects of religious warfare and made a pragmatic compromise. Toleration was an expedient solution to violence based on religious difference. But this compromise stuffed faith into the private realm and flattened much of law into a question of process or form. The resulting risk was nihilism about the very materials of public life. Pujol calls for a reconstructed and richer genealogy of free speech that would place the toleration of extremity within a vision of the common good and of the discovery of truth. In this he mirrors a point that emerged in a 2004 discussion between two towering white-haired German professors born in the late 1920s, Jürgen Habermas and Joseph Ratzinger, the atheist critical theorist and the future Pope Benedict XVI: that modernity cannot be casual in its reliance upon the nonrenewable moral resources of Greek, Roman, Jewish, and Christian traditions. This book similarly engages in both a friendly and a serious exchange of views and a long-term vision of stewardship for our collective life.

Indeed, it is remarkable how systematically and scrupulously Pujol meets the liberal tradition on its own terms. He does not lead with his own theological framework or philosophical anthropology, though there is no question where he ultimately stands on the nature of God or humanity. Rather, he leaves his potentially partisan tenets in the background. In this book he seeks common ground and speaks the dominant secular language of scholarship. This was a point of Habermas—that people of faith bear an asymmetric burden in a secular public sphere because they need to be bilingual. They must translate their faith into terms that can pass through a plural and noncommitted public. (This is literally the case in that Pujol wrote this book in his second language, English, the current world tongue of scholarship as well as of the liberal tradition.) The decorum—along with, of course, respectful critique—displayed by the book's probing mode of analysis again proves its point. It also suggests something deeper: bilingualism is not only a burden but a blessing. One knows one's own language only if one learns another. In the same way, belief can grow in clarity and richness in being articulated for another. The public realm, at its best, can be the purifying distiller of belief.

Pujol, as noted, has an acute awareness of paradoxes. I appreciate his delicate dance around the question of the history of censorship by the Church. He is fully aware of the degree to which the history of fulminations against censorship has been anti-Catholic as well as anti-Muslim. Milton, for instance, is unremittingly sarcastic in *Areopagitica*, saying that popes act as if St. Peter had bequeathed them the keys to the press as well as the Church and that their censorship rakes "through the entrails of many an old good author, with a violation worse than any could be offered to his tomb." He observes that five imprimaturs can sometimes be seen "together dialogue wise in the piazza of one title-page, complimenting and ducking to each other with their shaven reverences." Milton's vituperation and harsh religious mockery shows that his support for extreme speech was not only an argument but a rhetorical practice.

Pujol argues instead, with qualifications, for the possibility of ecclesiastical censorship as pastoral care, as protecting the flock. More intriguingly, he shares a notion with Milton: that prohibition awakes desire. Perhaps, he notes, the Index of banned books even stimulated careful and engaged reading, borrowing Alasdair McIntyre's notion of reading dangerously. After all, Adam and Eve seem to have grown more interested in the tree of knowledge when it was forbidden, leading to the fortunate fall that made us all! Censorship, as G. K. Chesterton once observed, is a "theatrical problem." It is easy to get sucked into the melodrama and get outraged at the black-hatted villains, but none of us really believe in our heart of hearts that everything can or should be said or that the scarce real estate of the public realm should be completely without curation or moderation. Could liberalism learn something about pastoral care? Could it see that railing against censorship can stigmatize some groups? It is certainly worth a thought, especially if liberalism's core principle is humility, the conviction that there is always something to learn from the other. Milton put it beautifully: the free press "broke that triple ice clung about our hearts, and taught the people to see day." Perhaps the liberal tradition could unlearn its knee-jerk attack on censorship and recognize the costs of this unbending point of blind faith.

What would a Christian philosophy of free speech look like? Putting one forward is not Pujol's explicit task here, but his work tempts me to a few concluding reflections. The resources and challenges for such a philosophy are many. Milton quoted Paul with approval: "Prove all things; hold fast to that which is good." (Paul's word is *dokimazō*, which means to examine or test.) This could be the motto for a prosocial philosophy of free speech. Certainly, the Christian tradition authorizes an attitude of fearlessness in facing evil or extremity. As Milton suggested, the Holy

Spirit fears neither height nor depth. Jesus of Nazareth thus exhorted his followers to be wise enough to make friends with the Mammon of unrighteousness (Luke 16:9). What he meant is debated, but he seems to have endorsed the practice of living in the world in a savvy and active way. He also said that his followers should render unto Caesar and to God. You might find here a kind of separation of church and state, just as in the Roman saying that the gods can take care of their own injuries. The idea that the public realm must be left alone to make its mistakes and messes has a long warrant in the European tradition. Sometimes free speech is not pretty, and everyone knows that. (However, not everyone needs to celebrate it.)

But what do we do with all the biliousness and hostility in a thinker like Milton? Milton's call for free speech needed Catholics as a foil, just as *Charlie Hebdo* needed Islam as a foil. Yet enmity is the enemy in and of Christianity. The question is how to overcome enmity without succumbing to its logic. If one fights the other as an enemy, then doesn't one recreate the enmity one is trying to solve? In other words, could there be a philosophy of free speech that not only does not contradict itself by its deeds but also doesn't have (or need) enemies? What would a vision of free speech look like that was purged of disdain for the other (the prude, the believer, the untutored, the militant, the censor)?

Let's be honest: the Christian tradition has excelled not only in preaching charity but in producing harsh speech. Some contemporary theologians who call for an ontology of peace can do so in an extremely polemical (literally warlike) way (David Bentley Hart comes to mind). Milton, as we have seen, was a devout Christian with unparalleled gifts of sarcasm and invective. Martin Luther was also known for his sharp tongue, but so were the Church fathers. No one could outmatch a Church father in the art of chewing out a heretic; next to "De" (about) "Contra" (against) must be the most common word in the title of a patristic treatise! Paul of Tarsus was no slouch in meting out tongue-lashings ("You foolish Galatians") and neither, for that matter, was Jesus himself ("You strain out gnats and swallow camels")! Topping it off, God himself, as Milton insisted, used "vehement" language in scripture, using Hebrew vulgarities in the Torah. (Milton found the divine use of the F-word fully justified.) Christianity, in other words, has long been the breeding ground for antagonistic and hard speech and the justifier of its use. The apostles of love have long spiked their speech with fire.

On the other hand, Christianity, like Judaism before it, warns against othering. Both teach that the other is us. You are yourselves the strangers. The other is a self, and we might even discover, if we lose our life in love, that the self is an other. We might come to recognize the personhood of others and the strangeness of ourselves. This is also part of the adventure of free speech!

Pujol, fortunately, is not in the least a flame-thrower, and in this he taps into a deep well of Christian ethics: hospitality. Care for the homeless and the weak is where a genuine Christian philosophy and ethics should end up. I love his question about who is left homeless by all this talk of extremity and uninhibitedness that civil libertarians celebrate. Here he asks not only about the effects of extreme speech but the effects of advocating it. It is easy for such advocacy to become a kind of class warfare, an assertion of privilege, a claim to the higher moral and cultural ground. The well-educated, the secure, and males consistently favor free speech, as survey research shows. What would an account of free speech look like that aimed to care for the homeless and the weak? How would it handle the problem of innocence and experience? How can children be protected from inappropriate materials without infantilizing or patronizing the rest of the public? As one small and beautiful example, Pujol lauds the time that people in the New York City subway spontaneously started to scrub away racist graffiti using their small bottles of hand sanitizer! They never notified the police; they just came together as decent fellow-citizens contributing to the well-being, indeed the commonwealth, of public space. They weren't censoring; they were doing what public-spirited people in cities always do: they were cleaning up the trash. We do not need a legal proscription against hate speech to do something about it: openness and a robust civic culture can go together. Weak laws and a strong Church!

Christianity's doctrine is that hard hearts can be softened. Milton was right to see free speech's potential role in the melting of the ice around our hearts. But this is possible only where there is argument without enmity. Pujol rightly asks us to take *disputatio*, the long-standing practice of clashing arguments in Scholastic philosophy, as a more general model for public and personal growth. In the Jewish tradition, the similar practice of pairwise dialectical Talmud study is called *chavruta*. This word, at base, means *friendship*. I think this intuition lies at the core of Pujol's contribution, both in what he argues and in how he argues it. He marries the best parts of

Habermas and Ratzinger, of Milton and Rome. War interrupted by hospitality, tit-for-tat exchange turned into gift: this is what you call *grace*. It is the power of turning enemies into friends, the power of suspending all enmity.

In his first inaugural address in March 1861, President Abraham Lincoln spoke especially to the Southern states that had seceded from the Union: "We are not enemies, but friends. We must not be enemies." This was poignantly delivered on the eve of the Civil War, the bloodiest event in US history. If anyone had cause to fall into a logic of friend and enemy, it was Lincoln. But he didn't. Today, when every glance at Facebook or Twitter asks us to take sides and the news feed offers a parade of rogues for us to despise, Lincoln's wisdom bears repeating. There are no enemies. We must not be enemies. This is the deep insight at the heart of Fr. Jordi Pujol's work of outreach, understanding, and friendship.

John Durham Peters
New Haven, Connecticut
November 5, 2021

ACKNOWLEDGMENTS

I like to compare intellectual work to preparing a good meal. Ideas take time to mature within us. Writing an academic book is not preparing fast food but slow cooking. In this process, the flavors of different readings, conversations, and personal study blend together in a mysterious way. I want to acknowledge the people who accompanied me on this journey toward understanding the challenges posed by the exercise of freedom of expression. This project began in 2014 in Rome and matured throughout different research stays at the University of Notre Dame, the Columbia Journalism School, and Harvard University. I owe a debt of gratitude to my mentors and sponsors at the different universities: Norberto González Gaitano, José Maria La Porte, Ryan Madison, Carter O. Snead, Michael Schudson, and Urs Gasser.

My gratitude also goes to my colleagues at Santa Croce and at the De Nicola Center for Ethics and Culture for their support during my year at Notre Dame. I am extremely thankful to have been able share my thoughts with such outstanding scholars as Alasdair MacIntyre, Sean Kelsey, Rick Garnett, Randy Kozel, Gladden Pappen, Patrick Deneen, Paolo Carozza, and Brett Robinson, among others. I am also very much obliged to John D. Peters for his generous support and inspiration. What started as admiration for his work has led to the great blessing of true friendship. While attending some conferences around the United States, Steven J. Heyman, Ronald C. Arnett, Fred Turner, Edward Wassermann, Stephen J. A. Ward, Kathleen B. Culver, Catherine Waite, Paolo Granata, and Dennis D. Cali all provided particularly helpful feedback. The wonderful opportunity to be in touch with Michael Novak was limited to email, as he passed away some weeks before we had planned to meet.

I am grateful for the conversations and the advice that Michael Schudson, Richard R. John, Andie Tucher, Todd Gitlin, Emily Bell, and Hawley Johnson offered during the six months that I spent at the Columbia Journalism School in New York. My gratitude also extends to the fine people in the PhD program, particularly to Alex Gonçalves, Ros Donald, Efrat Nechushtai, Angela Woodall, and Bernat Ivancsics. We shared the anxieties that all PhD candidates have, as well as the pleasure of friendship and intellectual growth in our early-morning PEBC meetings led by Professor Richard R. John. I spent the last period of research for this book in Cambridge, hosted by the Berkman Klein Center at Harvard, where I was able to learn from the remarkable work of Urs Gasser, Jonathan Zittrain, and the online free speech team led by Amar Ashar. Their work on speech and content in the context of the Internet and the interplay of law and technology has been an inspiration to me. In the area of social media I also benefited from the digital mastery and research of Kevin De Souza.

Supplying this book's many ingredients has been facilitated by a large group of terrific librarians at the Pontifical University of Santa Croce, the Hesburgh Library at Notre Dame, Butler Library at Columbia, and the Widener and Langdell Library at Harvard, as well as the staff of the aforementioned centers. My gratitude goes to them for their patience and generous support. Also to Kira Howes and Marilyn Martin for their brilliant assistance in polishing the text, as well as to the many people who supported me, even with their prayers: my mother and siblings, Lucía Ramírez's family, and a long list of friends. Finally, there is an editor behind every book who makes the project happen. I am very grateful to Margaret Cabaniss, research and publications manager of De Nicola Center for Ethics and Culture; to the director of the University of Notre Dame Press, Stephen M. Wrinn, and to Rachel Kindler at the press; and to Carter O. Snead, editor of the series "Catholic Ideas for a Secular World." Like every good meal, each intellectual work is the result of the careful blending of ingredients provided by many important collaborators. This project could not have come to fruition without them.

Introduction

Freedom of expression is one of the most emblematic buildings on the skyline of democracy. By virtue of its visibility and centrality, it is more vulnerable than other such buildings to threats that take shape in every historical period in the form of restrictions (content censorship) or compulsions (the imposition of ideas). This book is a study of the sustainability of this building, this freedom of expression constructed by liberal architects between the seventeenth and the nineteenth centuries. The political project that Milton, Locke, and Mill contributed to and elaborated on broke with the earlier period but it did not arise out of nothing. These classical liberal authors borrowed some of their construction materials from preceding cultural traditions (from Athens, Jerusalem, Rome, and Medieval Europe), especially the notion of justice and the separation between morality and law.

This building, made from liberal stones, is supported by the various philosophical, theological, and juridical pillars that sustain it, such as the separation between church and state and the creation of a secular public sphere where all beliefs are freely expressed without any one being particularly privileged, as well as the institution of political power that would protect a person's inalienable rights, including the freedom to express one's own ideas in public without repression. Tolerance of evil and error is the key facet in the justification of the general limits of public order and public morality, as well as the boundaries between freedom of speech and other rights (equality, religious freedom, and so on).

Threats to a building's integrity can come from external actors or from internal flaws in construction. Damaging external agents can take the form of censorship of public discourse by governing authorities, or it can come from the imposition of ideas by *orthodox* factions that refuse to permit criticism or dissent. Among these are those engaged in the religious fanaticism that caused violent reactions against drawings of Mohammed and against the abuses of the illustrators of *Charlie Hebdo*, as well as an aggressive intolerance of anyone who dares to doubt new dogmas on gender identity or secularism. This book analyses these external and internal threats by looking at paradigmatic cases in Europe and the United States that are causing serious cracks in the edifice of freedom of expression.

Along with these threats, the development of the Internet and its deregulation have led to a real upheaval in the project of freedom of expression. The digital ecosystem, by its very nature, amplifies the violence of hateful discourse that—with words and images—tries to intimidate people on racial, sexual, religious, or ethnic grounds. The damage caused is indelible. This is a critical test of the moral and legal structure of the freedom of expression.

Moderators of digital platforms report that 60 to 70 percent of videos are spam and pornography.[1] Flourishing all over the Internet are "hate crimes and an alarming increase [in] youth suicides that result from social media vitriol; inciting mass shootings such as the 2019 attack in Christchurch, stabbings and bombings; recruitment of extremists, including entrapment and sex-trafficking of girls as fighter brides; threats against public figures, including the 2019 verbal attack against an anti-Brexit politician and hybrid (racist, anti-women, anti-immigrant) hateful threats of violence against a US member of the British royal family; and renewed anti-Western hate in the 2019 post-ISIS landscape associated with support for Osama Bin Laden's son and Al Qaeda."[2]

If we add that a high percentage of activity on these social networks is generated by automated bots, the conclusion that follows is disconcerting: the platforms seem to be losing the battle to generate rational and open debate in this networked public sphere.

In turn, the Internet has opened up many free spaces that had previously been the domains of people with more resources and a greater capacity for influence. Among these we can consider the access to texts, music, and art, as well as the distribution of ideas themselves, which were previously marginalized but not marginal.

The philosophy of freedom of expression, conceived in the context of paper and the political rhetoric of the seventeenth and eighteenth centuries, is rather well adapted to the audiovisual media of the nineteenth and twentieth centuries (newspapers, radio, film, and television). However, is it equally well adapted to the digital ecosystem of the twenty-first century, which is a mixture of all of the elements described above? We have always had bad actors, but their influence was limited thanks to constraints of time and space and the fact that public authorities worked to ensure the maintenance of legally defined limits of tolerance. The global reach of the Internet and its absence of authority have changed the rules today. Private companies now moderate the public conversation of millions of people (approximately three billion, in the case of Facebook) as an essential part of their business model (based on content, attention, and publicity), but without disclosing their criteria. The power wielded by these technology companies makes it necessary to regulate their activity.

This book identifies the deficiencies inherent in the European Enlightenment paradigm that weaken the foundations of freedom of expression and explain the cracks that threaten its strength. The Enlightenment separated freedom and tolerance from their natural allies — truth and good — to base them on an ethical relativism. It adopted legal positivism as the definitive solution, but its purview is limited because abuse of expression is also a moral question. The proposed neutrality of the public sphere turns out to be fictitious. Liberalism requires suspending moral judgment, but it has its own ideas about discourse and the person. The crisis of truth that caused concern for a good part of modernity has had many consequences, including the merely formal use of words and concepts. This has protected opportunists who use free speech in an abusive way. The contemporary tradition of freedom of expression is left without satisfying responses to those who suffer the consequences of the most harmful speech.

For many free speech theorists, only *actions* can produce objective harm. Anything else constitutes subjective offenses. But if words don't mean anything, then anything goes. Faced with the real harm caused by abuses of expression, the liberal formula suggests "more speech" as the only solution without providing justice for the damage caused. In this way, public speech becomes a kind of pitched battle in which he who yells louder has more influence and power, and he who imposes his view with violence wins.

In this book I have accepted John Durham Peters's invitation, in *Courting the Abyss: Free Speech and the Liberal Tradition*, to reconstruct the foundational ethics of freedom of expression. In describing his goal when writing that book, Peters said, "My aim was to purify the [liberal] tradition of some of its excesses and pathologies such as its tendency to glory in its supposed ethical superiority."[3] In these pages I delve into some of the "illiberal tendencies" that Peters mentions, which emerge in the examples discussed throughout the book.[4]

In addition to identifying the problem and its historical and philosophical roots, I propose a series of ideas for the purpose of reformulating them. These are taken from treasured legal and philosophical intellectual traditions, not in a nostalgic way but, as T. S. Eliot puts it:

> Time present and time past
> Are both perhaps present in time future
> And time future contained in time past.
> *Four Quartets* (1943)

Finding convincing solutions to the fundamental problems of contemporary freedom of expression requires seeking inspiration from the central ideas articulated by Milton, Mill, or America's Founding Fathers without taking them out of the context of the Christian ethos of the world in which these men lived or separating them from the principles in which their thought was immersed. Contemporary liberal speech has been centered around an academic justification of the expressive freedom of the transgressors (Nazis, the Ku Klux Klan, and others) and around rationalizing the ability of the marketplace of ideas to promote truth, but it has been incapable of distinguishing between freedom and license. The classical theorists of freedom of expression never posited a supposed "right to offend" that normalizes any and every expression in the name of the principle of freedom.

For the purpose of resolving the dilemmas of freedom of expression and re-examining the authors who proposed it, I suggest incorporating arguments that come from other disciplines. Pragmatics of language allow us to distinguish the internal rules proper to expression, thereby more objectively identifying where language is abused. Philosophy and moral theology shed light on human intentionality and frame these dilemmas as a question of justice, in the classical sense of "giving to each what is his own."

Identifying abusive uses of expression requires the examination of discursive actions (*speech acts*) in light of the rules of the philosophy of language. There are discursive actions that are not "expressions of ideas" so much as exaltations of insult or mockery. An expression does not always have the same meaning. In language and with the giving of information, it is not only what is said that is important (the speech dimension) but also the non-speech elements and what surrounds what is said, because words are actions, and some of their possible effects are foreseeable. The pragmatics of speech allow us to distinguish between the intent and the meaning of expressions.

With the evolution of analytic philosophy, especially the philosophy of language and theories on the act of speech, we have the tools for analyzing all expressions and classifying them according to the three categories of purpose (referential, fictional, and pragmatic discourse), thereby making ourselves able to judge whether they are fraudulent uses of expression that violate the internal "grammar" of each type of speech. What is happening is that these theories on the act of speech are unknown to the dominant school of thought on freedom of expression.

Transgression and harmful speech constitute a central question for freedom of expression. In theology a redemptive sense is given to the abyss of evil, to *mysterium iniquitatis*. There should also be room for this idea in our discussion. As in the construction of any building, contrary forces are key elements in the stress resistance of any material; the wear and tear of the weather or the vibrations of a subterranean train test the building. In the case of freedom of expression, the critical point comes when extreme or harmful speech is produced: up to what point should we tolerate it? The law, the philosophy of language, and moral theology give complementary reasons for a solution that will never be definitive and will always be "prudential." Theological traditions based on Aristotle, Augustine, and Aquinas underscore the need to tolerate transgressions to a certain degree for the sake of a higher good. We cannot—and indeed, should not—prohibit all offenses or immorality. This principle was inspired not by Enlightenment optimism or by a utilitarian calculation but by a tradition that looked at the common good and considered that evil does not have the last word.

The thesis of this book is that the liberal tradition of freedom of expression was built upon legal and moral foundations that were borrowed from an inherited tradition (based on Christianity, Greek philosophy, and Roman law) that has been taken for granted. Modernity disregarded these roots, trying to build a new order (a notion of tolerance based on skepticism, creating a "neutral" public sphere where faith has no impact, at least in public life), and redefined many key concepts under this new paradigm: a new "idea of man" and freedom, but also of law and justice, with its moral and legal positivism. As Adrian Vermule puts it: "The law has officially disavowed its own classical heritage but in practice draws upon and develops it, all while afflicted by a strange *amnesia*."[5] Modernity constructed something new but—de facto—lived out of an inherited ethos. These rational foundations were taken for granted for centuries. Now, in our contemporary, nearly post-Christian world, the new claims on free speech rely on "modern" ideas that have created a void and cannot hold the building together. With this epistemological vacuum left by modernity, the contemporary tradition of freedom of expression is left without the ability to give a convincing response to those who suffer the consequences of the most harmful speech. My call to refurbish the liberal building of freedom of expression starts from claiming the soundness of an inherited tradition.

On one hand, we must recover the realist concept of law and re-establish the natural link that tolerance and freedom had with goodness and the truth of what things are. The re-establishment of this objective moral link allows us to distinguish abuse from the legitimate right—individual and collective—to produce satire. On the other hand, we must rediscover the fact that words—in some circumstances—have the force of actions. With these premises we can recognize that some abuses of expression can cause objective damage and that, insofar as they do, they constitute a question of justice that is not merely emotional.

The philosophy of freedom of expression cannot continue to ignore the complaints of the various racial, religious, or ethnic minorities who point out the objective harm caused by hateful speech. It is not so much about recognizing identities as it is about respecting human dignity when faced with abuse. We must not forget that freedom of expression was not originally incompatible with equality. Its opposite is an imbalance that must be repaired. The path forward is nothing other than "pluralizing liberalism itself by discovering the liberalism of the other."[6] Only blind arrogance could impede this process of self-critique and reconstruction.

In the first part of the book we shall identify the main debates and tensions that affect the philosophy of freedom of expression by looking at paradigmatic cases. The *Charlie Hebdo* and *Jyllands-Posten* cartoons raise the question of offensive speech: does "anything go" in the name of freedom of expression? Is it OK to use freedom of expression to beat up on Islam? On American campuses, a tension is arising between freedom of speech and equality and inclusion: are they irreconcilable? Examples like the Masterpiece Cakeshop case point to compelled speech as a new form of intolerance. The fight between *orthodoxies* in the public sphere is not new. The danger is in the state taking sides, thus changing the project of pluralist coexistence. Both censorship and the imposition of ideas are threats to freedom of expression, as both co-opt individual conscience. New modes of censorship on the Internet and the private moderation of public conversation carried out by technological platforms challenge the foundations of liberal thought on freedom of expression in new and unprecedented ways.

The second part begins by offering a roadmap of the main criticisms of the contemporary liberal tradition by communitarians, libertarians, feminists, and critical race theorists to then analyze the gaps and contradictions of these criticisms. These include a fabricated notion of tolerance, with no solid reference to good and truth. This could function in the context of the Enlightenment, but subsequently, opportunistic use of transgression amplified by Miltonian tolerance betrayed the emptiness on which it was based. The liberal tradition has paid almost no attention to the philosophy of language and its rules for identifying abusive use, limiting itself instead to a uniform understanding of speech. The neutrality of the public sphere has been shown to be fictitious, and liberalism — particularly in its *comprehensive* version — has a partisan idea of humankind. Modernity's crisis of truth has destroyed trust in the ability of practical reason to objectively distinguish evil from error and has led to mere formal use of words.

In the third part we shall look at the philosophical roots that explain the gaps and contradictions identified earlier and we shall recount the historical journey of these ideas. Political freedoms have their origins in two very different liberal revolutions: the French and American Revolutions. The distinct foundations of these freedoms and the differing European and American legal traditions crystalized two ways of resolving the critical question of harm caused by expression. The first one protects human dignity with hate speech laws, and the second defends freedom against any interference by the state. Both show their limitations when faced with a timeless dilemma. The abuse of anti-discrimination laws can undermine the principle of freedom, and the absolute defense of freedom can be turned into a refuge for opportunists. The defense of rights and freedoms has taken on a distinct Harvard School and Holmesian disposition. Finally, in this historical-philosophical context, we confront the question of the legitimacy of censorship and of the new kinds of censorship that are currently arising.

The fourth part contains a proposal for rebuilding the basis of freedom of expression. From a theoretical standpoint, this is an appeal to find inspiration for more solid legal and moral foundations for freedom of expression in our inherited tradition. That is to say, it is an appeal to evaluate the limits of legal positivism and consider the readoption of the classical concept of justice that governed the law for many centuries. Then, in a much more applied way, we shall revisit the limits of freedom of expression. Additionally, I propose incorporating the field of pragmatics of language as well as theological and ethical concepts of human intentionality as new, complementary disciplines that can help to reform Mill's concept of harm. This reconstruction project involves bridging the chasm created between the secular and the sacred and recognizing how religion is a font of meaning for millions of people and so, as such, it too has an inescapable place in the construction of a pluralist public sphere.

PART I

Freedom of Expression under Threat

Emblematic Cases

ONE

I Am Not Charlie Hebdo

Defending Freedom of Expression
but Not Its Content

THE TERRORIST ATTACK AND THE HISTORICAL
DEVELOPMENT OF THE MAGAZINE

On January 7, 2015, two armed terrorists entered the Paris headquarters of the satirical weekly magazine *Charlie Hebdo*,[1] killed twelve people, and wounded eleven others. The terrorists carried out the attack while yelling, "Allah is great" and other similar expressions as signs of vengeance for the magazine's continued offences against Islam and its prophet Mohammed. The attack resonated widely throughout the world. Four days afterward, there was a public demonstration with the motto *Je suis Charlie* in which hundreds of thousands of citizens and public figures in forty countries participated.

This was not the first time the weekly publication had been attacked by Islamic radicals. In November 2011, after having published cartoons from the Danish magazine *Jyllands-Posten* on its cover and mocking

Mohammed and Islamic law, the French weekly suffered a Molotov cocktail attack that damaged some of the magazine's facilities. After this episode, the director and other members of the editorial board lived under police protection, and the headquarters of *Charlie Hebdo* was guarded by the French police. Despite the threats and defamation litigation they faced, the editors did not change the publication's editorial bent, which is based on insults and offensive and denigrative humor.

The magazine not only satirized political life but focused especially on attacking religions (particularly Christianity and Islam) and on racist themes. For example, in 2012 they characterized a black minister as a monkey and showed the prophet Mohammed naked or engaged in pornographic activities. They treated the Christian God with similar blasphemies and published offensive and grotesque caricatures of Pope Benedict XVI.

CITIZENS' REACTIONS: *JE SUIS CHARLIE* AND *JE NE SUIS PAS CHARLIE*

From the first moment of the latest tragedy, several different viewpoints were captured under the motto *Je suis Charlie*, which made it difficult to have a clear understanding of the arguments in play. It was unclear if the demonstrations were in support of the victims and in denunciation of terrorism, in defense of freedom of expression, or both. On one side, the terrorist attack was castigated and support for the victims expressed; on the other, this feeling was identified with support for the principle of freedom of expression, typical of Western democracies. But the motto *Je suis Charlie* went further, because it identified freedom of expression with the content and offensive style of the magazine. The attack was also associated with a feeling of animosity toward Islam.

In order to properly analyze the reactions, I believe three types should be distinguished: citizens' reactions in the streets and via social media, the reactions of the media, and the reactions of politicians and public authorities.

There was a massive reaction in the streets of the major European capitals, including demonstrations of solidarity at French consulates and embassies, with particular intensity in Paris, where gatherings, banners, candles, flower offerings, and so on were especially abundant. The motto *Je suis Charlie* went viral on social networks in the form of memes, avatars, or hashtags.

Not long after the attack, the French artist/journalist Joachim Roncin published a message via Twitter that immediately went viral: *Je suis Charlie*.[2] In a few hours the phrase had spread as a slogan in support of the victims in the form of a hashtag (#JeSuisCharlie), garnering 3.5 million tweets worldwide that day.[3] The hashtag peaked on January 7 at 9:30 p.m., with 6,500 tweets per minute. A study by Giglietto and Lee found that most of the tweets were written in French (30 percent), English (25 percent), and Spanish (12 percent), even though all of them kept the hashtag in French.[4]

In turn, other mottos came out that showed the above-mentioned confusion. Some who did not identify with the offensive editorial choices of the magazine did not hesitate to reply with *Je ne suis pas Charlie/Ne pas Charlie*. Between January 7 and 11, some 74,047 tweets were posted using the hashtag #JeNeSuisPasCharlie. Muslims who felt offended because the magazine ridiculed their faith and culture started the hashtag *Je suis Ahmed*[5] in reference to the Muslim police officer who died in the attack, or *Je suis juif* (I am Jewish), showing the discrepancy of the racist and blasphemous style of the magazine and as a reminder that on January 9 four Jews were also assassinated, in a Kosher restaurant.

Giglietto and Lee report that "the hashtag #JeSuisCharlie was reported to have been created at 12:59 p.m. on January 7, immediately after the shooting at around 11:30 a.m. The first tweet with #JeNeSuisPasCharlie was published at 1:46 p.m. in its local time zone, less than an hour later than the original, affirmative hashtag."[6] The message that #JeNeSuisPasCharlie expresses was reactive and brought together diverse opinions.[7] It functioned more as a "crisis/emergency–related hashtag" than as a "media spectacle–related hashtag."[8] According to Bruns and Stieglitz, crisis hashtags (#tsunami, for example) exist to cite external sources and incite retweets, while media event hashtags (#royalwedding, for example) exist more for sharing information.[9] In the case of #JeNeSuisPasCharlie, 41 percent of the messages contained links to other sources and 70 percent were retweets.[10]

Several studies of the above-referenced hashtags have been conducted.[11] In the literature written, this new idea emerged: "The language used to criticize the counterpart hashtag was emotionally charged and provocative. On one hand, #JeSuisCharlie supporters criticized the emergence of the negative hashtag by describing it as 'shocking,' 'insulting,' and 'disgusting' and addressed their criticism specifically to #JeNeSuisPasCharlie."

And, "on the other hand, #JeNeSuisPasCharlie tweeters described #JeSuis Charlie as an inherently 'Islamophobic bandwagon' full of 'bigotry' and 'hypocrisy.' In what was one of the most recurring arguments, #JeSuis Charlie supporters were accused of invoking the 'free speech' argument only when it conformed to their ideals and beliefs."[12]

Therefore, the social media conversation on Twitter was mostly emotional and supportive of the hashtag #JeSuisCharlie. There was some disapproval (#JeNeSuisPasCharlie) that didn't achieve the same spread, though. A more reflective conversation unfolded in the mainstream media.

THE MEDIA'S REACTION

European media outlets aligned themselves almost unanimously with the magazine under the motto *Je suis Charlie*, identifying the attack as an assault on the principle of freedom of expression. The critical outlook expressed by the mottos *Je ne suis pas Charlie* and *I am not Charlie Hebdo*[13] came mostly from Anglo-Saxon outlets, which distinguished between solidarity with the editors and illustrators who lost their lives and the ideological position of the magazine and its ideas.

On the day following the terrorist attack, *New York Times* editor Dan Baquet wrote an article that appeared on the editorial page outlining a way to determine what goes beyond satire: "We have a standard that is long held and that serves us well: that there is a line between gratuitous insult and satire. Most of these are gratuitous insult."[14] This line of demarcation between freedom of expression and gratuitous insult drew strong criticism,[15] but the *New York Times* took the lead, and their approach was echoed by other international outlets.

In the first few hours after the attack, there was an initiative to create solidarity with the magazine and honor the victims by republishing the blasphemous cartoons from *Charlie Hebdo*, but it was not unanimous. On one hand, some were amenable to the idea of republishing the cartoons, like David Callaway, editor of *USA Today*: "If it's news, we publish."[16] Or the well-known multimedia journalist Jeff Jarvis: "If you're the paper of record, if you're the highest exemplar of American journalism, if you expect others to stand by your journalists when they are threatened, if you respect your audience to make up its own mind, then dammit stand by *Charlie Hebdo* and inform your public. Run the cartoons."[17]

The editors of the *New York Times* decided not to publish the material,[18] a decision shared by other major international outlets like the BBC, CNN, and the *Washington Post*. Martin Baron, executive director of the *Washington Post*, argued, "[The Post] doesn't publish material that is pointedly, deliberately, or needlessly offensive to members of religious groups."[19] The associate editor of the *New York Times*, Philip B. Corbett, said that his paper did not publish material that was "deliberately intended to offend religious sensibilities."[20] The editor of the *Guardian*, Alan Rusbridger, indicated that his paper shared many of *Charlie Hebdo*'s journalistic values, including the need to offend, but claimed that there is some offensive material "that the *Guardian* would never in the normal run of events publish."[21] The Associated Press also reasoned that it would not publish the pictures because it did not want to be the "conveyor belt for images and actions aimed at mocking or provoking people on the basis of religion, race, or sexual orientation."[22] The vice president of the agency, Santiago Lyon, explained why they decided not to publish: "We've taken the view that we don't want to publish hate speech or spectacles that offend, provoke or intimidate, or anything that desecrates religious symbols or angers people along religious or ethnic lines.... We don't feel that's useful."[23]

The dilemma for and the pressure on European media to get in line and publish these cartoons was great. Timothy Garton Ash, a well-known professor at Oxford and expert in freedom of speech, led the initiative on the day after the attack: "All of Europe's means of communication should respond to the Islamic terrorists in Paris by a coordinated publication next week of selected drawings from *Charlie Hebdo* and a commentary on why they're doing it."[24] To advance this initiative, he took the argument to the extreme: "If the newspapers don't publish the images the terrorists win."[25] Such a coordinated solidarity action never took place.[26] Ultimately, some newspapers published the drawings, but many others did not, especially in the United Kingdom and the United States. Some papers did not publish the images in the papers but did publish them in their online editions.

The majority of cartoonists honored their colleagues at *Charlie Hebdo*,[27] but there were some critical voices that emerged, like those of Joe Sacco and Carlos Latuff. Two days after the attack, Sacco expressed his concern for the victims with a page containing ten cartoons, and he said: "My first reaction to the murders at the Charlie Hebdo offices in Paris was not bold defiance. I did not feel like beating my chest and reaffirming the principles of free speech."[28] Plus, he described *Charlie Hebdo*'s style as a "vapid way to use the pen," which in many ways is in accordance with its objectives. "When we draw a line we are often crossing one too, because lines on paper are a weapon, and satire is meant to cut to the bone. But whose bone? What exactly is the target? And why?"[29] In the same sense, the Brazilian cartoonist Latuff sent off his own cartoon with a tweet on January 15, 2015: "Freedom of speech? Not if you're dealing with Israel! #JeNeSuisPasCharlie."[30]

Two broader lessons emerge from assessing these views of journalists: the fact that the magazine labeled itself as *transgressive* does not excuse its irresponsible journalistic practices, nor should it shield it from criticism. The exercise of satiric power is not a license to act as if "everything goes"; it comes with certain ethical responsibilities to meet publishing standards. And secondly, although the magazine claims that it spares no political sides, social groups, or religions, the slant of its resume speaks for itself.

Two debates began (which we shall look at in Part II). The first is about whether there is a right to offend. Amos Guiora, from the Center for Global Justice, said: "*Charlie Hebdo* published cartoons deemed offensive to Islam. That is true. So what? Journals publish articles, satire and cartoons that offend other faiths and ethnicities. That is what satirists and cartoonists do. Edgy artists perform an invaluable public service. They deserve our fullest support and protection. Their voices must be heard, no matter how offensive an opinion might seem or the discomfort it might cause. Otherwise, the most precious values of our society will 'not be.'"[31] On the other hand, academics like Paul Cliteur, a professor of law in Holland, posed the dilemma thus:

> Should we exercise restraint? No. If we want to uphold the principles of a free society we certainly should not. But because there are hardly any private individuals left who want to take the role of the martyr, anonymous publishing will become more prevalent. We're back in 17th and 18th century Europe when religious criticism as exercised by Spinoza, Voltaire, Rousseau, Diderot and others, was published anonymously or under nicknames.[32]

Returning to the arguments against supporting Garton Ash's initiative, the editor of *Guardian* contended that the real reason was not to betray the newspaper's principles,[33] and Chris Boffey, the former news editor of the English publications the *Observer*, the *Sunday Telegraph*, and the *Mirror* concluded that even though there is an ingrained tradition of satire in English culture, "in this country being offensive for offensive's sake, has never been a tradition."[34] This seems like another version of the *common sense* moral argument, in defense of a responsible exercise of the freedom of expression.

Glenn Greenwald (of the *Intercept*), a jurist and well-known journalist, questioned the underlying premise in a tweet: "When did it become true that to defend someone's free speech rights, one has to publish & even embrace their ideas? That apply in all cases?"[35] Greenwald established a key distinction between defending the *principle* and the *content* of expression, noting that if both are intermingled, it contravenes one of the classic principles of free speech theory, which holds that one can defend the right to "express harmful ideas" but that this tolerance is compatible with "condemning the idea itself" (its content).

The solidarity call of *Je suis Charlie* was not merely a defense of free expression; it required acceptance of the content of the magazine's drawings. This situation goes beyond mere support of the principle of freedom of expression, and that did not go unnoticed by many. The decisions to publish these drawings and not others, in this political-social situation, by this means but not another means, are carefully deliberated and calculated. If one decides that calculating the possible effects is not part of the decision, it means that one must choose the alternate option, which in this case is the irresponsible one. We shall take a closer look at this question in Part II when we look at intentionality.

POLITICIANS' ATTITUDES

We could provide a thorough exposition of the particular statements by politicians in solidarity with the victims and in castigating terrorism, but it would not add much to the substance of our discussion. Among these statements, that of UK Prime Minister David Cameron stands out. Cameron said that he was going to join the masses in Paris "to celebrate *Charlie Hebdo*'s values."[36] Although these are striking words, I think that they express volatile convictions. In the day-to-day world of political events there are many different interests at play and a variety of implicated actors, all of which creates an unstable vortex. At the same time, it is very much a reality that is constructed — in large part — by the declarations of these same politicians, which change as a function of the interests or tendencies involved. In this tempest of declarations, it seems as though some were buried in favor of others, but information technology is a means of documenting them. Take, as a brief example, what occurred with Manuel Valls, former prime minister of France.

During the days following the terrorist attack, Valls made grand gestures of admiration for *Charlie Hebdo*, making it out to be a defender of freedom, satire, and tolerance.[37] This contradicted the opinion that he had expressed some months before, when, as minister of the interior, he forbade certain performances by the comedian Dieudonné, condemning him publicly for ridiculing Zionism and for his criticism of Israel.[38] The limits of freedom of expression are difficult to determine, but the double standard hurts the credibility of politicians such as Valls.

In the same vein, a significant event was immortalized by a staged photograph that showed forty-nine heads of state behind a banner, as if they were at the head of the huge citizen mobilization that occurred on January 11 in Paris. The reality was that security constraints required the leaders to demonstrate on their own while protected and far from the front of the protest. The media hid this reality from the public and presented a photomontage as the image of a real populist demonstration.

THE EDITORIAL BENT OF THE MAGAZINE
AFTER THE TERRORIST ATTACK

At the beginning of this chapter, we gave a summary of *Charlie Hebdo*'s historical editorial bent. At this juncture it is relevant to refer to two polemics generated by the new director of the magazine, Laurent Sourisseau Riss, confirming that the offensive style of the magazine is not circumstantial but rather constitutive of its business model.

The manager of the magazine had no scruples about using the death of a Syrian child (Aylan Kurdi), left lying on a Turkish shore of the Mediterranean, and relating that to the immigration crisis in Mediterranean Europe. Riss signed the drawing from September 2015, which had words that read: "Proof that Europe is Christian" and showed a Jesus-like figure walking on the water while a child's figure wearing shorts is lying face-down in the water, with Jesus saying, "Christians walk on water" and a speech bubble coming from the dead child saying, "Muslim children sink." Nor did Riss refrain from publishing a cartoon from January 2016—a year after the Paris attacks—in which the artist criticized and satirized sexual abuses and robberies that took place on New Year's Eve in Cologne (Germany), presumably perpetrated by immigrants seeking asylum. The first small illustration shows a drowned child on the beach in Turkey with the question "What would little Aylan have grown up to be?" and a second drawing offering a response, with two young men chasing girls with las-civious intentions and the phrase "A groper in Germany."

The fact that the French magazine used Aylan shows that it remains faithful to values that go beyond satire and that it has no problem with humiliating the human condition. Although the general reaction was one of rejection, the magazine still benefits from its status as victim. The fundamental ethical debate is still eclipsed by the iconic status that the magazine has attained. I think that, with time and the reflection it affords, the critical position that the Anglo-Saxon media took regarding the confused messages and consequences of the slogan *Je suis Charlie* will help the intellectual debate to gain better clarity on this paradigmatic case.

The almost immediate spontaneous reaction of solidarity with *Charlie Hebdo* from millions of people shows the consistency of support for the principle of freedom of expression and the rejection of violence as a mode of censorship. From the communicative perspective, the difficulty was that the messages became muddled: support for the victims and for the principle of free speech was mixed up with the content of the speech of the magazine. It is clear to me that most of the millions of demonstrators were not adhering to Charlie Hebdo's agenda: they were not haters of Islam, against immigrants, or anti-Catholic. The thumbs-down given by Anglo-American media (for example, by opinion writer David Brooks in a column in the *New York Times* titled "I Am Not Charlie Hebdo" and others) sparked this remarkable debate. Mainstream media unmasked a tricky instrumentalization of free speech. That is why *Charlie Hebdo* is no "free speech martyr." As we shall see further on, the philosophy of freedom of expression stands in a difficult and unstable equilibrium between fostering maximum expressive liberty and protecting justice and human dignity to safeguard public order and public morality. In any case, freedom of speech is not intended to be a weapon against religion, race, or any human condition. The risk of tolerating too much is that those acting in bad faith can find refuge in the principle of free speech. But the option of censorship is not the solution. The rule of law and growth in morality are both needed. As we shall see later, there is a boundary between insult and satire that can be distinguished using common sense.

SATIRE AND GRATUITOUS INSULT

Álvaro d'Ors saw common sense as a necessary "practical philosophy for jurists" that is determined by "the simplicity of the common individual reason of each one: it is not the feeling of the multitudes, but that of each non-insane man whom we can face individually."[39] It is the simplicity of seeing things as they are. The Cambridge Dictionary defines *common sense* as "the basic level of practical knowledge and judgment that we all need to help us live in a reasonable and safe way" and as "the ability to use good judgment in making decisions and to live in a reasonable and safe way." Three key elements emerge from these definitions: it is a question of applied knowledge that involves a judgment that is reasonable. These are the very same elements that for many centuries we have called "natural law" or the "law of nature": an internal order in nature that manifests itself in biology and in human beings. It is an internal rational capacity to discern and a mandate to conduct our lives by doing good and avoiding evil. For the very reason of being a law of nature, this internal order is universal (for all cultures and civilizations) and permanent (for all times). That is why, according to Chesterton, "men do not differ much about what things they will call evils; they differ enormously about what evils they will call excusable."[40]

In the inner realm—which some call conscience or practical reason—we are able to see and distinguish what is true and grasp what is just: not in general, but in the here and now. As a result, I frame the distinction between insult and satire as a rational-moral judgment, looking at the object, the circumstances, and the purpose. This judgment is not only subjective but related to truth and justice, and anyone can grasp it because it is rational, universal, and permanent. For that reason, I consider that humor will adopt infinite ways of expressing itself, but our capacity to grasp "things as they are" makes men and women capable of judging whether a given expression is irony or sarcasm, satire or insult. We will touch on that issue, from different angles, in chapters 8, 18, and 19.

I believe that the production of genuine satire is an invaluable skill for the good of the community, one that draws public discussion and reflection (as well as amusement) from the audience. Princeton Professor Alvin B. Kernan tells an Irish story (*The Great Visitation to Guaire*) that illustrates how the arbitrary use of satiric power constitutes an aggression that society has curbed and channeled:

> The satirist Dallan demands from King Hugh a magic shield which makes weak all those who look upon it. Hugh refuses to part with his most precious possession, and Dallan then proceeds to curse (satirize) him. But since the curse of Dallan is unjust, used only for personal profit, and without truth, it rebounds on the satirist, and Dallan dies within three days, while King Hugh continues to live and prosper.

Kernan goes on to say: "The point is clear: satire is required to be both just and true if it is to work; if untrue, it harms the man who speaks it."[41]

Satire, as a genre, has its proper rules of language. Despite the obvious exaggeration of its fictitious world, the satirist, when denouncing and shocking an audience, is also bound to truth because he or she is saying, "This is the way the world really is."[42] Therefore, satire's constructs will be necessarily subjective but not arbitrary because the satirist must—like anyone else—meet the ethical requirement of truthfulness. Although I believe that common moral sense can grasp the difference between humor and scorn, it would be naïve not to decry the abuse of the mediating character of language, which has been increasingly corrupted by partisan interests, as we shall discuss in chapter 8.

TWO

The Paradox of Freedom
of Expression on Campus

WHAT IS THE PROBLEM?

In November 2015, the Pew Research Center published a survey on the global state of free speech. The situation in the United States, a champion of freedom of expression, was particularly interesting. The United States was the country that showed the greatest tolerance of offensive speech (offense to minorities: 67 percent; offense to religion and beliefs: 77 percent).[1]

On the one hand, American citizens strongly support freedom of expression as a principle, but at the same time, data shows that new generations of Americans are more inclined to set limits on harmful speech.[2] New surveys by the Knight Foundation published in 2018, 2019, and 2022 confirmed these essential trends, first detected in 2015, and have painted a fuller picture. A growing number of people in the United States (between 70 and 90 percent) think that government and both public and private institutions such as schools, colleges, and social media companies should prohibit certain types of speech that somehow threaten or endanger people.[3]

From 2015 on, polemics related to freedom of expression have increased in some American Universities, such as the Universities of Chicago and Missouri, Northwestern University, Columbia, and the University of Colorado, as well as Yale, Princeton, and Harvard. There are many students demanding "safe spaces," which are places without offensive speech that might hurt anyone's feelings. These students demand that offensive speech be prohibited.

Some cases are particularly interesting. Judith Shulevitz, a journalist at the *New York Times*, reported on many of these situations in 2015.[4] Recent scholarly work has completed the picture, gathering a fair number of cases from many reporters, such as the ones below.

At a student meeting at the University of Chicago, a Muslim student rebuked the guest speaker (a *Charlie Hebdo* journalist) for his magazine's lack of respect toward Islam. The guest did not yield, and the dialogue grew tense. A few days later the organizer of the event had to apologize. Similar situations were seen in the turmoil caused by the distribution of pamphlets against homophobia at Columbia and the opposition by a group of students from Brown University at a conference where a speaker's topic was "rape culture." UCLA suspended the chapters of a fraternity and a sorority for co-hosting a "Kanye Western," deeming it racist. At Yale, a dispute arose about how Halloween costumes can be "potentially offensive." At Princeton, students blocked the rapper "Big Sean" from giving the commencement speech because they claimed that his lyrics were misogynistic. Students at Harvard protested against a law professor, claiming that he should not mention rape crimes in their classes because of the risk of stirring up traumatic memories. In Colorado, students blocked the screening of the film *Stonewall* because it did not represent the role of African Americans in US history.[5]

In all these cases, activist students pleaded for the administration to provide safe spaces, that is, to protect the campus environment from offensive speech that might hurt the feelings of any of the students. The consequences of these protests and demands have, on several occasions, driven some university leaders to apologize publicly, to interrupt events, or to request a speaker to call off a discussion.[6]

There are many groups involved in this phenomenon, including students, faculty, parents, alumni, administrators, trustees, citizens, and politicians. I will focus only on the three main groups of participants in this debate: the students, the faculty, and the university administrators—and their core points.

Activist Students

The main group in this debate are student activists. Their core points are as follows:

1.   They demand that campuses be free from offensive speech related to sexuality, gender, race, and religion.
2.   They demand protection from images, words, and ideas that could offend them.[7]
3.   Their goal is to turn their campuses into safe spaces in themselves.[8] The placement of "safe space stickers" around campus (in colleges, faculty offices, and so on) indicates support for such attitudes, and it means that potentially harmful stances should be left out, even before a discussion begins.[9]

Faculty

The second main group is university faculty, whose core points include the following:

1.   Safe spaces attempt to immunize academic life from the intellectual challenge of debating conflicting views. A university is a place to confront different standpoints and to cultivate the intellectual courage to argue against ideas that one could disagree with, oppose, or even find offensive. The goal of higher education includes acquiring skills for critical thinking. Safe spaces create an atmosphere of immaturity.[10]
2.   Restricting the free exchange of ideas is like destroying an open and democratic society. Universities need to identify freedom of thought and discussion as their central value and educate students in this principle.[11]
3.   Notwithstanding these arguments in favor of free speech, it must be mentioned that some members of the faculty support at least part of the student activists' position.[12]

University Administrators

The final main group of interest is that of university administrators, who broadly advance the following viewpoints:

1. Administrators stand for pragmatism. The statutes governing universities require them to respect and balance two requirements: preservation of the campus from any "hostile environment," that is, providing protection and security but also guaranteeing freedom of expression.
2. The plain fact is that a student's family, paying around $60,000 a year, becomes a customer, and the concern of the administrators is to satisfy the customer.
3. Administrators have to deal with budget requirements, investments, and donations from trustees. Therefore, their first principle may ironically not be freedom of thought but rather serving donors and "customers."

FREE SPEECH AND THE UNIVERSITY

Universities are not, strictly speaking, "public spaces" but places that serve the purpose of private or public education.[13] According to Robert C. Post, "Within the classroom, university professors do not have freedom of speech, as measured by the classic First Amendment Tradition."[14] Professors have academic freedom that is guided by the principle of competence within a disciplinary community.[15] The fact is that universities hire faculty and allow projects not on the basis of the marketplace of ideas or content neutrality but on their ideological mission. "They do not," Post says, "consider all ideas to be equal. . . . That is why history professors who deny the Holocaust are not hired or promoted."[16] The same happens with "outside speakers" invited by professors or students; such speakers are authorized by the university because they also serve educational purposes.

At the same time, to achieve the educational mission of what John Henry Newman called the "real cultivation of the mind,"[17] many universities embrace free speech values voluntarily and give their support when student groups organize activities and invite speakers in order to create a diverse and vibrant campus debate. So there is some confusion over the debate about freedom of speech within universities. One reason for the confusion is that from the 1960s on, campuses became safe harbors in the fighting of cultural battles regarding sexual liberation and civil rights.

It is not my intention to elaborate on the political and ideological interests that cloud these debates. I will focus my attention on the universities as places of human growth and education in citizenship. As Robert George and Cornel West stated: "The pursuit of knowledge and the maintenance of a free and democratic society require the cultivation and practice of the virtues of intellectual humility, openness of mind, and, above all, love of truth. These virtues will manifest themselves and be strengthened by one's willingness to listen attentively and respectfully to intelligent people who challenge one's beliefs and who represent causes one disagrees with and points of view one does not share."[18] Bearing in mind this idea of a university, I shall explore the "paradox" of a new generation asking for safety and not for challenge.

After a quick overview of the main points of the three key actors above, it is clear that some of the liberal tradition's values relating to freedom of expression are under siege: primarily tolerance in the face of all kinds of discourse and the openness of a free marketplace of ideas. But the question is this: How can freedom of expression be restored when so many of those who should defend it on campus (faculty and administrators) have turned against it, surrendered, or at least subordinated it to other ideals?[19]

Stanley Kurtz suggests that, to restore free speech on campus, it is necessary to recover the policy modeled in Yale's Woodward Report of 1974 and the University of Chicago's Kalven Committee Report of 1967.[20] Going into the details of these reports is beyond the aims of this research, but I shall make a brief mention of each.

It is worth noting that the Chicago Report was written during the Vietnam protests and the cultural revolution of the mid-1960s and '70s.[21] It was, in short, a different era. Yale's Report was particularly focused on defending intellectual growth through unfettered freedom of thought and expression.[22] The Chicago Statement, which contained similar ideas, appeared in 2015.[23] However, in many areas of US politics, liberals and non-liberals appeal to this era as an "idyllic past" in which, despite all the tensions, they overcame problems with free democratic politics.

The context of the safe space complaints that we are exploring here is very different from the atmosphere of the 1960s and '70s. It is not my intention to draw a parallel between them. My aim is to show the paradoxical situation that the safe space cases today set against the classical values of tolerance and openness for a democratic society.

COLLEGE STUDENTS' PERCEPTIONS OF FREE SPEECH ISSUES ON CAMPUS

We cannot forget that today's generation of students has received a strong cultural formation of protection and security that started after September 11, 2001. They belong to a culture of prevention of attacks by different enemies: Al-Qaeda, AIDS, financial crises, Covid, and so on. Education on safety and prevention is thus widespread and concerns health, sexual life, happiness, personal aims, and so forth. These young people have been born digital. As John Palfrey and Urs Gasser say, they are not very much worried, as children, about posting inappropriate content that they may regret in the future. "Our data," they write "show that many young people have already developed approaches to managing their privacy and reputation in this respect — and others are learning from the savviest users."[24] This is not the place to offer a complete overview of the sociological situation, but the above offers a peek into the educational background of these students.[25]

In 2018, the Gallup-Knight Foundation published a study on how college students in the United States saw free speech issues, including views of First Amendment rights, tensions between free expression and inclusion, the campus climate on free expression issues, the role of social media in campus life, and students' views on how to limit speech. The results reflect an abstract acceptance of the principle of free speech, but when asked about specific details — tolerance of harmful speech, inclusion, campus climate, and the policies adopted by universities (like safe spaces and free speech zones) — they are not supportive of the liberal philosophy behind free speech.

Summarizing these surveys, there are the four key takeaways:

1. College students, when asked if they are supportive of free speech, say yes (89 percent say it's very important or extremely important), but when they are asked about speech that is intentionally harmful, 64 percent (71 percent of women and 56 percent of men) think that such speech should not be protected by the First Amendment.[26]

When asked about campus policies that restrict certain types of expression, 73 percent of students think universities should restrict racial insults, and 60 percent say the same about stereotypical costumes. But only 30 percent think the expression of offensive political views should be restricted on campus.[27]

2. Colleges in the United States have instituted a variety of policies that limit free speech. Some of the more common campus policies govern speech codes, free speech zones, and safe spaces.

    College students show widespread support for free speech zones (83 percent), which are campus areas set aside for students to protest or distribute literature. They also show broad support for safe spaces (87 percent), which are designated campus areas where students can go to be sure they will not be confronted by offensive or hateful speech.

    Students are divided on speech codes (49 percent to 51 percent), which are policies that are intended to prohibit offensive speech on campuses even though that kind of speech would be permitted in society more generally.[28]

3. If you ask them to choose between free speech rights or promoting an inclusive society, they favor inclusion (53 percent), and this is stronger among women (64 percent), blacks (68 percent), and Democrats (66 percent).[29] Students think that feeling safe, respected, and included is more important than free speech.[30]

4. The discussion has shifted to online practices. According to Gallup, "More students say discussion of political and social ideas at their college takes place on social media rather than face-to-face in public areas of campus."[31] They increasingly think that anonymity is one of the big problems with social networks (83 percent) and that "social media can stifle expression because of a fear of being attacked (59 percent) or because people block those with whom they disagree (60 percent)."[32]

    College students see the Internet as one factor in a significant increase in hate speech (83 percent), and they think that tech companies should be responsible for limiting hate speech (68 percent: 74 percent of women, 61 percent of men).[33] This data illustrates that the younger generations do not endorse the liberal rationale on freedom of expression.

THE MODERN NOTION OF TOLERANCE AND ITS FRACTURING

As we shall examine in Part II, Enlightenment philosophers, especially Voltaire (1694–1778), rebuilt the classical notion of tolerance.[34] They suppressed any reference to truth and good and pointed to subjectivity and ethical suspension: that is, to relativism.[35]

The classical understanding of the tolerance of evil[36] is an attitude that recognizes the objective difference between a positive and a negative fact or behavior and then allows this negative fact or behavior to effect the lesser evil.[37] That is why it is important to note that tolerance is different from permissiveness. The first allows room in society for error and evil but considers that good and truth are permanent values. Permissiveness implies a lack of objective moral values.

The distinction between tolerance and permissiveness is very much present in classic and contemporary literature on moral philosophy and theology, particularly in the debate about cultural relativism. The idea of tolerance presupposes a system of principles that evaluates a given conduct as evil. Tolerance is about not banning a behavior while not necessarily approving of it, whereas the principle behind permissiveness is relativism, understood as meaning that every conception of the good has value in itself, each choice has equal value with all the others, and one's choice is independent from the values of other people. Here I'll carry this rationale of tolerance into the area of freedom of expression to point to noxious speech in order to expose the roots of some of the problems of free speech theory.

Do We Stand for Tolerance or Permissiveness?

John Milton became one of the heralds of free speech by writing *Areopagitica* (1644) and elaborating on the principle of tolerance.[38] In that work he sets forth the idea that good and evil grow up together, so truth and falsehood must grapple in a free and open encounter.[39] Toleration of transgression and evil to a certain degree and in view of a higher good belongs to the ethos of the tradition in which Milton lived.

Milton's theory of tolerance and liberty comes from this dialectical conception of truth; allowing all kinds of speech is socially healthy and wise because "truth has been broken into a thousand pieces and scattered to the four winds."[40] The purpose of Milton's grappling is "confuting of error," not finding out what "is true." The Miltonian "exploration of evil without limits" is fully allied not to the classical virtue of tolerance but to permissiveness.

Furthermore, I believe that Milton's sympathy for evil gives rise to a certain alleged right to evil and error as necessary values. For many scholars, this framework would validate and justify the right to offend. It is on this conceptual basis that most contemporary theorists of freedom of expression have founded their intellectual development.

What Is the Liberal Approach to Tolerance of Harmful Speech?

There are two basic positions that one can take in defense of harmful speech in the name of tolerance. The first claims that legal systems are more influential in exerting authority to "protect dissenters" than they are in teaching about tolerance.[41] Others advocate for a pedagogical understanding of tolerance as the best protection for free speech against an individual's impulse toward intolerance.[42] In either case, harm is seen as a subjective emotion of the victim. The liberal understanding of harm is that only acts can cause verifiable damage, not words. As a result, speech is an unrestricted and ambiguous area in which Milton's principle of tolerance reigns, through which all harmful speech is allowed, in a free and open confrontation of ideas. Claims of equality challenge the arrogance of the free speech rationale on harm.

There are words that can harm, and there are acts that intimidate. The meaning and interpretation of acts and words is often an open question, but it is not completely without boundaries. The "ambiguity" and "elasticity" of meaning that is sometimes attributed to them is unnatural: ambiguity cannot be forced endlessly.[43] On the other hand, saying, "Let speech compete and be balanced by society's reactions" is based on an optimistic but irresponsible assumption: permitting "more speech" is pointless because it leads only to further abuse or could place the offender in a position of power over the victim.[44]

As we saw above, students agree that there are some values, such as respect or inclusion, that have to be safeguarded because not everything should be permitted. I am advocating not the enforcement of hate speech laws but a reconsideration of tolerance and the principles that sustain it. Common moral sense resists Milton's tolerance (permissiveness) of insult and hateful speech. Certainly, strong academic criticism is actually necessary, and so is sound intellectual debate. There is also a need to unmask transgressions that are acts of visual or verbal abuse rather than constructive criticism. The moral of opposites advocated by Milton is a kind of ethical neutrality and skepticism that ends nowhere because reality is not paradoxical, as if to say: "To defend freedom it is necessary to defend enemies of freedom." Evil exists, and it is useful for human growth, but evil and offense are not moral rights to be defended. Those who advocate absolute freedom of expression must weigh the social price to be paid by this intellectual position.

THREE

The Threat of
Religious Fanaticism

Jyllands-Posten and
the Regensburg Address

THE CARICATURES OF MOHAMMED

On September 30, 2005, the Danish magazine *Jyllands-Posten* published twelve drawings under the title "Muhammeds ansigt" (Mohammed's face). In one, Mohammed appeared in a turban shaped like a bomb. An editorial note signed by Flemming Rose accompanied the drawings:

> Modern, secular society is rejected by some Muslims. They demand a special position, insisting on special consideration of their own religious feelings. It is incompatible with contemporary democracy and freedom of speech, where one must be ready to put up with insults, mockery, and ridicule. It is certainly not always attractive and nice to look at, and it does not mean that religious feelings should be made fun of at any price, but that is of minor importance in the present

context. . . . We are on our way to a slippery slope where no one can tell how the self-censorship will end. That is why *Morgenavisen Jyllands-Posten* has invited members of the Danish editorial cartoonists union to draw Muhammad as they see him.[1]

The drawings were immediately interpreted as an insult. Danish Muslim leaders tried to get the government of Denmark to intervene. Muslim ambassadors protested and sent a formal letter to Prime Minister Rasmussen, but he responded that he had to respect the freedom of the press, offering only judicial redress as an option for the Muslim diplomats.

At the same time, violent reactions in other countries soon sprang up. Over the following months, Danish embassies in several Muslim countries (Syria, Indonesia, Iran, Lebanon, and others) had to close for security reasons. A few weeks later, some of these embassies were set on fire. The threats and disturbances were growing in Arab countries, leading to deaths that would total around 150 by the end of the controversy. While Western flags were being burned and other violent protests were going on, an Iranian newspaper began publishing drawings from a contest asking people to submit jokes about the Holocaust.

The European press backed *Jyllands-Posten*.[2] Nonetheless, the reaction of European, American, and Russian politicians was to condemn the drawings' publication, calling it "insulting and insensitive," "imprudent," and "an unacceptable provocation to religious and ethnic hatred."[3] The magazine's editors kept silent, probably because judicial proceedings were in progress.

Danish imams began to contact the magazine directly since dialogue with the government was closed. The editors' response was regret for having offended anyone's sensibilities. In no case did they invoke the defiant right to offend attitude in the name of freedom of expression. Before the judges absolved the publication, the imams had already obtained a public declaration from the editors (in January 2006) in which the editors admitted their guilt and said that it was not their intention to insult the Islamic religion.[4] This was their declaration:

In our opinion the 12 cartoons were moderate and not intended to be insulting. They did not go against Danish laws, but have evidently offended many Muslims, for which we apologize. Meanwhile a couple of offending cartoons have circulated in the Muslim world which were never published in *Jyllands-Posten* and which we would never have published if they had been offered to us. We would have dismissed them on the grounds that they breached our ethical limits."[5]

This kind of rational debate between imams and editors, as well as the fact that this sort of insult did not reappear in later years, makes this Danish case quite different from that of *Charlie Hebdo*. Rose alleges that publishing the drawings was an act of "cultural integration" of Islam in Denmark. "The cartoonists treated Islam the same way they treat Christianity, Buddhism, Hinduism and other religions. And by treating Muslims in Denmark as equals they made a point: We are integrating you into the Danish tradition of satire because you are part of our society, not strangers. The cartoons are including, rather than excluding, Muslims."[6] Leaving aside the question of Rose's sincerity, it is relevant — as Alasdair MacIntyre suggests — that Danish critics of Islam and Muslim leaders debated the significance of being Muslim and being Danish.[7]

Several studies have looked at the influence this case has had on the relationship between stereotypes of Islam and freedom of expression.[8] Currently, the term *fundamentalist* has a mainly pejorative connotation, referring to a person or reactionary group that is not predisposed to discussion, is uncompromising in its position, and takes its beliefs literally.[9] One way to characterize fundamentalism is as fanaticism, which is considered a passionate and exaggerated attitude toward an idea or belief, mixed with the psychological conditions of uncompromising intellect and stubbornness of will.[10]

It is intuitive that the temptation to engage in religious fundamentalism is a threat for believers of any religion. As Pope Francis said on his return flight from his first visit to Africa, "Fundamentalism is a closed-mindedness that exists in all religions. . . . The fundamentalist religious person is not religious. Why? Because God is missing. It's idolatry."[11] That being the case, saying that the risk of fundamentalism is a phenomenon common to anyone supporting an idea or belief is not new or exclusive to religions. Insofar as it has to do with faith, John Paul II highlighted the necessity for faith to become culture so that it does not deviate into ideology, and Benedict XVI also highlighted the necessity that faith be accompanied by reason.[12]

On the other hand, Francis highlighted the pathological character of fundamentalism, in whatever form it takes, because, as in all closed-mindedness, there is something unhealthy and abnormal about it since it goes beyond what is reasonable and tends toward physical and psychological violence. There is not any real faith behind these fundamentalist stances and attitudes, only ideology.[13] Hence, the problem is not with religion[14] but with humankind, which, with the transformative power of religion, can convert certain beliefs into an ideology.

That being the case, we must distinguish between two questions related to Islamic religious fundamentalism as a threat to freedom of expression—on one hand, if it is possible to distinguish between the Islamic religion and terrorism perpetrated in its name and, on the other, how to confront the question of blasphemy and freedom of expression.

THE REGENSBURG ADDRESS

During the summer of 2006, Benedict XVI took a six-day trip to Germany (September 9–14), intending to visit some places that were especially important to him: his native land, the city where he had been bishop, and the university where he had been a professor. Over the course of this trip, on September 12 he presided over a conference at the University of Regensburg, where he had previously been a professor. Two days after this conference, the day he returned to Rome, British and American media outlets began reporting on "angry reactions in the Muslim world" to the papal lecture that he had given two days earlier at the university.[15]

The conference was titled Faith, Reason, and the University: Memories and Reflections. The topic tied the past with current events, mentioning all sorts of things, from ancient Jewish and Greek thought to Protestant theology and even modern secularism. The discourse centered mainly on Christianity and the tendency to exclude the question of God from reason. It also touched on the dialogue between religions and dealt with religious justification of violence. The polemic stemmed from three paragraphs at the beginning of Benedict's discussion, those in which he cited a text written in 1391, from a discourse by a certain Persian, Digno Mouterizes, in Ankara of Galatea, as an expression of the Byzantine emperor Manuel II, a paleologist on Islam.

Jeremy Kryn did a study on this polemic,[16] analyzing the coverage of four Anglo-American news media outlets on this question.[17] We shall base our discussion on his results.

As revealed by this investigation, the reactions in the Muslim world against the three paragraphs cited by the Pope were less than civil. There were threats, violent acts, and various assassinations that we shall briefly look at here to give an idea of the magnitude of the reaction.

In the West Bank city of Naplusa, a Greek Orthodox church and an Anglican church were bombed, and a Greek Orthodox church in Gaza was attacked.[18] In Turkey, certain state employees responsible for organizing Muslim worship called on the Turkish government to arrest Benedict XVI during his visit to the country[19] so that he could be brought to justice for violating Turkish laws against "insulting" Islam.[20] A fatwa was declared against the Pontiff in Pakistan for his "blasphemous declaration," and, similarly, Al-Qaeda called for a jihad due to Pope Benedict's declarations.[21]

In Mogadishu (Somalia), on September 17, 2006, two armed men killed an old Italian nun, Sister Leonella, and her Somali bodyguards. No specific motive was found for this assassination, but, given the words of a member of Somalia's Supreme Council of Islamic Tribunals, which did not rule out the concrete possibility that the murder was a "reprise for the Pope's declarations on Islam,"[22] the connection is fairly clear.

On the other hand, in Basora (Iraq), a group of people burned the flags of Germany, Israel, and the United States, as well as crosses and images of Pope Benedict and Jesus. In Bagdad, two Christians were killed by stabbing. All over the country, churches were bombed or attacked in acts of vandalism, and Christians were threatened with death at the doors of the churches. An Assyrian Orthodox priest was kidnapped in Mosul. His kidnappers demanded a condemnation of the Pope's comments and payment of a ransom. The priest was decapitated.[23]

During his Angelus address on Sunday, September 17, Benedict XVI made his first public comment on the worldwide reaction to the Regensburg discussion. The Pontiff expressed his regret for the reactions that a medieval text had incited, and he clarified that this citation did not express his personal thoughts. He also clarified that his intention was to invite dialogue.

The initial reaction of politicians and academics from the Muslim world was rejection. The first declarations from the Vatican's spokesperson and the Vatican's secretary of state were ineffective in calming Muslim ire.

Calm began to return only after the Pope's apologies and several days of diplomatic mobilization.[24]

After the analysis of the international coverage of the negative reactions in the Muslim world using the four outlets analyzed by Kryn, some figures are worth mentioning: the BBC published twenty articles on the subject in one month, the *Guardian* published twelve in ten days, the CNN website published twelve in ten days, and the *New York Times* published six in one week, five of which were written by the same author. The first three of these outlets started reporting on the negative reactions to the Regensburg discussion on September 15, 2006. Ian Fisher of the *New York Times* was the only one that began on September 13, 2006.[25]

It is curious that the media's reaction was not immediate but came two days after the discussion, perhaps because the journalists did not have a clear idea of the focus of the Regensburg Address.[26] As Kyrn suggests in his investigation, surely the journalists must have made a connection between Regensburg's text and the *Jyllands-Posten* Danish drawing polemic from a few months earlier.[27]

Nonetheless, as we saw above, the Muslim reaction to the Regensburg text was not merely verbal but consisted primarily of violent acts. It became clear how religious fundamentalism does not allow for rational disagreement and debate of ideas but represses them with extreme violence, thereby constituting a great threat to freedom of expression.

As for as the Anglo-American media analyzed by Kryn, it is striking how it put so much emphasis on recounting in detail the international reactions against the Regensburg discussion but never denounced Muslim leaders for their failure to condemn these violent reactions, including the assassinations in Somalia and Iraq. From this we can discern a nexus between the two kinds of fundamentalism: the relativist kind and the religious kind. Benedict XVI affirmed this in his message for World Peace Day in 2011: "We must not forget that religious fundamentalism and secularism are extreme, mirror images of the rejection of legitimate pluralism and of the principle of secularism."[28]

The fundamentalists—the relativists as much as the Islamic ones—do not recognize the freedom of others and presume to impose their beliefs. In both cases, it is clear that violations of freedom of expression are closely related to the breakdown of religious freedom. One sheds blood in the name of God, the other with the motive of God, outraging and denigrating him through words and images. Both types of fundamentalism are atheistic in the sense that in the end there is not God, but an ideology that instrumentalizes him for the purpose of imposing its own ends, whether it be Sharia or secularism. Both threaten freedom of expression. Here we are faced not with an academic problem or debate but rather with a challenge of coexistence that affects men and women the world over.

Finally, in light of the spread of fundamentalist terrorism in Syria and Iraq and of the alarming number of its victims,[29] Pope Francis gave a speech to the diplomatic corps in January 2015 urging Islamic religious leaders to more strongly condemn religious fundamentalism: "I ask the international community not to be indifferent to this situation; I hope that religious, political and intellectual leaders, especially Muslims, condemn whatever fundamentalist or extremist interpretation of the religion that justifies such acts of violence."[30]

As the reaction in the Muslim world to the Regensburg Address shows, violence based on expression is never justified. An in-depth analysis of this phenomenon is beyond the scope of our topic, but it is useful for us to look at one aspect of it.

Religious fundamentalism — in this case, Islamic fundamentalism — rejects Western modernism in all its manifestations. The reason for this rejection can be summarized by saying that Islam considers Western culture corrupt and decadent, contrary to Allah's desired order.[31] It is totally understandable, since its cultural and religious perspective includes ideas contrary to the secularism that flourishes in the West. The problem starts when this opposition is no longer limited to rational debate but instead manifests itself as violence. Thus, if dialogue among Islamic intellectuals were to increase, it could contribute to the improvement of society.[32]

The Beirut Declaration is an initiative among certain Sunni Muslim leaders and academics that "clarifies Islamic teaching on subjects like recognition of religious freedom and education, respect for individual conscience, respect for human dignity, the right to disagree, respect for diversity, adherence to the Bill of Rights, etc."[33] There was an attempt to build a consensus around this declaration, with the intent to create debate within the Sunni Arab world with the aim of condemning the extremist demonstrations and the terrorism that harm Islam.[34] At the end of 2015, the Lebanese mufti Abdel Latif Deriane met in Egypt with the imam Al-Azhar and with other Sunni leaders, declaring, "We should form a common front against extremism." And he added that Islam "must face serious challenges . . . , we must raise our voices to denounce these abuses that harm Islam."[35] This doctrinal development can serve to counteract extremism within Islam. As Noun says: "We can't be satisfied with empty declarations like 'this isn't Islam.' We must convince Muslims with arguments taken from the Muslim faith, from the Koran."[36]

FOUR

The Rise of a New Orthodoxy

The Intolerance of Secular Relativism

FREEDOM OF THOUGHT:
THE MASTERPIECE CAKESHOP CASE

In July 2012, David Mullins and Charlie Craig walked into the Masterpiece Cakeshop in Lakewood, Colorado, a well-to-do Denver suburb,
to order a cake for their upcoming wedding. The shop offers a variety of
baked goods, ranging from everyday cookies and brownies to elaborate
custom-designed cakes for birthday parties, weddings, and other events.
The owner, Jack Phillips, declined the order, explaining that he did not
create wedding cakes for same-sex couples because doing so would violate
his religious beliefs. He said that he would be happy to make and sell them
any other baked goods, but they left the shop.[1]

As stated in the resulting court case, "Jack Phillips is an expert baker
who has owned and operated the shop for 24 years. Phillips is a devout
Christian. He has explained that his 'main goal in life is to be obedient to'
Jesus Christ and Christ's 'teachings in all aspects of his life.'" And he seeks

to "honor God through his work at Masterpiece Cakeshop" (App. 148). One of Phillips's religious beliefs is that "God's intention for marriage from the beginning of history is that it is and should be the union of one man and one woman." "To Phillips, creating a wedding cake for a same-sex wedding would be equivalent to participating in a celebration that is contrary to his own most deeply held beliefs" (App. 149).[2]

Further:

> The following day, Craig's mother, who had accompanied the couple to the cakeshop and been present for their interaction with Phillips, telephoned to ask Phillips why he had declined to serve her son. Phillips explained that he does not create wedding cakes for same-sex weddings because of his religious opposition to same-sex marriage, and also because Colorado (at that time) did not recognize same-sex marriages. He later explained his belief that "to create a wedding cake for an event that celebrates something that directly goes against the teachings of the Bible, would have been a personal endorsement and participation in the ceremony and relationship that they were entering into" (App. 153).[3]

The couple then brought a claim against Mr. Phillips and the cakeshop on the grounds that they had been discriminated against, in violation of Colorado state law.[4] On summary judgment, an administrative law judge ruled in favor of the couple, finding that Mr. Phillips's actions constituted prohibited discrimination under the Colorado Anti-Discrimination Act (CADA) on the basis of their sexual orientation. The Colorado Civil Rights Commission affirmed the previous decision and ordered Mr. Phillips to cease and desist from discriminating against same-sex couples by refusing to sell them wedding cakes or any products they would sell to heterosexual couples. The Commission also ordered staff training, changes to company policies, and quarterly compliance reports over a period of two years. The decision was reviewed and upheld by the Colorado Court of Appeals. That court's decision was appealed to the Colorado Supreme Court, which declined to hear the case. The decision was then appealed to the Supreme Court of the United States.[5]

Justice Anthony Kennedy delivered the opinion of the Supreme Court, noting that this case involved the need for a reconciliation between two principles, one being the authority of the government to protect the rights of gay people from discrimination when they seek goods and services and the other being the right to exercise one's freedom of speech and religion.[6] But Colorado's anti-discrimination law protects individuals from discrimination on the basis of sexual orientation as well as religion. In this sense, Kennedy's majority opinion admits that the Colorado Civil Rights Commission had violated the state's obligation to provide religious neutrality by not giving Phillips "neutral and respectful consideration."[7]

Commissioners repeatedly "endorsed the view that religious beliefs cannot legitimately be carried into the public sphere or commercial domain, implying that religious beliefs and persons are less than fully welcome in Colorado's business community."[8] Kennedy writes that one commissioner suggested during the hearings on May 30, 2014, that "Phillips can believe 'what he wants to believe' but cannot act on his religious beliefs 'if he decides to do business in the State.'"[9]

Commission members also stated that religion has historically been used to further all kinds of discrimination, "and to me," Kennedy states, it is one of the most despicable pieces of rhetoric that people can use—to use their religion to hurt others."[10]

The Court held that the Commission's treatment of his case had elements of a "clear and impermissible hostility toward the sincere religious beliefs that motivated [Mr. Phillips's] objection."[11] In this sense, Kennedy pointed out that during the hearings on July 25, 2014, one commissioner "even went so far as to compare Phillips's invocation of his sincerely held religious beliefs to defenses of slavery and the Holocaust."[12]

Following similar criticism of the Commission's lack of neutrality, Justice Neil Gorsuch emphasized that, in the United States, "the place of secular officials isn't to sit in judgment of religious beliefs, but only to protect their free exercise. Just as it is the 'proudest boast of our free speech jurisprudence' that we protect speech that we hate, it must be the proudest boast of our free exercise jurisprudence that we protect religious beliefs that we find offensive."[13]

Justice Kennedy ends his opinion with a crucial remark: "These disputes must be resolved with tolerance, without undue disrespect to sincere religious beliefs," pointing to the lack of fairness and neutrality with which the case had been treated by public officers. In the same vein, Justice Elena

Kagan said: "State actors cannot show hostility to religious views; rather, they must give those views 'neutral and respectful consideration'"[14] because, as Kennedy highlights: "The Constitution commits government itself to religious tolerance, and upon even slight suspicion that proposals for state intervention stem from animosity to religion or distrust of its practices, all officials must pause to remember their own high duty to the Constitution and to the rights it secures."[15]

Justice Clarence Thomas declared: "In future cases, freedom of speech could be essential to preventing *Obergefell* from being used to 'stamp out every vestige of dissent' and 'vilify Americans who are unwilling to assent to the new orthodoxy.'"[16]

The fact that important civil rights groups like the Cato Institute, the Reason Foundation, and the Individual Rights Foundation backed the cake baker's right to freedom of expression in reports that they wrote,[17] even though they support gay marriage, shows the doctrinal fracture within the liberal tradition of free speech. The Cato Institute's brief sees the cakeshop case in line with *Wooley v. Maynard*, 430 US 705 (1977), the New Hampshire "Live Free or Die" license-plate case. This case "makes clear that speech compulsions are as unconstitutional as speech restrictions. *Wooley*'s logic applies to custom wedding cakes and other types of visual art, not just verbal expression."[18]

The British gay rights activist Peter Tatchell changed his mind about the prosecution of the Christian-run Ashers Bakery in Belfast over their refusal to provide a wedding cake to Gareth Lee with the slogan "Support Gay Marriage," to which the "QueerSpace" logo was attached. Prior to the appeal in the Northern Ireland Court of Appeal in February 2016, Tatchell wrote in the *Guardian*: "Much as I wish to defend the gay community, I also want to defend freedom of conscience, expression and religion."[19]

One of the dangers that Tatchell recognizes is that banning dissent or compelling businesses to promote ideas with a chosen agreement, sets a disturbing pattern: "Northern Ireland's laws against discrimination on the grounds of political opinion were framed in the context of decades of conflict. They were designed to heal the sectarian divide by preventing the denial of jobs, housing, and services to people because of their politics."[20]

Tatchell warns about the slippery slope of enforcing compelled speech without respect for freedom of religion and conscience, saying such enforcement will backfire:

The judge concluded that service providers are required to facilitate any "lawful" message, even if they have a conscientious objection. This raises the question: should Muslim printers be obliged to publish cartoons of Mohammed? Or Jewish ones publish the words of a Holocaust denier? Or gay bakers accept orders for cakes with homophobic slurs? If the Ashers verdict stands it could, for example, encourage far-right extremists to demand that bakeries and other service providers facilitate the promotion of anti-migrant and anti-Muslim opinions. It would leave businesses unable to refuse to decorate cakes or print posters with bigoted messages.[21]

In January 2022 the European Court of Human Rights (ECHR) affirmed the UK Supreme Court's verdict in favor of freedom of expression and conscience that was handed down to the owners of Ashers Bakery in Belfast, ruling that Daniel and Amy McArthur should not be punished for refusing to bake a cake for Gareth Lee with the slogan "Support Gay Marriage" inscribed on it. At the same time, the Court stated: "As such, there had been no discrimination on grounds of sexual orientation."[22] The decision by the Court is final.

The editor of the *Telegraph* wrote: "We are in the realms of thought crime here and even Peter Tatchell, the veteran gay rights campaigner who initially welcomed the prosecution, has changed his mind about it. He said the law against discrimination was meant to protect people with differing views, not to force upon others opinions to which they conscientiously object. Indeed so. The conviction must be overturned."[23]

There is a form of intolerance that comes from secularist doctrines: banning dissent and compelling ideas in the name of a new orthodoxy. The *Cambridge English Dictionary* defines "secularism" as "the belief that religion should not be involved with the ordinary social and political activities of a country." As a *belief*, as a doctrine, secularism must not be imposed on those who do not adhere to it. The liberal tradition of free speech is based on, among other things, the principles of tolerance of all speech, the neutrality of the public sphere, and maintaining a free and open marketplace of ideas. Freedom of thought and discussion for liberals should consist in not assuming a position of infallibility but rather allowing truth to grapple with falsehood under a notion of tolerance sustained by a skeptical understanding of the good. So, in classical liberalism, tolerance of ideas regarding the "good life" means that the proper reaction should be "I don't know." Acting otherwise will be an illiberal tendency. The attitudes of imposing or banning ideas are anti-liberal according to liberalism's own notion of tolerance.

As we shall see with more detail in Part II, and particularly in chapter 6, Milton and Mill lived and formulated their theories in a Christian ethos, so the moral consequences of their formulations on free speech live on the basis of presuppositions. When this foundational ethos is removed, the structure of freedom of expression trembles, as we see in these examples.

PROVIDING NO PLATFORM FOR SOME IDEAS AND SPEAKERS

Pope Benedict XVI was invited to give the inaugural lecture at La Sapienza University in Rome on January 14, 2008, as Paul VI and John Paul II had done before him. A frenetic situation prevented the Pope from speaking. The events evolved rapidly: a group of professors sent a manifesto ("Keep the Pope Out of the University") to the university's president, providing the basis for the controversy.[24] They argued that Benedict was an enemy of science, that the Church had invaded the civil sphere, and that religion was opposed to reason.

After New Year's, protests were organized on campus to boycott the event. These demonstrations were composed of a minority of students but received extensive media coverage in Italy. The scheduled events, some of them strongly irreverent, included assembly meetings and public readings of manifestos and were intended to attract the attention of other students and the press.

A group of students took over the main building on campus two days before the event. That same morning, the Vatican confirmed the Pope's visit in order to dispel any concerns about the event, but there were riots and a high risk of violence. In a new statement later that evening, the Vatican announced that the Pope would not visit La Sapienza. That same night, the president of Italy wrote a letter to the Pontiff regretting the intolerance shown by some groups in not allowing him to speak on campus. The Pontiff's speech was sent to the president of La Sapienza and was read at the beginning of the academic event.[25] Some Italian newspapers published it in full. In sum, secular and religious authorities considered these events an affront to the principles of free speech.

There are two similar paradoxes here. Benedict was presented as a threat to science and reason when in his undelivered speech he defended the autonomy of the university in regard to political and ecclesiastical authority, stating, "It must be exclusively linked to the authority of the truth."[26] The Pope advocated the need for the university as an institution in modern society, precisely as a means to seek truth, because "the truth means more than knowledge: the knowledge of truth is aimed at knowledge of the good. The truth makes us good, and goodness is true."[27] In short, Benedict XVI presented the Christian message as a stimulus to the truth precisely because of its divine origin and, for that reason, a force against the threat of power and vested interests.[28]

The conclusion is clear: whether or not we agree with the Pontiff, his speech was neither threatening nor noxious to life in a democracy. The only hostile attitude toward democracy comes from intolerance that leads people to refuse to listen to the arguments of the other and to ban people from speaking. This partisan response easily leads to intimidation and fear, and even to physical violence.

The journalist Mercedes de la Torre did a detailed investigation of this case involving the Pope, for which she studied the news from the ten days surrounding the controversy, analyzing 494 articles published in eleven Italian newspapers. I am using the data from this study to reflect on some important aspects as they relate to freedom of expression.[29]

De la Torre's investigation documented the "boomerang effect" of the polemic at the level of public opinion. Until Benedict XVI announced that he would not give the speech, the narrative was dominated by pointed reasons given by the letters and demonstrations referred to above: Benedict is an enemy of science, the Church is invading the civil sphere, faith and reason are opposed, and so on. Nonetheless, as soon as Benedict announced that he would not proceed, the polemic took another direction and the focus was on the demonstrations in support of the Pope, which came from many different directions, not just from religious circles.

Most people reacted in recognition that the Pope was a victim of an act of intolerance, and most in the political and academic sectors saw that act as a defeat for freedom of expression.

The liberal idea of absolute tolerance of speech failed. Disagreement with Benedict's ideas materialized into disturbances and riots, using force, which had nothing to do with rational debate. The dissent turned into intolerance, including threats of censorship and violence. The idea of the university as a place for debate and confrontation of opposing ideas through the rational discussion of arguments faded away.

The fundamentalist attitude of impeding speech, imposing one's own vision as the only and infallible one, with violence against things and people, was denounced by people from diverse ideological backgrounds: as De la Torre wrote: "The director of *Il Foglio*, Giuliano Ferrara, revealed in an interview that the professors from the University of Rome who fought to boycott Benedict's visit, who occupied the administration building, and who threatened the place where a dignitary such as Pope Benedict XVI was supposed to be welcomed, had committed an act of intolerance."[30]

On the Sunday after the incident, from the balcony at St. Peter's Square, Benedict himself explained what the fundamental problem was. He began by explaining that he had accepted the invitation because of his predilection for the university environment, of which he was a part for so many years: "It unites love for the search for truth, for confrontation, for frank and respectful dialogue between different positions."[31] Then he pointed, in a positive way, to the qualified nature of freedom of expression that goes beyond mere self-expression: "I encourage you all, dear universitarians, always to be respectful of distant opinions and to seek, with a free and responsible spirit, the truth and the good."[32] In this way Benedict advocated not for political correctness but for a peaceful pursuit of truth motivated by the force of truth, over the power of force, permitting honest, responsible, and free debate.

Our contemporary liberal tradition of free speech was developed by focusing on an academic justification of those who transgress (Nazis, Ku Klux Klansmen, and other harmful speakers) and the ability of the marketplace of ideas to promote truth and civility. However, the turn in its development that we have seen in above examples has made us unable to distinguish between speech and insult, satire and sarcasm. One reaction to certain abuses of speech has been the "deplatforming" position,[33] which posits that harmful speech should not be prohibited but that instead institutions should not provide a platform for it or a space for it to spread.

Professor Deborah Lipstadt's decision to decline an invitation to a debate that she knew David Irving (famous for denying the Holocaust[34]) would also attend, represents an alternative to "deplatforming." The debate between creationists and evolutionists is similar. Some scientists, such as

Richard Dawkins, would say, with salty irony, something along the lines of this: "Whenever a creationist invites me to hold a formal debate on the evidence of evolution, I respond: This would look very good on their resume, but not on mine."[35]

In the chapter about freedom of expression on American campuses we looked closely at the censorship of speakers whose ideas were considered noxious, dangerous, or radical. In these cases, as Warburton explains, there is a distinction between what the law prescribes and what is a moral requirement. Legally, they can express themselves, but morally they should not be allowed space in the communication channels because that would mean conceding credibility to these people, normalizing their ideas and giving respectability to their ideas. This attitude reveals an ethical superiority that liberalism should not have on its own terms. At the same time, calls for laws against hate speech follow part of this argument.

This line of reasoning is dangerous for public life. Not giving space to some kinds of speech (deplatforming) is really an a priori decision about what is indisputably harmful, which, in the end, is a contradiction: if there is no space for expression, what is the point of talking about expression? An argument without a platform for discussion is like a circular square. Not only does it result in a silence that is arbitrarily imposed, but it is one in which the arbitrariness takes on the form of honorability, denying the possibility of discussing the merit of that presumed honor, which is nothing other than pure will. This position contravenes the liberal thesis of tolerance and the marketplace of ideas.

Arguments for deplatforming are a side effect, an unexpected turn, a bitter fruit of "modern hubris." The Enlightenment's theory extols the autonomy of reason and one's own subjectivity over all other values, leaving out the spiritual element of mankind and the role of religion as something mythological and supernatural. With a certain ethical arrogance, it seeks to construct a program of citizenship based on classical virtues, mainly self-control and excellence. With this outlook, for example, in 1741 Benjamin Franklin created the American Philosophical Society, inspired by the British Royal Society, both institutions that were created to develop a civic program that created a public sphere where good manners and self-correction proper to cultivated people reigned.[36] The rules of these societies did not permit heated discussion or debate of subjects related to deep personal convictions, as religious beliefs can be. They considered reason and the virtue of self-control to be enough to keep expression civil in the public sphere. These rules were sustainable because people were all educated in and living out of the inherited ethos of Christian thought. Currently, in what some people call a post-Christian society, when the moral foundations that we long took for granted have been removed, it is difficult for the younger generations to justify and hold together the principles of tolerance and unfettered freedom.

WHY ARE WE HERE? THE MENACE OF CULTURAL RELATIVISM IN RELATION TO FREEDOM OF EXPRESSION

After the disenchantment that followed the great European wars, postmodernism replaced ideological modernity (of a rationalist and secularist mold). Postmodernity wipes the slate clean of all the grand narratives and advocates relativizing everything. Now there is a movement from the pride of modern reason to another type of dogmatism, this time from a nihilistic mold. This new paradigm speaks of "fluid values" in which forms of softness prevail but is based on indisputable principles. Its neutral mission is to guarantee social rights to build one's individuality according to an absolute freedom of choice that is unquestionable. I believe that many of the challenges of free speech find their roots first in modernity and then in some postmodern developments.

One of modernity's key features was an emphasis on the individual and his or her subjectivity, a rejection of any moral normativity and the establishment of autonomy as a paradigm. Today, in the postmodern context of cultural relativism, references to reality and nature, to what is good or bad for the human person, have been erased. This prevailing relativism has led to a blurring of the foundation of society and man, imposing an agnostic view on the public sphere, guided by ethical suspension (called "neutrality") as a cornerstone of the pluralist society. However, this neutrality is indeed neutralism, because religion and faith are excluded from the public sphere. Jürgen Habermas, among others, denounced this cognitive discrimination.[37]

As John D. Peters said in an interview, revelation and inquiry, debate and discussion go together and are part of life. They are not a matters of either faith or reason. Peters is "sympathetic with Habermas' idea that there's a kind of educational responsibility for people to be reasonable before they participate in the public sphere, because reasonability is also an ethical position, because to be reasonable is to respect otherness."[38]

I see two main problems with some of the contemporary developments of free speech that are rooted in relativism. The principle of freedom of expression exercised exclusively in a self-referential way leads speech to become an end in itself. This freedom becomes narcissistic and easily evolves into a weapon, a mere instrument of conflict, because controversy becomes an end, negating rational dialogue and the confrontation of ideas and opinions.

On the other hand, this self-referential freedom of speech backed by relativism forgets that liberal freedom also requires relativizing one's own opinion or vision of things, opening oneself up to dialogue with the ideas of others. Moral relativism justifies the exercise of self-referential and acritical freedom, falling into illiberal and intolerant attitudes toward what is outside of one's worldview, with the censorship and silencing of uncomfortable voices as potential results. As Peters states, "The danger in moral liberalism is the sin of pride. Liberalism should be a matter of: we don't know."[39]

Relativism as a background philosophy narrows the understanding of free speech because it does not grasp that free speech is a medium that aims to display truth itself. I think that relativism helps to imprison free speech in its narcissistic circle of self-affirmation, preventing true dialogue—true listening to the arguments of others—and prohibiting the construction of a paradigm for responsible free speech that defends the rights of speakers and listeners beyond our own whims.

That is why I understand relativism as a real threat to freedom of expression: if it is impossible to discern what is good and true, then there is no rational dialogue but only self-affirmation and individualistic exhibition of one's own ideas. In this situation, the only alternative is to speak louder, resorting to offensive verbal or physical violence to dominate the public sphere. Arbitrary violence easily results in physical and psychological violence. When expression becomes self-affirmation it is called the "right to offend." In this case, it is more than an expression of one's own ideas; it becomes a weapon, a demonstration of verbal or physical violence.

This raises the moral question of the internal link between freedom of expression and reason and between freedom of expression and the common social good. Acts of expression are called to be morally reasonable and open to respect for the other and not to be empty affirmations of self. As I understand it, the state must be interested not only in protecting individual interests but also in ensuring a just system for solidary social life. Freedom of expression is a negative right, so the state must not intervene unless harm is done to a common good (public order, social peace, public morality). This lack of action expected on the part of the state does not mean it should be indifferent.[40] The original meaning of "tolerating evil" for a greater good meant "offering no repression," but whereas tolerating can lead to legitimization of evil that harms human dignity, other types of positive action are possible and needed: prevention, education, and so on. One of the purposes of this book is to explore conditions for better speech.

Part of the task of rebuilding the principles of free speech involves recovering its roots in harmony between reason and faith, between the autonomy of the intellect and the nature of what things are, which means rediscovering that free speech was never meant to be unlimited. It constitutes a baseline freedom but is not an end in itself. It is necessary to rediscover its foundations beyond modern ideologies so that humankind can continue the passionate search for the truth and full development as a human family.

FIVE

Facebook's Content Moderation Rule

Private Censorship of Public Discourse

THE CONCEPT OF SOCIAL NETWORKING:
CONNECTING WITH PEOPLE . . . BUT NOT ONLY THAT!

When Facebook came onto the public scene in 2006 it marketed itself as a social network that helped users connect and share with the people in their lives. Apart from an age restriction (13 years or older), anyone and everyone could sign up on Facebook. The platform's attractive design easily coaxed people into signing up so that they could stay in touch with family and friends everywhere.

Sixteen years later, Facebook is the world's largest social media platform. Its mission statement has evolved, and it now purports to "give people the power to build community and bring the world closer together."[1] At the 2017 Facebook Communities Summit in Chicago, Mark Zuckerberg, Facebook's founder and CEO, admitted, "I used to think that if we just give people a voice and help some people connect that that would make the world a whole lot better by itself. Look around and our society is still so divided. We have a responsibility to do more, not just to connect the world but to bring the world closer together."[2]

If giving people a voice means granting free expression as "say-whatever-you-want," it does not work. Absolute freedom harms and divides. The company has a responsibility to promote authentic freedom of expression on its platform. We shall see how the company tackles this question with content moderators.

The platform has grown rapidly. Today Facebook has almost three billion users, making its user base bigger than the population of China. However, rapid growth also has its burdens, like internal management difficulties and transparency issues. The privacy abuses that the Cambridge Analytica files showed, along with the lack of transparency of the rules changed the conversation and has led to a credibility crisis.[3] A good number of users, mostly in the United States and Canada, quit the social network. Europe, led by Germany, has enforced tougher privacy regulations, and countries like the United Kingdom and France have sued the company for huge sums of money.

Public networks have enjoyed growing popularity with social networks in general, and with Facebook in particular. They bring together like-minded individuals who frequently post, comment, and share topics of common interest. This new dynamism has had a strikingly powerful influence on forming opinion.

Social media platforms outshine traditional media outlets in three ways: they provide the drama of instantaneity, key players create a whirlwind of attention to the networked public through their social media pages, and the news circulated is often a mixture of fact, opinion, and emotion blended into expressions uttered in anticipation of events that have not yet been recognized by the mainstream media.[4]

A case in point is what people sometimes call the "Facebook Revolution," which is said to have led to the resignation of President Hosni Mubarak of Egypt in 2011. Only history will be able to tell how much Facebook and other social media platforms influenced the turn of events that year.

On June 8, 2010, Egyptian-born Wael Ghonim, working in Dubai, saw a startling image on Facebook: it was the disfigured and bloodied body of a young Egyptian who had been killed. The young man's name was Khaled Mohamed Said, and he had been beaten to death by Egyptian police.

Ghonim was outraged at the brutality and decided to create a Facebook page that he called "Kullena Khaled Said"—"We Are All Khaled Said." According to Jose Antonio Vargas, just "two minutes after he started his Facebook page, 300 people had joined it. Three months later, that number had grown to more than 250,000. What bubbled up online inevitably spilled onto the streets, starting with a series of 'Silent Stands' that culminated in a massive and historic rally at Tahrir Square in downtown Cairo."[5]

Wael Ghonim was not an activist until he saw that picture on Facebook and decided to take up the fight for justice. As an online marketer, he considered the available public-outreach options. Finally, he decided it would be better to create a page on which he would maintain an informal tone that would appeal to the sentiments of the people. He has since written: "Using the pronoun *I* was critical to establishing the fact that the page was not managed by an organization, political party or movement of any kind."[6]

Digital platforms pave the way for a "crowd-sourced" form of leadership. Ghonim's appeal to the sentiments of the average Egyptian citizen was the spark that ignited a fire in Egyptian politics. There was no pause to cross-check the information presented. Combined with the networked and "always-on" character of social media, the affective aspects of such messages nurture and sustain involvement, connection, and cohesion.[7]

Facebook's Community Standards

As of February 4, 2022, Facebook employed 71,970 full-time people and had 2.91 billion active users monthly.[8] Every sixty seconds, more than 510,000 comments are made, 243,000 photos are uploaded, 317,000 statuses are updated, and four hundred new users join the network. Facebook accounts for over 45 percent of monthly social media visits.[9] On average, users spend thirty-four minutes on Facebook every day, followed by TikTok with thirty-two minutes and Twitter with thirty-one minutes daily.

Since its inception, Facebook has been rating college girls. But it had to take certain measures due to the nature of some of the content being shared. A team of twelve people was formed in November 2009 to specialize in content moderation. Facebook hired lawyer Jud Hoffman to draft what would later come to be known as the Facebook Community Standards.[10]

The goal of these is "to encourage expression and create a safe environment."[11] Some of the reasoning behind this goal is difficult to understand and even contradictory. Facebook explains: "Our mission is all about embracing diverse views. We are on the side of *allowing content, even when some find it objectionable, unless removing that content can prevent a specific harm.* Moreover, at times we will *allow content that might otherwise violate our standards if we feel that it is newsworthy, significant,* or *important* to the public interest. We do this only after weighing the public interest value of the content against the risk of real-world harm."[12]

The Facebook Community Standards page offers guidelines on violence and criminal behavior, safety, objectionable content, integrity and authenticity, respecting intellectual property, and content-related requests. And some of these guidelines have subheadings, such as

- Hate speech: "Direct attack on people based on what we call protected characteristics—race, ethnicity, national origin, religious affiliation, sexual orientation, caste, sex, gender, gender identity, and serious disease or disability."[13]
- Adult nudity and sexual activity: "We restrict the display of nudity or sexual activity because some people in our community may be *sensitive* to this type of content. Additionally, we default to removing sexual imagery to prevent the sharing of non-consensual or *underage content.*"[14]

The company highlights the fact that threats to national security deemed to be genuine will be reported to law enforcement authorities.

There are just over twenty bullet points that describe what should not be posted. There is also a reference to fake news under the section "integrity and authenticity."[15] The paragraph on fake news raises the question of whether public discourse can be productive when it is untrue. Why would Facebook keep untruth in circulation? Instead of reducing the news feed distribution of fake news as suggested, it should be removed.

The site makes it clear to users that violation of these standards carries different penalties according to the degree of violation. Some people may receive a warning and, if they ignore it, Facebook may restrict their posts.

The bone of contention is not the existence of these Community Standards. It is obvious that Facebook wants to moderate content to keep the business and its profits going. But this moderation should be done for the benefit of the public interest. To add to the conundrum, the teams of people dedicated to content moderation "backstage" are following fine-tuned rules written in elaborate rulebooks. The rules do not always reflect what the Standards lay down, and this creates a transparency gap. On the other hand, as we will see now, those who moderate content *need* rules.

THE RULES BEHIND THE COMMUNITY STANDARDS

Standards are "principles of conduct informed by notions of honor and decency,"[16] while a *rule* is "a principle that operates within a particular sphere of knowledge, describing or prescribing what is possible or allowable."[17] When you see a speed limit sign by the roadside with the figure "55" on it, it means that there is a speed limit of 55 miles per hour; it is saying to you: "Do *not* drive faster than 55 miles per hour."

General standards are vague and subject to arbitrary enforcement by decision makers. A traffic cop would have a difficult time if, instead of the rule above, drivers were told, "Do *not* drive *fast*." The adjective "fast" is subject to the driver, driving conditions, and other factors; it remains unspecific.

Rules are clear-cut, though they may be over-inclusive or under-inclusive, making them unfair. Rules limit the whims of decision makers. Facebook has had to switch from standards to rules for content moderation for three main reasons: the rapid growth of users and the volume of content being posted, the internationalization of the online community, and the globalization of the cleaners.[18]

The Geneva Art Museum posted on Facebook images of two statues for an upcoming exhibition. One statue was a half-naked Venus, and the other was a nude man kneeling down. Facebook removed this content. Whereas algorithms can be written to trace certain patterns that point to illicit content, there are cases, such as this one, that need a person to decide. And, depending on where you were born and how you were brought up, the images could be seen as art or pornography.

Content Moderation before and after Publication

In this battle to remove sites that promote hatred, tech companies rely both on technology and on human judgment. Kate Klonick, professor at St. John's University who studied the rules and processes of these powerful digital platforms, shows how they are moderating hate speech in daily life online. These companies are using technology to block content automatically through sophisticated software: PhotoDNA, ContentID, and geo-blocking. As she says: "Platforms can determine within micro-seconds between upload and publication if an image contains child porn."[19]

When someone uploads a video to Facebook, a message appears to say that the video post is being processed and a notification will be sent when it is ready for viewing. This is an example of ex ante content moderation, which happens between the upload and final publication.

Microsoft developed PhotoDNA to try to stop the spread of online photos of child sexual abuse. They offer a short video to explain how this picture-recognition algorithm works.[20] Some 1.8 billion photos are uploaded every day; of these, 720,000 are illegal images.[21] While many sexual abuse photos can be tracked down, their modification in size or other attributes by those who pass them on lead them to go undetected.

PhotoDNA uses the "hash"-matching technology to identify known illegal photos even if someone has altered them. According to Tracy Ith, "It works by converting images into a grayscale format, creating a grid and assigning a numerical value to each tiny square. Those numerical values represent the 'hash' of an image, or its 'PhotoDNA signature.' The program protects user privacy in that it doesn't look at images or scan photos; it simply matches a numerical hash against a database of known illegal images."[22]

Geo-blocking is a form of ex ante content moderation. It prevents both the publication and the viewing of certain content depending on the location of users. Sensitive material such as the video "Innocence of Muslims," which went viral can be blocked at the request of the governments of the countries involved. This video was blocked in Egypt, Libya, Saudi Arabia, Malaysia, India, and Singapore.[23]

Another form of moderation is ex post proactive manual content moderation. This is an important development, as platforms must constantly strike a balance between national interests such as security and free expression. At the moment, ex post proactive moderation targets terrorist activities. As of February 2016, Facebook had formed teams dedicated to removing all posts or profiles with links to terrorist activity.[24]

Except for proactive moderation of terrorism, almost all user-generated content that is published online is moderated manually by users who "flag" posts and content moderators who review them. This is ex post reactive manual content moderation.

One flags a post by selecting "Give feedback on this post." This kind of moderation is a very practical way of reviewing hundreds of thousands of posts every day. It also gives Facebook a good excuse when other users protest in the name of freedom of expression. In 2012, the company had four teams: a safety team, a hate and harassment team, an access team, and an abusive content team to address flagged material.[25]

Once material has been flagged and passed on to the teams, decisions must be made about whether to take down a post, warn a user, suspend a user account, or something else. This decision-making process is not always clear. Sometimes content that is permissible according to the Community Standards is removed. Until recently, users could not appeal these decisions.

COO Sheryl Sandberg announced that Facebook is reviewing its free expression policy so that people can appeal what can be shown on Facebook through an independent body. She said that the platform will adhere to what the independent body decides.[26] Ex post reactive manual moderation is in the hands of human moderators. They are the ones who enforce the rules according to the rulebooks that Facebook provides to them.

The Tiers of Content Moderators

In October of 2008, Facebook announced that it would be setting up its International Headquarters in Dublin. At that time, Sheryl Sandberg explained: "As we grow and strive to make Facebook into a place for people around the world to connect and share information, we need local operations to better advance our efforts."[27] She did not explain that this move was also made to outsource content moderation, first to Dublin and then to Hyderabad, India.[28]

This was a significant change, since the company had until then maintained a homogenous base of content moderators in Palo Alto. The outsourcing of this job may have initially been conceived as a plus for Facebook, which had to cope with an increasing amount of content being uploaded. But it posed a new challenge, because moderators working in regions to which information was outsourced came from different cultural backgrounds. "One man's meat is another man's poison," goes the English saying. What would not be offensive to a North American might not be perceived the same way in Africa, Asia, or Latin America.

David Willner drafted the first set of Abuse Standards, a comprehensive online document for moderators. These were rules about what could and could not be posted. Because of the new cultural factor, the rules had to be more specific about Community Standards. For instance, "hate speech" is not permitted on Facebook. An American would not hesitate to flag a post with the "N-word," while someone in Turkey or the Philippines would not share the same sensibility. Moderation without specific rules becomes very subjective because it relies not only on the context of the post, but also on the context of who is moderating.

In order to unify moderation policies, Facebook devised a three-tiered moderation model. When material is flagged by users, the content is sent to a server to await review by human content moderators. Of these we have the following:

- Tier 3: Some moderators work in call centers in the Philippines, Ireland, India, Mexico, Turkey, or Eastern Europe.[29]
- Tier 2: More specialized moderators with experience review content escalated by Tier 3 moderators. Sometimes the same content is sent to different Tier 3 moderators; if there are varying opinions, this content is escalated to Tier 2 moderators. They are usually based in the United States.
- Tier 1: moderation at a legal or policy level is carried out in the United States.

The challenge for this model is that in order to operate effectively, Tier 3 moderators must be well trained and "culturally neutral," or "culturally neutralized." Sasha Rose, who worked with David Tillner to train the first team in Hyderabad, India, said in a telephone interview: "I liked to say that our goal was [to have a training system and rules set] so I could go into the deepest of the Amazon, but if I had developed parameters that were clear enough I could teach someone that had no exposure to anything outside of their village how to do this job."[30]

The Backstage Rules for Moderators: Abuse Standards

Tier 3 moderators have three possible courses of action when they receive flagged content. They can "confirm" or "unconfirm" that content violates the Community Standards, or they can "escalate" the content to Tier 2 supervisors for further review.

In a bid to help Tier 3 moderators to make uniform judgments, regardless of their cultural backgrounds, Facebook developed an online Abuse Standards tool that is reviewed frequently. Here we will look at versions 6.0 and 6.1. These online tools were leaked by a Facebook moderator and give a valuable insight into the intricacy of the rulebooks being followed.

The first page of Abuse Standards 6.1 describes major changes to version 6.0 regarding a number of topics, such as sex and nudity, hate speech, graphic violence, attacks, photoshopped images, international compliance, and photo comments.[31] I shall focus on hate speech.

Content moderators are supplied with definitions of people, examples of types of attacks, and protected categories. There is a note on the same page about protected categories: it says that users may not create content that degrades individuals based on race, ethnicity, national origin, religion, sex, gender identity, sexual orientation, disability, or serious disease. The protected-category status should over-ride the person's status as a public figure or as head of state. Example: "I hate Obama" is unconfirmed, while "Can't stand that [N-word] Obama" is confirmed for flagging as inappropriate.[32]

To establish the credibility of an attack, the rulebook proposes a credibility test based on three parameters: consequence, specificity, and practicability.[33] It is true that in the ethical realm, to say that "Obama is a fool" holds greater weight than saying that "Harry Potter is a fool" because the reputation of a president needs to be defended more assiduously than that of a fictional character. There is also a difference between a post that says, "I'm going to stab (method) Lisa H. (target) at the frat party (place)" and another that says, "I'm going to blow up the planet on new year's eve this year." The first is something that should be escalated because the action is not impossible to carry out. The second does not need to be escalated because it is not credible.[34]

I have deliberately made detailed reference to the online rulebooks because it becomes patently clear that the job of content moderators is not at all easy. The platform itself acknowledges this in Abuse Standards section 6.2, on assessing credibility, which says: "The expectation from moderators is to research where language and context hint at loaded history. We understand that this is an operational burden and *ambiguous* in some cases. We'd still like to give it a try to protect more vulnerable targets. We'll *try* and make sure that *you're not penalized* for *unreasonable expectations*."[35]

Although it is commendable that Facebook is going to great lengths to track down hate speech, violence, and other online crimes, Tier 3 human moderators are the ones who have to make the final call. They must judge whether content should be unconfirmed or confirmed and escalated to Tier 2 moderators.

Tier 3 moderators ultimately pay the price for their mistakes. What happens if they make a "wrong" call in what the company calls ambiguous cases? Can ambiguous cases be correctly or incorrectly judged? Why would the company speak of penalizing moderators for unreasonable expectations?

The Woes of Tier 3 Content Moderators

In May 2017, Zuckerberg went on a hiring spree to enlist 3,000 extra content moderators. This followed the broadcast of a father killing his daughter in Thailand live on Facebook. After more than a day and 370,000 views, Facebook took down the video. Another video of a man shooting and killing another man in Cleveland also had to be removed.[36]

These kinds of problems have grown significantly. COO Sheryl Sandberg announced at Digital Life Design, an innovation conference in Munich, that the company was investing heavily in keeping Facebook safe. It was in the process of hiring 30,000 moderators and continuing research on moderation by artificial intelligence.[37]

The platform pledges its commitment to creating safer spaces for its base of 2.9 billion active users. But it says very little about the tens of thousands of content reviewers who spend full workdays watching raw violence, sexual abuse, offensive content, conspiracy theories, and so on. Two reports by Casey Newton revealed the unhealthy conditions of US content moderators' work, being exposed to nonstop violence and hatred.[38]

In 2017 Mark Zuckerberg stated that artificial intelligence will take a period of years to really reach the quality level that Facebook wants.[39] As of 2019, artificial intelligence was not yet up to the mark. Tier 3 moderators receive low wages for a job that is taxing and almost inhumane considering that they spend full working days sifting through raw footage containing harmful material.

Facebook needs to be more transparent about who works behind the scenes to keep the network safe. This might draw a great deal of criticism at first, but there would also be a positive effect. Many of the 2.9 billion users would be motivated to think differently when they post material and flag unworthy content. The platform, too, would have an incentive to defend freedom of expression, which seeks truth. Transparency can help the platform formulate less ambiguous Community Standards. These can be based on what is ethically good and discourage those expressions that dehumanize.

CONTENT MODERATION OF A COMMUNITY
OF ALMOST THREE BILLION PEOPLE:
A QUESTION OF PUBLIC INTEREST

Some cases of hate speech, violence, pornography, and suicide began to shed light on Facebook's decision-making process as to what content should be censored. Documents leaked to the *Guardian* show that Facebook's rules and guidelines governing censorship remain unknown to the public.[40]

Facebook's opaque policy related to its algorithms and censoring activity has led to suspicion among journalists. For this reason, Margaret Sullivan, an opinion writer at the *Washington Post*, and Emily Bell of the Tow Center for Digital Journalism, have called for Facebook to appoint an editor (and staff) who will judge its content and have the power to censor it. It requires, they say, more than algorithms; it requires real people, able to distinguish between a famous photo of a naked and napalmed girl in South Vietnam, which was temporarily blocked, and child pornography. Facebook is, by virtue of its size and activity, a media company, not just a social platform.

All media outlets have rules about participation, but a question of magnitude arises: Facebook guides the conversations of almost 3 billion users, and for this purpose, it is training a crowd of content moderators that continues to increase (in 2019, to more than 30,000).[41] According to the NYU Stern Report, 3 million times a day posts, pictures, and videos are flagged by AI or reported by users. And, as Mark Zuckerberg admitted, moderators "make the wrong call in more than one out of every 10 cases." That means 300,000 times a day, mistakes are made.[42] Given its size, as Bell has pointed out, "Facebook does not have the luxury of the 'our house, our rules' approach of smaller communities."[43] The public has the right to know what criteria are used to moderate content, the actors involved, and the methods these giant companies use to shape public opinion. As Michael Schudson has noticed, transparency is not an absolute value but a value that expresses a kind of procedural morality. In the end, transparency is expressed in processes, and these practices promote trustworthiness.[44]

Legally, these platforms can moderate their content in the United States "to preserve the vibrant and competitive free market" (of ideas) and can also restrict it in order to protect the public by blocking and screening harmful content: "No provider or user of an interactive computer service shall be treated as the publisher or speaker of any information provided by another information content provider."[45]

Common sense dictates that Zuckerberg cannot be responsible for content posted by third parties. Mary Ann Franks, professor of cyber policy and law at the University of Miami, says that "§230 [of the The Communications Decency Act, or CDA] protects intermediaries from liability for the actions of others, not individuals from liability for their own illegal conduct."[46] This distinction points to a blurred frontier where platforms such as Facebook sometimes operate disingenuously when they host interactions while also suggesting content. Franks asserts, "The CDA distinguishes providers of 'interactive computer services' from 'information content providers.'" The basic question is this: Should these social media companies lose their immunity if they act as authors or architects and not just as facilitators? In this context it is difficult to maintain that these companies are not editors, that is, media actors.

US law considers Internet service providers to be mediators that foster debate and innovation on the Internet. For this reason, they are protected against laws that would otherwise make them legally accountable. Some scholars consider this situation a privilege; others think that a combination of technology, public policy, and law protecting mediators will ultimately foster freedom of speech online. The framework in Europe is much different and includes the requirement for platforms to take down content within forty-eight hours.[47]

Fearing any link to terrorism or hate, some big companies like Johnson & Johnson and Verizon—among others—are pulling their advertising dollars from Facebook and Google.[48] Facebook has declared its commitment to tackle the problem of violent extremism online several times, but its reluctance to be transparent is a worrying sign. It seems that their statements are meant to convey a sense of serenity and trust more to investors and consumers than to the public. M. Bickert, Facebook's director of global policy management, and Brian Fishman, counterterrorism policy manager, repeat the nice slogan "We believe technology, and Facebook, can be part of the solution."[49] Of course they are part of the solution, but their lack of transparency regarding the criteria used to implement algorithms and artificial intelligence contradicts their words. This statement was made in an idle effort to explain their commitment but not the exercise of transparency required by the public.

Facebook's attitude seems to have changed recently. It has gone from covering up editorial decisions under the framework of technology (as Bickert said: "Ideally, one day our technology will address everything"[50]) to Zuckerberg's words in 2019:

> Lawmakers often tell me we have too much power over speech, and frankly I agree. I've come to believe that we shouldn't make so many important decisions about speech on our own. . . . I believe we need a more active role for governments and regulators. . . . From what I've learned, I believe we need new regulation in four areas: harmful content, election integrity, privacy and data portability.[51]

On April 21, 2020, news broke of a new case of censorship by Facebook. This time the company had been pressured by the Vietnamese government to censor content posted by dissidents. This government pressure on social media companies to take down content that "offends the authorities" within twenty-four hours has been a regular occurrence since the cybersecurity law went into effect in January of 2019.[52] These companies have sometimes resisted such requests. However, the new pressure was aimed at Facebook's business. According to a Reuters report, through February and March 2020 the Vietnamese government compelled Internet service providers in Vietnam (which are basically controlled by them), to disrupt Facebook's activity by slowing down the custumers' access to its services (WhatsApp and Instagram).[53] James Pearson, author of the report, said, "Once we committed to restricting more content, then after that, the servers were turned back online by the telecommunications operators."[54]

A statement from Facebook (on April 22), the day after the Reuters report broke, showed that their pronouncements on principles are not reliable: "We believe freedom of expression is a fundamental human right, and work hard to protect and defend this important civil liberty around the world. . . . However, we have taken this action to ensure our services remain available and usable for millions of people in Vietnam."[55] Public social deliberation cannot depend on their decisions, which are based on profits.

We are facing some important political and moral dilemmas regarding the Internet. The balance that must be struck between freedom and safety cannot be exclusively in the hands of these huge companies and their partners. It is urgent to have a public conversation about moderation policies and the specific criteria used to remove content, as a matter of public interest. This is not possible if said companies are not fully transparent and we do not have a global legal paradigm.

PART II

The Liberal Tradition
of Freedom of Expression
and Its Contradictions

SIX

The Sustainability of
the Liberal Rationale

Main Critiques

It is not my purpose here to present a genealogical history of the authors who have focused on freedom of expression, much less a history of the juridical-legal dimensions of freedom of expression or the full extent of its social repercussions. Instead, my purpose is to identify and list the moral presuppositions of various authors that form the foundation of this freedom. Moreover, I will show how these presuppositions emerge in the debate between the different schools of thought.

Freedom of expression comes not from a uniform tradition but from a variegated one. The exposition of ideas is organized according to four different schools of thought: libertarianism, the thought of contemporary liberals who are critical of the liberal tradition, communitarianism, and finally, the thought of those with feminist and anti-racist standpoints. I believe that they cover the most important arguments on freedom of expression. The main criticisms of the liberal free speech tradition made by these schools of thought (limits to harmful speech, antagonism between freedom and equality, a formalistic understanding of language, and the limitations of some ethical programs like individualism and utilitarianism in solving these problems) mirror some of the main shortfalls that I am emphasizing in these pages. That is to say, that the liberal tradition of freedom of expression is floundering because of the epistemological and anthropological gaps in the structure of Modernity in which it was theorized.

FREEDOM OF EXPRESSION IN THE LIBERTARIAN SCHOOL OF THOUGHT

Libertarian thought can be observed in the origins of American republicanism. Liberty is understood in the absolute sense, as a natural and inalienable right, and freedom of expression is an essential manifestation of these individual rights—although we do find an unresolved contradiction in the American Founders: advocating human freedoms and countenancing slavery at the same time.[1]

For libertarians, the role of the state consists in protecting the rights we receive by nature. In the particular case of freedom of expression, the state ensures it in two ways: by protecting those who engage in controversial writing or speech from violent private responses and by establishing limits on the government's tendency to exert control over public discourse or limits on a state's tendency to limit the speech either of those who dislike those in power or those considered inconvenient by the ones wielding power.[2]

John Durham Peters characterizes civil libertarianism as a diverse school of thought ranging from those with the most anarchistic position regarding the role of the state to those who believe in the need to establish "strong laws" in sensitive areas, such as laws protecting the secularism of the state and laws regarding life, family, education, and health.

There are two authors who frame the libertarian approach as not restricting any type of speech or discourse, and they do so based on two distinct perspectives: Edwin Baker invokes the principle of autonomy as it pertains to individuals, and Ronald Dworkin claims absolute liberty as a principle of democratic legitimacy.

Baker, a professor at the University of Pennsylvania, departs from the classic tradition of Milton and Mill and from the arguments of social utilitarianism to formulate a theory of free expression that revolves around the self-actualization of the individual, leaving aside the common good.[3] He argues that the government should respect and preserve this individual autonomy, which is understood as the self-expression of the individual who lives in society and interacts with others.[4] As Baker acknowledges at the beginning of his article "Harm, Liberty and Free Speech," the harmfulness of speech never justifies limiting an individual's free expression.[5] He argues that the paradigm of autonomy includes respect for the other, since each person freely shows his or her values to others and chooses how to respond. Thus, the government should not interfere or discriminate.[6] Considering the devastating consequences of hate speech, especially as regards the dignity of individuals and of racial, religious, or sexual minority groups, Jeremy Waldron believes that arguing against any type of regulation of hate speech on the grounds that it violates individual autonomy is to invoke autonomy as a mere slogan.[7]

Professor Dworkin has developed what some have called an egalitarian stance,[8] which emphasizes that government intervention must be minimal, not prescribing on foundational ethical matters to show equal concern and respect for all ways of life and to avoid spoiling the democratic process with preemptive legislation.[9] For example, despite the consideration that pornography constitutes an offense to and degradation of women, it should not be regulated since it has not been proven that it results in sex crimes, based on the fact that such censorship is not covered by the Constitution.[10] Dworkin believes that it is fundamental for the process to be legitimate and equal for all so that, in the end, fanatics, racists, and others all comply with the democratically adopted laws—even those who are bothered by them.[11] Freedom of expression, understood in this way, would be the price to pay for political legitimacy, but Dworkin's idea conveys a moral stance of imposed neutrality.

In the twentieth century, this libertarian school of thought developed a nihilistic undertone that could be characterized with the well-known aforementioned phrase of Holmes and Brandeis: "Defend the thought you hate." Both jurists advocated learning to coexist with reviled speech as a program of civic education. This implies the defense of harmful speech in the public sphere, as a theoretical position, for education in political and democratic liberty through tolerance. However, both Peters and Waldron criticize the idea that tolerating thought that one detests automatically builds democratic character.

Holmes followed in the footsteps of Mill and the stoic classicists when it came to controversy and confrontation as necessary means. Holmes conceived of the public sphere as the "battleground" on which fighting must be permitted to the extreme, followed by education in self-discipline and tolerance.[12] Brandeis's position was more romantic. He thought that the dangers for freedom of expression come both from the intrusions of the state and from citizens' apathetic attitudes toward the truth, concluding that "dangerous speech" must be part of the debate because a passive society is a stagnant society.[13]

The libertarian approach is not found only in the United States. There are also theorists in Europe who favor an absolutist view of freedom of expression, such as the Belgian thinker Raoul Vaneigem. Vaneigem defends an unlimited freedom of expression, including hate speech, in which everyone can express any ideology or belief, however aberrant or hateful.[14] This author proposes the rejection of the idea that any idea or preconception is untouchable, such as, for example, the idea of sanctity: "What sacralizes kills. . . . Sacralized, the child is a tyrant, the woman an object, life a discarnate abstraction."[15] Vaneigem believes that "no truth deserves that one be made dessert in its presence, and every pre-concept held as eternal and incorruptible exhales that stinking stench of God and tyranny."[16]

It is interesting to see how Vaneigem absolutizes freedom of expression to an irrational extreme. He ends up, for example, encouraging the rekindling of all possible fires, in reference to harmful and hateful speech: "Racist, xenophobic, sexist, sadistic, spiteful, and contemptuous opinions have the same right to be expressed as nationalistic ones, as religious beliefs, and as the sectarian ideologies of the corporatist groups that encourage it openly or subtly, according to the fluctuations of demagogic ignominy."[17] It seems that he even dispenses with the content and meaning of words and gives value to communication in itself, regardless of whether it informs or insults.[18] He disconnects communication from any outside category and reference and therefore from realities such as truth, equality, or justice.

THE LIBERAL CRITICS OF LIBERALISM

Among the liberal ranks of contemporary authors, there are criticisms from within, which recognize that abuses of freedom of expression do occur. Timothy Garton Ash advocates for as little government limitation of free expression as possible, but at the same time he advocates doing "more to develop shared norms and practices that enable us to make the best use of this essential freedom."[19] Ash summarizes his opinion by saying that he fights for "more and better free speech."[20] Presented with the challenge of hate speech, Steven Heyman highlights the need for mutual recognition of and respect for the intrinsic value of the human being.[21] He argues that the rights model is useful both for defending freedom of expression and for justifying its limits.

I find the most pervasive criticism to be that of John D. Peters in his book *Courting the Abyss: Free Speech and the Liberal Tradition*, which deals with the ethical dilemmas posed by freedom of expression in the twenty-first century. Peters examines the strength of the principle of tolerating the most extreme speech, exploring the classical and contemporary liberal approaches. The notion that tolerating these extreme transgressions and offenses strengthens citizenship is not just moral gymnastics but dangerous acrobatics. So is the belief that everything is permissible because it all adds to the public good in the end or that one can learn something from any speech or discourse — however harmful. In this sense, Peters claims that the paradigm of "civic self-discipline" practiced by Anglo-American culture from Locke to Smith and from Mill to Holmes is in tatters. The liberal morality of opposites is an "agnostic" neutrality that has not led anywhere.[22] And he notes that confidence in freedom of expression has actually weakened in today's Anglo-American culture (as seen in the defense of Nazi ideas, the burning of flags, obscenity and pornography, and other instances).[23]

Peters seeks to offer a response to the mystery of evil and iniquity behind many of these extreme transgressions and offensive expressions in the public sphere. This response is inspired mainly by the stoics, Milton, and Saint Paul. Peters examines the Miltonian idea that good and evil go together and the idea of the catharsis produced by the "servants of evil." In Saint Paul and in the Christian sense of Jesus's death and crucifixion, in that *felix culpa* (happy crime), Peters finds a justification for redemption through transgression.[24] When contemplating an image of the crucifixion, Christians see beyond the offense and the wounds; they see grace and forgiveness. The most degrading death can be, for them, a sign of triumph and devotion. Christian culture prepares us for a certain kind of ironic reading.[25]

As Waldron recognizes in his analysis of Peters's book, liberal discourse has focused on academically justifying fanatics' freedom of expression (such

as the speech of Nazis and other harmful speech) or on providing the reasoning in favor of the ability of the marketplace of ideas to promote the
truth. However, there is no reflection on the moral alchemy that can
arise—in the form of virtue—from the journey through the abyss of hell
and evil. He recognizes that this self-criticism is important and has been
neglected in the history of liberal thought.[26]

In a similar way, Owen Fiss states that free expression is not an end in
itself (it is not like a moral code), but the autonomy that it defends is important for democratic values.[27] On this point, his thought is very compatible
with the concern of Peters, who attempts to reconstruct the true relationship between communication and democracy within the liberal free speech
theory but believes that there are positions (which are presented as unquestionable dogmas) within this school of thought that must be cast aside.[28]

In *Courting the Abyss*, Peters urges an ethical reconstruction of the liberal school of thought on freedom of expression through the intellectual
tradition of the authors who defend this freedom with a deep sense of the
central values of morality, such as Saint Paul and Milton, Thoreau and
King, Arendt and Havel. This is a rich cultural synthesis of authors whom
he describes as the "radical center" in order to reconcile critical freedom
(openness) with the orthodoxy of faith (the sacred) under the conditions
of postmodernity.[29]

Peters identifies the roots of free speech theory in stoic ethics, which
call for recognition of the other, and in Saint Paul, who goes one step further and calls for love of the other. Peters defends a public sphere that is
pragmatic and oriented toward mutual understanding, openness, care, and
growth (Peirce's evolutionary love[30]). Thus, in Paul and Milton, Peters sees
two thinkers who believed that debates about opinions should be based on
love and a deep sense of the human moral heritage. He emphasizes the
fact that Milton established the concept of provocation[31] and, on the other
hand, that Paul "recognizes the right of the other to think differently, even
though he is very convinced that there's one universal truth."[32]

Peters believes that these two authors did not conceive of freedom of
expression as an end in itself. He warns of this danger when he says that a
policy of self-referential or absolutely open debate that does not take sen-
sitivities or vulnerable minorities into account may not be the only way to
discover the truth. What the philosophy of freedom of expression needs
today is the delicate mix of freedom and love.[33]

Part of the reconstruction of the edifice of freedom of expression goes through the demolition of a certain contemporary secularism—rooted in the Enlightenment—that conceives of the public sphere as a space where only secular reason is appropriate. Peters's thinking on the marginalization of religious argument is clear: "Revelation and inquiry, debate and discussion go together and are part of life. It is not a matter of either faith or reason,"[34] as if they were mutually exclusive. "Belief is public," Peters says, "and we enact our beliefs in everything we do. Reason operates in many languages. Paul again, in 1 Cor: 12, 14, says that the spirit speaks voices, and reason has many languages in many tongues. I would say, secular reason is only one of these languages."[35]

As Peters says in the preface to the Hungarian translation of his book: "My aim was to purify the tradition of some of its excesses and pathologies such as its tendency to glory in its supposed ethical superiority, its lack of reflection on the pragmatic conditions and consequences of communication, and its contradictory dependence on and distaste for strong opinions."[36] It is in cases like that of *Charlie Hebdo* and its incontestable defense with the slogan *Je suis Charlie*, which in Europe did not admit any opposition, that one can see this arrogance of the liberal ethical paradigm, which makes it "illiberal." In this sense, Peters comments: "In a similar way it is very difficult to love and support the rights of gay people, and still hold to a vision of marriage as exclusively male and female. That is a very difficult position to articulate in this culture. Just like it's a very difficult position to say: I don't like *Charlie Hebdo* but I do like free speech."[37] And Peters goes on to reflect on how difficult it is to have a rational discussion about religious freedom and marriage in North America today: "In a robust liberal public sphere, it would be possible to stage a healthy debate about what, for example, marriage means without some members of the debate being reduced to 'phoebes' or 'haters.' But that is not the climate."[38]

THE SOCIAL THESES OF THE COMMUNITARIANS

I do not claim to include here the full scope of the debate between liberals and communitarians.[39] I only want to touch upon the arguments that can shed some light on the rational foundations of the exercise of freedom of expression.

Communitarians believe that each person must be understood within a social framework, since there is an intimate relationship between the person and the society in which he or she lives.[40] For adherents to this school of thought, society constitutes and decisively influences the identity of the individual. In the words of Alasdair MacIntyre: "The individual is identified and constituted in and through certain of his or her roles, those roles which bind the individual to the communities in and through which alone specifically human goods are to be attained; I confront the world as a member of this family, this household, this clan, this tribe, this city, this nation, this kingdom. There is no 'I' apart from these."[41] Those horizons of relation form us as human persons.

As Charles Taylor argues, the social framework to which every individual belongs is expressed in, among other things, the fact that we have a sense of respect for the dignity of the other and an awareness of our duties toward others: "Frameworks provide the background, explicit or implicit, for our moral judgements, intuitions, or reactions. . . . Doing without frameworks is utterly impossible for us."[42] More than relating to our identity as persons, this social reference framework implies a sense of the natural justice of "what is owed to the other." This argument will be very important for the exercise of freedom of expression because, unlike an individualism that postulates autonomous and self-referential freedom, communitarianism retains the sense of responsibility that accompanies the exercise of personal freedom, which is always an act of social community.

The communitarians criticize the liberal dissociation between the public and private spheres to define the individual and his or her autonomy (the public sphere would be governed by justice and the private sphere by a certain conception of the good), which seems artificial. Thus, they criticize a conception of the individual whose "autonomy entails the absolute primacy of the freedom to choose one's lifestyle over any conception of the good."[43] The question then arises of who decides what is good or bad. Liberalism promotes neutrality, thereby choosing to forfeit thinking about what is good for the human being and opting for an ethical relativism.

In this sense, MacIntyre recalls the classic doctrine on virtue: only the virtuous person sees the true good as a good:[44] "For what education in the virtues teaches me is that my good as a man is one and the same as the good of those others with whom I am bound up in human community."[45] He goes on to say: "There is no way of my pursuing my good which is necessarily antagonistic to you pursuing yours because *the* good is neither mine peculiarly nor yours peculiarly—goods are not private property."[46] In other words, every concept of what is just necessarily includes a mode of understanding, a vision of the good. There are things that we all want: not to be victims of torture or of slavery, the right to a fair trial, and not to be victims of insults and public falsehoods.

Martin Rhonheimer, however, objects that the consequences of projecting MacIntyre's argument of the "community of virtue" onto the political-institutional sphere would be unclear, since it is not the mission of the political system to give "public validation" to a particular conception of the "good life."[47] Rhonheimer goes on to say that, through the recognition of fundamental rights, liberalism claims an "independence of man *as man* over values that dominate through specific traditions, communities, or collective practices."[48] That is, he says, that an objective conception of the good should not be imposed out of respect for the liberty and conscience of the human being and because doing so would deny legitimate pluralism.

Charles Taylor argues that some liberals conceive of the human being as an individual who possesses a "self-understanding" that is independent of and prior to the society that he or she existentially inhabits. Taylor calls this strictly individualistic conception of autonomy and of the human being who pursues only individual ends *atomism*,[49] and he adds that this conception of freedom has a clear connotation of procedure; that is, it is not substantive (it does not form part of a human being's practical reason), and thus on its own it cannot make important ethical judgments about the good of a person.[50] Taylor believes that atomism affirms the self-sufficiency of the individual and results in the primacy of rights above all else, which is a contradiction because, if "we assert the right to one's own independent moral convictions, we cannot in the face of this social thesis go on to assert the primacy of rights, that is, claim that we are not under obligation 'by nature' to belong to and sustain a society of the relevant type."[51] Taylor's intuition reveals a frequent contradiction in the exercise of the freedom of expression: absolute autonomy is invoked on the one hand, but the social importance of fundamental rights for living in a democracy is sustained on the other.

Taylor proposes a liberalism that is not "atomistic" but "whole," that is, a concept of justice that does not take priority over the substantial concepts of the good:

Since the free individual can only maintain his identity within a society/ culture of a certain kind, he has to be concerned about the shape of this society/culture as a whole. He cannot, following the libertarian anarchist model that [Robert] Nozick sketched, be concerned purely with his individual choices and the associations formed from such choices to the neglect of the matrix in which such choices can be open or closed, rich or meagre.[52]

The theory of freedom of expression can draw from Taylor's comprehensive approach the sense of social responsibility that must accompany the exercise of artistic or written expression, beyond the mere self-affirmation of the artist.

Taylor continues: "It is important to him [Nozick] that certain activities and institutions flourish in society. It is even of importance to him what the moral tone of the whole society is—shocking as it may be to libertarians to raise this issue—because freedom and individual diversity can only flourish in a society where there is a general recognition of their worth."[53] Freedom of expression is valuable not only as the exercise of individual self-determination but also as a social contribution. In this sense, it is not helpful to dig a chasm between a public act and a private act, because the individual acts are performed within a social context and, in this sense, they can be more or less valuable, depending on their contribution to the social good.

The debate between liberals and communitarians is an interesting source of arguments that have direct implications for freedom of expression. The debate shows where some of the underlying problems lie when it comes to obtaining a moral foundation for the exercise of freedom in the public sphere, the necessity of finding a common horizon of meaning, the social meaning of each individual act, and the appeal to responsible communication, precisely because of this dimension of community and respect for human dignity.

RACIAL AND FEMINIST CRITICISMS RELATING TO EQUALITY AND HARM

"Critical Race Theory": Freedom of Expression and Equality

In the 1980s, a school of thinkers critical of absolute freedom of expression formed. They compiled a series of articles about what they called "assaultive speech" in which they denounced the use of words as weapons to hurt, humiliate, or degrade. They established a direct relationship between offensive speech and racial exclusion, both on university campuses and in different social structures.[54] In turn, they criticized some of the liberal foundations that support free speech theory, such as the neutrality of the state and the distinction between public and private, where offense pertains only to the private sphere. They also argued that impersonality in the public sphere is a "refuge" for transgressors and criticized the view of evil and transgression as educators in virtue, objecting that the irony can be gleaned only by some.[55]

This school of thinkers started from a realistic presupposition: there are words that hurt and acts that intimidate. The meaning of acts and words is open to interpretation but not to such an extent as to permit an abusive usage. The "ambiguity" and "elasticity" of the meaning that is sometimes attributed to them is artificial: ambiguity can go only so far.[56] On the other hand, to let speech compete and reach equilibrium with society's reactions relies on an optimistic but irresponsible assumption: "More speech frequently is useless because it may provoke only further abuse or because the insulter is in a position of authority over the victim."[57]

A field study cited by Richard Delgado shows that the richest, most educated, and usually male groups accept and encourage more absolute freedom of expression.[58] The suspicion that is automatically implied (but not exactly implicit) is that this is surely the case because they have more mechanisms for dealing with the consequences of absolute freedom of expression. Peters concludes that, as was the case with stoicism in antiquity, the liberalism that sustains free speech theory is a philosophy of the privileged.[59]

Freedom of expression is not only an action, but also a condition: there is an innate value in each human being, and each one is called to a dignified life. Insult and verbal violence, especially toward minors, impedes people's dignified development because they can react with only hostility or passivity when faced with the offense, and in both cases the results they obtain are detrimental.[60] This situation damages individuals, groups, and society as a whole.

For the authors of critical race theory,[61] the objective of the First Amendment, to put public discourse above other considerations, is not possible in a marketplace of ideas that is distorted by coercion and privilege.[62] However, theories based on race have been strongly criticized, sometimes being called the etiquette of the new censors.[63]

Feminist Critics

The feminist theses on freedom of expression have been connected from the start with the question of pornography, which analyzes the extent to which this phenomenon does or does not benefit women. So far, studies have focused on heterosexual pornography that is aimed primarily at men.[64] On one side, feminist Wendy McElroy is in favor of tolerating pornography and justifies it as something that benefits women's liberation, highlighting the importance of privileging individual choices.[65]

McElroy distinguishes three ways that pornography benefits women: it provides an overview of the different possibilities of sex, it allows one to imaginatively experiment with and safely explore new sexual alternatives; and finally, it facilitates the provision of information about different forms of sexual interaction, which allows one to see one's personal emotional response to these stimuli.[66] Without engaging here in a deeper and broader moral evaluation of McElroy's position, we can perceive the fact that the author does not see beyond the mere right of individual choice, closing her eyes to the consequences of this industry for women and society.

Other feminists have gone further and studied whether there is a direct relationship between pornography and physical and psychological violence against women. In a study from October of 2010, four researchers looked at four popular pornographic films and sought to analyze the degree to which these two types of violence against women (physical and psychological) occurred. For this purpose, they observed 304 scenes of pornography and found that 88 percent of the scenes contained physical aggressions against women (mainly whipping, gagging, slapping, and so on) and 49 percent of the scenes contained verbal aggressions (insults and barbaric expressions).[67]

As described in a report by the American Academy of Pediatrics from June of 2016 on a project directed by the physician David Perry, women see pornography as a way of being treated as sexual objects. "When women view the pornography their partners are viewing they can develop a lower self-esteem, feelings of inadequacy, and begin to feel sexually undesirable."[68]

Catharine MacKinnon's studies were similar. She sees physical, psychological, and social damage for women in the ease of acquiring pornography.[69] One of the most serious implications that MacKinnon sees is the relationship between pornography and the crime of rape. Studies of the fantasies of those who consume violent pornography, with scenes in which women are intimidated (through masochism, rape, and so on), show that sooner or later such fantasies are brought to reality in the form of sex crimes. MacKinnon cites the *Shiro* case in her book,[70] reporting the testimony of a rapist who admits the connection between the images that he saw in films or magazines and his desire to carry out the rape he committed. The same author, despite not having the evidence provided by statistics, establishes a similar relationship between consumers of racist propaganda and those who commit crimes of racial harassment.[71] The authors of the above-cited study by the American Academy of Pediatrics observed that a group of young adults exposed to pornography considered the crime of rape to be less serious than did the control group.[72]

Warburton, on the other hand, does not see a direct relationship between pornography and rape. Moreover, he thinks it is an exaggeration to consider pornography as an incitement to violence against women because most people do not go beyond the mere consumption of pornography. However, Warburton does recognize that the psychological mechanism that MacKinnon describes seems plausible for some criminals.[73]

In any case, the social damage emphasized by the feminist discussion is that pornography communicates an offensive message about the dignity of women for several reasons. Women are presented as having a sexual availability that turns them into objects of pleasure. Distorted physical models of women are shown, which lead to false expectations about real women. Not only is it particularly humiliating and degrading when they are presented showing attitudes of submission and even of enjoying that treatment but these presentations communicate a totally false image of a woman's real feelings.[74]

Authors like Warburton and Dworkin who oppose these feminist theses argue that pornography should be censored only in the case of direct harm, such as when its production involves minors or adults who are coerced (through human trafficking).[75] But an approach based only on statistics falls short. MacKinnon's figures show that there is a statistically significant problem. Those who aim to build legality and morality into statistics are correct that there is no proven direct evidence of the connection between pornography and violence against women. But at the same time, they forget that statistics do not offer a causal relationship. Statistical studies can manifest meaningful problems fostering further reflection but are not causal science.

SEVEN

A Fabricated Notion
of Tolerance

Tolerance of evil and of error are key human and social dilemmas for political and moral philosophy, which have a solid tradition in the classical thought of Aristotle, Augustine, and Thomas Aquinas.[1] Starting from the European Enlightenment of the seventeenth and eighteenth centuries with Voltaire, Hobbes, Locke, and Rousseau, the notion of tolerance has taken on a different shade depending on each thinker's concept of social order. In the thought of John Milton and John Stuart Mill, among others, the literature of freedom of expression has specific applications regarding the tolerance of different forms of expression in the public sphere.

JOHN MILTON AND THE VALUE OF TRANSGRESSION

The English writer John Milton wrote an essay, published on November 23, 1644, for Parliament in favor of the freedom to print without needing a license: *Areopagitica: A Speech for the Liberty of Unlicensed Printing, to the Parliament of England.* This pamphlet has become an obligatory reference text for scholars of freedom of expression. *Areopagitica* is a reaction to an order of the Parliament of England from June 14, 1643, whereby no "book, pamphlet, or paper shall from henceforth printed . . . or put to sale, unless the same be first approved and licensed."[2] This order reintroduced the previous limitation and censorship of publishing companies, which would now be required to have a license to print. The queen granted this publishing license to only twenty publishers.[3]

There were additional factors that could have influenced Milton. He married in 1642, but the relationship was short-lived. During 1643 and 1644 Milton wrote four essays in favor of divorce,[4] which scandalized Parliament and much of the clergy, who tried to censor these writings. A reaction to that censorship could have been one factor that led him to write *Areopagitica*.

Throughout the essay Milton praises wisdom and culture in an epic and persuasive style, citing the classics of antiquity. In order to emphasize the importance of publishing without censorship, he compares people to books: "Who kills a man kills a reasonable creature, God's image; but he who destroys a good book, kills reason itself, kills the image of God, as it were in the eye."[5]

Milton explores the question of evil profusely in his work *Paradise Lost*, in which, as in some passages of *Areopagitica*, his intellectual fascination with the penetrating power of evil becomes apparent. He offers a political reading of its power as a catalyst of human affairs, to the extent that he maintains that the role of the law as a regulator of behaviors should be heavily restricted, so as not to inhibit the growth in civic virtues of citizens, who grow in virtue precisely in their confrontations with damage, evil, and lies.[6]

Drawing on Saint Paul, he says in a heroic tone: "Good and evil we know in the field of this world grow up together almost inseparably."[7] The knowledge of good and evil are equally inseparable, so that one leads to the other and vice versa, as if they were twins. "Let [Truth] and Falsehood grapple; who ever knew Truth put to the worse, in a free and open encounter?"[8]

Many authors have identified the above-cited words of Milton (allowing "a free and open encounter") with the economic metaphor of the marketplace that is used to describe how the economy—and, by extension, communication—grows and expands when it is not regulated. Peters shows that this attribution is incorrect because that concept was not

used in communication until the middle of the twentieth century.[9] Moreover, he points out that Milton uses not the language of *markets*, but that
of *construction*: he speaks of building the house of truth with the contribution of individuals.[10] Naturalism and the enlightened optimism that the
truth will make its way on its own[11] are very present in *Areopagitica*: "See
the ingenuity of Truth, who, when she gets a free and willing hand, opens
herself faster than the pace of method and discourse can overtake her."[12]

What Milton wants to emphasize with his dialectic conception of
truth and the utility of evil is that one also ends up "knowing good by
evil."[13] Milton starts from the premise that evil acts as a catalyst, and this
is the basis on which he expands his argument about the necessity of
knowing and studying vice in order to form virtue — to analyze error in
order to confirm truth, to explore the region of sin and of what is false. It
is for this reason that the author ridicules the practice of not unnecessarily
exposing oneself to dangers and the attitude that one should not waste
time on vain things. He criticizes the fear of the "danger of contagion" on
the part of some Catholic authors, reproaching their notion of virtue as
"fugitive and cloistered virtue."[14] He argues that this is cowardly behavior,
typical of those who never venture out to face the adversary. Milton instead proposes the necessity of indiscriminately reading books.[15]

Vincent Blasi highlights the strong character of the Miltonian framework, which extols the courage and boldness that citizens must have in
order to deal with error and evil. And he contrasts it with the cowardice
contained in the naïvete, purity of ideas, and submission to authority of
those who support censorship. Milton encourages freeing oneself from
what he considers a certain formal dependence on civil and religious authority (the need for criteria and previous authorization and so on).[16]
This is a call not to political rebellion but to intellectual rebellion. He
understands freedom of expression as a way to renew society with intellectually transgressive attitudes. As Blasi states, Milton does not understand freedom of expression as "a mechanism for deliberation and persuasion so much as a phenomenon shaping the character and aspirations
of the population."[17]

Thus, Milton's civic framework poses a certain need for evil as a condition of moral progress. Nevertheless, Milton admits excluding from this
system children and immature people, who can be discouraged from reading some texts but should not be forcibly prevented.[18]

For Peters, the dialectic between good and evil that is discussed in *Areopagitica* is not so much a defense of unhindered freedom as an account of the benefits of transgressive discourse.[19] For Milton, publishing has theological and aesthetic connotations, that is to say, exposure to evil can produce beneficial effects.[20] Milton is confident that truth and God will prevail in the struggle between good and evil, but in the interim, evil will have a catalytic effect on the moral life of society. That is why Milton postulates a negotiated coexistence between good and evil.[21]

Within the context of books, Milton interprets evil in conformity with Saint Paul's passage in his letter to the Romans in which he talks about food: "Nothing is unclean in itself; still, it is unclean for someone who thinks it unclean" (Rom. 14: 14).[22] The starting point that Milton takes from Saint Paul is certain: everything is pure for those who have a clean heart. However, in presenting the good and evil binomial as interlaced, Milton leaves out that one cannot directly do evil to obtain good. This ability is beyond the human being. For Milton, truth and error (theoretical and practical or moral) are not interchangeable.

Thus, evil and error are like shadows in a painting, which provide a contrast that we need in order to see the light. In this sense, error is tolerated, even though we know that it is not something good or true in itself. From the artistic standpoint, evil can be used as a catalyst (making recourse to the redemptive sense of evil: dramatis personae) to show the good. In this context, Peters sees Milton as an "abyss redeemer," a provocateur who flirts with evil in the abyss, without falling into it.[23]

John Henry Newman encountered a similar dilemma: how can the false be discovered if it is not confronted by the truth? The English author considered that there are many perspectives on reality, emphasizing the need to compare one's thinking with other perceptions of the same problem. "No conclusion is trustworthy which has not been tried by enemy as well as friend," he wrote.[24]

The implicit moral ethos that exists in the meaning of Milton's idea of transgression would cause many problems for the authors who would formulate freedom of expression from the twentieth century onward. For Milton, there was truth, grace, and sin, but centuries later, those who came after him would reject all transcendence and disregard the reality of good and evil. Milton's artistic-theological interpretation of seeing a certain need for evil (for sin) in order for humans to be saved has not been fully understood. The problem is that the authors who came after Milton did not have that transcendent spiritual sense, so transgression lost this instrumental sense of serving "character formation" and became an end in itself.

JOHN STUART MILL AND THE VALUE OF CONTROVERSY

The English author wrote an essay about freedom (*On Liberty*, 1859) that includes a section dedicated exclusively to freedom of expression. Mill, two centuries after Milton, takes up the call for an almost unlimited freedom of expression, but with other nuances.[25]

Mill's thought lies mainly in the field of economics. In the sphere of communication, some American jurists such as Holmes, Brandeis, and Brenan adopted his thesis and made Mill an academic source for free speech.[26] As in the case of Milton, the expression "marketplace of ideas" cannot be explicitly attributed to Mill because he did not formally use it.[27] Mill does not believe in the automatic victory of the truth in competition with falsehood, as does Milton; nor does he believe in an open and unlimited public space since he recognizes the role of the tyranny of the majority. As a utilitarian, he understands freedom of expression as open-mindedness and identifies it with being exposed to a wide variety of arguments.

But Mill explicitly distinguishes himself from Milton: "The dictum that truth always triumphs over persecution, is of those pleasant falsehoods which men repeat after one another till they pass into commonplaces. . . . It is a piece of idle sentimentality that truth, merely as truth, has any inherent power denied to error of prevailing against the dungeon and the stake."[28] Peters uses a very striking image to distinguish Milton from Mill: "If Milton imagines truth as an undefeated wrestler, Mill's sporting metaphor might be a batting average: truth gets hits some of the time, but strikes out other times."[29]

The essence of Mill's thesis on freedom is found in the harm principle. The sole criterion for preventing individual freedom and autonomy by force is harm to others:

> The only purpose for which power can be rightfully exercised over any member of a civilized community, against his will, is to prevent harm to others. His own good, either physical or moral, is not a sufficient

warrant. He cannot rightfully be compelled to do or forbear because it will be better for him to do so, because it will make him happier, because, in the opinions of others, to do so would be wise, or even right. . . . These are good reasons for reasoning with him or persuading him, but not for compelling him.[30]

Mill's words point to the two main faces of the harm principle: On one hand, expression can be repressed only if it has generated objective harm to others or, in exceptional cases, to prevent it.[31] On the other hand, expression can never be forced ("compelled"). The *Masterpiece Cakeshop* case is emblematic of a liberal inversion that would involve forcing an expressive act against someone's freedom.

There are three ideas that Mill sets forth in the chapter dedicated to the liberty of thought and discussion that are key for the edifice of the liberal philosophy of freedom of expression. First, Mill considers discussion a decisive element for each person to build and form his or her own individuality. He believes that individuals need to listen to all points of view, however immoral they may be. The human being needs to compare and discuss ideas. On the other hand, he claims that "all silencing of discussion is an assumption of infallibility,"[32] which hurts everyone (in the present and in the future) because it prevents the dissent of those who think otherwise. Third, referring to positions that are true, Mill also warns: "If [the truth] is not fully, frequently, and fearlessly discussed, it will be held as a dead dogma, not a living truth."[33] It will be defended as "prejudice, with little comprehension or feeling of its rational grounds."[34]

All three arguments are sensible and correct. This framework stands in contrast with the attitudes of censorship and insulation on North American campuses. The censorship hurts everyone. Those who approve it are hurt because they are denied the opportunity to change their minds if they discover that the doctrine they previously held was wrong. And if their ideas are true, they are unable to refine their formulation because of the lack of comparison with error.[35] Robert George and Cornel West declare: "A recognition of the possibility that we may be in error is a good reason to listen to and honestly consider—and not merely to tolerate grudgingly—points of view that we do not share, and even perspectives that we find shocking or scandalous."[36]

The free expression of thought, as conceived by Mill, admits few exceptions, one of which is incitement. That is to say, the opinion pronounced may be punishable when the circumstances in which it is offered involves an incitement to commit actions that hurt others.

Thus, as Kevin O'Rourke observes, this limit has to do not with the content but with the circumstances under which it is expressed.[37] This essay does not establish criteria for determining what constitutes a "harmful incitement" or how to distinguish it from "innocent debate." In fact, if the criteria were not to offend, everyone whose opinion was attacked would always be offended. Perhaps that is why O'Rourke recognizes that there are ways of proclaiming an opinion that are reprehensible and blameworthy but difficult to prove so.

Mill rejects the notion that discussion should be regulated: "The free expression of all opinions should be permitted, on condition that the manner be temperate, and do not pass the bounds of fair discussion."[38] True morality in public discourse is found in self-discipline, a stoic-inspired mix of honesty and loyalty, which leads Mill to allow attacks made with self-control (apathy, tranquility, equanimity, and so on). For him, it is not that anything goes in the name of free expression but that the measure of allowability cannot be to *not offend* because "[the] experience testifies that this offence is given whenever the attack is telling and powerful . . . and when they find it difficult to answer."[39] In all of these cases, says Mill, the opponent appears lacking in moderation. What Mill categorically condemns are different forms of manipulation: "The gravest of them is, to argue sophistically, to suppress facts or arguments, to misstate the elements of the case, or misrepresent the opposite opinion,"[40] because these threaten truth and justice.

On one hand, comparing ideas and opinions is how people grow intellectually. This is not an abstract task, but, in the words of Peters, it requires "real contact" between the interlocutors.[41] However, unlike Hannah Arendt's way of seeing the issue, Mill's view on listening to different voices is completely open. According to the English author, the public space must include the whole bestiary: the evil, saints, the insane, prophets, terrorists, fanatics, and others. Arendt, rather, thinks that putting all voices at the same level contravenes the system because it demands an unrealistic Socratic deliberation. On the other hand, Mill's framework presupposes an ethical substrate of moderation, rectitude, self-discipline, and self-control afforded by the social and cultural context of nineteenth-century Europe, which had Christian roots.

THE REFORMULATION OF TOLERANCE
IN THE EUROPEAN ENLIGHTENMENT

Tolerance can properly be considered not a virtue, as John Paull II saw it,[42] but rather a philosophical formula for confronting the abyss of evil. Tolerance understood in the classical sense is the attitude of allowing an evil or an error and being able to avoid it in view of a higher good. Thomas Aquinas followed this same tradition, stating: "A wise lawgiver should suffer lesser transgressions, that the greater may be avoided."[43] The inexorability of evil is affirmed while recognizing the difference between good and evil, as well as the existence of degrees.

The notion of tolerance poses a critical question about the reality of evil that we cannot address in depth but only insofar as necessary for the purposes of this work. Saint Augustine was looking for the source of evil and got nowhere, saying of himself that he posed the question "Whence is evil? — and found no answer."[44] The Christian and biblical answer is that evil is not an autonomous entity. Evil is "performed" by the exercise of freedom; evil does not exist by itself (it is not a thing). We experience human-caused evil in very specific ways: lies, hatred, violence, torture, war, genocide, public shaming, and so on. Evil can be performed not only individually but socially, generating wicked structures or systems. However, government is not called to guide or prevent the development of liberty. Public authority is the guardian of common good and public order. The evil conduct that calls for public action is only external behavior, carried on in public, and relevant legally.

The degrees of evil is a moral subject that it is not addressed by law but that social norms can tackle. Some limits must be clearly drawn by law, others considered case by case in jurisprudence, and yet others depend on a common moral sense that guides individuals as members of a community. The pervasiveness of hackneyed evil is what Arendt denounced during the Eichmann trial.[45] Adolf Eichmann was found guilty of war crimes, crimes against humanity, and crimes against the Jewish people. He was condemned and put to death after the trial, on May 31, 1962. But Arendt focused not only on "the little man" as the origin of evil but on the banality of evil, which suggested a structural moral failure of modernity, because Eichmann was not only a careerist man obeying orders but was "obeying the law." Arendt's account was trying to unmask a larger evil; however, it is possible that she fell into Eichmann's trap if he was merely playing the role of a mindless functionary in the hope of gaining a more lenient sentence. Nonetheless, the banality of evil is a rich concept, even if the crimes of Eichmann himself may not fit it perfectly.

The European Enlightenment thinkers of the eighteenth century theorized tolerance in various ways, but they shared a common vision, seeing tolerance as the opposite of fanaticism. Many modern philosophers see fanaticism as coming from tradition and religion. They want to build a "scientific ethic" that does not refer to any permanent criteria, value, or truth, because truth is understood as an "experimental verification."[46]

The classical concept of tolerance was reformulated during the European Enlightenment, eliminating the objective reference to moral good or evil and replacing them with ethical subjectivity.[47] The Enlightenment formula bears the seed of transformation from tolerance into permissiveness. The former distinguishes error and evil, and it considers that good and truth are permanent values. The latter implies a lack of objective moral values — it is mere indifference. For the European Enlightenment authors, skepticism is the foundation of tolerance.[48]

Some of these authors proclaim the spirit of tolerance as the definitive formula and remedy for the sake of social order. The issue is that their concept of tolerance is unique and admits only a relativistic approach.[49] Milton considers it wise and healthy for society that all types of speech be permitted, because Truth has shattered into a thousand pieces and is scattered to the four winds.[50] Milton's tolerance is not absolute, however, as he banished Catholic ideas in different ways.[51] Nevertheless, with this competition or battle of ideas, Milton's intent is not so much to seek the truth as it is but to "contrast the truth with error" in the most experimental and strategic sense of the method.[52]

Milton understands tolerance not in the pure classical sense of tolerating an evil or an error to seek a greater good but as an instrumental necessity, that is, in the sense of allowing the transgression — as harmful as it may be — as a catalyst to strengthen life in democracy. This intellectual approach places all ideas at the same level, authorizing transgression as an end in itself and promoting a certain right to error and evil as necessary weapons. What is problematic from the standpoint of value in Milton's transgression are the later developments.

On one hand, Lee Bollinger, paraphrasing Mill, presents the common understanding of free speech theory, stating that only acts can harm, not words.[53] This allows for an ambiguity in language, as well as a margin of offense in all types of discourse, which this Miltonian concept of tolerance (permissiveness) ends up authorizing. Bollinger criticizes the contemporary liberal standpoint that views speech in an abstract way: "In my judgment," he writes, "this literature generally pays insufficient attention to the potential psychological costs (both individual and social) of some speech acts."[54] In the following chapter I shall discuss the question of the pragmatic dimension of expression, but as one can intuit, when we are talking about offensive speech, the distinction between doing and saying has consequences that are not insignificant. There are words that can perform actions, and that can intimidate. That is why the freedom to offend that is authorized by Milton's theory of tolerance may lead to abusive and irresponsible attitudes, because trusting only in the fact that these discourses will balance one another does not remedy or grant justice for the social damage that harmful expressions can cause to their victims.

The framework of civic tolerance cannot be sustained in a moral vacuum. As Fernando Ocáriz says, "If tolerance is, above all, a moral issue, then it is clear that the general principle that sets it forth will have to be a moral principle, and it can be expressed briefly: in some circumstances, it is morally licit to not prevent an evil—while being able to prevent it—in view of a higher good or in order to avoid more serious troubles."[55] That is to say, "Tolerating an evil" does not mean being satisfied with evil. The issue lies in defining the limits of "intolerable."

When presented with those who advocate for the absolute tolerance of all kinds of speech, the need to establish some limits to tolerance must be raised as an objection, as Locke also thought: "I say, first, that a ruler should not tolerate any doctrines which are detrimental to human society and prejudicial to the good morals which are essential for the preservation of civil society."[56] From the moral standpoint, the fundamental issue will be determining what these "moral rules" are and what is meant by "opinions contrary to human society," beyond the naturalism and Enlightenment relativism that have drained them of their content.

As we have seen in the case of *Charlie Hebdo*, there are expressions (words and images) that constitute real actions and cause real harm and a real threat. Mere tolerance does not solve the problem. That is why it is necessary to distinguish free expression from insult. Some responsibility should be demanded for the abuse of freedom of expression because this constitutes individual and collective harm. The case of *Charlie Hebdo* demonstrates how gratuitous or arbitrary insult is an act of mere self-affirmation (artistic, ideological, or other), which is far from satire. Critical humor and satire are indispensable for coexistence in a democracy, but they have embodied limits that are imposed by the common good.

The Protestant Notion of Freedom and Its Implications

In English-speaking countries Protestantism provided the "cement" for the liberal account of justice. As George Parking Grant puts it: "This co-penetration of Protestantism and liberalism must not be understood in terms of a simple passive overriding in which Protestantism gradually lost itself. It was a veritable co-penetration in which Protestantism shaped as well as being shaped."[57]

Different notions of freedom have been used throughout this study. We alluded to the distinction that Isaiah Berlin postulates between negative (liberal) freedom, in which the state refrains from intervention, and positive (social) freedom, in which the state is the dispenser of freedoms. Michael Novak argues that there is a third type: ordered freedom,[58] which was the classical conception of Aristotle, Plato, Seneca, and Cicero, a political freedom associated with a telos. It is a freedom understood as responsible self-governance (personal and imposed by the republic) that would lead to virtuous citizenship, emphasizing that the exercise of freedom corresponds to a responsibility (toward others and society).

However, modern governments are based not on virtue but on utility and interest. Positive law defends the maximization of well-being. With Hobbes the law ceased to have a link with others, performing a social function like the *ius* had performed, which implied the three notions of classical justice (*debitum, alteritas, aequalitas*, or debt, alterity, equality) and the resulting duty of restoration. The concept of "subjective right" arose with Hobbes, and it links the subject with the law.[59] With this, Michel Villey writes, "the *ius* no longer evokes the duty that moral law imposes on us, but, on the contrary, a *permit* that the law leaves us—a license—or a freedom—liberties."[60]

The conception of individual liberty finds its roots in Protestant thought. Following in the nominalist footsteps of Ockham, Luther separates freedom from its relationship with the being of things: there is no telos, that is, a natural order or purpose. On the other hand, Luther separates freedom from practical reason, which does not capture the "good to do." Luther does not understand that "the exercise of freedom is an act of a reasonable will," according to Francisco Mateo Seco.[61]

Luther's notion of freedom, found in his work *The Bondage of the Will*, is an unbound freedom. Only God is free, because he has no owner,[62] and his freedom is absolute, that is, not conditioned by anything (including evil and absurdity), which makes God arbitrary.[63] Luther understands freedom as being linked only to will (without beginning or end) and to power, becoming despotic and unpredictable. For Luther, *free will* is a divine term that means *divine power*.[64] In Lutheran logic, human freedom ends up competing with divine freedom.

Luther believed that human freedom is not reasonable because it is "blind, deaf, stupid, impious, and sacrilegious,"[65] fit to move only in the realm of the inferior, of necessity; that is why on higher questions it is possible only to have faith, and on the peripheral matters to use freedom as choice, as the dominion of the individual over the inferior. As we can deduce, freedom then becomes self-referential and autonomous: our words and knowledge cease to be true because they penetrate and coincide with the being of things (ontological truth) and become true (subjective certainty) due to the simple fact of saying them or thinking them. The essence of freedom, then, is the act of exercising it: of choosing.

The voluntarist subjectivism of Protestant thought encapsulates freedom in its pessimism (enslaved freedom) and arbitrariness ("the mere right to use and abuse, without reference to the order of being and, therefore, of the End," in the words of Mateo Seco[66]). The substitution of the morality linked to reason by the morality of will leads to a concept of justice that makes it so that the new morality is necessarily a justice of the prevailing opinion.

The distinction between liberty and license is that the latter brings the nuance of abuse. Freedom without responsibility (individual and social) is license. As seen in the previous chapters, there are exercises of free expression that are abuses of freedom (license) and not true freedom. In a meeting with representatives of the world of culture in Paris, Benedict XVI said that "freedom has an inner criterion."[67] And, of the tension between bonds and freedom, he said: "This tension presents itself anew as a challenge for our own generation as we face two poles: on the one hand, subjective arbitrariness, and on the other, fundamentalist fanaticism. It would be a disaster if today's European culture could only conceive freedom as absence of obligation, which would inevitably play into the hands of fanaticism and arbitrariness. Absence of obligation and arbitrariness do not signify freedom, but its destruction."[68]

The Tolerance of Comprehensive Liberalism Leads to an Anti-Liberal Framework

Milton's and Mill's conception of tolerance as the political value of "open-mindedness" has given way—in many nations—to tolerance as a moral value. In the latter case, the government imposes a comprehensive view of what a good citizen is,[69] with policies that have elevated all interests and options to individual rights (multiculturalism), placing all of them at the same level.

If the state promotes a moral paradigm to sustain a view inspired by another framework (a religion) regarding the basic aspects of a social institution, such as marriage between a man and a woman or respect for life from conception to its end, it is seen as something negative that threatens the new civic morality. In this form of liberalism, which orders respect for a new orthodoxy, if one leaves the framework of the "good liberal citizen" he or she is reprimanded or aggressively silenced.

An example of this intolerance occurred in Australia when Andrew Denton, a television producer and bioethics activist, gave a speech to the National Press Club in August of 2016. Denton was speaking about the need for a law that would admit euthanasia in Australia when he openly urged people to exclude from the debate ethical opinions based on religious convictions: "[Those] whose beliefs instruct you that only God can decide how a human being should die. I urge you, step aside."[70]

Similarly, Robert George recounted during an academic debate how "Chai Feldblum, who is very active in the gay marriage movement, said a few years ago that there will be hundreds of points of conflict between gay rights and religious liberty. 'But,' she said, 'I have trouble thinking of any conflicts on which the religious liberty interest should prevail, over sexual interest.'"[71]

The desire to impose one's own ideological paradigm is nothing new, nor is trying to eliminate dissent. What is incredible is the notion that it should be done in the name of tolerance and liberalism. John D. Heydon, former justice of the High Court in Australia, puts it this way: "The modern elites are tyrants of tolerance. They say: 'You must listen to what I am going to say. Then you must either praise my virtue or shut up.' . . . Modern elites do not demand tolerance. They demand unconditional surrender."[72] This dominant and despotic position is irrational and therefore contrary to the classical liberal paradigm.

Milton Friedman warned of the risk of anti-liberal liberalism years ago, stating emphatically: "The society that puts equality before freedom will end up with neither; the society that puts freedom before equality will end up with a great measure of both."[73] Inclusion and diversity are worthy goals, but the freedoms of religion, conscience, and expression cannot be sacrificed on the altar of equality. As Peter Kurti writes: "Individuals in an open, liberal society should enjoy the fundamental right to live in obedience to any religion of their choosing, as long as no threat is posed to the stable, secular social compact."[74]

This new liberalism considers tolerance a tool to serve individuals or groups that have suffered discrimination in any of these new rights related to identity. "Tolerance in the name of relativism has, indeed, become its own form of intolerance. We are commanded to respect all difference and anyone who disagrees can expect to be shouted down, silenced or, often, branded a racist. Everyone must be 'tolerant.'"[75]

Classical liberal political tolerance distinguished between law and morality, and it proposed the coexistence of different views of the good citizen. Under comprehensive liberalism, the state is the promotor of a civic order in which it also uses the law to change the culture. The "illiberal left" as it has been called by the *Economist*, "put their own power at the center of things, because they are sure real progress is possible only after they have first seen to it that racial, sexual and other hierarchies are dismantled."[76] Progressives imposing equity are using the same blueprint as populists on the right. According to Michael W. McConnell, "In the case of liberalism, this is not merely overextension. It is inversion. When government insists that all citizens be neutral, tolerant, and egalitarian, it ceases to be liberal government."[77]

Abuses of Freedom of Expression as a Cause of Objective Harm

As we have seen in Milton and Mill, classical liberal authors defend trans-gression and controversy to the fullest, which some have taken as a right to offend but without the implicit rights of responsibility that Milton and Mill took for granted. The problem of the modern notion of tolerance (permissiveness) based on moral relativism is that it does not recognize the objectivity of harm.

As we saw explicitly in Mill, "offending" cannot be an objective crite-rion for settling anything either ethically or legally. This sentiment is con-firmed in Martha Nussbaum's reflections on the relationship between dis-gust, shame, and law[78] and in Peters's distinctions between "offense" (disgust) and "indignation" (anger).[79] For these authors, offense is not a ra-tional criterion but an emotional one, and they justify it by arguing that those who offend rarely consider themselves offenders. Offense is some-thing that "is perceived" and not something that "is done," Peters would say. That is to say, it is something attributed rather than perpetrated.[80] That is why, for liberal authors, indignation and anger (for example, at child abuse), are more rational and can therefore be universalized.[81] For them, anger includes a sense of justice in terms of what is right and what is wrong, unlike offense, which — as an emotion — does not.

In Spanish, offense (*ofensa*) is different from outrage (*indignación*). It is only the latter that mainly connotes the subjective dimension. One can be offended and not necessarily be outraged. To be offended implies that there is a real harm, and to feel offended is the psychological dimension of harm. If there were no real harm, any feeling would be arbitrary and every-thing would be susceptible. Thus, rather than focusing on the issue of per-ceptions as Nussbaum does, I think it's crucial to focus on the harm itself: sarcasm is not the same as satire; the first humiliates (we laugh at), and the second releases (we laugh with).

As Peters self-critically acknowledges, "Liberalism often fails to ex-tend this analysis to its own analysis."[82] Those who offend rarely consider themselves offenders. Surely, Peters continues, this is because they do not admit that there can be a view of the public sphere that is not theirs, based on agonizing debate and on a self-perception that is not enthusiastic about self-criticism.[83] As we are seeing, the notion of tolerance emptied of objective moral references becomes tyrannical and unilateral, denying any room for other worldviews. One of Peters's striking images can be applied to this new orthodoxy: when talking about the case of *Jyllands-Posten* and its cartoons of Muhammad, Peters says that liberal arrogance in favor of freedom of expression can be perceived as a "Crusade" advanced by those who take the most absolutist positions on freedom of expression.[84]

EIGHT

The Epistemological Shortfall

A Homogenous Concept of Discourse

The liberal philosophy of freedom of expression has focused on promoting the marketplace of ideas and preserving the neutrality of the public sphere. Presented with the most extreme speech, the protection of expression has had different focus areas: sometimes the protection of the individual's (the transgressor's) rights has been emphasized, and other times the social interest has been accentuated, differentiating between worthwhile speech and worthless speech,[1] favoring the former for reasons of social order. In both cases, free speech theory has considered discourse to be univocal and homogenous when it is not.

Language encompasses a whole universe of sense and meaning, and it has its own rules that the philosophy of language helps to unravel. For example, a headline that reads "A Wave of Immigrants Crosses the Border" is not informative-descriptive speech, point-blank. As the famous Dutch linguist Van Dijk said in an interview, alluding to this metaphor: "If someone uncritically assumes it, then he or she is accepting that immigration is undesirable and dangerous, because *a wave* is capable of drowning you.

And that idea of a wave has already conditioned everything you will say about immigration."[2] Several types of language can be distinguished, and their use is not neutral. The philosophy of freedom of expression has paid much attention to harmful ideas, but it has neglected this area, which is key to being able to grasp the abusive uses of language or to objectively distinguishing between information and manipulative propaganda.

FREE EXPRESSION, NOT HOMOGENEOUS: TYPES OF SPEECH

It is impossible to find an exhaustive way to classify all speech or texts in the broad sense. The list would be very long and would include notes, orders, diagnoses, narrations, pamphlets, prophecies, summaries, announcements, jokes, doctoral theses, and so on. We can classify texts according to different criteria: according to style (poetry or prose, narrative or persuasive); according to medium (oral, print, audiovisual); according to genre: journalism (chronicle, interview, analysis, news, editorial), novels (thriller, historical fiction, romance), films (comedy, drama, horror); and according to format (talk shows, live broadcasts, series). These criteria can also be combined. For example, in journalism there are narrative texts (e.g., current affairs) and argumentative texts (e.g., editorials), as there are various formats of television series (e.g., soap operas, mini-series, game shows, talk shows). The possibilities of speech and discourse are endless, but as Antonio Vilarnovo and José Sánchez explain, any speech or text can be classified by a single criterion: that of its purpose.[3]

As Aristotle described, there are three types of language: apophantic logos, a text guided by logic that states truth or falsehood; poetic logos, a text that creates a world (fiction) with its own internal meaning that is not necessarily real; and pragmatic logos, a text that pursues action.[4] Each type of discourse has its own internal rules for construction. This classification allows us to analyze all expressions and identify them according to this categorization.

Of course, any speech or discourse can have a combination of these three dimensions, so we can find that the types of discourse are mixed within the space of the same locution, but this particular division based on the goal of the discourse allows us to identify what we are dealing with. Thus, a text can be created by mixing a logical discourse with fiction, but there is an internal rationality that makes a fiction a fiction. This reality of the internal meaning of the text or speech should not be ignored.[5] For example, I can order from a menu by informing the waiter of my choice in very different ways: plainly and simply, by saying, "Bring me X," or more poetically, by saying, "My mood today demands *spaghetti ai fiori di zucca.*" However, there is only one way to interpret the speech, and that is according to its purpose—that is, what the speaker intended by saying these words—which is nothing other than the meaning of the speech or discourse. Thus, discourse is not a conglomerate of words with their meanings but the meaning (as a whole) that is intended when the words are pronounced. This includes not only the words themselves but also the context in which they are uttered and the relationship between the people in that specific situation.

As Aristotle explains in his essay *Rhetoric*, every act of communication involves three elements: a sender, a recipient, and the content itself[6]—all three in a specific context, because communication does not occur in an abstract world, in a "nowhere space," but takes place in specific circumstances between specific people.[7] In pragmatic language, the interactions among these three elements (that is to say, the relation of the speech with the communicative situation) form the first pragmatic dimension.[8]

To analyze an author's intent in relation to the context of the recipient, we look at a case that took place almost fifty years ago in Illinois. In 1977, a Neo-Nazi organization decided to organize a march, complete with Nazi uniforms and insignias, in the Chicago neighborhood of Skokie, where many Jewish survivors from the World War II concentration camps lived. The village council had banned the demonstration, but the decision was denounced by the ACLU (American Civil Liberties Union), and it was ultimately determined that the ban was a violation of the freedom of expression protected by the First Amendment.[9] The state Court dismissed the decision made by the Skokie village council, so the march did take place, although it was moved to a different part of Chicago.

The Skokie case is an example—even a symbol—of the principle of tolerating harmful speech advocated by the liberal tradition of freedom of expression. As we have already seen, the liberal attitude encourages pushing back on hate speech with more speech, with what is called *counterspeech*, but never prohibiting or censoring it. Let us look at the problem in detail.

First, communication is not something indeterminate or generic, a kind of abstract idea outside of space and time, but rather is a discursive action that takes place under specific circumstances. The argument that the Nazis, in a free and open society, have to be tolerated so that they can express their ideas in the public sphere is a general judgment, even theoretically acceptable as such, but a universal practical validation does not follow from this argument. The concrete damage suffered by individuals is not justified by the theoretical truth of that proposition. We all agree with the general statements in favor of the pluralism of human rights, but the reality is that human rights are "experienced" in a specific way — and so it is with tolerance. Sustaining Nazi ideas in general is not the same as expressing those ideas in a particular Jewish neighborhood, in front of people who have survived concentration camps. In principle, the people who support Nazi ideology have to be tolerated in a free and plural society; however, expressing this speech in a specific context (Skokie) and with particular recipients (Holocaust survivors) changes everything. The demonstrators were not only saying something in general, something theoretical; they were also doing something specific and concrete: causing harm to the Jewish inhabitants of that community.

In this sense, it would be absurd to argue that the Skokie demonstrators only wanted to express their ideas in the public sphere for two main reasons: their speech was pragmatic, which means that they were not just saying, "Heil Hitler!," and, since that speech was linked to a communicative situation, they intended to cause harm. The three elements of the communication are related (sender, recipient, and the content itself), and they work in a pragmatic way. Second, there is an additional pragmatic dimension beyond the interaction of the three elements, and that is the fact that the speech itself is a communicative action. As Vilarnovo and Sánchez explain, the first pragmatic dimension (the three elements of communication) is based on the second (speech as an action), but, at the same time, the second is possible because of the first.[10] That is to say that the speech is not a mere dissertation or disquisition but an act of communication in society. The circumstances of the Skokie event are fundamental for illustrating how this march, as a discursive action, was *objectively* harmful, because it was intended to offend. For this reason, from the standpoint of the pragmatic purpose, the Skokie march was not just a "tolerable" instance of speech in line with principle; it was an action (a speech act).[11]

Vilarnovo and Sánchez highlight two notions of the speech act that are relevant to our topic. First, the act of expression works according to an agreement between the sender and the recipient. Both are real persons—not unreal or fictional subjects—with predictable intentions expressed in the message and in the purpose of the (historical, fictional, or propaganda) text or content. That is why subverting the rules of what is "expected" would be a violation of this agreement—for example, presenting a book as a piece of literature when it was a book of propaganda, as occurred with *The Satanic Verses* (by Rushdie), as it is not a literary work but a pragmatic text against Muslims.[12]

The second notion of the speech act is that the text has a value in itself, as well as some constitutive internal rules: a newspaper article is different from a fictional story or an academic article. News in which the facts are false or in which the sources are not verifiable is a fraud as an informative text. An academic article that confuses a hypothesis with a result is a fraud as a scientific contribution. A work of fiction in which the "implicit recipient" is constructed with the intention of manipulating the "real recipient" is also a fraud.[13]

Thus, these two agreements—between the sender and the recipient and within the construction of the text or content—build a relationship and loyalty between the sender and the recipient, regulating the pragmatic value. Oftentimes the narratives and representations are shown to be neutral when it is important to remember that the difference between saying and representing an action is the difference between saying it and doing it. The speech act does the action, or it is the trigger for others to act.[14]

In her book *Only Words*, Catharine MacKinnon stresses that some words and expressions have this performative power of motivating action. They are not only words, ideas, drawings, photographs, or scenes. "Pornography contains ideas, like any other social practice. But the way it works is not as a thought or through its ideas as such."[15] This is the pragmatic force of expression, which is not just speech but discursive action.

This pragmatic dimension of language certainly has significant social repercussions; however, its nature is not theoretical but eminently effective. That is why analyzing freedom of expression from this perspective adds a dimension that is not fully contemplated by modern law or political philosophy.[16] For classical political philosophy as well as Roman law, this was evident. The practicality of language allows one to evaluate the social interaction of the expression and, as Van Dijk said in the interview mentioned earlier, it can be a good way to "understand the deep undertones of a society and its power and political structures."[17]

MacKinnon establishes a comparison showing the operative power of words, comparing pornography with law: "Like law, pornography does what it says."[18] For MacKinnon, sexual words and images presented in a certain context, like pornography, are operative: in a certain way, they *are* sex.[19]

In addition to pornography, MacKinnon points out an example of racism, saying that if someone finds the words "Die negro!" painted on their office door, the liberal discourse's reasoning that the person should not feel insulted or threatened because it is an "impersonal graffiti" is not convincing, since it is clearly directed at that person.[20] As I have stressed, the damage caused by the exercise of freedom of expression is not experienced in an abstract way—it can have a personal and collective effect.

The legal scholar Paolo Carozza has developed the idea that "human rights" must be conceptualized so as to produce both theoretical substance and development practice. Human dignity, if taken seriously, must be *experienced.*[21] In this context, Carozza and Clemens Sedmak talk of "doing dignity."[22] Conversely, the abuse of freedom of expression is not only a theoretical concept but a practice really experienced, as in the case of the targeted individuals living in Skokie village.

SPEECH ACTS AND THE FRAUDULENT USES OF EXPRESSION

The idea of a speech act was developed in the twentieth century by philosophers of language with the purpose of explaining thought through language. Among the founders of this discipline are the British philosophers Grice and Austin.[23]

Herbert P. Grice (1913–1988) argued that language is not only a semantic act but is also used to convey intentionality.[24] As Sergio Tapia explains, "If two people are capable of establishing a dialogue—even during a heated discussion—it is because they have managed to understand not only the semantic meaning of the words they are using, but above all, the speaker's meaning."[25] For Grice, the natural meaning (the words spoken) is not solely literal but is subject to an *intentional* meaning that allows the listener to understand the speaker's intention. Grice goes beyond the logical implications, speaking of the *implicatures*, in order to highlight the intended meaning.[26] Grice's intuitions opened the door to other developments on linguistic value and the rules that govern conversation.[27]

John L. Austin (1911–1960) was the one who, studying language, distinguished between declarative or constative utterances and operational or performative utterances.[28] Performative utterances are those that do not simply say things but do things when pronounced in a certain context. He calls this the "theory of Speech Acts,"[29] which (as Tapia recalls) is Austin's, even though the expression was popularized by John Searle.[30] Austin distinguishes between three speech acts: "saying something" (locutionary act), "doing something" (illocutionary act), and "making [others] do something" (perlocutionary act).[31] This distinction is very useful for analyzing conversations because it allows us to distinguish between intent and meaning. As Tapia explains: "We have to consider the whole situation in which the expression is emitted—the whole linguistic act—in order to be able to see the parallel that exists between the statements and their performative expressions."[32] Not all statements can be considered true or false depending only on how they conform to facts; their intentions and purposes must also be taken into account.[33]

As Tapia says, one of the moral consequences of Austin's "speech acts" is that, if in certain cases saying implies doing, then the possible actions derived from our speech acts must be submitted to the same factors that determine responsibility—as in the case of any other action. An action may, then, be meaningless, or it may turn out to be null or illicit. The factors that mitigate against or exempt one from responsibility, or those that imply that the act may be void because of violence or duress, are also applicable.[34] For example, any expression pronounced in a given scenario supposes a circumstance of place that, because of its own characteristics, implies that this expression is vacuous or "hollow."[35] One example is theater actors promising themselves in marriage on stage: they say but do not perform this action.

Many authors think the origin of the paradigm of discourse that was developed by these twentieth-century authors is found in Aristotle's *Rhetoric* and *Poetics*, albeit not formulated in the same way. For Aristotle, literature is the imitation (mimesis) and representation of reality.[36] Vilarnovo and Sánchez stress that it is imitation not of specific people but of human actions, placing the emphasis on the meaning.[37]

The comparison that Aristotle draws between literature and history offers an important clarification. Both focus on human actions: history says "what has happened," while literature says "what is possible according to what can be expected or to the internal need of the work."[38] A difference is also shown by the fact that in literature there are characters, while in history there are people.[39] Aristotle says that "the difference between the historian and the poet is not that between using verse or prose."[40] And he explains that "poetry relates more of the universal, while history relates particulars."[41] Along these same lines, Arendt qualifies the work of art as something permanent and believes its lasting nature is of a higher order (immortality) than the tools of ordinary use (perishables).[42] Moreover, as Norberto González Gaitano recalls: "Literature and history are 'liberal arts' in the Aristotelian sense, that is, they are written and read 'for their own sake,' *without ulterior motives* or as a means to something else."[43]

This universal character may seem contradictory to the pragmatic purpose of speech acts, but it is not. That is because what this "saying the universal" expresses is that there is a unity of meaning in literature.[44] This unity of meaning is broken when two facts that do not tend toward the same end meet.[45] For example, the universe created by Dickens includes a critique of certain aspects of nineteenth-century industrial British society, "but," as González Gaitano writes, "no historian would use them as a documentary source to reconstruct life in London at that time."[46] For that reason, as González Gaitano points out when speaking of the universal nature of literature: "A novel is not written *to do* something in the real world in which the author is writing"[47] but to do something in the perennial world of literature.

The novel *The Satanic Verses* is a negative example of the subversion of this order. Rushdie's characters live in a fantasy world of imagination and dreams that intermingles with facts of the Muslim faith and Muslim reality, which the author wants to criticize. For example, Rushdie creates a brothel called *Hijab* (the name of the veil that covers Muslim women in public), employing this term with a meaning that is the opposite of how Arab culture understands it. Moreover, within that brothel the protagonist is surrounded by twelve prostitutes that have the same names as the twelve wives of the Prophet Muhammad. These twelve women perform pornographic acts that are totally contrary to the wives of the Prophet, who enjoy great respect in Islam. Rushdie's text does not have the *impartiality*[48] of a universal work. *The Satanic Verses* is neither a fantasy nor a historical critique of the Muslim world. It is a text that outrages Muslim reality with symbolic inversions coated in fantasy.

On the other hand, according to Aristotle, there are only two ways of carrying out the "imitation of actions" in literature: narrative (indirect discourse) or representation (through dialogues or monologues).[49] Both are modes of artificially (as artifacts) recreating reality that must act in accord with a series of functional elements.[50] Narrative implies an interpretation, because when reality is recounted (actions, intentions, modes, circumstances, consequences, and reactions),[51] "something is taken and something is necessarily left," according to Vilarnovo and Sánchez.[52] The defining feature of representation is that there is no mediation of a discourse, even though, like the story, it is an artifact. There are two different representations within representation: an external one between the author and the recipient, called the "situation of enunciation"—the implicit (simulated) author and recipient that are the images of the real author and recipient (which are given in the text itself).[53] That is to say, the author influences and leaves her mark on the text by means of what is said (or not said) and by means of how she says it. So "it is represented" in one way or another, depending on the recipient.[54]

In this context, Vilarnovo and Sánchez distinguish various types of fraud in the relationships and pacts of loyalty that are generated in representation: in what they call the vertical plane (the relationship between empirical sender and recipient) and the horizontal plane (the construction of the text, between the implicit author and recipient).[55] They distinguish five types of fraud,[56] some of which we want to emphasize because they are especially grave and also common to our object of study. One refers to the confusion or concealment of the object of communication, as is the case of books like *The Da Vinci Code* (by Dan Brown) or *The Satanic Verses* (by Salman Rushdie). In the first book, the planes of fiction and reality are confused and mixed with pragmatic purposes (attacking the Catholic Church). In the second book, what is actually an attack on Islam is presented as a literary work.[57]

The deception may also be due to a partial reproduction of the facts, as is common in poor "journalism." This can be observed in the classic informative genres: news, reports, and interviews. The case of the crisis generated by Benedict XVI's lecture in Regensburg could, in a way, also be of this type. A positive case in this regard could be the film *Spotlight*, which deals with the crisis of the sexual abuses committed by Catholic clergy in Boston. The film represents a controversial case thoroughly and without falling into partiality.

González Gaitano distinguishes another fraud that is related to the confusion between reality and fiction regarding the identification of the who (person or character) being written about, and he distinguishes two types of such fraud. On one hand, in an informative story the identification of the who is a mere description and is thus partial, while in a fictional story the identification of the who is much richer and is revealed as the story unfolds.[58] On the other hand, in the sphere of hidden intentions, "the novelist has them and the informant does not, because he or she does not know them."[59] As González Gaitano emphasizes, "It is not legitimate to assume them . . . [because] he or she ceases to be an informant in order to become a fiction narrator."[60] Those intentions may very well exist and be plausible, but they are not true.[61] This relates to the author's ethical commitment to respect the internal rules of stories. Interpreting and judging are parts of both fictional and informative stories, but in the case of the latter, the inner world that is not known must be respected.

Finally, as Vilarnovo and Sánchez highlight, the most widespread form of fraud is the manipulation of the recipient who does not have the tools of judgment to critically assess something presented in an attractive way. Based on what has been said above, that there are no neutral narratives because, in the words of González Gaitano, "telling the concrete truth about human actions implies making an ethical judgment,"[62] one can distinguish between persuasion and manipulation because they imply different intentions of the author.

An example of manipulation are hate fictions (racial or religious), such as the book *The Protocols of the Elders of Zion*.[63] The "Protocols" are a literary invention of the minutes of a supposed meeting that took place at the end of the nineteenth century in which a group of Jewish leaders decided to take over world hegemony, subverting Christianity and controlling the press and economies of the world. The book has proven to be a fraudulent invention with the objective of making readers hate the Jews. A case similar to that of the "Protocols" was the book *The Da Vinci Code*, which in this case was against the Catholic Church and, in particular, against *Opus Dei*, an organization within the Catholic Church.[64]

The Da Vinci Code also uses conspiracy theory and mixes the fictional with reality. Alasdair MacIntyre argues that if the fraudulent use of history, language, and so on is shown, the damage caused and the potential future damage must be repaired with measures beyond the judicial sphere, such as requiring that a satisfactory explanation be published in subsequent editions so as not to foster prejudices or feelings of hatred.[65]

Oftentimes, the pragmatic dimension of speech acts is not immediately perceived. As Vilarnovo and Sánchez explain, stories and representations are often presented as *neutral* to a recipient who has not been made aware: "It appears that they only say (and it is thought that these are only objective things), but the reality is that they also *do* and they also lead the recipient to do something in a certain direction."[66]

Pragmatic speech employs the three elements of discourse (sender, recipient, and message), stimulating one or the other in order to obtain the desired ends of action. For convincing, persuading, and "making others do," we can first look at the sender. Among the various characteristics of the speaker, Aristotle emphasizes reliability as the most important quality. If we focus on the recipient, our efforts will probably go toward studying what passions to stimulate to achieve the desired reactions (emulation, imitation, and so on). This would be the case of the pragmatic goal of a political speech or advertisement. Finally, we can focus on the content of the message. Following Vilarnovo and Sánchez, we see that there are necessary, probable, and possible propositions. Necessary propositions produce certainty because they express that things are one way (as in the case of science). Probable propositions produce opinions since they seem to be one way but could be otherwise. Possible propositions produce doubt because they express a reality that may be the opposite, without going against logic.[67]

This distinction is useful for highlighting how pragmatic speech employs the three propositions (necessary, probable, and possible), and perlocutionary speech — in particular — employs the probable and possible propositions as necessary. The possible and the probable appear as true and plausible (believable). This fact emphasizes the dilemma as to whether the criteria for judging an expression should be external or internal. That is to say, should works of art (literary, pictorial, or cinematic) or advertisements, as pragmatic logos, be governed by external criteria as to the usual or common way in which things happen? Aristotle does not understand it this way in his *Poetics*. The criterion for interpreting a literary work is the work itself and not external reality: what is possible according to what is expected of (and necessary to) the work itself.[68] That is to say that "the work itself is the norm," write Vilarnovo and Sánchez.[69] Gianfranco Bettetini and Armando Fumagalli warn of the tendency of contemporary semiotics, which requires reading texts from the outside.[70] Even though there were no films or advertisements in Aristotle's time, the same criteria that apply to literary works can apply to them.

Therefore, fiction and poetry can introduce impossibilities or exaggerations because the criterion of subjection is not its adaptation to reality,[71] making it believable, but the internal perfection of the work: that the qualities and actions of the characters are consistent with the internal parameters of the work.[72] Vilarnovo and Sánchez, taking up Aristotle's idea, conclude: "What is introduced in a poem, even though it is rationally impossible (and thus not believable), is good if it serves the end of the art itself."[73]

Every narrative involves an ethical compromise for the author, and González Gaitano highlights two reasons: because the author projects himself in the work—totally or partially—to create his world and because "there is no neutral narrative when talking about *the* world, be it the possible world of a work of fiction or the real world of past or current history."[74]

Artistic creativity builds on knowledge of the world and of reality: knowledge of the human condition, with its values, longings, desires, contradictions, and more. In fact, literary protagonists are *types* of human characters.[75] Artistic creativity reflects the existence of good and evil, but all in the service of the internal meaning and purpose of the work. As González Gaitano says, "We are interested in narratives—historical, fictional, and journalistic narratives—about human actions, because we need to know society, as well as who we are to be."[76]

Very often in the world of communication, this thesis of verisimilitude is taken as a dialogue value of what the audience is willing to accept or support as the measure of an artistic work. In some cases, verisimilitude turns into a strategy of "making one believe that it is true," as Bettetini and Fumagalli put it,[77] and therefore, it becomes an instrument of manipulation.[78] However, as Vilarnovo and Sánchez point out, this verisimilitude thesis does not allow for the distinction between fiction and nonfiction, because there may be realistic and unrealistic fictions, and it does not get to the heart of the issue of the "proper end of the art," to which Aristotle constantly alludes and which is so helpful for making an objective assessment.

NINE

The Anthropological Shortfall

Modernity's Idea of Mankind

MODERNITY'S CRISIS OF THE "IDEA OF MAN"

An essential element of modern philosophy was becoming liberated and unbound from the tradition that came before, taking an anthropocentric turn: exalting the autonomy of reason and one's own subjectivity above any other value. Severed were the roots that freedom has, by nature, in truth and goodness. Throughout this process, behavior would no longer be based on the objective principle of natural law—"Do good and avoid evil"—and the criterion of good or evil became dependent on individual subjectivity: "Do not do to someone what you would not want them to do to you."

As Charles Taylor assesses the situation, society was cast as an aggregate of individuals pursuing individual objectives, governed by a social contract.[1] From this approach emerged the figure of the modern state that operated in a sense that guaranteed individual rights and duties, dissolving the common substratum of what it is "to be a man or a woman," that is, one's nature. Over time, the "defense of rights" morphed into a cause in which what mattered was not the *why* but rather the practical solution that it provided in the face of the conflicting goods.[2]

In this paradigm of citizenship, the individual gave his or her freedom to the state in a social contract whereby the individual was responsible for protecting his or her rights and eventual conflicts of interest. The state sought to maximize freedom, and for that reason it was also established as a creator of social rights that exist in all areas—moral, social, cultural, scientific, artistic, religious, economic, and so on—forgetting that rights are not concessions of the state but rather belong to a person by virtue of his or her dignity.

Modernity reformulated certain key notions of political philosophy (law, reason, nature, rights) that imply a perspective on the world and the human being. As we shall see, these have affected the discourse about freedom of expression. Legal positivism—reductively—imposes a functional view of the human being, reducing rationality to the scientific method, and it establishes a chasm between faith and reason, expelling from the public debate reasoning that comes from faith.

The modern promise that autonomous freedom and unlimited progress were the keys to a definitive triumph of humanity proved false. The world wars, the perpetuation of social inequalities, and environmental destruction are parts of the price we are still paying. In this modern paradigm of liberation in which the individual seeks to be totally free and not dependent on anything or anyone, freedom does not look to its origin or its destination. The natural relation to the "Creator" is abolished, and relations to good and truth disappear. If society continues like this, it is inevitably heading toward dehumanization.[3] Freedom without responsibility, detached from the nature of what things are and without an orientation toward truth and goodness (as opposed to subjectivity itself), also permeated the liberal philosophy of freedom of expression. Some consequences have been revealed in the cases presented in Part I. Freedom of expression as a mere right, without duties or responsibilities, is easily turned into a weapon to attack and destroy (hate speech), to provide a refuge for those making money at the cost of the dignity of women (pornography), or to compel the speech of those who have different beliefs (the *Masterpiece Cakeshop* case).[4]

As Mariano Fazio observes: "This is fundamentally about a crisis regarding the truth of man. . . . The world is going through a crisis caused by anthropological reductionisms that prevent an integral view of the human person."[5] The author sees a direct relationship between the rejection of God and the loss of human values. Getting into a justification of the causes and trajectory of this phenomenon would divert us from our objective. The cultural battle that takes place in modernity leads us to bury, and in some cases to subvert, the meanings of certain fundamental philosophical and legal concepts, such as nature, justice, law, freedom, and natural law, among others. The philosopher Marcello Pera summarizes the situation in the following way: In the seventeenth century, political thought went from a communitarian, organistic, and teleological perspective inherited from the Middle Ages to the individualist, atomist, and mechanistic perspective of the Modern Era.[6]

This crisis of the "idea of man" has led society to cast the individual as the "creator of himself." In this sense, says Jean Grondin: "The principles, the rules, the values are nothing more than functions invented by individuals, and no assignable reality corresponds to them."[7] The Canadian philosopher attributes this phenomenon to those who live in a "nominalist era" that recognizes the existence only of observable elements, which has eliminated metaphysics and any concept that goes beyond the individual: "The perspective of nominalism, when it is radicalized as it is today, leads to nihilism. That means that there are no (nihil) principles, norms, realities, or measures that exceed spatial-temporal realities — the only ones that exist."[8]

In fact, Grondin verifies this argument by referring to our experience that seeking a common substrate arouses suspicion. This is the case, for example, with human rights: "They are principles that are only proclaimed in declarations, without being based today on an essence of the human being."[9] In this way, we speak of human dignity because it is a useful term, not because it is thought to be an essential principle, but rather because it is "a useful fiction."[10] Moreover, Grondin warns of the danger of atheistic humanism (that of Sartre and Nietzsche) and of contemporary anti-humanism,[11] for which "humans are fundamentally free beings, and therefore, without a definition. It is up to each person to define himself or herself."[12] Something these philosophers have in common is rebellion against the human condition as something prior that was given to us.[13]

In the following sections, we shall briefly look at two developments of individual freedom that have inspired the philosophy of freedom of expression. On one hand, the utilitarianism of Bentham and Mill takes the concepts of individual autonomy and state neutrality as an inheritance from the modern European Enlightenment and applies them to the ethical, legal, and political spheres. John Rawls would later reject the postulates of utilitarianism as incompatible with liberalism and formulate his proposal of comprehensive liberalism and his subsequent return to classical political liberalism.

MILL'S CONCEPT OF "AUTONOMY"

As we saw in chapter 7, Mill draws a safe zone around the individual's autonomy of action and choice in order to preserve it from society's ability to restrict and limit individual freedom, using as a pretext "making one happier," "more just," or "a better citizen."[14] For Mill, freedom is the affirmation of individual autonomy, which should be limited only if and when it harms any absolute need for general utility. For the English author, autonomy means absolute freedom in everything that concerns a subject. Any choice of the individual, by virtue of the very fact of being autonomous, is likewise valuable. "Independent freedom" prevails over "freedom for good."

As Ángel Rodríguez Luño and Arturo Bellocq argue, it has been a mistake to sacrifice freedom on the altar of truth, but it is also a mistake to sacrifice the truth — expelling from philosophical reflection everything that refers to the truth of the human good. There is a human dignity that is guaranteed by fundamental rights, which must be recognized and protected independently of the philosophical position that each individual holds. The error, according to Luño and Bellocq, has been in not having a good understanding of the distinction between personal ethics and political ethics: wanting to guarantee peace, freedom, justice, and so on, and relegating the truth concerning the human good to a private sphere.[15]

The only part of an individual's conduct that he or she is responsible for is what affects others. Mill had to clarify this claim by adding that everything that concerns an individual can fall upon others. As Maria Ferrari points out, however, the division of the consequences of human action into two dimensions (public and private) and its practical application introduce a great amount of complexity. However, it is difficult to separate the good and evil of the individual from the happiness of those connected with him or her.[16]

Mill believed that an individual is motivated not by moral reasons but by the pursuit of happiness through maximizing pleasure. He considered the individual as a "unit of happiness" based on the fact that the subject is totally autonomous. We must keep in mind that in utilitarian morality, pleasure and good are the same. Thus, pleasure and happiness determine the meaning of the concept of freedom.

According to the utilitarian paradigm, in social and political life there are those who favor the principle of "maximizing the happiness (pleasure) of individuals." This behavior is underpinned by an understanding of happiness as something measurable, and thus material. This assumes a reduction of the concept of human happiness but restricts it to those merely material aspects. In turn, the rights and duties that derive from political freedoms understood in this way admit only material principles (e.g., a greater number of votes for an ideological position). For Mill, the challenge is to promote and increase freedom and subjective satisfaction without threatening or harming society, that is, to make the two principles of individual and general maximization mutually compatible. This is impossible with a logic of mere quantitative calculation, for how is someone—following that logic—to sacrifice his or her individual satisfaction to preserve social happiness?

Giuseppe Abbà disagrees that there are no reasons for acting independent of my desires for pleasure and autonomy. He believes there are "reasons of good" that motivate and perfect human beings and society.[17] There are motivations of human action that have to do with transcendent convictions: friendship, love, gratitude, and self-giving, which give meaning and happiness to men and women and go beyond the scale of utility. The issue is that these reasons do not fall within the utilitarian way of weighing happiness. The latter considers only a single type of happiness, one produced by sensory satisfaction and pleasures, excluding all spiritual and transcendent elements.

The main point of contention and incongruence in Mill's morality lies here: on one hand, political freedom must preserve the free and autonomous character of the utilitarian subject, and on the other hand, his or her behavior must be compatible with others, who represent a limit on the personal project of that utilitarian subject.[18] J. C. Smart and Bernard Williams object that it is absurd to ask a theory that advocates the maximization of individual happiness to move away from the individual's personal project for the sake of a "network of utility."[19]

Mill does not contemplate the normative reasons that are prior to the subject's decisions and independent of his or her desires.[20] Ferrari concludes that, with these premises, it is not possible to establish morality as a network of intersubjective relationships. It is necessary to recognize that there are some human interests and desires that correspond to objective values: goods that are good by virtue of their real perfection, toward which subjects are naturally inclined. Without this normative telos that is beyond subjective desires and decisions, aspirations constitute only subjective values, and consequently there is no reason for some subjects to sacrifice all or part of their own interests for the benefit of the interests of others, just as there is also no reason to collaborate so that others can actualize their subjective conceptions of happiness.[21]

Mill's paradigm excludes any nonscientific influence because the highest criterion of morality are happiness and utility—achieving the greatest possible happiness for the greatest number of people. The consequence of this criterion is that the goodness or the evil of actions is determined by the happiness that they produce. Thus, following this logic, the good is defined before and independently of what is just or unjust in a "calculation of happiness."

The utilitarian ethic that conceives of the human being as a utilitarian and radically autonomous being understands a subject's relationship with moral law as a third-personal ethics. This means that the human being has an original autonomous freedom to which a morality is subsequently applied. Thus, moral law is understood as something external and foreign to the human being, something that is imposed from outside. The ethics formulated by utilitarians focus on convincing the subject that it will be "useful" to act ethically.[22]

As Abbà notes, "A will naturally inclined toward a normative *telos*, toward a transcendent good in the human being himself, is not recognized in the agent subject."[23] Such an ethic leads to paradoxical and ambiguous situations: when one is trying to collaborate with others, ethics are reduced to a weighing of conflicting interests, since the ethical decision is guided solely by personal interest in the face of a multitude of utilitarian subjects who limit one's autonomy.

Ferrari shows that the job of the government and of society to maximize human good fundamentally relates to the moral sphere, that is, the promotion of virtuous conduct and lifestyles. Utilitarianism does not grasp this nuance because it identifies happiness with pleasure and social good with the maximum overall amount of happiness. In reducing the unit of measure for promoting happiness exclusively to a mathematical calculation, it proposes that governments function with a merely arithmetic logic in their decision making, exclusively promoting external and material factors.[24]

THE LIBERAL CONCEPT OF "MAN":
SOME RELEVANT CONTRADICTIONS

The philosopher John Rawls (1921–2002) claims that the human being is capable of formulating a conception of the good[25] and has a sense of justice.[26] This distinction of human action proposes that there are actions at two levels: some that are guided by "the good" (the good or the good life that I rationally intend to achieve) and other actions that are governed by "the just" (action in the public sphere).[27] However, as Martin Rhonheimer warns: "According to Rawls, human society is an enterprise of cooperation for mutual advantage. Therefore, society must be regulated by principles that can be shared by all."[28] This leads to putting "the just" before "the good"[29] because this cooperative sense must lead to the pursuit of an equity (fairness) that everyone can share. Therefore, the good life that one wants to live must be compatible with the principles of common justice (rules of fairness). Thus, according to Rawls, "in a well-ordered society" there is a common substratum of rules of justice politically agreed by all that serve as the basis of life in society. And, in turn, divergent conceptions about the good exist on the private level. He believes this allows people with different conceptions of human good to coexist and cooperate, admitting a reasonable pluralism.

Years later, in what is known as the "Second Rawls," the American philosopher abandoned his comprehensive liberalism and formulated a proposal for political liberalism without a particular anthropology. Rawls's proposal of political liberalism purported to be impartial: "Political liberalism does not attack or criticize any reasonable view," he wrote.[30] Rawls thought that the liberal institutions coordinate the lives of individuals who are enriched by diversity.[31] As Da Re points out: "The objective is to justify the neutrality of the state with respect to particular conceptions of the good. In the second instance we could say that the objective is also to justify the value of tolerance."[32]

According to the Second Rawls, order in society would be the result of an "overlapping consensus" that would form a "public reason" based on the "rules of fairness." This consensus by intersection intends to include within political liberalism all comprehensive views that are reasonable. So, as George points out, they could agree to political liberalism: "not only supporters of the liberalism of Kant and Mill, but also Catholic faithful, evangelical Protestants, and observant Jews . . . , without compromising their basic religious and moral convictions."[33] Unfortunately, as Robert George pointed out in an academic debate in December of 2013: "The attempt to drive religion into the purely private sphere, out of the public square, to design a system in which the public reasons—to use John Rawls' famous phrase—are drawn so narrowly so as to exclude the religious witness, is simply to cut the heart out of the right to religious freedom."[34]

The neutrality that excludes from public debate reasoning about what is good for the human being actually ceases to be neutral because it is embracing relativism as a doctrine.[35] To exclude "convictions of the good" from the public debate would be an anti-liberal measure because, as Rhonheimer points out: "Such a restriction would attack the very ideal of liberalism that is based on the mutual respect that citizens have for their profound convictions."[36] It is true that one way of respecting their deepest convictions is to wall them off, but for Michael Sandel and Charles Taylor, a more serious and profound form of respect would be to subject them to reflection, without putting them aside.[37]

Pluralism expresses, better than neutrality, the task of getting different conceptions of the human good to coexist. This is about each individual's being able to run his or her own life as he or she sees fit but also allowing for reflection within that plurality. It would be a sham to impose the premise of giving up the philosophical evaluation of the conceptions of life while defending tolerance. It is in this sense that Rodríguez Luño denounces the danger of exiling the philosophical reflection on true and false conceptions, preventing the rational illumination of the decisions that everyone has to make about his or her own life.[38]

There are those who object that the philosophical search for truth and respect for autonomous freedom are incompatible, and they suggest that this incompatibility be resolved with the "sacrifice of truth on the altar of tolerance."[39] This is where the consensual theory of truth emerges.[40] It is a sham to purport to guarantee peace, freedom, and tolerance by relegating the truth about human good to the private sphere.

From the personal and social standpoint, sequestering a person in his or her subjective conscience to make his or her decisions, renouncing open discussion, and discerning between true and false conceptions of what constitutes human good would be self-destructive to the person.[41]

THE CRISIS OF THE CAPACITY FOR OBJECTIVE JUDGMENT

The elevation of subjectivity leads us to consider another underlying problem related to conscience because it is often understood not as an authority that is closely connected to reason and reality[42] but as one confined to oneself (one's tastes and choices). That is why practical reason ceases to be a universal rational phenomenon. It is in this context that the question arises how to reconcile freedom and authority.

The thought of John Henry Newman and Benedict XVI brings attention to errors about freedom and conscience that are present in utilitarianism, individualism, atheism, consequentialism, and cultural relativism. As we have already pointed out, there is a set of concepts surrounding freedom that seem to have been drained of their meaning and original reference: terms such as law, authority, conscience, and truth.

If subjective conscience is the bastion of freedom against the limitations imposed by authority, then we have two opposing models: the "morality of conscience" and the "morality of authority."[43] In the first, conscience is the supreme norm that should always be followed despite the dictates of authority. However, if the judgment of conscience were infallible and closed in on itself, it would mean that there is no truth at the foundations of our existence in the moral sphere. It would mean that there are no universal natural ethics that allow us to make objective judgments. The Christian model is based on the connection between freedom and truth and on the existence of practical reason. Christian ethics are not based on a model like that of a "morality of authority," which is based on the subjection of all existence to God, who controls and regulates even the most intimate aspects of human beings.[44]

The problem is that, according to the skeptical and relativistic paradigm of modernity, conscience is not "open to truth"—because truth does not exist—but it is precisely "the faculty which dispenses from truth. It thereby becomes the justification for subjectivity."[45] If the choices themselves have no connection with the authority that comes from reality and nature, then we lose sight of the fact that conscience is the opening of the human being to that common world of what it is to be men and women.

Another consequence of a subjective conscience that is closed in on itself is that "the obligation to seek the truth ceases. . . . Being convinced of oneself, as well as conforming to others, are sufficient."[46] According to this logic, "doing evil in following one's conscience would be moral" because one has chosen it. However, it would lead to embarrassing contradictions, such as that of whoever claimed that "the Nazis acted morally because they acted in accordance with their subjective conscience." It is clear that there is something erroneous and equivocating in this sort of "morality of subjectivity."

For this reason, placing subjective conscience in opposition to authority (truth) is one of the deepest problems of modernity because it means, as a matter of fact, denying that reality precedes freedom. That is to say, "Freedom is tied to a measure, the measure of reality—to the truth."[47] For this reason, a project of freedom that understands liberation as the dissolution of references to reality and the continued expansion of individual freedom is a false (and dangerous) notion.[48]

Thomas Aquinas formulates it another way. Human beings have autonomy and are the personal owners of their actions. The moral law that comes from God and that is also a law proper to human beings is what Aquinas calls the "rightful autonomy" of practical reason.[49] That is why the autonomy of reason cannot mean creation, by reason itself, of moral values and norms.[50]

In his *Letter to the Duke of Norfolk* in the chapter called "Divided Allegiance," John Henry Newman presents different dilemmas concerning freedom and authority in the form of hypothetical situations to show the supremacy of conscience: "Certainly, if I am obliged to bring religion into after-dinner toasts (which indeed does not seem quite the thing), I shall drink—to the Pope, if you please—still, to Conscience first, and to the Pope afterwards."[51] With these words Newman recognizes papal authority, but he interprets it together with the primacy of conscience and challenges the traditionalist positions of his interlocutors. In this regard, Ratzinger adds: "Modern man, who presupposes the opposition of authority to subjectivity, has difficulty understanding this. For him, conscience stands on the side of subjectivity and is the expression of the freedom of the subject. Authority, on the other hand, appears to him as the constraint on, threat to and even the negation of, freedom." And Ratzinger continues: "For Newman, the middle term which establishes the connection between authority and subjectivity is truth."[52]

This transformation of the notion of conscience pushes everyone to construct his or her own truth and morality. The result of this reformulation of conscience as the supreme judge of this good is that discussion of the truth is shelved. According to John Paul II:

Once the idea of a universal truth about the good, knowable by human reason, is lost, inevitably the notion of conscience also changes. Conscience is no longer considered in its primordial reality as an act of a person's intelligence, the function of which is to apply the universal knowledge of the good in a specific situation and thus to express a judgment about the right conduct to be chosen here and now. Instead, there is a tendency to grant to the individual conscience the prerogative of independently determining the criteria of good and evil and then acting accordingly.

To judge acts of incitement toward hate from an ethical standpoint, we are presented with the challenge of overcoming this subjective and individualist focus, this "atomism,"[53] using Charles Taylor's expression, for which each individual faces his or her own truth that is different from the truth of others. If the expressions of hate speech are analyzed from the perspective of conscience as a purely subjective judge, then the results will lead to an increasingly abusive use of freedom of expression.

The truly critical issue of the Modern Era, according to Ratzinger, is this: "The concept of truth has been virtually given up and replaced by the concept of progress. Progress itself 'is' truth. But through this seeming exaltation, progress loses its direction and becomes nullified. For if no direction exists, everything can just as well be regress as progress."[54]

The crisis of truth that occupied the better part of modernity has had several consequences, including the merely formal use of words and concepts, as well as the divorce of truth, speech, and action. As James Carey explains, when language is defined as "an instrument for manipulating objects," something "to get others to believe what we want them to believe,"[55] it devolves into "propaganda or polemic."[56] For Carey, "The divorce of truth from discourse and action" hinders and deforms "the very notion of truth, and therefore the sense by which we take our bearings in the world is destroyed."[57]

TEN

The Neutrality of
the Public Space

A Useful Fiction

THE CREATION OF THE PUBLIC SPHERE

The French and American liberal revolutions ushered in a new political and social order that is characterized by the separation between religious and political power, as well as the creation of a neutral public sphere that is not dominated by any specific option of human good. These new states were endowed with constitutions that protect the freedom of their citizens and recognize their rights by law, and the power of the government is limited. In the classical liberal paradigm, community development is carried out by intermediate institutions (educational, cultural, charitable, religious, and so on) created by civil society.

One of the central aspects of the project of political liberalism is the neutrality of the state. Any possibility of using the government to determine the thinking or lifestyles of its citizens is rejected. As Locke stated in *The Second Treatise of Government* (1689), to ensure the freedom of the individual, the government must focus on its "great and chief end," which is the preservation of three properties: "life, liberty, and estate."[1] Each citizen's freedom to pursue happiness is protected.[2] For this reason, the state recognizes certain individual rights, including religious freedom. The American Enlightenment assumes the necessity of religion for people's moral lives, but without an official state religion.

North American legal culture uses a metaphor of Thomas Jefferson (one of the founding fathers of the United States) to show the relationship between the church and the state: "[A] wall of separation between the church and state."[3] This is based on the words of Locke in his *Essay on Toleration* (1689): "I believe that we must above all distinguish between political and religious matters, and properly define the boundary between church and commonwealth."[4] Highlighting that "their boundaries must be kept, and their names not confounded."[5] As McConnell shows, Hobbes did not share this separation between church and state in *Leviathan* (1651),[6] nor would Rousseau later in *The Social Contract* (1762).

At first, there were no complaints in this regard, but in some court cases following World War II, the need to codify this principle in law was confirmed: "The wall between Church and State ... must be kept high and impregnable" was the ruling in one case.[7] Leonard Levy shows how federal legislation did not affect the states at first, so that six of the thirteen original states maintained "religious establishments."[8] Unlike in the Christian kingdoms in Europe, in the United States the establishments were of different religions. It was in 1947 that the Supreme Court established the criterion that the state must be neutral "between religions" or "between religion and non-religion." This neutrality is described by other courts as "strict and lofty neutrality," "wholesome neutrality," "benevolent neutrality," and "complete neutrality."[9]

In this country, conflicts about the practice of religion in public schools began to arise in the 1960s. As Michael Sandel recounts, as more than a matter of state neutrality, the establishment of the religion of secularism began to permeate the schools.[10] Prayer and nativity scenes or Christmas trees in schools were prohibited in the name of this "neutrality." In 1985, Supreme Court Justice Warren Burger dissented from these prohibitions, saying that this exercise of so-called neutrality "manifests not neutrality but hostility toward religion."[11]

The principle of neutrality that underlies the First Amendment to the US Constitution, that "both religion and government can best work to

achieve their lofty aims if each is left free from the other within its respective sphere," is a legitimate and just premise, but it is not easy to put into
practice. In fact, as Sandel shows, jurisprudence has several interpretations,[12]
with two main ones: the voluntarist interpretation that highlights "autonomy" and "choice," which is preponderant in contemporary jurisprudence,
and that of freedom of conscience. "By invoking the voluntarist conception
of neutrality," Sandel writes, "the Court gives constitutional expression to
the version of liberalism that conceives the right as prior to the good and
the self as prior to its ends."[13] This position is not neutral, he says: freedom
of conscience was traditionally understood "as the right to exercise religious
duties according to the dictates of conscience, not the right to choose religious beliefs."[14] What makes freedom of belief respectable is not the way in
which these beliefs have been acquired but the human good in itself.

The voluntarist theory has led to the empowerment of all subjective
interests and alternatives in the name of "autonomy" and "choice." According to this view, the state has established itself as a defender of these
new rights of identity, given potential forms of discrimination.

Hannah Arendt criticizes the creation of the "social sphere" into
which the public and private spheres have been absorbed. In antiquity, the
author explains, "freedom" developed in the public sphere (*polis*), whereas
life's "necessities" developed in the private sphere (family).[15] Modernity
would completely erase this distinction, and a new "nation-wide administration of housekeeping" would take on full prominence, excluding any
possibility of action,[16] and, in the place of action, society would express a
certain kind of behavior from each person through the imposition of in-
numerable norms that would tend to normalize and standardize its members.[17] Arendt concludes her criticism by saying: "Behavior has replaced
action as the foremost mode of human relationship."[18]

Arendt claims that the political sphere, characterized by action, is severely damaged by the disappearance of the distinction of spheres because
this destroys the "common world,"[19] characterized by "human plurality,"[20]
which, as those last two words express, is unity and differentiation. This
destruction takes place in tyrannies but also in the society of the masses
where everyone behaves in a standard way, "imprisoned in the subjectivity
of their own singular experience."[21]

As happened in the Greek *polis* and the Roman *res publica*, according to Arendt, action and speech are united in the political sphere of
our time: "Finding the right words at the right moment, quite apart from

the information or communication they may convey, is action," and, she adds, "Only sheer violence is mute."[22] Thus, Arendt saw human plurality (equality and differentiation) as the basic condition for both action and discourse. "If men were not *equal*," she writes, "they could [not] understand each other. . . . If men were not *distinct*, each human being distinguished from any other who is, was, or will ever be, they would need neither speech nor action to make themselves understood. Signs and sounds to communicate immediate, identical needs and wants would be enough."[23]

In the classical liberal context, neutrality meant that the government would not take part in ideological disagreements among the people (content neutrality), it would not impose any particular view (not taking sides), and it would not force anyone to take a position against his or her own convictions (no compelled speech). According to McConnell, "Tolerance meant something like 'live and let live.' It did not mean that everyone in the nation was expected to approve of the conduct or beliefs of everyone else."[24]

THE PUBLIC SPHERE: PLURALITY OR NEUTRALITY?

A transversal principle that runs through the liberal theory of freedom of expression is ethical neutrality, a mix of indifference and skepticism, understood as the exclusion from the public sphere of any conception of the good about the human being, because the public space must include all voices aseptically. This neutrality carries a specific ethical position, of the relativistic variety. Thus, it is not simple impartiality, but it is taking an axiological position, to affirm that "all values are equally valuable," or, the same thing taken to the extreme, "none of them are."

The positing of a public space with no ethical norm is a theoretical position that takes two forms: the non-contentious one, which promotes the civic attitude and stoic self-discipline,[25] and the contentious one, which encourages transgression considering that everything is permitted because, in the end, everything adds to the public good and that public opinion balances out and is self-regulating.[26]

A fundamental principle of the freedom of expression is the search for knowledge as an individual and social objective,[27] through a free and open debate of ideas.[28] The competition between ideas is presented as a program for civic education in reaching the truth. No received truths should be

taken as untouchable, and erroneous or harmful ideas should not be silenced (partially or totally) but vigorously refuted. The defenders of an absolute marketplace of ideas,[29] even admitting that false ideas can do great
damage, think that *reason* is the greatest instrument that humanity has for
its progress. Justice Holmes, despite his skepticism about the Millian possibility that there is an objective truth that people can achieve, supports the
principle by saying that "the ultimate good desired is better reached by free
trade in ideas—that the best test of truth is the power of the thought to get
itself accepted in the competition of the market, and that truth is the only
ground upon which their wishes safely can be carried out."[30]

As I have repeated throughout these pages, liberalism bases civil or
political liberties on freedom of choice as an expression of individuality
"but without any consideration of the good for which this freedom is
used."[31] For the liberal tradition, the important thing is to foster people's
own choices as long as they do not hurt others. However, the a priori ban-
ishment of morality exclusively to the private sphere has created a moral
vacuum in the political sphere that legalism cannot resolve.

The political and the moral spheres are distinct but inseparable because, according to Ángel Rodríguez Luño, "politics essentially relates to
the common good, which includes the promotion and teaching of the
goods that are relevant for the common life of human persons, such as the
public order and peace, freedom, justice, equality, etc."[32]

In some modes of secular liberal reasoning, the "neutral state" is often
confused with the "secular state."[33] There are concepts such as pluralism or
state neutrality that are sometimes equivocally invoked, giving them an
ideological component. The distinction between the church and the state,
between the religious and the political, does not mean we should cancel the
ethical references rooted in the human being.[34] As Alexis de Tocqueville
recalled with a touch of irony: "Christianity, which has made all men equal
before God, will not be loath to see all citizens equal before the law."[35]

The political-philosophical struggle to impose a naturalistic view of
the human being introduces confusion in these terms and makes it difficult to properly understand legitimate pluralism in political and religious
matters. So-called ethical pluralism is introduced, which is a relativistic neutralism that separates the political plane from natural moral principles.[36]
In many cases, there is a distorted understanding of the desire to be nondenominational, which leads to the projection of a public space with no

ethical norm. Tocqueville himself laments that the natural link between acts and beliefs, as well as the union of free action with reality and good, has been broken: "You cannot establish the reign of liberty without that of mores, nor found mores without beliefs."[37]

Human rights rest on this principle of dignity (both civic and political), which underpins the democratic commitment: the dignity of the person includes his or her freedom. This principle owes its validity to a political-legal ethic that corresponds to a European metaphysical and religious tradition.[38] Without God, the concept of person, dignity, and sacredness, to which human rights refer as the ultimate justification, cannot be explained.[39] The idea of "person" introduced by Christianity and culturally accepted by everyone until the twentieth century, is more stable, and it transcends the various political formulations. Now the appeal to God is made not in a religious sense of adherence to a faith but as an appeal to a natural resource of reason that does not rule out a metaphysical contribution in its philosophical way of reasoning.

The logic of neutralism aims to expel teleological moral meaning from the public space, substituting a scientific morality that is positive legislation. This approach presents a paradox in that it proclaims, first, that true freedom means there is a place for all speech and the possibility for it to be expressed, however harmful or radical it may be, and second, that the law cannot and should not anticipate everything. Rules cannot be contemplated for every situation because that would be both impossible and stifling. The result is that legalism offers no convincing solutions when it comes to abusive exercises of expression. The reaction of the Anglo-American media of not identifying with the content of *Charlie Hebdo* and not publishing its cartoons showed a sense of common morality that does not fit with more extreme tolerance (permissiveness) or with legalistic ethics.

As we have seen, this is a recurring contradiction: the liberalism that admits an extreme license to transgress (Skokie, *Charlie Hebdo*, *Satanic Verses*) also becomes oppressive in practice (intolerance against the cake baker or against Ratzinger in his lecture at La Sapienza). It becomes clear that, by protecting expression in an absolute and unlimited way, some elites (political, economic, media) or those who take strong positions (transgressive artists, aggressive lobbies, and so on) are protected and the weaker ones (insulted groups such as immigrants, believers, and some racial minorities) are left homeless. The underlying problem is the same one

Tocqueville identifies in speaking of the desirability of integrating received beliefs with those discovered. The secularist form of liberalism does not accept any received heritage (from ethical-moral and religious roots) because it wants to establish something completely new (neutral, adherents say), but in turn there is the de facto contradiction that they live in the cultural ethos of that Judeo-Christian and Greco-Roman moral tradition.

THE EXCESSES OF NORMATIVISM AND LEGAL POSITIVISM

Hannah Arendt observes that the foundation of freedom that modernity establishes and that gives rise to these rights and political freedoms protected by law required a source of authority that could not be identified with the liberal revolutions. This authority would guarantee a certain stability and would be the source of the justice from which laws derived their legitimacy.[40] In the American Revolution, the "great Law-giver of the universe" was invoked, and in the Declaration of Independence, Jefferson himself appealed to the "Laws of Nature and of Nature's God."

It may seem contradictory that a revolutionary movement that sought to create a new political body and rid itself of the earlier tradition (the Old Regime), and which believes in the necessity of emancipating the political sphere from the religious, would invoke the Divine Lawgiver as a principle. In this respect, Arendt gleans that "even Locke, who so firmly believed that 'a principle of action [has been planted in man] by God Himself' [so that men would have only to follow the voice of a God-given conscience within themselves, without any special recourse to the transcendent planter]."[41] Thus, the need for an absolute that underpins the public sphere was commonly recognized by pre-revolutionary theorists.

The model on which the West built its constitutions and civil law (corpus iuris civilis) was a combination of the divine law of Judeo-Christian origins and Roman law. The most indelible contribution of ancient Rome was building, for the first time in history, a body of law with a message, language, concepts, and principles that served as the basis for building a civilization.[42] Subsequently, the principles of Roman law were reformulated by Leibniz, Wolff, Kant, and Hegel (among others), who transplanted these principles into a new system of thought with different categories of property, rights, law, justice, and so on.[43]

Arendt recounts how, with the advent of modernity in the eighteenth century, the model was not altered: "Natural law stepped into the place of divinity."[44] She goes on to say, "For the trouble with natural law was precisely that it had no author, that it could only be understood as a law of nature in the sense of a non-personal, superhuman force."[45] Jefferson, as I pointed out earlier, invoked the "Laws of Nature and of Nature's God," which gives us the extent of what natural law meant: a right sanctioned by God that is in the nature of persons as a measure and that conscience recalls.[46]

The recognition of an "Immortal Legislator" that sanctioned human laws also required a belief in further rewards and punishments. This point was incompatible with the new revolutionary airs, but it was not removed. Arendt claims that if the men of the revolution did not write off the reference to a transcendent authority, it was for mere political utility.[47] Kriele confirms this opinion when he claims that the Enlightenment thinkers of the eighteenth century adopted an anti-ecclesial stance against the dominating pretensions of the churches in the confessional state, "but almost spontaneously, they lived in the ethos of tradition that was still alive and that marked the spiritual climate of the time as well as their ethical and political culture."[48]

As Kriele recalls, the emergence of the idea of human dignity in the political sphere was due to its Christian roots. The political Enlightenment did not discard these roots.[49] This provides an explanation (among other reasons) for why the subsequent attempts to base morality on reason or on utilitarian calculation failed to explain—convincingly—the reasons for defending human dignity in the face of the aggressions of unlimited freedom of expression.

The fact is that there are some axiomatic truths that do not require consent or political discussion because they are self-evident. Such is Jefferson's assertion in the Virginia Declaration: "We hold these truths to be self-evident"; these truths are "the opinions and beliefs of men (which) depend not on their own will, but follow involuntarily the evidence proposed to their minds."[50] They are truths that inform reason but are not produced by it. And finally, Jefferson said, the only immutable things are the inalienable and innate rights of human beings, because they are not the work of human beings but of their Creator.[51]

It may be surprising that, in the century of the Enlightenment, its authors were aware of axiological truths but the question of the purpose and meaning of things was not settled. As Jean Grondin recognizes, the evidence of order in the world, of a direction and meaning that exist independently of us, is evidence that it does not depend on our constructs. Ethical principles come from this experience of life that resides on the universal plane and not the cultural plane (that is, on the plane of changing constructs that would limit its scope).[52]

Up to the time of the Enlightenment, the question on the fundamentals of law and justice was undisputed. Social natural law was developed by the stoic philosophers (in the first century CE) and adopted by the Roman jurists of the first centuries in a shared way. As Benedict XVI explained in his speech in the German Federal Parliament, questioning this is a very recent phenomenon. Referring to the period after the Declaration of Human Rights was ratified in 1948 by the United Nations, the Pontiff states: "There has been a dramatic shift in the situation in the last half-century. The idea of natural law is today viewed as a specifically Catholic doctrine, not worth bringing into the discussion in a non-Catholic environment, so that one feels almost ashamed even to mention the term."[53] This is due to the fact that the legal positivism formulated by Hans Kelsen, among others, separates human nature (his or her ontological dimension: "being"), from his or her moral performance (moral imperative: "ought to be"), as if they were absolutely different areas.[54] Legal positivism has rejected universal natural law as a solid base of all rights and duties without giving convincing reasons.

The doctrine of legal positivism holds that rights receive their force exclusively from the law and they precede the goods they protect. The positivist school of thought reformulates the concepts of nature, reason, and law, understanding them in a merely functional way, as the natural sciences do. According to this logic, Benedict says, nature "is incapable of producing any bridge to ethics and law, but once again yields only functional answers."[55] In the same sense, through the positivist lens, reason is equipped with a scientific vision:

Anything that is not verifiable or falsifiable, according to this understanding, does not belong to the realm of reason strictly understood. Hence ethics and religion must be assigned to the subjective field, and they remain extraneous to the realm of reason in the strict sense of the word. Where positivist reason dominates the field to the exclusion of all else—and that is broadly the case in our public mindset—then the classical sources of knowledge for ethics and law are excluded. This is a dramatic situation which affects everyone, and on which a public debate is necessary.[56]

The exclusively functional positivist way of reasoning proves incomplete and reductive. This problem directly affects the philosophy of freedom of expression and the discussion on hate speech laws, as well as the legal status of the Internet. In Part IV we shall discuss the need for a global law that responds to the challenges that the Internet poses to freedom of expression and the desirability of recovering the debate on common rational criteria as a way to overcome the situation created by positivism.[57]

PLURALISM: ABOUT NOT "BUILDING COMMON GROUND" BUT "RESPECT FOR DIFFERENCE"

As in our discussion about tolerance, one can see when speaking of the neutrality of the public sphere that comprehensive liberalism contradicts the classical liberal program's principle of impartiality because the state assumes the role of imposing a civic moral program. Not only is the large number of anti-discrimination laws promoted by liberal governments a simple over-extension of state power, but they also constitute a true inversion of the liberal program.[58] Especially pronounced in Europe with its hate speech laws, this trend is also present in American academic literature. In the name of inclusion and diversity, we want to build a fabric of laws that protect those values. Such values are empowered for some ideological reasons that the liberal state cannot and should not make its own.

I agree with what McConnell says:

It is essential to recognize that secularism is not a neutral stance. It is a partisan stance, no less "sectarian," in its way, than religion. In a country of many diverse traditions and perspectives—some religious, some secular—neutrality cannot be achieved by assuming that one set of beliefs is more publicly acceptable than another. We need, instead, a pluralistic conception of neutrality: a neutrality not based on spurious common ground but based on respect for difference of opinion.[59]

According to Ronald Arnett, a healthy public sphere is based on having an "abundance of public spaces" for deliberation, in which "elites could be called out and questioned."[60]

Pluralism as Arendt understands it, with the two elements of a "common world" characterized by "human plurality,"[61] responds better to the needs of the public sphere than does Hobbesian liberal individualism, or the "state promotion of an identity" (multiculturalism), which "promotes a civic coexistence that cannot be achieved," in the words of Pierpaolo Donati.[62] Anti-discrimination regulations celebrate difference, multiculturalism, and diversity as long as the system of secular citizenship is not compromised. According to this logic, individuals enjoy religious freedom within the parameters of an imposed moral relativism. That is why when the dissent that results from a plurality of convictions emerges, the framework of these new rights breaks down. This is the case when the religious convictions of gynecologists or the consciences of nurses are required to be left at the door so they can intervene in abortions or fertility treatments that go against those convictions. It is also the case of bakers, florists, tailors, and others who are compelled to perform expressive acts with their work that go against their ways of thinking.

The manifestations of religiosity in the public sphere constantly put pressure on this secular civic program, as we have seen in Europe when Islamic women choose to wear the veil (the burka or niqab).[63] For many women, wearing the veil is an expression of religious piety and of belonging to a community and a particular religious tradition. For others, it may be imposed by their families or community. From a progressive perspective, the veil is an icon of submission that lowers the dignity of women. The underlying issue is that these mandates of "religious clothing" come from sharia, a law that is both political and religious. For this reason, invoking such obligations in a liberal democracy presents several complex problems that I am not going to deal with here. I want to focus only on the ways in which various countries have dealt with the tension between an individual's right to religious freedom (and its expressions) and their obligations of citizenship in a liberal state.

In France, the veil was prohibited by law with the goal of integrating and preserving a certain idea of "living together."[64] In Australia, a nation known for its great interculturality, challenges posed by the coexistence of different cultures and religions are being addressed in a more positive way.

Instead of establishing a general ban, the country is drawing limits, such as the need to see people's faces to identify them in a public process. In turn, solutions are needed that respect cultural-religious diversity and the principles of a liberal democratic society. For example, in public graduation events at a school, Muslim boys are not required to shake hands with the female teachers who preside over the official and public act as long as they express appropriate forms of respect.[65] This way, graduates are not required to perform expressive acts that are against their religion, while the sign of respect owed to their teachers is still protected.

If we compare this last example with the Japanese code of education and public morality, in which there is no physical contact between people (no handshakes, much less hugs or kisses), most can agree that it is not offensive for a Japanese person to not shake an outstretched hand but to respond with an elegant nod of the head. The openness shown by some sectors of Australian society to expressions of a religious nature is not found in the *laïcité* of the French state. This is not a matter of geography but an issue that is rooted in the French Revolution of 1789, which intended to confine religion to the private sphere and to close the public sphere to anything that was not secularist.

PART III

The Historical and Philosophical Development of Freedom of Expression

ELEVEN

The Origins of Freedom of Expression

MODERNITY: A NEW PARADIGM OF FREEDOM AND AUTHORITY

On Gutenberg and the Printing Press

Gutenberg's invention of the printing press in 1450 brought about the possibility of the mass publishing and dissemination of ideas in Europe, which had previously been in the hands of copyists who reproduced the texts by hand. Wide-distribution print newspapers began 150 years later. News sheets, literary brochures, gazettes, and pamphlets abounded during the fifteenth and sixteenth centuries; all of them were nonperiodic publications that were sold in bookstores or by street vendors in the cities.[1] According to Pierre Albert, all these forms of "flyers in this way illustrated from their beginning, the three main functions of journalism: current information, the account of minor events of human interest, and the expression of opinions."[2]

In medieval Europe, Christianity held a dominant position as the source of doctrine and as an institution. It was a powerful agent of cultural development, which is why the first impressions of "incunabula" (printed books) were made in the abbeys, bishoprics, and universities of the Church. The printing press was in the service of the Church and monarchs, as well as people with less honest interests. All of them found an excellent ally in printing.

With the increase of translations of the Bible into vernacular languages and their spread with the printing press, bishops grew concerned about the integrity of these unofficial translations. In many cases, they were done by people with no pastoral experience or those who were not authorized by the ecclesiastical hierarchy. Hence, the first interventions of the Church's authority were related to that issue. It is in this context that censorship in the Church appeared, as an internal measure for her members. We shall address this in the following chapter.

A Political and Philosophical Change

The Enlightenment postulated the dominion of reason — and reason alone — over any other form of knowledge. There was a desire to give thought to new foundations, that is, to provide rational principles detached from God. Presented with a hierarchical social order that was stratified on the basis of variant conditions granted by birth, a new social structure that would be based on reason was now defended. According to the Enlightenment thinkers, we would thus go from a society based on privilege to the equality granted by reason.[3]

A key aspect of all this is that the Catholic Church formed part of the system of the Old Regime, which was based on the alliance between the throne and the altar, a stratified view of society, and economic interventionism, and she had strict relationships of power with the civil authority. As Gonzalo Redondo has written, "The Church's position in Catholic countries was ambiguous at the end of the eighteenth century. And this ambiguity was accentuated as the need for a change in social structure became more evident."[4] The people who led movements of social change and political renewal had a difficult time distinguishing between the interests of the absolute monarchies and those of the Church. The social change that was advocated was based on equality of the law and before the law and on freedom in all areas: freedom of thought, expression, and association, as well as economic and political freedom.

The innovative rationalist doctrines, coupled with the tensions coming from the Catholic monarchies and the infiltration of Jansenism that also affected the structure of the Church, "allows us to understand the well-defined and almost exclusively defensive attitude that the Catholic Church adopted in the eighteenth century," writes Redondo. "There were almost no great popes or great saints. The Church seemed to be withdrawn in safeguarding the faith of the vast peasant masses that were substantially faithful to her."[5] Thus, in an adverse doctrinal environment, a large group of educated Christians was missing—in the era of the Enlightenment no less.

In light of the serious doctrinal threats posed by the Enlightenment, Pope Clement XIII insisted on the *Index librorum prohibitorum*. In 1759 he condemned the *Encyclopédie* of Diderot and D'Alembert, the first two volumes of which had appeared in 1751 and 1752. In 1766 the Pope published the encyclical *Christianae Reipublicae Salus*, in which he came out against the modern distribution of books in order to defend the spiritual health of the Christian people.

The progress of the press was hampered by strict political control. "The press of the Old Regime was subject to the system of privilege and that of prior authorization," Albert writes.[6] Thus, with strict regulations and no possibility of competition, the authorities were able to direct the development of the journalistic press. Along with being subject to these limitations, the contents of publications were tightly controlled, and there were prohibitions against writing about politics and censorship proceedings. There was, moreover, the official press.

We must bear in mind that the press was not yet prestigious at the end of the eighteenth century, despite having improved technically as well as in terms of its contents. As Pierre Albert argues, "The privileged instrument for expressing ideas remained the book and the booklet." The press, a reflection of the world, was still passive; it informed without really arguing, leaving traditional literature to take care of conflicts and controversies. In the eighteenth century, the gazetteer was still an undervalued character, and the social and intellectual elite viewed journalism as a kind of subliterature with no value or prestige. This is what Rousseau expressed in 1755: "What is a periodic book? An ephemeral work with no merit, with no utility, whose distained and belittled reading by people of letters is only good for giving women and fools vanity without instruction."[7]

It would not be until after the French Revolution, well into the nineteenth century, that freedom of the press would be claimed as a great principle of modern liberty. As Article 11 of the Declaration of the Rights of Man of August 26, 1789, states: "The free communication of ideas and opinions is one of the most precious of the rights of man. Every citizen may, accordingly, speak, write, and print with freedom, but shall be responsible for such abuses of this freedom as shall be defined by law."[8]

Dilemmas Posed by Modernity

Between the eighteenth and the twentieth centuries, important social and cultural changes were taking place in Western society, including in the Church. She faced the need to respond to the dilemmas posed by modernity, and one of the main issues was the foundation of freedom and authority. Popes Gregory XVI and Pius IX denounced certain manifestations of modernity that, in the name of freedom of thought and the press, were an attack on the Church.

After the French Revolution and the brief period of the Restoration of the European monarchies, the old continent suffered new waves of revolution (in 1820, 1830, and 1848), which spread liberal ideas definitively. The so-called Old Regime was on the verge of disappearance.

In this historical context, there were not the necessary tools for conceiving of the political, social, and religious spheres separately. Pius IX convened the First Vatican Council, which dealt with the question of authority within the Church, but the council was never completed. Thus, the task of examining the nature and mission of the Church and her relationship with the world would culminate in Vatican II.

The Church was pushed from several different directions to offer a new synthesis of her approaches: she received the pressure of liberal ideas from the political sphere; from the social sphere, a new class arose out of industrialization that did not fit into the framework of the Old Regime in which the Church was entrenched; and, as for the sphere of communication, the press was already considered the "fourth estate" by the end of the nineteenth century, and through the press liberal and secular positions were spread.

However, the early nineteenth century in Europe was a time of relative peace and intellectual rebirth. The new freedoms of thought and expression that were recognized in the constitutions of many countries, as well as new scientific and technical discoveries, fostered a climate of development in thought at many levels.

The nationalism that emerged in the nineteenth century was based on the democratic principle, which was opposed to the monarchical legitimacy system, and materialized into a state that assumed the representation of the interests of its citizens. Nationalism affected the Church in regard to the "Roman question": the Papal States did not fit in well with the new sociopolitical schools of thought, and the threat of losing their territories also threatened their spiritual autonomy.

On the other hand, nationalism involved a dis-integrating element; some Christian denominations boosted national consciousness (Lutheranism in Germany and Anglicanism in Great Britain), while the Catholic Church saw in those nationalist sentiments a danger to the universality of the mission of the Church.

TWO VERY DIFFERENT DECLARATIONS OF LIBERAL FREEDOMS

The public recognition of human rights had two historical moments: the propagation of the Virginia Declaration of Rights in 1776 and of the Declaration of the Rights of Man in France in 1789. The latter had a clear anti-clerical tone, which led the Church to not adhere to that proclamation.

At first blush, it can be shocking that the Church opposed the recognition of the rights of man, as it was an important recognition of the dignity of the person, but if one takes into account the context surrounding this declaration, one can see that it included a strong element of rejecting transcendence. The reasons for the Church's reticence were not so much political as they were philosophical and theological: the authority on which these declarations were based, as well as their underlying individualism and naturalism, eschewed the spiritual dimension.[9]

Consideration was given to freedom, and above all to freedom of conscience, which was radically opposed to faith because it completely disconnected it from the truth about the human being and Christian truth, which has its ultimate basis in God. Freedom was exalted to the detriment of truth, which became almost eclipsed. That is why one can understand that the civil liberties that were advocated, especially those of religion and the press, drew the suspicion and revulsion of Church officials. The esteem for this concept of autonomous freedom, built rationally by the state, was part of a path toward the secularization of the structure of the state, of its authority, and of civic life. Thus, the Church lost her role as guarantor of the foundations of society, and thereby lost her public status.[10] The US Constitution, on the other hand, introduced the novelty of declaring its government separate from any ecclesiastical organization, which implied a new way of carrying out Church-state relations, with a real separation of both powers.

The French Revolution's proclamation of human rights in August of 1789 consecrated freedom of opinion and expression as a fundamental right.[11] The declaration proclaims liberty, equality, the right to property, and the separation of powers as some of the basic pillars of human rights. It also recognizes the primacy of Catholicism as a religion.[12] However, the events that followed this first declaration were completely anti-Catholic. In the following months, the property of the Church was seized and religious orders were dissolved. Pope Pius VI had to intervene, condemning revolutionary principles with the document *Quod aliquantum*, a text that was addressed to the French National Assembly in which he strongly protested against the Civil Constitution of the Clergy as an unfair political intervention to restrict the action and the independence of the Church in France and confiscate a large number of the Church's lands and buildings and denounced the conception of the human being that underpinned the Declaration of the Rights of Man.[13] At the end of his pontificate, the Papal States were invaded by General Bonaparte, who required the Pope to sign the harsh Treaty of Tolentino (1797), agreeing to surrender, the annexation of regions, payment of a large amount of money, and the confiscation of art. Some months later the treaty was completely disregarded; Napoleon's troops invaded Rome and the Pope was exiled.

In *Quod aliquamtum* Pius VI alludes to the right to print whatever one wants in matters of religion as "foolish." He writes that autonomous freedom based on naturalism declares that men "can freely think as they please and write and even publish in the press anything about Religion. . . . But what greater foolishness can one imagine than considering that all men are free and equal in such a way that nothing is granted to the reason with which man was originally endowed by nature and by virtue of which he is distinguished from beasts?"[14]

A small event is instructive about the historical context in which these protagonists operated. In French revolutionary propaganda, the news of the death of Pius VI on August 28, 1799, was relayed with the expression:

"Death of Pius VI and last,"[15] which includes the prediction that the pontificate of the Church would die with him.

The pontificate of Pope Pius VI (1775–1799) coincided precisely with the years of the bourgeois revolutions in Europe and America. Pius VI dealt with these revolutionary events by trying to exercise diplomacy in the face of the constant abuses to which the Church was subject.

The Church began her journey in the early part of the nineteenth century between two fires, that of the Old Regime, which would take some time to definitively extinguish, and that of a new regime based on the ideas of political liberalism. The life of the Church in the nineteenth century revolved around three major elements: her relationship with the state as a new social structure that would be adopted throughout the world; the relationship between faith and reason; and the unity around her head, the Pope, so attacked by the pretensions of the national Churches, which had the backing of the temporal powers.[16]

THE "INSTITUTIONAL" CRISIS OF THE CHURCH AND HER NEW RELATIONSHIP WITH THE TEMPORAL POWERS

A starting point of liberalism was the rejection of a world conditioned by two closely linked powers: the monarchy and the Catholic Church. As I mentioned earlier, one facet of the Old Regime is being an absolute monarchy, with a hierarchical social organization and a very interventionalist economic system.

At the root of many liberal criticisms we see the confusion between the Church as an immutable guardian of the faith and the Church as a historical institution. If we don't understand that we are dealing with a temporal and circumstantial option for a certain social structure (one that lasted for centuries) by confusing the historical-political plane with the deposit of revealed faith, then we do not properly understand the Church.[17]

These premises are fundamental for understanding the Church's trajectory in the past two centuries. The Church is not identical to the political and cultural context that she inhabits, even those in which the Church lives and is materialized. As Pope Francis explains, Christianity does not have a single inculturation: Quoting Pope John Paul II, he continues: "The history of the Church shows that Christianity does not have simply one cultural expression, but rather, 'remaining completely true to itself, with unswerving fidelity to the proclamation of the Gospel and the tradition of the Church, it will also reflect the different faces of the cultures and peoples in which it is received and takes root' (John Paul II, *Novo millennio ineunte* no. 40, January 6, 2001)."[18]

In the First Vatican Council, the "ecclesiastical problem" was a central aspect, with various views and conceptions of the Church inherited from the eighteenth century. The ultramontanes conceived of the Church as a perfect society in which the idea of a community of love also dominated. For German traditionalist ecclesiology, the Church was the body of Christ under the guidance of the Holy Spirit, highlighting the aspect of authority, especially that of the Pope. Thus remained the issue of reconciling the ideas of the "visible Church" (society) with those of the "invisible Church" (spiritual).[19]

In Vatican I, the authority of the Pope was reinforced and, as a result, the centralization of the Church and the hierarchy as well. The reaction to modernism led to an emphasis on authority and institution.[20] The understanding of the Church as "Mystical Body" in Pius XII's encyclical in 1943 groups the two concepts of the visibility of the Church in the societal sense and the mystical and spiritual dimension of the Church.[21] Not only is the Church a supernatural organism but she also exists in time. Her "social corporeity" is an essential element, along with her spiritual element. This unity of the "Body of Christ" gives way to a sacramental conception of the Church that better reflects the distinction and complementarity of the two aspects of ecclesial reality.[22]

This ecclesiological debate is not the result of a theoretical theological distinction, but it presents the need for a closer examination of the nature and mission of the Church since she wants to recover a presence in and dialogue with the contemporary world.[23] Starting from the Second Vatican Council, writes Mariano Fazio, "the defensive attitude of the Church has been transformed into openness, dialogue, and constructive criticism with respect to Modernity."[24]

The exercise of freedom of expression is directly related to religious freedom and political freedom. Therefore, without a sufficient framework for understanding the relationship between political power and religious power (in the twelfth through the twentieth centuries) or, better yet, between the political sphere and the religious sphere (both public, let us not forget) or between Church and world (put in ecclesiological terms), it is impossible to properly resolve the issue of freedom of expression. Hence the difficulties of the Magisterium prior to Vatican II.

The Origin of Political Freedoms:
The Christian Cultural Substratum in Which Freedom of Expression Is Formed

The "freedom of the moderns,"[25] which had its origins in the American and European revolutions of the late eighteenth and early nineteenth centuries, breathed an idea of freedom associated with a new origin, a new authority, and a new law.[26] It therefore had a public nature,[27] not the quality of human will. The awareness of "doing something new" at the political level took on a radical air. According to Hannah Arendt, the idea of the modern revolutions consisted of a foundation of freedom, of constituting (in the case of France) and of founding (in the case of the United States) a public space, that is, "a body politic which guarantees the space where freedom can appear."[28] As Arendt points out, this public and secular space already existed in classical antiquity,[29] but it had become invisible with absolutism. In the modern world, the act of foundation meant drawing up a constitution.[30]

In America the political sphere of the "pursuit of happiness" was established,[31] and that became the term for the freedom and right to access and to participate in public life. In France a new political space was built in which to exercise what Arendt calls the "passion for public freedom."[32] For her, revolution established civil rights for "happiness or public liberty" that in France were stifled by Robespierre's revolution[33] and in America were channeled toward a civil and political construction.[34]

Arendt frames the distinction between liberty and liberation in the difference between those two models of revolution: the French one that wanted "the liberation of man" from all that the Old Regime meant and the American one that wanted "the foundation of freedom."[35] This dual tradition involves some perplexities with respect to human rights, giving place to two traditions (French and American).[36] In the French case, the ownership of individual rights is given by virtue of birth, regardless of the political body, which is distrusted.[37] And the American model is characterized by rights as a limitation of both the power of the government and the power of the majority over individuals.[38] In both cases, the revolutionaries sought to establish a new authority and the Christian heritage was part of the core of their societies in the form of customs, principles, educational institutions, and more.

Alexis de Tocqueville also distinguished two traditions, although he expressed them differently than Arendt. He contrasted the motives of each revolution: in the face of the irresistible and anonymous trend of violence, he thought that the free actions of people and the power of virtue could prevail. He advocated a society based on the strength of human virtue.[39]

In the book *Democracy in America* (1835–1840) Tocqueville highlighted the idea that the revolutions have the effect of upsetting old beliefs, weakening authority, and eclipsing common ideas.[40] In this sense, it seemed to Tocqueville that eighteenth-century European philosophy was more revolutionary than democratic insofar as the eighteenth century exalted the individual and, with a certain intellectual anarchy, received beliefs were expelled from the debate.[41] On the other hand, he noted that in the United States "Christianity itself is an established and irresistible fact that no one attempts to attack or defend."[42] As we can see, the distinction between liberation and liberty emerges once again, and it confirms the presence of a Christian heritage that forms the sociocultural background of America.

The formulation of freedom of expression in the modern era was conceived and developed in a Christian cultural and social context. With the overthrow of the Old Regime and the separation between political and religious powers, these two areas of jurisdiction were also separated. From the political-historical standpoint, this separation was bidirectional, as Arendt points out. Thus, "just as one speaks of an emancipation of the secular from the religious, one may, and perhaps with even more right, speak of an emancipation of religion from the demands and burdens of the secular."[43] The author is referring to the political responsibilities that the Church was forced to take on after the fall of the Roman Empire and until the fall of the absolute monarchies in the eighteenth century.

As we have already seen, some wanted this relocation of the Church to be a displacement, and since the twentieth century the most secularist schools of thought have wanted it to mean the disappearance of her influence in the public sphere. Certainly, the Founding Fathers and some theorists of free expression, such as Milton and Mill, lived and thought about freedoms within a Christian ethos. When they spoke of total and absolute freedom, they contemplated only certain general limits of public order.

TWELVE

Old-School and
New-School Censorship

"OLD-SCHOOL" CENSORSHIP

"Censorship" means "the action of the public authority by which the expression of certain ideas and opinions in various media of social communication is controlled, limited, or suppressed,"[1] which is justified as upholding morality or a public life ordered toward the common good of society. This power was originally exercised by a king, who, in turn, professed a religious faith as either a Catholic king or a Protestant king: *cuius regio eius religio* (whose realm, his religion). This law prescribed that his subjects would follow the monarch's authority and religion.

Thus, the state exercised censorship through an agency, and, in issues related to faith or morals, the civic power delegated the criteria to the Church, enforcing what she decided. For example, according to Del Pozo: "In 1521 [Holy Roman Emperor] Charles V issued an edict punishing the publication of books prohibited by the Church, which examined potentially heretical or immoral works through the Congregation of the Holy Office."[2] As a matter of fact, censorship existed in the Protestant kingdoms as well as in the Catholic ones.[3] This power was not disputed by subjects until the arrival of liberalism, which brought a greater awareness of individual rights and freedoms.

The Pope's first official conformity with censorship was affirmed in 1479 with the document *Accepimus litteras vestras* (March 17, 1479), whereby Sixtus IV praises, supports, and grants the use of ecclesiastical censorship,[4] and some years later Pius IV confers this authority to the University of Cologne.[5]

This document of the Pope was the first norm of ecclesiastical censorship established within the Church; in this case, it was directed toward printers, merchants, and readers. Within a few years, the first pronouncement for the entire Church would arrive with the bull *Inter multiplices* (November 11, 1487).[6] In it Pope Innocent VIII arranged for the ecclesiastical censorship of books for all Christianity, entrusting the bishops with the execution of the task of control. All texts were examined before going to print, and the approval of the ecclesiastical authority was required in order to print them (via a certificate of *imprimatur*); otherwise penalties of varying intensities were incurred. The institution of the Indexas, an organized mode of censorship, was completed at the Council of Trent.[7]

As one can infer, the origin of the conflict between censorship and freedom of expression was due, on the one hand, to its arising during a historical period in which religious power and political power were undifferentiated and, on the other, to a notion of individual autonomy that implies an ideological view of the human being. The different conception of the person, as a being called to perfect himself by the search for and attainment of truth or, in an individualistic way—that is, one that is carried out by means of his own self-affirmation—determines his general attitude toward censorship. Depending on one's perspective, censorship can be understood either as a prudential orientation or as a measure that restricts freedom. Tensions surrounding freedom of expression and its limits are found in this context. Let us look at their evolution throughout the years.

Censorship as a Prudential Act of the Church with Her Faithful

As early as the modern era, Pope Leo XIII justified the Index of books that were prohibited for Catholics, arguing that, in the words of Leticia Soberón, he "wished to defend common folk by regulating the Index, and at the same time, he opened the Vatican archives to researchers with the goal of responding with truth to the murmurings" of the suspicious.[8] The

Pontiff condemned the manipulation of truth and the spreading of error among people who did not have the resources to work out the truth of what was presented to them.[9] Several years later, Leo XIII reformed some of the earlier measures of his predecessors regarding the censorship of books,[10] and shortly thereafter he updated the *Index librorum prohibitorum*,[11] preserving the substance, but making the rules less strict.[12]

At the beginning of the twentieth century, the great problem of the Church was doctrinal (modernism) within the Church herself. Just as Leo XIII had focused on the dialogue of the Church with the world, it was up to Pius X (1903–1914) to cast his gaze within the Church. Pius X summarized the modernist errors and their agnostic philosophical roots in the encyclical *Pascendi*.[13] He also established some prudential measures, like paying attention to seminarians, needing an *imprimatur* for doctrinal publications, establishing a supervisory board in each diocese, and so on.[14] Pius X maintained the disciplinary norms of his predecessor while also taking a clear position against the integralism that arose from the ultramontane Catholics.[15]

The Holy See granted bishops the right and the duty to prevent harmful writings that were printed and distributed in their dioceses from falling into the hands of the faithful without preparation.[16] Interpellation to bishops included not only said prevention but vigilance over priests and consecrated people issuing permits to carry on journalistic and editorial jobs.[17] That is why Pius X ordered the bishops to establish a commission of censors in each diocese for the review of writings.[18]

Pius X was adamant about the ideological implication of European liberalism, which banished faith to the exclusively private sphere. The Church could not agree to be relegated to the privacy of consciences and sacristies. He concluded, in the words of Gonzalo Redondo, that "there were no agreements or transactions—much less capitulations—when it was the life of the Catholic Church at stake."[19] Twenty years later, Benedict XV would eliminate the Congregation of the Index (*Index librorum prohibitorum*),[20] and his censorship powers would be subsumed under the jurisdiction of the Holy Office.

The Holy Office (today the Congregation for the Doctrine of the Faith) has exercised censorship in this prudential sense in the name of the Church for several centuries. The problem of censorship was not legitimacy but the confusion between the political and religious spheres, which was introduced in the modern age in the national confessional states.

It should be noted that in abolishing the Index in 1965,[21] Paul VI declared that its mission endured as a moral force. Thus, the document that the Congregation for the Doctrine of the Faith published at the request of Pope Paul VI stated that "the Index remains *morally binding*, in light of the demands of natural law, in so far as it admonishes the conscience of Christians to be on guard for those writings that can endanger faith and morals. But, at the same time, it no longer has the force of ecclesiastical law with the attached censure."[22]

It is important to distinguish political censorship (of books and the press) exercised by governments at a time when temporal and religious power were united (in the the sixteenth through the eighteenth centuries) from the moral censorship carried out in familial, academic, or religious spheres.

Self-Censorship in the Film Industry:
The Motion Picture Production Code and the Legion of Decency

In 1930, the Motion Picture Producers and Distributors of America (MPPDA) established a set of moral guidelines that formed a production code for the industry that was applied to most films until 1968, when it was transformed into a set of classifications based on the age of the intended audience.[23] This production code was called the Hays Code, after Will H. Hays, who, as president of the MPPDA from 1922 to 1945, directed the preparation of the Code, which went into effect in 1934. The final product was defined by some as "a Jewish owned business selling Catholic theology to Protestant America."[24]

In a Puritanical society like the United States with public decency laws, the film industry was primarily concerned with avoiding eventual government censorship but also with looking like a moral watchdog. Hays proposed the creation of an internal Studio Relations Committee that had no connection with the government that would review film content. This resulted in the industry's taking on its own "production code," which consisted of self-imposed decency standards revised by the Committee,[25] which oversaw production and proposed necessary cuts and changes.[26]

In a speech to representatives of the press, Pope Pius XI, paraphrasing Dante and Manzoni, said that neither the press nor the film industry should become "intermediaries of evil."[27] This Pope was responsible for putting together the first teaching on film. Pius XI begins his first encyc-lical about film with these words: "There does not exist today a means of influencing the masses more potent than the cinema."[28] The document fo-cuses on pointing out the moral dangers and threats inherent in film, and, on the other hand, it highlights the possibilities of apostleship that opened up with this new tool.[29] Pius XI thus expressed the first considerations of the Church regarding film in two words: "concern" and "hope."[30] The for-mer led him to promote mobilization, and the latter to recognize the pos-sibilities of the seventh art.

In the 1930s, faced with the production of many immoral films and films with obscenities, the Church in the United States came out with an initiative: the National Legion of Decency.[31] The Legion was an organiza-tion promoted by the US Catholic bishops that, from 1934 on, promoted the self-regulation of content on the part of the industry (not censorship by the state).[32] One of its initiatives was to identify and denounce immoral content in film. The institution also had the support of Protestants and Jews.

The National Legion of Decency had great influence on the Ameri-can motion picture industry until the 1960s. Starting in 1964, large cine-matic productions began to make a lot of money, and interests in promot-ing obscenity became more powerful.[33] The representatives of Protestant denominations first, followed by those of Jews two years later, abandoned their involvement with production codes, and the Church was left alone in this struggle.[34] The decisions of the Supreme Court on issues of decency began to change at the end of the 1960s. Leo Pfeffer, an influential Jewish American lawyer at the time, said: "Supreme Court decisions did not cause the sexual revolution of the 60s and 70s; it is closer to the truth to say that they reflected it."[35]

In 1968 the US Supreme Court limited censorship to content for mi-nors,[36] and in 1972 the MPAA (Motion Picture Association of America) established a national voluntary rating system based on the age of the au-dience: G– general audiences, M– mature audiences; PG– parental guid-ance required; R– required a 16 year-old to be accompanied by a parent; and X– under 17 not allowed. In 1990, X was replaced by NC– no children under 17, to differentiate an artistic film from pornography.[37]

In 1972, the Supreme Court ruled that there is no general rule for ob-scenity; it would be determined based on "contemporary community stan-dards.[38] Thus, we can say that from one perspective, the battle for decency in Hollywood movies was lost in the mid-1970s, although calling for personal responsibility and community standards was an important contribution in the long run. However, after *Miller v. California* (1973), films began to be released without the moral stamp of the MPAA. The system of voluntarily submitting to the production code and the scrutiny of the Legion was set aside. The Legion had no power to compel Hollywood to edit its films, nor could it require the arrest of those who went to see those films. What it could do was to urge Catholics not to attend and to rely on the credibility that the movie ratings had among people of other religions. Catholics could participate by enrolling in the Legion, making a public promise, and signing a pledge,[39] which was done by more than 10 million Catholics in the United States.[40] In addition to distributing the moral classifications of films, the Legion organized to boycott those that were immoral.[41]

With the encyclical *Vigilanti cura* in 1936, the Pope gave publicity to the American initiative and sought to involve the universal Church in its purpose.[42] He suggested that the bishops imitate the system used in the United States through schools and parishes and that a "permanent national review office," dependent on Catholic action, be established in each country to carry out this task and distribute information to priests and the faithful.

After twenty-five years of activity by the Legion of Decency, the Vatican's secretary of state wrote a letter to the US Bishops' Committee for Motion Pictures, Radio, and Television on April 25, 1959, affirming and encouraging them in their work:

> Many Christians of the separated Churches, as well as Jews, gave their support to the movement, animated as they were by the desire to join in defending the primacy of the moral law, the sole true guarantee of the welfare of peoples and the future of nations. This remarkable commencement of the Legion of Decency, and its many years of efficient activity, provide an evident proof that it is possible for our modern age even while respecting just individual liberty and legitimate private interests to obtain in public spectacles the observance of the natural law engraved by the hand of God in the heart of every man.[43]

As has been frequently repeated in these pages, the main role of public authority is to safeguard public order, and this notion includes public peace and public morality. We shall discuss that in the final chapter, but it is important that we frame decency (and its opposite, indecency) within public morality and as a necessary consequence of human dignity, one that especially affects women and children. This was the main goal of the battle for decency in Hollywood, and the fruits of the Legion of Decency's work have not been completely obscured: the code promoted by the Legion still serves as a reference. The standards of decency have been challenged repeatedly by people who argue that cultural and moral habits change and evolve and that they should not be regulated.[44] Moral relativism has damaged common understanding on this ground. However, recent scholarship advocating decency has focused on its legal value,[45] as well as the social costs of pornography and obscenity, highlighting the addiction and dependency that come with pornography and that frame it as a health issue.[46]

THE "NEW-SCHOOL" CENSORSHIP

In the environment of today's super-connected society, where the flow of messages and live interactions is millions of messages, photos, videos, and comments every minute, one might think that censorship is impossible. In this sense, it should be the "golden age of free expression." However, as Zeynep Tufekci puts it, this is how this golden age of free speech actually works:

> In the 21st century, the capacity to spread ideas and reach an audience is no longer limited by access to expensive, centralized broadcasting infrastructure. It's limited instead by one's ability to garner and distribute attention. And right now, the flow of the world's attention is structured, to a vast and overwhelming degree, by just a few digital platforms: Facebook, Google (which owns YouTube), and, to a lesser extent, Twitter.[47]

Thus, "censorship during the internet era does not operate under the same logic [as] it did under the heyday of print or even broadcast television."[48] As the historian Richard John puts it, free expression in the past presupposed "content creators that were spatially bounded, temporally limited, and accountable to the public. Content and not connectivity was king."[49] In the new digital environment, it is not so much expression that counts but attention. Rather than silencing an inconvenient speaker, the new methods of censorship aim to capture the attention of listeners, mainly with "troll armies" mobbing someone on social media or with "flooding tactics" of the mass distribution of disinformation.[50] These methods use the capacity of expression and information as a weapon not so much to debate ideas as to attack, "confuse, blackmail, demoralize, subvert, and para-lyze,"[51] in the words of Peter Pomerantsev.

We live in this reality: technology companies are designed to capture and keep our attention, which is why they offer a personalized presentation of information that is adjusted to our tastes, ideas, and interactions. This process of filtering the content we consume has resulted in a fragmentation of public discourse into filter bubbles. We then see that, in this context of superabundance of information, fragmentation, and attention deficit, the difficulty lies in being heard. It is not enough to be on the Internet; one must get on that short list designed by the companies that monopolize attention — to which users do pay attention.

This "new-school" censorship does not replace the previous model, but it adds new possibilities. The issue of previously censoring ideas, controlling the discussion, and penalizing the heterodox is an enduring strategy, even in the twenty-first century. In the networked public sphere, tools of speech control have been decentralized and the shadow of the government that is mimicked with the digital environment and with the technological possibilities that it offers has become more subtle. As Jack Balkin writes: "Governments can target for control or surveillance many different aspects of the digital infrastructure that people use to communicate: telecommunications and broadband companies, web-hosting services, domain name registrars, search engines, social media platforms, payment systems, and advertisers."[52]

One way of silencing inconvenient speakers is through the abusive online mobs known as "troll armies." Russia was one of the first countries to use the systematic method that it called web brigades. As Tim Wu explains, there were three hallmarks of the Russian method of action: the obscuring of the government's direct influence (recruitment, funding), the use of swarmlike attacks (over email, telephone, or social media), and an international scope.[53]

In the past few years, this mode of censorship has affected both public and private discourse. It has been used by groups on the left and the right, in political election campaigns, and for the causes of private lobbies. Dirty tactics have always existed, as have public operations to discredit a person or entity. The novelty here is in the speed, dimensions, and durability of the attacks.

This style is reminiscent of the one in *The Scarlet Letter* (1850), an American novel written by Nathaniel Hawthorne that tells the story of a woman in the puritan New England of the seventeenth century who, after committing adultery, is condemned to wear a scarlet letter "A" (which it is assumed stands for "Adulteress") on her chest and to stand on a scaffold to be seen and belittled by the entire village. She gives birth to a daughter but refuses to reveal the identity of her father.[54]

In his novel Hawthorne describes how public shaming was the weapon used in puritan cultures to punish those who failed to follow the rules of the community. The message to those who broke the laws was "We trample you down ... because you are a clog to our prosperity, and because the spectacle of your agony may discourage others of similar unlawful inclinations."[55] There is no space for reconciliation or for beginning a new life. The person is perpetually identified by her transgression.

To puritans, Church and state are two institutions that are intrinsically linked in nature and function.[56] On a practical level, puritan communities do not have clear boundaries between morality and law because specific laws and immunities are accorded to community members (e.g., tax exemptions, special subsidies, laws on liquors, and so on), along with norms of social behavior. Within puritan communities there is no space for dissent or toleration of other kinds of conduct.

There are two important elements of public shaming through trolling: on the one hand, we have norms that are enforced as rules of conduct by the zealotry of volunteer gatekeepers of morality. On the other hand, however, these social-moral norms prescribed by a group are subjective.

The Internet, like the seventeenth-century colonial puritan communities, "is quickly becoming a powerful norm-enforcement tool," according to Daniel Solove; it is a public platform for punishing people through digital shaming because, according to its civic secular rule, they are "bad" (rude, disrespectful, insolent) or, because of their ideas, they are "bigots," "dangerous," and so on. "The Internet can enable norm violators to be shamed in many instances. . . . Is this a good thing?," asks Solove.[57]

The Internet certainly fosters a proactive citizenship empowering the lone voices of everyday citizens to fight for their rights and voice their concerns (e.g., about bad custumer service). It also promotes transparency among institutions because "openness" is one of the key values of the Internet and the fear of a "shame storm" that could damage their reputations if they hide information is a driving force. A utilitarian ethicist could claim that the vices of digital shaming are greater than their virtues, but the question is not only quantitative; the perspective of the problem has broader consequences.

The use of "flooding tactics" is another contemporary method of manipulating speech;[58] it has also been called reverse censorship,[59] since it is intended to invalidate a message by flooding the digital ecosystem with disinformation. The false news distributed on the web has been dubbed "fake news," but we are dealing with an issue that is as old as humanity: the spread of falsehood through propaganda.

China is a paradigmatic example of a country whose government has bet on technology (such as video surveillance and facial recognition) to carry out its purposes of political control in the twenty-first century, and it has also engaged in information flooding by distributing disinformation or discrediting reliable sources of information. Gary King, Jennifer Pan, and Margaret Roberts write:

> The Chinese government fabricates and posts about 448 million social media comments a year.... [The] strategy is to avoid arguing with skeptics of the party and the government, and to not even discuss controversial issues.... The goal of this massive secretive operation is instead to distract the public and change the subject, as most of these posts involve cheerleading for China.[60]

Wu concludes that these methods are especially effective in an attention-scarce world because if "listeners have highly limited bandwidth to devote to any given issue, they will rarely dig deeply, and they are less likely to hear dissenting opinions."[61] But we are not dealing with a new phenomenon, because something similar has occurred—for a long time—in societies with high levels of illiteracy. In places where there are still large numbers of people who have trouble reading and writing, the people are left defenseless against the propaganda that bombards them. In many cases they lack the proper education to contrast what they see and hear. When they disagree with these things, they do not have the necessary preparation to discuss why they disagree at the same level as those who create these messages in the cultural and political sphere.

THIRTEEN

The Classical Tradition
of the Founding Fathers
of the United States

THE FOUNDING FATHERS AND THE PROTECTION OF FREEDOM

The term "Founding Fathers" is used to describe those leaders and states-
men during and after the American Revolution who designed and shaped
the political institutions of the United States. An expansive use of this
term to include only the signatories to the Declaration of Independence
(1776) and the members of the Constitutional Convention (who met in
Philadelphia in 1787) exceeds one hundred names. Further expanding this
definition to include every jurist, diplomat, military leader, member of the
Congress, and leading statesman of the various states, we assemble a vast
pantheon of patriots to whom the term "Founding Father" might apply.
It is not simple, therefore, to establish a unified sense of the beliefs of the
Founding Fathers. Even if one were to limit the list, as historian Richard
Morris did, to the seven key figures who had the greatest impact on the
nascent Republic,[1] one finds that disagreements ran deep and were plenti-
ful. Professor Thomas West distinguishes George Washington, Alexander

Hamilton, and John Adams as being on the "right," with James Madison, Thomas Jefferson, and Thomas Paine (not one of Morris's seven men) as being on the "left," while highlighting that despite their partisan views, they maintained a broad consensus regarding the basic principles on which to base the government and institutions of the country.[2]

The Declaration of Independence, framed by Jefferson and signed by the members of the Continental Congress during the American Revolution, is perhaps the best guide to the foundational principles on which the Founding Fathers did agree: "We hold these truths to be self-evident, that all men are created equal, that they are endowed by their Creator with certain unalienable Rights, that among these are Life, Liberty and the pursuit of Happiness. That to secure these rights, Governments are instituted among Men, deriving their just powers from the consent of the governed."[3]

These same basic rights, with similar formulae of inalienability and bestowal from the Creator, are restated and expanded in the declarations of rights that were adopted prior to the ratification of the Constitution by five states: Virginia (1776), Pennsylvania (1776), Vermont (1777), Massachusetts (1780), and New Hampshire (1784). The list is expanded to include the rights to life, to the exercise of freedom of speech and religion, to the acquisition and owning of property, and to the pursuit of happiness and security. In this conception of rights descending from the fundamental equality of men, Government is established as the guarantor of these rights that are received by nature.[4]

The Founding Fathers' concept of inherent rights, such as religious freedom or freedom of expression, is that of an absolute and inviolable freedom that comes with being a human person. Therefore, it is not something that is "granted," or "made available" by the state or by any other human being, because all people have been created equal. On the other hand, however, one must consider on a case-by-case basis whether the exercise of what Henry Kalven refers to as that "almost absolute freedom" involves an abuse of law or constitutes a damage to the common social good.

In this chapter dedicated to defining the Founding Fathers' project of protecting individual liberties as natural rights bestowed by the Creator of the universe, it is important to securely establish what constitutes the classical liberal tradition regarding freedom of expression. I am sympathetic to Kalven's understanding of legal tradition "as something more than a body of legal precedent."[5] The free speech liberal tradition in the United States is not an overall formula but a "living body, toughness, and inspiration" that emerges not only from common law but from an awareness of an "intellectual history."[6] Kalven used to tell his students: "In confusion and lack of overall formula . . . I see strength."[7] His notion of tradition relates to MacIntyre's living tradition: "an historically extended, socially embodied argument, and an argument precisely in part about the goods which constitute that tradition."[8] What is being described here is not a clear map of rules, but a living tradition hammered out through controversy.

THE LOCKEAN INTERPRETATION OF THE POLITICAL PHILOSOPHY OF THE FOUNDING FATHERS

The political philosophy that underlies the US Declaration of Independence, which was written mainly by Jefferson, is attributed to the influence of the English philosopher John Locke (1632–1704)[9] the so-called Father of Liberalism. This foundational text contains four mentions of God, a fact that some, starting in the nineteenth century, have considered problematic. Different contemporary authors who have studied Locke confirm that his political philosophy has a direct link with a natural theology that underpins the mentions of God in the Declaration of Independence and its conception of individual rights.[10] However, even though there is agreement on this undeniable substrate, there are different interpretations of how this natural theology forms the foundation of Locke's political theory. Some argue that he based his ideas on the God of Scripture, while others disconnect his theory of right from natural theology.[11]

It is from these different interpretations of the Declaration of Independence and of Locke's political philosophy that one of the main difficulties for many modern authors emerges: how should the relationship between politics and morality be understood?[12] In other words, what is the influence of natural theology and metaphysics in politics? That is to say, it is difficult to figure out how one should understand the influence of these disciplines on the intellectual development of the philosophers of the time and what foundational role that development played in the political institutions that were founded with the modern state. Readers can detect the strong desire of modern authors to erase any prior influence or tradition.

We have to remember that at the end of the seventeenth century the American colonies were mainly Protestant and Anglican and the Catholic presence was smaller.[13] As early as the eighteenth century, after the American Revolution, the new colonies formed by Anglicans, Calvinists, Presbyterians, Quakers, Catholics, Lutherans, Anabaptists, and other Christian denominations learned to live together in relative peace, creating a unique and novel regime in which religious freedom prevailed and in which there was a strong shared concept of natural law.[14]

The legacy that underlies the Founding Fathers' approach reflects the heritage of many centuries of human history. It is rooted in Greek philosophy, Roman law, and the Jewish and Christian religious traditions. This shared ethos assumes that there is an inherent order in creation and in creatures, and it does not hesitate to cite God as the architect, without mixing the political and religious order. As Charles Chaput says, the state does not have a specific religious view,[15] but it recognizes a person's right to profess the religion of his or her choice without any interference.[16] This equanimity was not possible in Europe because the continent was immersed in so-called religious wars in which civil and religious interests were completely combined. The eighteenth-century Enlightenment Europe of Voltaire and Rousseau expressed that violence to a certain extent.

In contrast, one can find certain universal and natural values in the new American political project. These values are something known and rationally accepted without the need for either theology or law. The American Declaration of Independence recognizes certain rights that are innate to the human being: the rights to property, life, truth, and so on. This declaration intended to protect such values from any violation. Opposed to these human values, stealing, killing, abusing the weak, and lying are inhuman crimes instinctively recognized by all human beings, whatever religion they profess.

Along with the Declaration of Independence (1776), a federal Constitution (1787) was written, as well as some amendments (1791) that protected and ensured the rights manifested in the declaration: "To secure these rights, governments are instituted among men."[17]

The federal Constitution did not originally include a bill of rights, but such rights were present in the states' declarations and, after its presentation by Madison, the First Amendment was understood as the first of the ten amendments that would constitute a Bill of Rights.[18] They are formulated as natural rights that are to be safeguarded from abuse by the power of the state and are limited by the rights of others.[19] Madison expressed this idea with a well-known image in essay no. 51 of the *Federalist Papers*:

> If men were angels, no government would be necessary. If angels were to govern men, neither external nor internal controls on government would be necessary. In framing a government which is to be administered by men over men, the great difficulty lies in this: you must first enable the government to control the governed; and in the next place oblige it to control itself.[20]

West adds a very interesting consideration by highlighting that the government is not the enemy; it is indispensable for guaranteeing and securing these rights that belong to individuals by nature.[21] This is a simple idea that is often forgotten in debates about rights between liberals and libertarians. It is important to remember that the government is not in itself evil because it tends to interfere. What West is emphasizing is that it must be effectively good and effective in the preservation of the rights that correspond, by nature, to individuals. This consideration expresses an idea that will be repeated throughout these pages — that rights are not a concession of the state but belong to every woman and man by virtue of their humanity. The mission of the public authority is to ensure that they are respected at the individual and social levels.

In the rights and freedoms that the Founding Fathers recognized (and especially in the principle of freedom of expression and thought) there are some "inherent values," as Eugene Volokh shows — "the search and attainment of truth, scientific progress, cultural development, the increase of virtue among the people"[22] — which also help to place them within the broad framework of human dignity.

As Jeffrey Langan explains, the period from the late nineteenth century into the twentieth saw the desire to restructure American liberalism in Hegelian, pragmatic, utilitarian, and Kantian terms. This restructuring was obliged by a premise that demanded that any reference to metaphysics, natural theology, or any philosophy that sustained a final causality be separated from public discourse.[23] The conclusion is clear: metaphysics and natural theology are confused with religious belief. When implicit or explicit references to God are presented in dealing with questions of political philosophy, they are treated as an intrusion. Thus, what we would refer to as this secularist redefinition does not fit with the real conceptions that Locke and the Founding Fathers were working with.

ALTERNATIVE INTERPRETATIONS OF
THE FOUNDING FATHERS' POLITICAL PHILOSOPHY

The basis of rights as an inalienable gift of the Creator became, as noted above, a problematic concept in the nineteenth century, with efforts to define rights within a utilitarian paradigm. In this paradigm, the self-evidence of rights as gifts proceeding from the Creator as a feature of our common humanity became difficult; it became necessary to define each right as an independent principle rather than a principle that is itself merely an instance of a higher principle. The attempt to reframe the Founding Fathers' project and political philosophy along these lines has led to an increasing effort to find justifications for individual freedoms.

Frederick Schauer distinguishes between these two types of principles as a foundation for this discussion: first, those principles of political philosophy that do not depend on the truth of another principle but stand on their own reasoning, which he calls "independent" principles,[24] and second, those that depend upon a broad independent principle. Schauer does not name this second kind but instead describes them as principles that "can be carried into acceptance as a component of a broader principle."[25] We can safely call these "dependent" or "contingent" principles. Schauer's analogy is the relationship between a general principle that holds that all killing of animals is morally wrong and a specific principle that it is wrong to hunt rabbits. If it is morally wrong to kill all animals, then it is morally wrong to kill a rabbit, but if it is not morally wrong to kill all animals, then killing the rabbit is unobjectionable. Should the prior principle fall, so, too, would the moral prohibition of hunting hares. However, if one can find independent reasons to oppose hunting rabbits (an argument, for example, about the evils of hunting for sport), then that principle becomes independent; one need not accept the premise that killing any animal is evil in order to accept the specific principle against rabbit hunting: even if the former principle falls, the latter survives. Schauer justifies classifying the principle of free speech as independent based on our collective approach to it; we treat it as independent, thus meriting an inquiry into the foundations of a possible independent free speech principle. Moreover, he argues that the foundations of freedom of speech (the quest for truth, the democracy principle, individuality, and so on) allow it to stand on its own.

Schauer treats several proposed foundations upon which one might independently defend the principle of free speech. Of particular interest are the principle of truth and the principle of democracy. I will briefly assess Schauer's arguments to demonstrate that each argument (and his final conclusion) depends on the basic assumption of a government constituted to protect the foundational rights of individuals that accrue to them solely because of their sovereignty as equal human beings (which comes as a gift from God, their Creator).

Schauer describes the first principle, the "argument from truth," as the "predominant and most preserving" of all the arguments to support free speech posited through the ages.[26] The argument from truth is (at its core) a simple one: seeking truth is a good, and the surest means of allowing man to seek the truth is to allow him to freely express his ideas, contributing to the "marketplace of ideas" in which good and bad ideas compete. Schauer rightly declines to dispute the fundamental premise that seeking truth is good or that the truth is, as a general principle, qualitatively better than a falsehood, commenting that whatever philosophical tradition one comes from, "Truth" has more or less universal acceptance as a good. Schauer concludes that the argument from truth provides only limited justification for the free speech principle; it is better to allow the freedom to question received wisdom not because the marketplace of ideas is necessarily effective but because giving the state the power to determine truth and falsehood has proven to be ineffective and unwise. In fact, Schauer's conclusion that "it is a wise caution to heed when we must decide how much authority we will give to those in power to determine what is right and suppress what is wrong" depends on the premise that seeking truth (a subset of the rights to liberty and the pursuit of happiness) is a good and that the government ought not to interfere with that good.[27] It depends implicitly on the argument that the fundamental purpose of government is to secure those basic rights.

Schauer makes explicit the dependence of the argument from truth on prior principles when he links it to a second "conditional" argument, the argument from democracy. This argument he refers to as conditional because it depends on the a priori acceptance of democratic government, which is to say it depends on the acceptance of the sovereignty of individuals with individual rights who delegate power to the government of their choice in order to secure those rights. Schauer moves the definition of democracy from strict majoritarianism into the liberal mainstream (and indeed the beliefs of the American Founding Fathers) that democracy requires an equal right of participation by all members of the sovereign people in the body politic. In this conception it is the pre-existing value of equality that is presupposed (not too far removed from "we hold these truths to be self-evident, that all men are created equal") in order to assert the requirement of access to information and the ability to express ideas freely.

While Schauer makes several other arguments, by his own admission none of his arguments alone is sufficient to establish the free speech principle as independent. Rather, he says that taking them as a whole, along with the over-riding assumption of governmental incompetence to decide what is true and what is false, one has sufficient reason to treat free speech as an independent principle. His strongest formulation for the independence of the free speech principle from the general principle of liberty is that the principle of free speech seems to break certain norms of the principle of liberty. The general principle of liberty, says Schauer, gives individuals freedom as long as they do not harm others; however, freedom of speech in the American context protects even some forms of harmful speech. This seeming rule violation touches on the discussion about distinguishing freedom from license that appears in the next section, and it is more closely related to arguments over the content of the right to free speech than to its nature. Insofar as this question touches the nature of free speech, the Founding Fathers were divided on the issue; the *Federalist* faction clearly supported limits on the freedom of speech for national security and the preservation of trust in the government (which resulted in the Alien and Sedition Acts of 1798), whereas the Jefferson-Madison faction took the view that these were too much of an intrusion into the right to free speech.

Contrary to Schauer's arguments that the principle of free speech is of the "independent" variety (and indeed was viewed as such by the Founding Fathers), it is my suggestion that each of these arguments depends on the pre-existing general categories of liberty and the pursuit of happiness, which the Founding Fathers believed to be inalienable. As I showed earlier in this book, there was an internal link (or interdependency) between freedom and truth that modernity disregarded. Moreover, I would add that a third category of principle exists outside of the dual structure suggested by Schauer, which we might call "interdependent" or "symbiotic" principles; their truth is dependent on the higher-order principles, yet the higher-order principles depend upon them to be realized. We create the fiction of an independent principle of free speech because we can find other arguments for its importance aside from the general principle, yet those arguments are themselves based on the premises established by the higher inalienable principles of liberty and the pursuit of happiness. The reason we speak so often of freedom of speech as if it were a freestanding right is precisely because of its symbiotic relationship to the foundational principles. Free speech is one of the means by which human beings can express themselves, guard their freedoms, and seek the truth, which is a road to happiness.

Using the Declaration as a lodestar, we can divide the rights enshrined in the US political and constitutional order into two categories. The first are the foundational rights, or the purpose for which the revolutionaries established the republic, namely "Life, Liberty, and the Pursuit of Happiness." These rights are inalienable and come from the Creator on account of our common humanity. They form the foundation for the second tier of rights, which are how the foundational rights are expressed and realized and the means by which they are protected. These rights exist in dynamic relation with the foundational rights because, in the absence of the second tier, the foundational rights would be unprotected and unarticulated. The right to freedom of speech is one such right, part of a body of rights that (like flesh covering bones) covers and expresses the God-given rights to life, liberty, and the pursuit of happiness, which form the foundation of the Founding Fathers' political philosophy.

THE DISTINCTION BETWEEN FREEDOM AND LICENSE

Before entering directly into the First Amendment's formulation of the freedom of speech and the press, it is relevant to keep in mind that, as Michael Zuckert argues, the elements that gave rise to the American project were the following: old English Whig constitutionalism, republicanism, the philosophy of natural rights, and the political religion.[28]

The First Amendment contains the same ideals as those expressed in the revolutionary declarations of individual rights in the different states: "Congress shall make no law respecting an establishment of religion, or prohibiting the free exercise thereof; or abridging the freedom of speech, or of the press; or the right of the people peaceably to assemble, and to petition the government for a redress of grievances."[29] With this statement the Founding Fathers expressed a general consensus regarding the formulation of freedom of expression and the press as inalienable and essential rights to be exercised against the possible abuse of power by the government. However, what this formula did not resolve was the tension that existed at that time between "libertarians," who desired a strong government that protected the freedoms of license and especially of property, and "conservatives," who supported individual liberties but were concerned with the seditious defamation of the government.[30]

Thus, even though there was a broad consensus on the main individual rights—personal liberty, safety, and property—and on the formulation of the First Amendment, behind this agreement lay deep divergences of opinions about the scope of this freedom of expression. Freedom of expression was a general principle that both sides upheld, but when this principle was to be applied in specific cases, various approaches inevitably emerged because of different approaches.[31] We could say that these past divergences are still repeating themselves today. There is widespread agreement on the general spirit of defending freedom of thought, belief, and expression as natural and inviolable rights of every person. However, there is a variety of interpretations in specific cases, especially when such rights are limited by the rights of others, even by what some recognize as rights of the community.[32]

With the Sedition Act, James Madison emerged as one of the main defenders of an absolute freedom of expression against the political class,[33] unlike those (such as Blackstone) who limited speech against the political institutions at a delicate political moment. In 1798, the nascent North American nation ran the risk of entering into war with France. In this context, the restriction of false, scandalous, or malicious publications against the government, Congress, or the president (qualifying them as seditious) was proposed as a means of internal political unity, but it had a provisional character (it expired in March of 1801).

This controversy resulted in two sects. On one side, the Federalists advocated on behalf of protecting institutions from falsehoods and defamations that had a negative impact on the nation, authorizing the limitation of certain rights to criticize. This view was theorized by William Blackstone (1723–1780), who argued that freedom of expression prevented prior censorship but not subsequent prosecution when it was of a criminal nature.[34] This position had a strong English character and is reminiscent of the debate in the English Parliament about the earlier censorship and Milton's reply in *Areopagitica*. On the other side, James Madison and other members of the Democratic Party argued that, despite the risks, total freedom of expression and communication was the only way to keep the government under control. For Madison, the greatest threat to political freedom was the "faction."[35] In no. 10 of the *Federalist Papers* he explains what he means by faction: a group of citizens—whether a majority or a minority—motivated against other citizens by passion or by a particular concern.[36]

Madison was ultimately concerned with the threat posed by the pressure exercised by those groups (which we call lobbies or lobbyists today) who are interested in imposing their agendas and interests. Presented with this threat, which is common to every system of government, Madison distinguishes two methods for "curing the mischiefs of faction": removing the causes of the faction or controlling its effects. The first method, Madison says, "is worse than the disease" because it destroys freedom.[37] Therefore, efforts should be focused on controlling the effects of the threat of faction, ensuring private rights and the public good.[38] The remedies that Madison sees are the freedom of expression; the principle of legality, which is a predominant power in a republic;[39] and the separation of powers as a system of mutual control that requires prudence.[40]

It is interesting to observe how, on one hand, Madison identifies the greatest threat to a republic in the endeavor to impose certain factional interests. In turn, he views the best remedy as risking freedom. In this sense, Madison supports the equal protection of those who speak and those who listen, without establishing a system of privilege for the means of communication.[41] On the other hand, we must remember that the English author Blackstone's conservative perspective was equally influential in the American tradition of free expression. As Steven Heyman writes, "According to that view, the state could regulate speech not only to protect the rights of others, but also to promote the common good."[42] For Blackstone the purpose of government is not just the protection of natural rights. Since human nature is corrupted,[43] the government must civilize human beings with laws made by the community in view of the common good.[44] Thus, the original tradition of freedom of expression includes the nuances provided by both authors. We shall resume this debate when dealing with the contemporary revisionisms of liberals, communitarians, and so on.

The underlying issue that the Founding Fathers raised about the limitations on freedom of expression was the discernment of whether the exercise of the law turns into an abuse of the law or into a danger to society—that is, when freedom under the protection of these natural rights becomes a license (a violation of the law of nature). The question is where this boundary of free expression is and when speech and expression become detrimental to the personal rights of third parties or to social peace.

Heyman quotes a text from the Massachusetts Bill of Rights, which clearly expresses that "the liberty of the press ought not to be restrained in this Commonwealth" but at the same time declares that "each individual in the society has a right to be protected by it [the Commonwealth]," and consequently, every subject "ought to find a certain remedy, by having recourse to the laws, for all injuries or wrongs which he may receive in his person, property, or character."[45] The concept of individual natural rights is present in this and other formulations. This is a right owed to an individual by others and by the community. On the other hand, it is not a solely physical right (life and property) but one that also affects an individual's inner dignity as a person. Thus, the role of the law does not restrict a priori but instead defends the rights and obligations of third parties and the community after the fact.

In several studies related to the Founding Fathers, Thomas G. West argues that the Founders' original meaning has been turned upside down, especially as regards the freedom of expression. He concludes that the Founders protected the freedom but not the license, while modern liberals protect the license but not the freedom.[46] West describes the positions of both. From the modern perspective, the Founding Fathers restricted what should be free: their restrictions on defamation seem inadequate, while their barriers to obscenity and pornography seem irrational and puritanical. On the other hand, in the Founders' time it was licit to impose religious convictions on workers; moreover, intimidation and racial and sexual harassment were allowed. As a result of the deregulation of finance in politics, the domination of the rich and powerful in political life was also permitted.[47]

West, changing perspective and putting himself in the Founding Fathers' shoes, reproaches the modern liberals, who currently enjoy less freedom of expression than did people at the birth of the Republic since they restrict speech where it should be free because they impose restrictions and control the presence of the media and they interfere in politics by imposing regulations when they think that too much money is invested in campaigns.[48] Finally, West argues that the original view of the Founding Fathers prevailed until the beginning of the twentieth century. From then on, he thinks, the liberal political theory of freedom of expression has been growing in importance and becoming increasingly prevalent, especially since 1965, in government and Supreme Court decisions.[49] We shall discuss this transformation of jurisprudence and the doctrine on freedom of expression in the following chapter.

NATURAL RIGHTS AND LEGAL RIGHTS

As I mentioned earlier, the beginning of the Declaration of Independence establishes that the government's raison d'être is to ensure natural rights: "We hold these truths to be self-evident, that all men are created equal, that they are endowed by their Creator with certain unalienable Rights, that among these are Life, Liberty and the pursuit of Happiness. That to secure these rights, Governments are instituted among Men."[50]

The threat to these nature-given rights comes mainly from the government and our fellow human beings, and thus the government must establish civil and criminal laws. As Locke points out: "A well-constructed government provides clear laws (defining injuries and the appropriate punishments), impartial judgment (through jury trials), and reliable punishment (by fines, imprisonment, or execution)."[51] There is much talk about the threat posed by the government, to such an extent that protection is reduced to that area, when many free speech violations come from other people. In this sense, West argues that injurious discourse was not originally protected, and in making this claim he relies on the testimony of the two Founders who, according to him, devoted the most attention to freedom of expression: James Madison and James Wilson.[52]

In his *Lectures on Law* (1790–1791) Wilson worked out the general principle that the government must allow any activity that is not injurious or harmful, be it in word or in deed.[53] This nonprotection of injurious speech proves itself consistent because the freedom of expression exists not only for political speech but also for the search for truth, as well as science, morality, and so on. That is to say, nuance that is not harmful is compatible with a view of freedom of expression that should protect those who speak and those who listen.

On the other hand, in Madison's speech for the presentation of the First Amendment to the House of Representatives (on June 8, 1789) he makes a distinction between the declared "natural rights" and those "rights created by the Government," such as the right to a trial by jury.[54] Similar to Wilson and Madison but with different nuances, Thomas Paine also distinguished between natural and inalienable rights and the civil rights created by the government.[55]

From all that has been said so far about the Founding Fathers and their conception of freedom, one can conclude that they were of a mind that there is "an absolute right to freedom of speech" in the sense that there is what West calls a "right to liberty in general"[56] that is natural and inalienable and thus originally absolute. A truly interesting element is that this approach connects with the classical Roman conception of right (*ius*) and justice, in which it is just to give to each individual the right that corresponds to him or her in such a way that attacks on freedom of expression are acts of injustice, as we shall see in Part IV. The absolute human freedom that underpins the approaches of the Founding Fathers is a personal freedom (not mere freedom of choice), and it is coherently linked with the other rights that they hold sacred: security (life) and property. As a matter of fact, in no. 10 of the *Federalist Papers*, Madison equates the protection of opinions to the protection of property, treating freedom of expression as a "property right": "A man has a property in his opinions and the free communication of them."[57] This comparison helps clarify the idea outlined above, that justice involves a right owed and, consequently, in the case of a breach, there is a need for restitution.

For the Founding Fathers freedom of expression simply formed part of the whole of the natural right to freedom that the government must guarantee. The Founders recognized the social benefit of freedom of expression for the progress of truth, science, morality, and the arts in general, but they did not understand it as a mere right of self-expression. These interpretations, argues West, belonged to twentieth-century authors.[58]

FOURTEEN

The Contemporary Redefinition
of the Free Speech Tradition
in the United States

NEW EMPHASIS OF FREEDOM OF EXPRESSION:
FROM DEFENDING INDIVIDUAL RIGHTS TO SOCIAL INTEREST

The tradition of freedom of expression, understood as an individual right inherent in the human condition and limited by the rights of other individuals and the community, gave way to a more positivist and utilitarian conception of the law. According to this perspective and after the bloody experience of the world wars, some authors thought that the mission of the law is not so much to protect fundamental rights as to promote social well-being in the terms in which the state has defined them.[1]

Among the works that bear witness to this transformation, we can distinguish the jurisprudence of various Supreme Court justices, among whom I will highlight Oliver Wendell Holmes, as well as the influence of the writings of several professors from Harvard Law School, like Zachariah Chafee and Roscoe Pound. The study of these authors here is not intended to be exhaustive. The perspective of my analysis will be predominantly philosophical-juridical.

Steven Heyman reviews many cases of the judge Oliver Wendell Holmes Jr. and shows that in his writings he rejected the Lockean and Kantian notions of the inherent rights of the individual and the essential value of the person. Moreover, Heyman states that Holmes argued that the constitutional interpretation of rights should be divorced from any notion of human rights having a moral sense.[2] According to this reasoning, rights receive their force from positive law (not from nature), and it is the law that provides for their social purpose; there is no purpose in nature. Pound argues that there are many conflicts of interest in social coexistence that are resolved with social principles and considerations established by the state. The classic concept of common good is replaced with that of public interest. For Chafee, the purpose of freedom of expression is to serve the "social interest."

As one can intuit, the fracture with the earlier paradigm has been tremendous since it affects many of the classic foundations of freedom of expression theorized by the Founding Fathers.

JUSTICE OLIVER WENDELL HOLMES

The judge Oliver Wendell Holmes Jr. (1841–1935) came from a Calvinist family tradition, although he seemed to be personally agnostic. He studied in a private school, and when the American Civil War began he enlisted as a soldier and underwent the experience of war for three years. He then studied law at Harvard, and shortly after he began practicing as a lawyer he was called to work as a judge in the state of Massachusetts. A few years later he was nominated by Theodore Roosevelt as a Supreme Court justice, as which he worked for thirty years.[3]

Holmes is one of the recognized interpreters of the First Amendment in the United States, and he stands out for having set the criterion of "clear and present danger" as a boundary of and limitation on freedom of expression in the *Abrams v. United States* decision of 1919. This author's theses are displayed in his jurisprudence and not in research works.

Holmes saw the public sphere as a "battlefield" on which fighting must be allowed to the extreme: "Even if it is futile, war may be necessary. Wasted blood is still glorious,"[4] he wrote. And he advocated stoic and militaristic virtues of self-discipline. The stoic virtues of neutrality and tolerance must lead to the defense of the other's right to express ideas that one may abhor ("defending the thought we hate"), to the extent of creating a public arena in which all arguments have a place because "the Constitution is a fighting faith."[5] He admits only the exception of incitement to physical violence. That is why John Peters considers Holmes one of the main civil libertarians.[6]

In his vote on another paradigmatic decision (*Schenck v. United States*), Holmes used an image that all the scholars of that subject matter keep repeating:

> The most stringent protection of free speech would not protect a man in falsely shouting fire in a theatre and causing a panic. . . . The question in every case is whether the words are used in such circumstances and are of such a nature as to create a clear and present danger that they will bring about the substantive evils that Congress has a right to prevent.[7]

It was by then recognized that the pronouncement of certain words can sometimes have the same effect as physical force. This argument has already been discussed in Part II of this book as one of the problems posed by freedom of expression. It is interesting to note that this 1919 decision was offered in a historical context (the period 1919–1927) in which political criticism of the government and of involvement in the world war were common, and this dissent was penalized by judges. According to David Strauss, both Holmes and Justice Louis Brandeis understood that justices were yielding too easily to the suppression of critical speech.[8]

In order to sustain such an extreme notion of freedom of expression, to the point of "defending your enemy" (with the exception of incitement to violence), Holmes introduced a concept that would have broad appeal in the legal world: that the judge must have two minds, or two bodies, completely separating the private sphere from the public sphere. This rendered the judge's feelings or personal opinions irrelevant. The truly important thing is that the principles that the Constitution dictates be applied. As we shall see when talking about Chafee, his influence on Holmes seems decisive and was made explicit in *Chaplinsky v. New Hampshire* (1942), where Holmes adopted Chafee's doctrine of the "social interest" of freedom of expression.

In this sense, the limit on transgressor discourse established by Holmes, that of a "clear and present danger," now had the connotation of causing a "substantive evil."[9] For the purpose of controlling or limiting free expression Holmes suggested analyzing the types of words spoken and the circumstances in which they are said in order to determine whether they create a serious and present danger. He also points out that "it is a question of proximity and degree."[10] However, the proximity of the danger is not easy to determine. As a matter of fact, Holmes did not determine exactly what constitutes a clear and present danger and where the lines should be drawn.[11]

Kent Greenawalt conducts a detailed analysis of the meaning of the phrase "clear and present danger" in the *Schenck* decision, comparing it with other decisions by the same justice, and he concludes that for Holmes the harm must be immanent and grave and the actor must have premeditated it, in the sense of having intentionality.[12] Strauss thinks that the interpretation of clear and present danger was complete with the dissent of Holmes and Brandeis from the *Abrams* decision,[13] in which they remarked that not only must the threat cause damage but it must be very likely, immanent, and serious. In turn, they added a caveat that has also become memorable: "We should be eternally vigilant against attempts to check the expression of opinions that we loathe . . . unless they so imminently threaten imminent interference with the lawful and pressing purposes of the law that an immediate check is required to save the country."[14] However, as Strauss recalls: "Holmes and Brandeis opinions represent an early recognition of what *New York Times v. Sullivan* later called 'the central meaning of the First Amendment,' and their opinions provided the raw material from which later justices fashioned First Amendment doctrine protecting political dissent."[15]

As we can see, we are looking at a defense of freedom of expression (political in this case) and the establishment of a limitation on speech that does not aim to restrict or censor the contents but that addresses the circumstances and intensity of the damage caused. However, it is a defense that has ceased to emphasize the individual right in itself, moving the center of gravity to the circumstances, in the context of the social interest. The fear of an excessive public intolerance requires a "buffer zone" for extremist speech, Lee Bollinger says: "This speech is protected not for its intrinsic value but because that protection better insulates what is intrinsically valuable."[16] Judging case by case, justices must protect a framework of common values in which all of society can recognize itself.

Although this debate is closely linked to the specifics of the American legal experience, it offers some general points for our fundamental study. On one hand, this "buffer zone" is never neutral because it is inseparable from the ideological views of the world and of human beings. On the other hand, even though at first glance it seems that it would allow us to attain a moral minimum, this framework of values will always exist within a utilitarian logic of calculating conflicting goods and not so much one of determining the true good of the human being.

The Skokie case is an emblematic example of the limits of free expression. In 1977 a Neo-Nazi organization decided to organize a march wearing Nazi uniforms and insignias in Skokie, a neighborhood outside Chicago where many Holocaust survivors lived. The Village Council prohibited the demonstration, but the case was reported to the ACLU (American Civil Liberties Union), which considered the ban a violation of freedom of expression as defended by the First Amendment. The Court of Appeals dismissed the decision of the Skokie Village Council, but the demonstration was moved to a park inside Chicago.[17] This case is cited as an example and as a symbol of extreme tolerance of harmful discourse, of which the liberal tradition advocates not censorship but defeat with more speech or with counter-speech—but never with prohibition. It is interesting to note that in the Skokie case the courts considered the need to prohibit that public demonstration of racist offense but decided that there was no clear and present danger of social harm.

Beyond the particulars of the case that we have dealt with before, it is interesting to relate it to the fact that in the same year there was another case in the United States that was even more controversial and consequential from a social standpoint: that of the civil rights marches of black people in the South. Authors such as Bollinger thought that if the offensive discourse of Skokie was prohibited it would mean that "Southern whites could ban civil rights marches by blacks."[18] Underpinning the argument of the judges who decided the Skokie case is the idea that it is necessary to tolerate offensive speech—as if it were a toll to be paid to safeguard the freedom of everyone and to live in a democracy.[19] Thus, with the judges' recognition of the abuse of freedom, if evil is not tolerated for a greater good, then the line between human good and evil will become blurred.

Bollinger considers Holmes's criterion of "clear and present danger" of social damage to be insufficient, and he distances himself from that proposal by betting on a line of thinking that is more jurisprudential than legal: judging on a case-by-case basis to improve the protection of freedom of expression. As we shall see later, Bollinger and Meiklejohn aim to show that the juridical-legal solution has a limited scope and that all the problems presented by transgressive speech cannot be resolved only with rules.

In short, with Holmes, the freedom of expression ceased to be understood as an individual right and became an interest that is weighed on the balance of social interests. In this way, the traditional meaning of freedom of expression as defined by the Founding Fathers is transformed. Heyman points in the same direction when he says: "Holmesian positivism and sociological jurisprudence had the effect of undermining the traditional American rationale for freedom of expression."[20] Next we shall look at the influence of certain authors from Harvard Law School.

THE LEGAL DOCTRINE OF HARVARD LAW SCHOOL

Professor Nathan Roscoe Pound (1870–1964) was an important jurist in the United States and was dean of Harvard Law School for twenty years. His doctrine is sociological in nature, emphasizing the importance of social interest as a way to shape society with the law as a tool.

Pound rejected the traditional doctrine on natural rights and instead argued that the state and the law have a social mission. That is to say, these institutions are called to preserve the social interests determined by the state. In this sense, a leadership role is attributed to the state as a legal entity (public interest) and to society as a community (social interest).[21] Although it may seem like a play on words, Pound thought the law should try to prioritize "social interests, since it is the social interest in securing the individual interest that must determine the law to secure it."[22]

He went on to defend the individual rights—to life, liberty, property, and so on—that are bound to the human condition and thus absolute, as well as "social interests" that the state determines: peace, coexistence, and so on. This was a change of perspective, but, as I will examine further in Part IV, it is not only a change in nuance.

Professor Zachariah Chafee (1885–1957) taught at Harvard Law School for forty years, and he was influenced by, among other things, Pound's sociological doctrine. Following the classical liberal thesis, Chafee distinguished public from private by differentiating two types of exercise of expression: those motivated by an individual interest and those motivated by a social interest. This author's main concern was to protect the social interest, and to this end, the decisive thing would be to determine in what circumstances the political discourse of social interest should be protected.[23]

Chafee's criticism of Holmes in the *Schenck v. United States* case (1919) is well known. In this case Holmes focused on denouncing the treatment of freedom of expression as a merely individual interest when the main objective of it is the social interest of discovering and spreading the truth in "subjects of general concern."[24] Chafee established two elements of social interest: "public safety" and the "search for truth," which form the boundary of freedom of expression.[25]

Chafee's doctrine had a decisive influence on Holmes, who explicitly incorporated his social doctrine in the decision on *Chaplinsky v. New Hampshire* when he wrote that the Constitution does not protect obscene words or insult. He further stated that such expressions (insults) do not form part of an exposition of ideas and that they lack social value since they do not constitute steps toward the truth and that all the social benefits of order and morality matter more than these expressions.[26]

According to Thomas Tedford, Chafee supported preserving the peace and penalizing defamation and obscenity under some circumstances.[27] Thus, worthwhile speech is set apart, in the interest of society, allowing forms of expression to be limited to those that benefit the community. On the other end is worthless speech, slanderous or obscene speech that contributes nothing constructive to the debate of ideas.[28]

The change in nuance is evident: it goes from a view based on individual liberties founded on human nature and the concept of republicanism to a view of freedom of expression as a democratic tool of self-governance in which the social interest is sought, balancing individual interests.[29] The difference between the two concerns the very nature of the freedom of expression. The classic model based on natural rights, says Heyman, is "objective," so that boundaries may then be worked out. While the modern standard of balance and finding an equilibrium of interests is more "subjective," it considers needs, desires, necessities, and more.[30] The two views also differ from the standpoint of their formal structure since the actors in the classical model are the speakers, individuals in general, and the state, while in the contemporary model there are two main groups: the social interests and the interests of the state. Individuals are absorbed into social interests.[31]

BRIDGING THE TWO TRADITIONS

There are two authors, Alexander Meiklejohn and Thomas I. Emerson, who try to reconcile the two above-cited models, protecting freedom of expression as an individual right but also serving the social interest.

Alexander Meiklejohn (1872–1964) agrees with Chafee's distinction of two types of freedom of expression based on value. In this case he distinguishes one as absolute and the other as subject to legal regulation. When speaking of the expression of ideas in democratic life, Meiklejohn uses the illustrative example of a town where there must be an open and strong debate with no limitation of ideas or fear of reprisals. However, the author points out that this does not mean listening to every single townsperson but rather ensuring that everything important is said.[32]

Thus, Meiklejohn explicitly argues that the Constitution establishes two different forms of freedom of expression.[33] On one hand, he considers expressions that are not made in the public forum to be private. He believes that they pertain to the "liberty of speech" that relates to the Fifth Amendment (such as life and property),[34] not to the First, which he thinks refers exclusively to discussion in the public sphere ("freedom of speech"), which he attributes to political life.[35] As Meiklejohn says:

> Individuals have, then, a private right of speech which may on occasion be denied or limited, though such limitations may not be imposed unnecessarily or unequally. So says the Fifth Amendment. But this limited guarantee of the freedom of a man's wish to speak is radically different in intent from the unlimited guarantee of the freedom of public discussion, which is given by the First Amendment.[36]

A question that spontaneously arises when one reads this argument is whether the Founding Fathers truly distinguished between these two freedoms of expression. If not, then it is a theoretical fiction. Considering that one of the foundations of classical liberalism is the division that Locke introduced between the public and the private and that philosophy has always distinguished between human freedom and political freedom, it seems plausible that this distinction could be implied in the Framers' approach when defining freedom of expression. Thus, correctly choosing which aspects fall into the public sphere and which belong only to the private sphere is much more difficult, since the range of realities is endless. However, attempting to justify this choice falls outside the scope of this work.

One of the most interesting aspects of Meiklejohn's thought is that his fundamental thesis goes beyond how to protect certain forms of extremist speech, bringing up the moral and intellectual foundations of a society that governs itself. This author aims to construct a vision of liberal tolerance as a tool for affirming certain values. While Holmes looked with skepticism on tolerance and value codes, Meiklejohn believes that there is a truth about things, and he distinguishes between ideas that are good and bad and those that are true and false. He criticizes irresponsible individualism and encourages the search for a collective good.[37]

On the other hand, Professor Thomas I. Emerson (1908–1991) thought that the American system of jurisprudence and the classic criteria of incitement and clear and present danger are vague and do not quite solve the problems posed by freedom of expression. Instead of proceeding case by case, the author argues for the need to provide a comprehensive theory of freedom of expression.[38] He establishes the distinction between behaviors that are "expressions" and those that constitute "actions." He believes that expressions must be encouraged and allowed with total freedom, while actions may be subject to some controls by the Constitution.[39]

Thus, for example, Emerson understands obscenity (in all media: books, films, paintings, theatrical productions, and so on) as an expression that can be prohibited as a behavior when it has a negative public dimension (for example, obscene contents intended to shock).[40] On the other hand, he considers defamation an expression when it is in the public sphere, but in the private context, when the feelings of an individual are offended, he considers it an action.[41] When offensive words are said in public, he understands insult as an expression that the audience has to tolerate, but when that insult is addressed to an individual in a direct encounter, with the intention to provoke, he considers it an inciting action, a true "verbal act," as the authors of critical race theory would more fully develop it and as we saw in Part II.

So the dilemma of the contemporary doctrine of and jurisprudence on freedom of expression will be found in this conflict between freedom of expression and the efforts of the state to promote social interests and values.[42] Thomas West reinforces this idea of a transformation of or break with the original idea when he says: "The founders did not hold a 'self-expression' or a 'democratic governance' theory of free speech. Such theories, which became fashionable in the twentieth century, leave unprotected many forms of non-injurious speech. For the founders, speech is simply a part of the overall natural right to liberty, which it is the main job of government to secure."[43]

The different views on freedom of expression held by liberals, libertarians, communitarians, constitutional originalists, and feminist and racial defense groups exist on the spectrum of these two great models, with various nuances.

THE REDEFINITION OF FREE SPEECH IN THE LATE TWENTIETH CENTURY

Having been made aware of this conflict in the academic background between free speech and the state's legitimate rights to protect societal interests, we will examine the Supreme Court's redefinition of the right to free speech into the latter half of the twentieth century, in which several landmark cases defined the precise limits of the government's power to censor, control, and penalize expression. Four lines of jurisprudence emerge from this era in distinct groups: cases seeking to define the "clear and present danger" criterion applied by Justice Holmes in *Schenck*; cases exploring the "defend your enemy" principle in the realms of offensive speech, obscenity, and expressive protest; cases involving defamation of and distress to public and private figures; and cases involving censorship or control over the press. Each of these will be discussed in turn, excluding a fifth line of cases, on campaign finance, which are not the subject of this work.

Holmes's dictum in *Abrams*, that speech that had the effect of a "clear and present danger" (with the archetypal example of shouting "fire" in a packed theater) would not be protected by even the most stringent protection of free speech, opened the door to new restrictions on free speech. In the decades following *Abrams*, successive Supreme Court cases attempted to define and apply the dictum of a clear and present danger. The results have been mixed; early applications of the rule were broad, allowing certain forms of speech (even of political speech, certainly not within the ambit of Holmes's doctrine) to be restricted by criminal penalties, whereas later cases have rolled back the broad permissions to restrict speech acts, especially in the realms of public and political speech.

The broadening of the clear and present danger doctrine can be seen in a series of cases from the 1950s brought under the anti-Communist "Smith Act." In *Dennis v. US* eleven leaders of the Communist Party had their convictions for conspiracy to overthrow the government upheld on the grounds that the First Amendment did not protect conspiracy to overthrow the government,[44] and the Court's decision expanded the doctrine of a clear and present danger elucidated in *Schenk* to permit prior restriction[45] (though those convicted had, in fact, not actually planned any definitive action to overthrow the government). It is of note that in *Dennis*, Justice Hugo Black dissented, arguing that the permission of prior censorship of this kind watered down the First Amendment to a mere "admonition" to Congress. He wrote: "The indictment is that they conspired to organize the Communist Party and to use speech or newspapers and other publications in the future to teach and advocate the forcible overthrow of the Government. No matter how it is worded, this is a virulent form of prior censorship of speech and press, which I believe the First Amendment forbids."[46]

The Supreme Court clarified its position in *Yates v. US*,[47] diluting the broad permission of prior restriction in *Dennis* to allow only those instances of actual advocacy to overthrow the government as a concrete action (and not merely those to overthrow the government as an abstract concept). As Kalven states: "The Court's idiom changed."[48]

In *Watts v. US* the Supreme Court reversed the conviction (for threatening the president) of a man who, at a protest against the draft, had said, "If they ever make me carry a rifle the first man I want to get in my sights is LBJ." In reversing the conviction, the Court limited the ambit of the restriction to "true threats," noting that political discourse often had the character of "vehement, caustic, and sometimes unpleasantly sharp attacks on government and public officials."[49] The broad permissions granted in the aftermath of *Dennis* finally came to a screeching halt in another 1969 case, *Brandenburg v. Ohio*.[50]

Unlike previous cases, which had involved Communism and antigovernment protest, *Brandenburg* was a race-relations case. Clarence Brandenburg, a KKK member, had given numerous speeches attacking Jews, African Americans, and the organs of the U.S. government, suggesting that some violence might be done to them. He was convicted under an Ohio law. The Supreme Court, in the per curiam opinion overturning the conviction, reformed the *Schenk* ruling on a "clear and present danger" (which it held as giving too broad a power to restrict the First Amendment), stating that "constitutional guarantees of free speech and free press do not permit a State to forbid or proscribe advocacy of the use of force or of law violation except where such advocacy is directed to inciting or producing imminent lawless action and is likely to incite or produce such action."[51] The *Brandenburg* case implicitly reversed *Dennis*, protecting even extreme political speech that does not amount to advocacy or incitement of an imminent crime.

The shift from 1919 to 1969 was remarkable and, as Kalven stresses, this turn reveals how important majority decisions and dissenting opinions are in the common law system. In this case, the dissenting opinions on subversive advocacy matured and became majority doctrine in *Brandenburg v. Ohio* (1969), which states that "radical speech cannot be cut off until it reaches 'incitement to imminent lawless action.'"[52]

The second line of development post-*Schenk* concerned the defense of objectionable speech, which was categorized above as a "defend your enemy" principle. This principle was developed along two lines: cases involving objectionable expression and protected classes of symbol or person and cases involving obscenity. As with the "clear and present danger" cases, two clear developments are evident here: first, an immediate broadening followed by a narrowing of the government's powers to restrict freedom of speech, and second, a reinforcement of a public-private divide that (in this case) provided stronger protections to private and political expression. In an early development, the Warren court formulated a "governmental interest" test, in *O'Brien v. US*, holding that a law prohibiting the symbolic burning of a draft card was constitutional.[53] The per curiam judgement, written by Justice Earl Warren, formulated the test thus: "A government regulation is sufficiently justified if it is within the constitutional power of the Government; if it furthers an important or substantial governmental interest; if the governmental interest is unrelated to the suppression of free expression; and if the incidental restriction on alleged First Amendment freedoms is not greater than is essential to the furtherance of that interest."[54]

The government interest in the case of draft card burning was considered sufficient to justify the restriction on free expression under this test. This can be contrasted with the Court's later rulings on burning the US flag. The per curiam judgment in *Texas v. Johnson* restates the strength of the First Amendment in protecting those forms of political speech (and, by extension, expression) that society at large finds to be distasteful: "If there is a bedrock principle underlying the First Amendment, it is that the government may not prohibit the expression of an idea simply because society finds the idea itself offensive or disagreeable."[55] Justice Anthony Kennedy, in his own concurring opinion, described the case as one of those rare occasions on which the justices might express personal distaste at the outcome, stating that burning the flag *was* offensive and yet must be protected:

> Though symbols often are what we ourselves make of them, the flag is constant in expressing beliefs Americans share, beliefs in law and peace and that freedom which sustains the human spirit. The case here today forces recognition of the costs to which those beliefs commit us. . . . Whether or not he [Gregory Lee Johnson, the draft card burner] could appreciate the enormity of the offense he gave, the fact remains that his acts were speech, in both the technical and the fundamental meaning of the Constitution. So I agree with the Court that he must go free.[56]

Though a minority in the court, including Chief Justice Rehnquist, sought to abrogate the right to free speech where the flag was concerned, the majority held that the State of Texas could not legitimately establish a protected category of symbol. The Court ruled consistently with *Johnson* in *US v. Eichman*, ruling the US Flag Protection Act unconstitutional.[57] Perhaps the more controversial development on this line of reasoning came in another race-relations case, *R.A.V. v. City of St. Paul*.[58] The City of St. Paul had prosecuted a teenager under a Bias-Motivated Crime Ordinance that made it a misdemeanor to use certain forms of expression (including images like burning crosses and swastikas) to arouse "anger, alarm or resentment in others on the basis of race, color, creed, religion or gender."[59] In finding the law to be unconstitutional, the Court's majority (in a decision written by Justice Antonin Scalia) found that the establishment of certain protected classes of people, against whom certain forms of speech were prohibited, was unconstitutional: "Selectivity of this sort creates the possibility that the city is seeking to handicap the expression of particular ideas. . . . St. Paul has no such authority to license one side of a debate to fight freestyle, while requiring the other to follow Marquess of Queensberry rules."[60] Not only are protected classes of symbol unconstitutional; so, too, are protected classes of people.

Though political speech and expression gained significant protections in the latter part of the twentieth century, there were some significant restrictions; obscenity and defamation of character were put firmly outside the remit of the First Amendment. Obscenity was widely agreed to be beyond the general protection of free speech,[61] although there is some disagreement about what exactly constitutes "obscenity."[62] But the Supreme Court formulated several tests that diluted this general rule, allowing the publication of sacrilegious material for the sake of artistic expression in *J. Burstyn v. Wilson*[63] and formulating tests to determine whether obscene materials might be permitted. In *Roth v. US* the Court ruled that obscene materials could be restricted only if they were "utterly without redeeming social importance."[64] This test was watered down in *Miller v. California*, restricting such materials only if they lacked "serious literary, artistic, political, or scientific value."[65] Moreover, since *Roth*, the standard for obscenity has been linked to the moving goal of "contemporary community standards"—enforcing only the standards of the day and not some preexisting absolute standard to decide what constitutes obscenity.

In *Beauharnais v. Illinois* the Supreme Court placed criminal libel outside of the constitutional protection of free speech granted by the First Amendment.[66] A significant challenge to this principle came in the 1964 defamation case *New York Times v. Sullivan*.[67] In *Sullivan* an Alabama public safety commissioner brought a libel charge against the *New York Times* for running advertisements to raise funds for imprisoned civil rights activists. A unanimous Supreme Court ruled against his claim, formulating a strong defense for press freedoms going forward: the "actual malice" test. Under the actual malice test a news-media outlet could be held accountable for false information it published about the government (including state governments) only if it could be shown to have had "knowledge of its falsity or with reckless disregard of whether it was true or false."[68] In *Curtis v. Butts* the Court applied the same test to publications about so-called public figures,[69] and in *Hustler Magazine v. Falwell* it exempted the press from "intentionally inflicted emotional damage" claims if the emotional distress was caused by a caricature, parody, or satire of the public figure and if a reasonable person would not have believed it to be true.[70] This raft of protections, though not applicable to libel involving private persons,[71] has created an exceptionally high bar for the restriction of falsehoods published by the press and has made prosecution of or suits against such defamation difficult. As Justice William Brennan put it, "The protection of such speech follows from a profound national commitment to the principle that debate on public issues should be uninhibited, robust, and wide-open."[72] The Court spoke of "the central meaning of the First Amendment,"[73] a fundamental protection of speech "without which democracy cannot function."[74]

Perhaps the strongest guarantees of free speech under the First Amendment were conceded in cases involving censorship of or control over the media. In the late twentieth century, broad freedoms were granted to the press, and the government's ability to interfere with those freedoms was severely limited. We have already examined the higher burden of proof of defamation imposed in *New York Times v. Sullivan* and the special protection against claims of intentionally inflicted emotional distress provided in *Hustler Magazine v. Falwell* as emblematic of the courts' jealous protection of press freedoms. Now we shall turn to cases explicitly involving freedom of the press in its dealings with government.

The landmark development in this area came about as a result of a government leak to the *New York Times* and the *Washington Post* concerning the "Pentagon Papers" (which detailed the background to the US government's entry into and prosecution of the Vietnam war). On the grounds of protecting national security, the executive branch sought to use a system called "prior restraint" that prevented the two outlets from publishing at all. The case would eventually arrive at the Supreme Court as *New York Times v. US* (1971). In the *per curiam* decision, the Court restated an earlier precedent[75] that "any system of prior restraints of expression comes to this court bearing a heavy presumption against its constitutional validity"[76] and restated another precedent regarding the "heavy burden" on the government to justify such a restriction.[77] Finding that the government had not met that burden, Justice Black sharply criticized both the government and his fellow justices who concurred with it and restated the purpose of press freedom in the First Amendment:

In the First Amendment the Founding Fathers gave the free press the protection it must have to fulfil its essential role in our democracy. The press was to serve the governed, not the governors. The Government's power to censor the press was abolished so that the press would remain forever free to censure the Government. The press was protected so that it could bare the secrets of government and inform the people. Only a free and unrestrained press can effectively expose deception in government.[78]

Following this case, two notable exceptions emerged. The first was given in *Branzburg v. Hayes* (1972), which required reporters to testify before grand juries in criminal cases,[79] and the second in *Turner Broadcasting System v. FCC* (1994), which permitted the government to require TV networks to allocate a minimum amount of airtime to local TV stations as an exercise of their legitimate interest in ensuring a multiplicity of broadcasters, balanced against the editorial control exercised by network TV.[80] In all of these cases we can see a familiar line developing, that of a stronger protection for political speech and speech that touches on the public sphere.

The jurisprudence of the latter twentieth century followed a general pattern, common to almost all the families of cases brought for review under the First Amendment: the rules established in the early part of the twentieth century to allow the restriction of free speech were given a broad application in the 1950s before being gradually rolled back or narrowed from the 1960s to the 1990s. The exceptions to this pattern have been in the spheres of freedom of the press and political speech, whose restriction is presumed unconstitutional unless a high bar for restrictions is met.

As Kalven highlights: "The central problem of free speech is to determine when, *if ever*, the content of communications may be interdicted by law. American law has attained a very considerable consensus on what we have called untouchable content. And over time it has worked through various categories of censorable content with pretty fair success."[81] However, the threats to freedom of expression that we are analyzing in this work come from not only an "unwarranted censorship" but also, in Kalven's words, "the danger that a doctrinaire orthodoxy will harden around the norm."[82]

As Kalven told his students, the challenge of the liberal tradition of free speech is to maintain the necessary "sympathy for the grievance against speech" and to "honor the countervalues" at the same time.[83] There is no legal formula to encapsulate the wisdom of this principle that protects freedom so vigorously rather than a strong moral tradition that holds all together, as we have been repeating throughout these pages. The liberal call to protect even the most noxious speech must not be upheld in an arrogant way, as if harm were not real and objective. I think Kalven grasps this when he says in a side note published by his son: "Speech has a price. It is a liberal weakness to discount so heavily the price. It is not always a 'witch-hunt,' it is not always correct to win by showing danger has been exaggerated."[84] A common pattern among liberals is to classify harm as emotional and danger as exaggerated by default. To purify liberalism from its arrogant tendency to say, "This is how it is; I am right" is part of the process of rebuilding the edifice of the free speech tradition.

FIFTEEN

The European Tradition

Hate Speech Laws

THE DIFFERENT HISTORICAL TRADITIONS
OF THE AMERICAN AND EUROPEAN MODELS

At the beginning of Part II we looked at the two traditions of political liberty that came out of the revolutionary periods in North America and Europe in the eighteenth century. The development of individual rights would materialize later in Europe after the painful experience of World War I and the tragedy of its prisoners of war and after World War II and the damage caused by Nazi ideology. In this postwar context, freedom of expression in Europe would be limited through the legal system.

In the United States, however, the approach to citizens' freedoms, especially their freedom of expression, was the opposite: expression in the public sphere was robustly protected. In the States, freedom of expression is protected in two ways: by protecting transgressors from private violence that they may suffer as retaliation to their extreme speech and by curtailing the state's power to limit any expression that it finds inconvenient, prohibiting the government from establishing any law in this regard.

As we saw earlier, there were originally just a few laws that prohibited pornography, blasphemy, and defamation as measures to safeguard public order.[1] Besides, the debate on freedom of expression in the founding era was limited to defamation of government officials at times of political instability, but no issue of offensive speech (burning of flags or crosses and so on) was raised.

In European countries, the historic tradition began with the Bill of Rights (1698) in England and the revolutionary Declaration of the Rights of Man and the Citizen (1789) in France. Each has a context and focus that is totally different from that of their American counterpart. In summary, we can say that in the case of Britain, Parliament imposed conditions on the monarch after a period of absolutist rule; in that of France, rights of man were declared in a revolutionary period in which the feudal system was crumbling, and consequently these rights had a strongly defensive sense. Finally, as the most recent historical precedent, we have the International Declaration of Human Rights (1948), which forms the frame of reference for the European model.

Regarding the idea of the origin of both traditions that was mentioned at the beginning of the chapter, Jeremy Waldron does not think it is exactly accurate to distinguish the European sensibility from the American based on a supposed European trauma at the hands of Nazism and its consequences. Waldron argues that the United States, as a nation of immigrants, also harbored many who had suffered in the Holocaust. Moreover, the States have had a painful two-hundred-year history of suffering with slavery, racism, segregation, and so on.[2] However, in the next couple of pages focusing on the "rights projects" of the United Nations, we'll be able to better grasp some commonalities and particularities of the different political and legal traditions.

THE RISE OF HATE SPEECH LAWS IN EUROPE

The United Nations was created after World War II as an international organization for dialogue, and its first document was created on December 10, 1948: The Universal Declaration of Human Rights, which had the purpose of ensuring certain inviolable individual rights. The central theme of freedom of expression in the public sphere has been determined by the fact that there is extreme speech and discourse with harmful content that require that boundaries be drawn between tolerable offense and impermissible damage to social peace and public order. These have recently been referred to as "hate speech."

In the first place, there has been some agreement between Europe and the United States on the identification of the human problem and in the defense of certain shared values, such as opposition to racism, blasphemy, pornography, that led these regions (among others) to sign three international documents — the Universal Declaration of Human Rights (1948) and a pair of treaties on human rights, the International Convention on the Elimination of All Forms of Racial Discrimination (ICERD, 1965) and the International Pact on Civil and Political Rights (ICCPR, 1966).

On the other hand, there has been some difference between Europe and the United States in the distinct mode of enforcing such treaties, from the juridical-legal and moral-philosophical standpoint and the political standpoint. In this sense, Paul Coleman points out that the issue of freedom of expression was hotly debated throughout the writing of these documents and that two standpoints emerged, standpoints that he considers mutually opposed. On one hand, there were Western liberal democracies (the United States, Canada, and Western Europe), which advocated not restricting freedom of expression, and on the other was the USSR and its allies, which supported banning the "intolerant" and "discriminatory" speech that was used by fascists and Nazis.

For the USSR, the difference between Nazi Germany and the Western democracies was only a matter of degree as regards the spread of ideas. A representative of the Soviet delegation argued: "It was of no use to argue that ideas should only be opposed by other ideas; ideas had not stopped Hitler making war. Deeds were needed to prevent history from repeating itself. Not only must ideas be fought by other ideas but fascist manoeuvres and warmongers' machinations must also and especially be made illegal and the necessary punitive measures must be provided for."[3]

The need for the power of the state to penalize the spread of dangerous ideas and the insistence that groups be expressly mentioned (in this case the common enemy was "fascism") were limitations that the Soviets wanted to impose in the article on freedom of expression. The negotiation process was arduous, but these proposals were ultimately not included in the final text of article 19, which reads as follows: "Everyone has the right to freedom of opinion and expression; this right includes freedom to hold opinions without interference and to seek, receive and impart information and ideas through any media and regardless of frontiers."[4]

Coleman shows in his book that the Soviet Union's efforts to impose its ideas were more successful in the writing of the article against discrimination (art. 7), which says: "All are equal before the law and are entitled without any discrimination to equal protection of the law. All are entitled to equal protection against any discrimination in violation of this Declaration and against any incitement to such discrimination."[5]

The Soviet Bloc went on to introduce language expressing the need to punish those who sow hatred (hate speech). Alexander Bogomolov, a Soviet member of the Human Rights Commission, expressed it with reasons that are very interesting in that they reflect the same rhetoric as that used by those who defend the distinction between free speech and hate speech today:

> The affirmation of the equality of individuals before the law should be accompanied by the establishment of equal human rights in political, social, cultural, and economical life. In terms of practical reality, this meant that one could not allow advocacy of hatred or racial, national, or religious contempt. . . . Without such a prohibition, any declaration would be useless. It could not be said that to forbid the advocacy of racial, national or religious hatred constituted a violation of the freedom of the press or of free speech. Between Hitlerian racial propaganda and any other propaganda designed to stir up racial, national or religious hatred and incitement to war, there was but a short step. Freedom of the press and freedom of speech could not serve as a pretext for propagating views which poisoned public opinion. Propaganda in favor of racial or national exclusiveness or superiority merely served as an ideological mask for imperialistic aggression.[6]

The American delegate to the United Nations (1946–1953), Eleanor Roosevelt, argued not only that speech restrictions (for racial, national, or religious hatred) were unnecessary but that they were also prejudicial, pointing out that "any criticism of public or religious authorities might all too easily be described as incitement to hatred and consequently prohibited."[7] However, countries under Soviet domination (Czechoslovakia,

Hungary, Poland, and Yugoslavia) argued that the freedom to not be discriminated against (because of race, origin, and so on) should have preference over freedom of expression or assembly.[8]

It is clear from the Soviet countries' intent to control and censor that they did not see anything positive in the freedom of expression; they saw only a dangerous risk. However, Coleman's work points out that perhaps the Soviets' insistence on safeguarding nondiscrimination had a positive influence by complementing the liberal Anglo-American position. Although we cannot stop to analyze this point, the contribution can be seen in article 4 of the above-mentioned International Convention on the Elimination of All Forms of Racial Discrimination that they signed in 1965.[9]

The fact is that since these international negotiations and agreements, the countries of Europe have paradoxically been incorporating laws against hate speech. In light of this trend, Coleman laments how those who defended freedom of expression on the international level, voting against restrictions on the part of countries in the Soviet Bloc, are increasingly restricting freedom of expression by regulating hate speech. How did we get into this discordant spiral?

ICERD was approved in 1965, and this marked the fight against discrimination as an EU objective. The ICCPR was approved one year later, and in article 20 it prescribes to the member states the following obligation: "Any advocacy of national, racial or religious hatred that constitutes incitement to discrimination, hostility or violence shall be prohibited by law,"[10] provided that these measures were compatible with article 19 of the ICCPR (freedom of expression). This international mandate was signed in 1966 and put into force in 1976. Thus, the member states began to implement the criteria of nondiscrimination in the 1970s and developed national laws to implement what was already established in the United Nations. The first laws protected race, age, sex, and religion. Starting in 2009, they were expanded to include the protection of "sexual orientation" and "gender identity."[11]

Within the Council of Europe, the European Commission against Racism and Intolerance (ECRI) is the organization that since the 2000s has been responsible for guiding and advising member states on the adoption of laws against public insults to individuals or groups on the basis of race or religion. It extended its recommendation to the LGBT collective in 2013.[12] Paradoxically, the ECRI text in which General Policy Recommendation No. 15 was adopted (December 8, 2015) recognizes that hate speech laws can be created "to silence minorities and to suppress criticism, political opposition, and religious beliefs." For this reason, it recommends that the member states amend them "to ensure that they are clearly and precisely worded."[13] Despite this notice, there seems to have been no change in the direction of European policy toward hate speech laws.

Faced with the possibility of yielding to the limitation of expression and qualifying the criticism of public and religious authorities as "incitement," Eleanor Roosevelt saw the danger that totalitarian systems would take advantage of these limitations to prohibit such criticisms. Her warning has continuously proven prophetic: "The communist proponents of such laws did regularly enforce them to suppress speech by political dissidents as well as by ethnic and religious minorities."[14] As Nadine Strossen argues, current advocates and lobbyists in favor of laws against hate speech criticize the American position on free speech, but this was the common view in most postwar liberal democracies.

Most defenders of hate speech laws in the United States argue that "such laws should punish only individually targeted insults,"[15] but experience shows that these laws have been used to investigate, persecute, and penalize political opponents, as well as religious leaders (Christian and Muslim), for speaking negatively of—for example—homosexuality using passages from the Bible. As Strossen explains: "The arguments to seek to justify hate speech laws are the very same arguments that always have been advanced to support restrictions on any speech whose message is disfavored, disturbing, or feared."[16]

As Johannes Morsink points out, despite the pressure of the Soviet Bloc, the amendment presented by the Russians was not formally adopted in the text: "While Borisov had proposed the outright prohibition of advocacy or incitement to hostility, hatred, and contempt, the Commission adopted the right to be protected against such incitement. In other words, the Commission did not revise what it had written in articles 18, 19, and 20 when it gave to 'everyone'—including Nazis and fascists—the rights to freedom of thought, conscience and religion and the right to express these thoughts 'through any Media and regardless of frontiers' and to do so with like-minded people."[17]

It may appear paradoxical that the arguments and rhetoric of the contemporary advocacy of hate speech laws are basically the same as the anti-discrimination narrative that the communists and their allies advocated in 1948. But it is no paradox. As Eleanor Roosevelt foresaw, the proponents of such laws enforce them to suppress speech that goes against their agenda. As far as I can tell, this is not pluralism or diversity but faction.

HATE SPEECH AND DANGEROUS SPEECH

International organizations do not have an official definition of the expression "hate speech," and indeed it is not easy to properly define since it does not have a univocal meaning.

As Waldron shows, the word "hate" can lead us to think that we are talking about passions and emotions, as when we are dealing with what are called "crimes of passion," which are crimes — such as murder or homicide — committed with the aggravating element of a relationship of kinship or friendship between the offenders and the victims. "Crimes of passion" refers to the feelings that motivate such crimes, while the "hate" in "hate speech" is understood as a possible effect of certain forms of speech.[18]

Thus, even though the word "hate" or "hatred" expresses "an extreme form of dislike,"[19] it should not be understood as if it were a totally subjective attitude of the speaker or listener. Professor Robert Post differentiates "hatred" from mere disgust or ordinary disagreement.[20] I have not found any author who argues that hatred is objectively evil in itself. Most experts limit themselves to justifying the calling of hate speech evil on the basis of the effect that it has on certain groups and minorities, not because it is something bad in itself, since from the modern age this ethical-moral category has not been admitted; rather, relativism as a moral and cultural paradigm has been imposed.

The word "speech," also leads to confusion in several ways. First, because it can refer to written or spoken discourse. Second, the general term "speech" can be used to talk about a mere conversation or about a public claim or declaration — what people say out loud as a problem[21] — which is very different. Finally, and most importantly, the fact that there are three types of discourse — apophantic, pragmatic, and poetic — implies that what is said is different in each type of speech or discourse, and a different moral evaluation is required for each of them, as we shall see later. This last facet of the pragmatic character of language has been almost absent from the literature on the issue. As we saw in Part II, this factor explains why the solutions that have been reached are partial and unsatisfactory.

Susan Benesch studies speech in the context of freedom of expression and hate speech. She speaks of "dangerous speech" instead of "hate speech" in a context of preventing violence caused by the use of language. Benesch defines dangerous speech as "any form of expression (e.g., speech, text, or images) that can increase the risk that its audience will condone or commit violence against members of another group"[22] and distinguishes it from hate speech: "[Dangerous speech] is a narrower, more specific category, defined . . . by its capacity to inspire a harm that is all too easy to identify—mass violence—and that almost everyone can agree on wanting to prevent."[23]

Benesch has not made lists of dangerous words, but she studies five elements: the message itself, its audience, the historical and social context of the message, the speaker, and the medium through which the speaker communicates it. The five elements are not always decisive, but "two elements are always required for speech to be dangerous: inflammatory content and a susceptible audience."[24]

An emblematic example of dangerous speech was the terrible massacre in Rwanda (1994), in which thousands of people from the Hutu ethnic group murdered hundreds of thousands of Tutsi with machetes (the death toll is uncertain but thought to be between 500,000 and 800,000). As it is described in the trial judgment of a court case resulting from the massacre:

Inflammatory speech against Tutsi had circulated in Rwanda for years before the genocide, and it was believed to have played such an important role that the International Criminal Tribunal for Rwanda (ICTR) made speech crimes a major focus of its cases. One of the best-known was the Prosecutor v. Ferdinand Nahimana, Jean-Bosco Barayagwiza, Hassan Ngeze, the so-called Media Trial, at which a newspaper editor and two executives of Radio Télévision Libre des Milles Collines (RTLM)—bitterly nicknamed Radio Machete— were all convicted. Much of the trial focused on ambiguous language, though, not explicit encouragement to kill.[25]

The radio transmitted dangerous speech from July 1993 to July 1994: "What RTLM did was almost to pour petrol—to spread petrol throughout the country little by little, so that one day it would be able to set fire to the whole country."[26]

It seems to me that Benesch's initiative is very good but insufficient. It is partially inspired by John Austin's speech act theory, which holds that language has the power not only to say something but to do what it says or trigger others to do it, and aims to prevent cases in which language is used as a weapon in a context of potential mass violence. However, Benesch seems more interested in the sociological aspect of such speech than in that of pragmatic discourse. Her reasoning is especially limited when analyzing the first element of the five (the message), where she does not consider that there are various types of speech depending on the purpose of the message.

Finally, rather than finding the definition of hate speech, I sympathize with Andrew Sellas's effort to study the main definitions of hate speech worked out by different disciplines and to extract common features: (1) the speech targets a group or an individual as a member of a group, (2) the content of the message expresses hatred, (3) the speech causes harm, (4) the speaker intends harm or bad activity, (5) the speech incites bad actions beyond the speech itself, (6) the speech is either public or directed at a member of the group, (7) the context of the speech makes a violent response possible, and (8) the speech has no redeeming purpose.[27] This is not an academic or legal definition, but it has the richness that multidisciplinarity gives to it so that the problem may be better understood.

SOLUTIONS TO HATEFUL SPEECH:
HATE SPEECH LAWS, MORE SPEECH, OR BETTER SPEECH?

In Europe, nations are sovereign and limit expression by law. This consideration is authorized by a nation's congress or the corresponding legislative chamber, in accordance with the EU treaties. In the American system, the states impose limits, but the Supreme Court is the authority that settles specific cases. American jurisprudence has defined some limitations on the freedom of expression[28] The *Regina v. Hicklin* case (1868) limited obscenity. *New York Times v. Sullivan* (1964) established the criterion of "actual malice" for falsehoods about a public official to be punishable. *Cohen v. California* (1971) held that insulting someone in public is considered impersonal; it is a crime only when done face-to-face. *Texas v. Johnson* (1989) established that public offense is allowed but not private offense. *R.A.V. v. St. Paul* (1992) allowed the burning of a cross in front of a house, which served as an example of the "two minds" required of a judge—

personally, he might find speech reprehensible, but as a judge he cannot do anything to prevent it.

These limits extend not only to political speech but also to religion, science, art, entertainment, and any demonstration of social morality, prohibiting forms of expression that are incitements to the violation of laws (*Brandenburg v. Ohio*, 1969); falsifications of proven facts (*Gertz v. Robert Welch, Inc.*, 1974); hard-core pornography (*Miller v. California*, 1973); child pornography (*Ashcroft v. Free Speech Coalition*, 2002); threats of violence (*Virginia v. Black*, 2003); plagiarism of ideas protected by copyright (*Harper & Row Publishers, Inc. v. Nation Enterprises*, 1985); or advertisements of alcohol and tobacco, which are subject to certain limitations (*44 Liquormart, Inc. v. Rhode Island*, 1996).[29]

The debate about tolerating harmful speech is not over. There are even voices in the United States that do not rule out the spirit that underpins the European approach. The criteria outlined by American jurisprudence protect free speech in the public sector that implies government action, but it does not affect the private sector. Manifestations of hate speech in private entities such as universities or private workplaces do not fall under the protection of the First Amendment. The leaders of these institutions may establish rules that penalize harmful speech.

Waldron refuses to condemn a priori the European option of legally regulating hate speech. He recognizes that the European countries' opinion that liberal democracies should have positive responsibilities to protect an atmosphere of mutual respect from certain vicious forms of attack is a valuable contribution and deserves to be taken into consideration.[30] In fact, the intention of his book is to develop a positive characterization of hate speech laws, trying to highlight the contribution they make.[31] Although I am sympathetic with treating the harm caused by speech as an objective damage that requires justice, I do not think hate speech laws are the way to solve the problem, for reasons I have been presenting in this chapter.

From the technical standpoint, the European Court of Human Rights, speaking of laws that restrict the freedom of expression, said that they should be "formulated with *sufficient precision* to enable the citizen to regulate his conduct."[32] Strossen criticizes the wording of these laws as inevitably vague and too broad, and she provides an eloquent phrase on this from Congresswoman Eleanor Holmes Norton: "It is technically impossible to write an anti-speech code that cannot be twisted against speech nobody means to bar. It has been tried and tried and tried."[33] Coleman reaches the same conclusion: "Once governments begin legislating restrictions on speech, there is no obvious stopping point. Rather than being narrow, well-tailored, well-understood legal concepts, Europe's 'hate speech' laws are the exact opposite: broad, over-reaching, and without limit."[34]

Most authors from the liberal tradition of free expression argue that hateful speech must be overcome with "more speech" and never by government prohibition (censorship). In this vein, Strossen and Coleman argue that, de facto, laws against hate speech are not effective. Coleman shows that almost no complaints end in criminal convictions. Strossen provides multiple cases of the ineffectiveness of hate speech laws in Western democracies, emphasizing that these laws have not reduced discriminatory or violent behavior.[35] One of the examples he provides is the rise of the Nazi Party in the German elections of September of 2017, in which it won 12.6 percent of the vote, or the recent increase in racist attitudes and verbal abuse against immigrants in some European countries, such as France.[36]

It is not only that laws against hate speech are ineffective; they are also counter-productive, as they are easily utilized by lobbying groups. The resonance of complaints about gender or race (homophobia, transphobia, xenophobia, feminicide, genocide, and so on) in public opinion and the fact that the people about whom these complaints are made (politicians, journalists, priests, bishops, artists, etc.) are investigated already shows the great success that the lobbies have had in achieving notoriety and in the social promotion of their interests.

Seeing the great number of people making a living out of lobbying, I sympathize with Madison's fear of "faction" regarding the common good of society. In the *Federalist Papers* (no. 10) we find what Madison meant by "faction": a group of citizens—whether a majority or a minority—moved by passion and by a particular interest against other citizens or the community.[37] In short, lobbies and pressure groups fighting "culture wars" don't serve the common good but fight "against" those they oppose and only "for" the factional. The scope is imposing their own agendas and advancing their own interests.[38] A political arena based exclusively on the clash and advancement of factional agendas I consider not "plural" but "fragmented." Pluralism of ideologies requires some civic virtues (respect, dialogue, toleration) and a common horizon of coexistence that faction does not allow by its own design, which is canceling, calling for "no debate," or publicly shaming rival worldviews.

Coleman reports fifty recent cases that show how protection with hate speech laws is used by some lobbying groups to impose their agendas.[39] The media pressure that is involved in denunciations and—sometimes—digital mobbing for an *alleged* crime of hate speech have the negative effect of self-censorship in public debate.[40] As Coleman says, "The criminal investigation may not be successful, but the stigma remains, and the conversation shuts down."[41] In most of these cases, the person accused of hate speech has been declared innocent in the eyes of the law, and the most optimistic will consider it a victory for freedom of expression. However, at the level of the individual's personal reputation, the damage caused is irreparable and its consequences are indelible. Due to the very dynamics of the Internet, the digital fingerprint in search engines that connect a person to a "hate speech scandal" is enduring.

The fact that hate speech laws can be used by lobbies damages public discourse because, in the name of counter-speech, what originates are new dogmas that are defined with (sometimes massive) group actions of public discrediting and witch-hunts: According to Coleman, "There is currently no adequate EU binding instrument aimed at effectively countering expression of negative opinions against LGBT people."[42] Recent cases regarding author J. K. Rowling[43] and the *Guardian* journalist Suzanne Moore[44] show this illiberal tendency.

Timothy Garton Ash adds a valuable nuance to this debate on the limits of freedom of expression when he says that we need "more and *better* free speech, since free speech has never meant unlimited free speech—everyone spouting whatever comes into his or her head, global logorrhea."[45] Social media facilitates counter-speech, but it makes it difficult to have better speech. We do not want lobbies, tech companies or mainstream media dictating what is or is not said. The path of anti-discrimination laws begun by the USSR and followed by hate speech laws are not the solution that will lead to better speech. The principle of tolerance of noxious speech must work together with the recognition of the principle of objective harm, as I shall argue in chapter 18.

The need for limits has never been questioned. What we need to recover are the rational bases (historical, philosophical, and legal) that underpin the foundations on which we rely in order to establish those limits. We need better free speech based on a common understanding of human good.

PART IV

Reconstructing
the Foundations of
Freedom of Expression

SIXTEEN

Reframing Freedom of Expression as a Human Good

WHAT "GOOD" DOES FREEDOM OF EXPRESSION PROTECT?

As we saw when we discussed the jurisprudence of several Harvard Law School professors and of Oliver Wendell Holmes, from their time on there was a change in the doctrine on freedom of expression: rights ceased to be defended as something inherent, and it would be the state that defined social interests. Freedom of expression went from being an ethical objective criterion based on human dignity to being an ethics focused on state-determined interests that change at the pace of sociological and cultural trends. The paradigm of the innate rights of the person had a universal and perennial foundation (the human being) that was replaced by something more subjective, despite the intention to impose a new neutral moral objectivity.

Freedom of expression protects the human and legal good and the good of a public sphere that allows men and women to grow in understanding and in their personal and social perfection. In this sense, freedom of expression is closely linked to other goods such as information, education, freedom of opinion, and the profession of certain religious beliefs.

Freedom of expression is not a mere freedom of choice on the part of the autonomous individual, as the enlightened narrative expresses. Expression is also an act, as evidenced by the pragmatics of language. John Garvey argues that the US Constitution protects the freedom to perform certain actions (freedom of speech, of association, of professing a religion, and so on)[1] because it believes they are intrinsically good.[2]

Garvey's approach inverts the classical liberal reasoning of prioritizing rights above human goods. Garvey argues that some actions are protected precisely because they are good.[3] For this reason, the utilitarian logic of understanding rights as interests does not completely grasp the fundamental element of rights as protecting human goods. Garvey believes that the good that freedom of expression preserves is that of reaching knowledge (as an activity).[4]

Thus, as we have seen throughout these pages, there are acts of expression that use this protection opportunistically since they are not aimed at achieving knowledge but are more like exaltations of violence (racist, gender-based, religious, and so on). In these cases, the right to free expression is abused because free expression is no longer protected as a good that has the goal of knowledge and truth; rather, expression is employed as a weapon with the goal of harm.

For John Peters as well as for Garvey, it is not suitable to identify the freedom of expression with the image of the "free market of ideas." Peters prefers to equate it to the stoic virtue of the self-control of a gentleman or a soldier.[5] Garvey sees it as a good with an intrinsic value that is objectively real: "Freedom of speech is not just a process for maximizing individual self-interest, but a rule for protecting an important human good."[6]

One central element that emerges from the reflections of Peters and Garvey is that the freedom of expression is not a meta-value that stands above everything else, like an absolute. Or, in Frederick Shauer's words: "Freedom of speech is not an end but a means, a means of identifying and accepting truth."[7] Garvey, however, distances himself from the liberal tradition of freedom of expression to argue that this activity of reaching knowledge that is protected by freedom of expression is intrinsically a good. However, it is a good not because one wants it, but in itself. In this sense, Garvey argues that the First Amendment of the US Constitution protects speech with a rational purpose and not as the mere satisfaction of subjective desires. Following this logic, pornography would be excluded from the protection that the First Amendment grants to expression because it does not lead to the achievement of knowledge, which is the good that the freedom of expression protects.[8]

Garvey rejects the view of those who consider freedom as the mere capacity to choose, in which one choice is as good as another—for example, those who believe that the choice between having an abortion and having a child is indifferent. Michael McConnell points out that in these cases freedom is equated to willfulness: "the ability to do what I want to do, when I want to do it, without being judged or constrained."[9] The new liberalism establishes skepticism as the moral attitude, eliminating the possibility of an objective standard of judgement: "This was not the early liberal conception," according to McConnell.[10] He concludes: "It is a sign of degeneration of our moral discourse that freedom is now seen as in opposition to virtue."[11] Garvey also calls into question the idea that everything is worthwhile (moral skepticism) and, on the other hand, that freedom is the mere satisfaction of what we desire (freedom as mere choice and not as rational action).

If freedom is based on human good and is understood as action, then reasonability and responsibility can be demanded since there is a justification that corresponds to every action. If the law should protect freedoms, it cannot disregard the meaning (including the moral meaning) of the actions. For example, "performing" a gesture of honor toward the flag is not the same as making similar physical motions in jest. The first is an honorary salute, but the second is an insult. Both are discursive actions, but they are not meaningless.

Not only does the human good that freedom of expression protects (the search for knowledge, as an activity) have to be identified and supported, as Garvey does, but it also requires certain conditions so that it can be carried out. Thomas Irwin Emerson also raised the issue of promoting the freedom of expression in the positive sense.[12]

WHAT "CONDITIONS" DOES FREEDOM OF EXPRESSION REQUIRE?

Access to Information and the Capacity for Criticism

The current communications situation, as a general rule, allows for a broad flow of information, except in some areas of the world such as China,

North Korea, Cuba, and Venezuela, as well as Bangladesh, the Democartic Republic of Congo, Egypt, India, Indonesia, Iran, Iraq, Myanmar, Sudan, and Zimbabwe, Human Rights Watch reports that citizens suffer from a lack of access to information.[13] As stated by Zeynep Tufecki and other experts, with the digital age (known as the Third Industrial Revolution) we should be living in the "golden age of freedom of expression." In the next couple of pages we will see that the situation is not one that can lead us to whistle a happy tune. Let's start by exploring some general conditions of this information ecosystem.

The good of information is not just the free flow of data and contents but also a set of conditions that allow for the development of an individual's knowledge and for political and cultural deliberation in the public sphere. Today, the information provided by information professionals intermingles with a torrent of data shared on the Internet by many individual sources that do not merit equal trust. Peters believes that "[this] erosion of professional authority without the collapse of the professions has created promiscuous knowledge."[14] He continues by saying: "What is at stake is the drift from *knowledge*, understood as disciplined generalizations about the social and natural world accepted by authority, to *information*, the massing of facts on particular topics by dispersed groups."[15]

The volume and speed of information transmittal can make it difficult to distinguish between true public debates and strategic distractions; to evaluate the credibility of different sources; to separate truth from falsehood or the relevant from the banal; to distinguish between information and disinformation; or to warn of ideological interests and the different agendas that are promoted.

The use of social networks such as Twitter, where rumors and messages (sometimes partial and not always contested) are spread, as a weapon turns the world of information into a battlefield that does not favor knowledge but rather achieving partisan objectives. These conditions make it difficult to form rational, independent, and free criteria for expression. Public shaming is an example of this "use of Twitter as a weapon," as Emerson Brooking and Peter Singer put it.[16] Jon Ronson dismantles the utopian thinking of those who proclaim that the Internet is a new democracy, showing the severity of mob justice through real cases of online shaming in which there is no possibility that one's reputation will ever recover. In such cases, he says: "There's no way back in. We don't offer any forgiveness."[17] The effects of public shaming are global and permanent.

To make full use of this capacity for judgment, it is necessary not only to access the information but also to have sufficient education to develop the skills of evaluation and discernment of the information described above. In this *promiscuous* environment of hyper-information, and in some cases of disinformation (flooding), the equality of educational possibilities is also a condition and a determining factor for being able to develop one's convictions without being manipulated. The universalization of compulsory school education has been a great advancement, but not everyone enjoys a sufficient level of instruction before participating in and following the different political and social debates.

A fair assessment of the health of the information we receive through the digital ecosystem is not very promising. Falsehood affects not just the contents but also the actors (e.g., bots with simulated profiles) and the metrics of interactions (bot farms).[18] There is a market for false profiles,[19] for buying popularity (the acquisition of followers, likes, and retweets),[20] and for deepfakes in videos and works of art.[21] In a networked public sphere it is not easy to gauge public opinion because, unless one is an expert, it is very difficult to distinguish true actors from bots. On the other hand, it is almost impossible to articulate a rational debate when the public conversation is artificially automized. It is naïve to think that the truth can break through in such a context. Peters believes that "we have always had promiscuous knowledge," but what is new in our time is the "attitude" of conceding the phenomenon.[22]

A Plurality of Voices

Emerson has confirmed the reality that there are voices and arguments that have gone unheard or that are very weak. The public conversation has been dominated by some elites who own media outlets and by politicians who share ideological interests with these outlets or with law firms that represent these media groups.[23] Emerson observes that, as a matter of fact, "the system of freedom of expression" lacks certain conditions of equality as to the right to speak, listen, and have access to information.[24] The framing of the First Amendment to the US Constitution focuses on preventing limitations on freedom of expression but not so much on promoting it through guarantees against discrimination in its exercise. The European legal system also favors a defensive attitude. The philosophy of freedom of expression coexists with this dilemma of emphasizing freedom or equality. The "system," in itself, does not solve the problem because, in the end, it must be used by individuals and by society.[25] And, if it does not work well, then it causes the edifice to collapse.

Thus, just as freedom of information requires basic conditions in order for a free opinion to be formed (free access, being able to evaluate the sources, the capacity to compare data and opinions, and so on) this freedom is not simply the formal possibility for all voices to be expressed without reprimand or censorship; it also requires certain conditions that allow for a public debate based on rational and free deliberation. In this sense, certain limitations already exist: the prohibitions against falsehoods, speech that violates intellectual property law, fighting words, or true threats. It is clear that absolute freedom of expression, with no rules or responsibilities, actually does not foster dialogue and public conversation; rather, it can lead to confusion, arbitrariness, and, in some cases, violence.

These conditions do not automatically function in the online universe, which has global outreach with nearly total deregulation. There are many experts who have raised their voices about the possibilities for manipulation that the Internet offers.[26]

The Rationality of Public Debate

Alasdair MacIntyre addressed the issue of freedom of expression in 2009 when giving the Philip Quinn Lecture at the University of Notre Dame.[27] He distinguished the two extremes in which freedom of expression operates: "Rational political deliberation can be threatened . . . by the extremes of tolerating too much and tolerating too little."[28] MacIntyre thinks that in many Western countries, the information situation (previously discussed) implies a lack of conditions for public deliberation. In the same vein as Emerson's diagnosis, MacIntyre adds that this situation makes the principle of freedom of expression into a "pseudodemocratic babble" that benefits very powerful special interest groups (political, economic, and media).[29] That is he MacIntyre suggests the need to establish some conditions of rationality and participation in the public conversation so that freedom of expression can be effective.

MacIntyre highlights the need to protect "rational grassroots public debate," creating "standards of intellectual and moral integrity" that would limit the abuse of freedom that involves the denial of reality and the spread of lies or falsehood in the public scene.[30] This would be about defending the public scene as a space for rational deliberation that is free and open to all voices except those make fraudulent use of freedom of expression. In this sense, MacIntyre believes that if an insult leads to an exchange between the insulting party and the insulted party, to the extent that both need to justify themselves and provide reasons, then rational debate has not been inhibited but has come alive.[31]

Thus, demanding accountability from those who insult others is an issue of justice (moral or legal) and of demanding reparation (when applicable), but it is also an issue of demanding rationality in public debate. This is because, as we have seen, if words do not mean anything, if an insult is answered by a louder insult, then we are increasingly moving away from the ultimate end of freedom of expression, which is fostering knowledge and rational debate to reach the truth.

A case that shows how insult may occasion a certain degree of rational debate was the one that arose after cartoons insulting Muslims appeared in the Danish newspaper *Jyllands-Posten*, which we discussed in Part I. The Danish imams, closing the road to dialogue with the government, began a direct dialogue with the newspaper. The editors took on not a defensive attitude in the name of freedom of expression but rather one of regret. In fact, they apologized in a public statement.[32]

This note of rational debate between the imams and editors, along with the nonrecidivism in recent years, makes the Danish case very different from that of *Charlie Hebdo* in France. Flemming Rose claimed that publishing these cartoons was an act of the "cultural integration" of Islam in Denmark: "The cartoonists treated Islam the same way they treat Christianity, Buddhism, Hinduism and other religions. And by treating Muslims in Denmark as equals they made a point: We are integrating you into the Danish tradition of satire because you are part of our society, not strangers. The cartoons are including, rather than excluding, Muslims."[33] Leaving aside the sincerity of Rose's words, it is relevant—as MacIntyre suggests—that Danish critics of Islam and Muslim leaders discussed what it means to be Muslim and what it means to be Danish.[34]

PROTECTION OF EXPRESSION:
RETURN TO THE INHERITED LEGAL TRADITION

In antiquity, justice was considered a virtue of social and political life that was fundamental for bringing about cooperation between members of the community. Plato understood justice as harmony between the three classes that compose a state (philosophers, warriors, and craftsmen), and Aristotle honed the more specific meaning of justice as a virtue that consists of observing the "golden mean."[35]

In Greek, within the concept of justice (*dikaion*), having the virtue of justice in oneself (*dikaios*) is distinguished from achieving justice outside of oneself (*to dikaion*). The first is a subjective justice (in one), and the second is an objective (general) justice, which for Aristotle was a just, or righteous, mean.[36] Thus, in Greece, "general justice" (*dikaiosne*) was distinct from "justice in oneself" (*dikaios*) as a virtue of the human being who respects the *dike*, the moral order of the universe.[37] There is a distinction between morality as a subjective virtue of the individual who is required to behave in a fair (moral) way and objective justice (the law), which does not regulate behaviors of individuals but defines principles of general justice.

Michel Villey states: "Thus the term law has been understood for a long time."[38] He goes on to say: "With Aristotle, law won its autonomy" from morality,[39] but this situation leads to a great deal of confusion. Villey continues: "[Currently] legal discourse would consist in *prescriptive, imperative,* and *deontic* propositions, as if the jurist turned immediately on the action of the individuals, assuming the role of the director of the behavior of those under jurisdiction"[40]—when the law (*dikaiosne*) should indicate the role that corresponds to each individual, remembering the universal principle but without getting into directing specific cases.

In Rome, *ius civile* (law that was applicable only to Roman citizens) was distinct from *ius commune* (law that is common to all people and all cultures). As Gaius wrote:

All peoples who are ruled by laws and customs partly make use of their own laws, and partly have recourse to those which are common to all men; for what every people establishes as law for itself is peculiar to itself, and is called the Civil Law, as being that peculiar to the State; and what natural reason establishes among all men and is observed by all peoples alike, is called the Law of Nations, as being the law which all nations employ. Therefore the Roman people partly make use of their own law, and partly avail themselves of that common to all men, which matters we shall explain separately in their proper place.[41]

As Hervada summarizes the matter, the Roman jurists distinguished between a law that comes from the *naturalis ratio* and another that comes from the human option (positive law). We see this same theory in Aristotle.[42]

William of Ockham replaced the realistic notion of right (as the right thing that is due) with the notion of subjective right. This separates the right of the licit use from the thing. For him, right is defined as a *potestas* or *facultas* (a licit power, not a just power).[43] The licit (moral) is distinct from the just (legal). Hervada explains that even though Ockham did not formally use the terms "natural right" and "positive right," the first appears as a moral precept—not as right in the strict sense—and only the second is truly a right.[44] Ockham's view of the right as a faculty or power was developed two centuries later by sixteenth-century Catholic authors and was definitively assumed starting in the seventeenth century.

From Ockham's formulation of the right as subjective right (a faculty or power) we get subjectivism and legal formalism (which I shall call legalism). The separation between the right and the thing (material or immaterial) gives rise to formalism, that is, a system of formal rights that, by virtue of being "declared," are owed to them, even though some of those rights are opposed (e.g., the right to life and the right to abortion).

Hannah Arendt also considers this true. She argues that the law as a catalogue of specific prescriptions is only three centuries old: "The law of the city-state was neither the content of political action (the idea that political activity is primarily legislating, though Roman in origin, is essentially modern and found its greatest expression in Kant's political philosophy) nor was it a catalogue of prohibitions, resting, as all modern laws still do, upon the Thou Shalt Nots of the Decalogue."[45]

Modern law rejected Aristotle's system and its division between morality and law and between universal and particular. In this process, between the sixteenth and eighteenth centuries, it stopped understanding the classical notions of justice (particular, distributive, commutative)[46] to the point that those notions almost disappeared from the study of law. Hobbes was the one to formulate the modern individualist philosophy of law in the seventeenth century, although its roots are in the nominalism of the fourteenth century. Hobbes was the "founder of the myth of the social contract and of the modern idea of the state," according to Villey.[47]

Aristotle thought that there was a "common view of the good" of all members of the polis. Being a good person was, for him, very closely linked to being a good citizen. For Aristotle, virtues had a place within the social context of the city-state.[48] Contemporary liberal ethics has relegated to the subjective realm this relation to the good as the perfecting of the human being's moral nature. The community has come to be seen as a set of individuals with divergent interests, with each one needing to autonomously formulate the determination of his or her goods. In this sense, we have gone from understanding justice as "human cooperation" to understanding it as mere "impartiality" or as an "ethic of rules" (legalism).[49] As Villey writes, "The law would no longer be the just solution [*dikaion* or *id quod iustum est*], but the set of laws. Which? Not the Torah, nor the universal natural law, but the laws established by the state to institute the social order that was missing from the state of nature."[50]

A century and a half after Hobbes wrote, Kant defined the law as "the set of conditions" that allow the coexistence of "the liberty of individuals."[51] The Kantian exaltation of freedom relegates morality to the subjective conscience and to being a matter of a religious nature. Roman law already separated morality from the law with great success, but it did not put them in opposition, as did the modern Enlightenment.

A CRITICAL EVALUATION OF THE MODERN PARADIGM
OF PROTECTING RIGHTS AND FREEDOMS

The philosopher Marcello Pera, in a book in which he specifically deals with the problem of the compatibility between the ethical tradition of the Church and modern declarations of human rights,[52] gathers the main disputants on the issue, which could be summarized as those who recognize that there are some rights and duties established by the Creator and those who deny it by placing the human being as the origin of his or her own individual rights.[53] As MacIntyre says, with modernity the "I" is freed from the burden of theism and the theological modes of thinking, which has obvious political and social repercussions.[54]

The Enlightenment legacy of human rights has taken a different turn from the one that gave rise to many of the declarations of rights of modern states. We could describe this legacy as legalist, that is, as declarations of rights that have lost the ethical-rational foundation that sustained them. And, stripped of these roots, they have become something that is available, something that has become a part of political marketing, of the interested multiplication of rights—something called social rights. As Patrick Deneen describes it, this expansion of freedom is secured by law, but "increasing freedom requires the expansion of law." Therefore, "one of the liberal state's main roles becomes the active liberation of individuals ... and the achievement of our desires."[55]

This argument was a central part of Benedict XVI's speech at the United Nations:

[Human rights] are based on the natural law inscribed on human hearts and present in different cultures and civilizations. Removing human rights from this context would mean restricting their range and yielding to a relativistic conception, according to which the meaning and interpretation of rights could vary and their universality would be denied in the name of different cultural, political, social and even religious outlooks. This great variety of viewpoints must not be allowed to obscure the fact that not only rights are universal, but so too is the human person, the subject of those rights.[56]

In his commencement address at Harvard University in June of 1978,[57] Alexsandr Solzhenitsyn referred to the set of rights organized starting from a system of laws. With respect to this system, Solzhenitsyn denounced the legalist massacre that leads to the consideration of the letter of the law as the supreme solution. That is to say, if one is correct from the standpoint of juridical science, no more is required. And it is not thought that the human being can have other motivations in the public sphere beyond the framework of positive laws. At this point, the author confesses:

I have spent all my life under a communist regime and I will tell you that a society without any objective legal scale is a terrible one indeed. But a society with no other scale but the legal one is not quite worthy of man either. A society which is based on the letter of the law and never reaches any higher is taking very scarce advantage of the high level of human possibilities.[58]

With the baggage of his traumatic experience under a totalitarian regime, Solzhenitsyn stands as a defender of the moral dignity of the human being while denouncing the human impoverishment represented by the model of freedom with no roots beyond what is stipulated by the law.

This bold criticism of legalism was also expressed by Hannah Arendt some years earlier when she attended the Adolf Eichmann trial as a reporter for the *New Yorker*. With her report *Eichmann in Jerusalem: The Banality of Evil* (1963), Ronald Arnett writes: "Arendt subordinated Eichmann, a single person, to a much larger critical agenda."[59] She unmasked the moral collapse of modernity. Like a contemporary Pontius Pilate, Eichmann "not only obeyed orders, he obeyed the law."[60] In this sense, Arnett stresses that for Arendt "Eichmann was a symptom, not the disease"; the "infectious disease" was individualism and modernity's legalism without an "enlarged mentality."[61]

When Solzhenitsyn talks about freedom of expression, he highlights the importance of defending not only "human rights" but also "human obligations." He then declares: "Destructive and irresponsible freedom has been granted boundless space."[62] The results seem to have proved Solzhenitsyn right. In the cases we referred to in Part I, it is clear that the legalistic structure of contemporary free speech has not supported the onslaughts that have come from moral decadence, particularly from online discourse (hate speech, pornography, bullying, violence, and so on). And he concludes that freedom in itself does not solve the problems of human life but "even adds a number of new ones."[63] As we have seen time and again, the autonomous freedom advanced by utilitarianism and individualism easily becomes self-referential and, when it stands as a law in itself, often leads to arbitrariness and violence. Solzhenitsyn's judgments are not an amendment but a challenge to political debate to re-examine the foundations of the "system of laws," suggesting that the question of what is good for the human being be placed back at the center.

Solzhenitsyn stresses that when American democracy was born, the individual rights protected in the founding documents came from the conviction that human beings are creatures of God, that is, that an individual's freedom is recognized conditionally, assuming his or her responsibility.[64] What happened next? The moral bond that accompanied the exercise of freedom was lost. Benedict XVI formulated this idea in his speech at the Reichstag in 2011:

The conviction that there is a Creator God is what gave rise to the idea of human rights, the idea of the equality of all people before the law, the recognition of the inviolability of human dignity in every single person and the awareness of people's responsibility for their actions. Our cultural memory is shaped by these rational insights.[65]

The solution to the dead end of the legalistic path would be, as Solzhenitsyn recalls at the end of his speech at Harvard, recovering the sense of principle of the search for freedom and happiness that gave rise to the modern democracies, calling for the "moral growth" of the citizens.[66]

As seen in the treatment of the *Charlie Hebdo* case and the content moderation on the Internet, there is a good number of liberal authors who admit that "not everything goes" and that it is necessary to draw some boundaries, but they rarely find another solution than that of judging this ethical dilemma in legalistic terms. Their efforts are focused on deciding on rules that establish which ideas or interests prevail, and this deliberation is based on some a priori assumptions that exclude from the debate the moral assets that are at stake. It is not permissible to ask, "What person am I going to be?" Rather, we should ask, "What rules should we follow?" and "Why should we obey them?" Liberalism does not allow for the formulation of questions about the human good or for the consideration of the purposes of human life in the public sphere. The fact that the religious-moral and the political orders are separated in practice does not mean that they are mutually opposed or that they are incompatible. The modern fracture between morality and legality directly affects the freedom of expression, which becomes a "morality of rules."

SEVENTEEN

Reconsidering
the Legal Grounds

PROTECTING FREEDOM OF EXPRESSION
IN THE CONTEXT OF A GLOBAL COMMUNITY

The paradigm illustrated by modernity that arises from the liberal revolutions of the eighteenth century is based on the creation of sovereign states under the command of the law. The law works as a limit on the exercise of power and ensures that social life is guided by justice. One of the issues that emerges is the sustainability of a framework based on the bureaucratic apparatuses created by the states.[1]

Does the law, centered on the sovereignty and territoriality (land, sea, and air) of nations, based on the division between the public and the private, achieve its purpose in the context of a global society? In an era in which the flow of financial transactions, that of information, and safety from terrorism are global issues,[2] justice should revolve not solely around the nation-states but also around the people.[3] Jürgen Habermas defines it this way: "A world dominated by nation-states is indeed in transition toward the post-national constellation of a global society."[4]

Rafael Domingo—among other authors—poses a legal reformulation and a global law (called the Common Law of Humanity, World Law, or Cosmopolitan Law),[5] inspired by the legal tradition inherited from the Roman *ius gentium*, from the Medieval *ius commune*, with elements of international law, from the *ius universal* and the international law forged in the Enlightenment.[6] Global law is neither a total legal system nor a completely new legal system; rather, it is a system of systems that has to be combined with international law, thus surpassing it—by the very reality of globalization—to be established in *ordo orbis*.[7]

The transformation that Domingo proposes is a transition from an international society of nations to a global community, which makes it a priority to center the system around the person[8] (and intermediate communities like the family), not just state sovereignty. Domingo suggests that the paradigm of a "global human community," requires nation-states to renounce specific aspects of their sovereignty through international treaties. At the other end of the spectrum is the idea of a "global civic society" that aims to consolidate a society of nations as a single body.[9]

The law regulates society at a certain time and place in history, but in turn, in the juridical development of humanity there is a common and permanent area between the different legal systems, along with some shared keys to understanding, some invariable problems, and lasting solutions.[10] Roscoe Pound planned the new paradigm openly: "Instead of formulation of precepts, should we not be seeking to create the universal ideal atmosphere in which the precepts may develop and be made living law in a world prepared for them?"[11]

In a similar way, Adrian Vermule proposes a return to the classical legal tradition, in which rights are not individual-autonomy-based but "delimited by a conception of justice that is in itself ordered to the common good."[12] This "common good constitutionalism" does not nullify rights but reframes them according to their original understanding as human goods. At the same time, Vermule's account aims to bypass the two dominant positivistic approaches in public law in the United States: progressivism and conservative originalism.[13]

As I showed briefly in the previous chapter, the enlightened model of rights that discarded a fundamental objective in natural law has been around for only three hundred years; thus, I suggest looking to the classical tradition—not with a melancholic eagerness but seeking an idea of law and justice not manipulated by temporal ideological interests. As we outlined in chapter 5 when we were talking about the moderation of contents (of violence, hate, and pornography) by digital platforms, we must consider whether there are ways of exercising the freedom of expression that are inhumane and therefore always and everywhere unfair. To answer this question, the status of individual rights and their pre-political foundations must be revised. In this sense, one of Greek philosophy's most important contributions to law has been providing an appropriate response to the tension that exists between the permanent and the changing, seeking a point of equilibrium that allows for progress without forgetting the past.[14]

DOING JUSTICE, BUT WHAT JUSTICE?
GOING BACK TO THE INHERITED TRADITION

After the Middle Ages, the concept of justice was studied in a different context than that of the moral theology of Thomas Aquinas. In the sixteenth century, great jurists and moralists (Francisco de Vitoria, Domingo de Soto, Martín de Azpilcueta, and more) dealt with this idea in light of the new social realities that opened up after the discovery of the New World. From then on, a sociopolitical, legal, and economic approach was studied, in addition to the theological approach. Starting in the seventeenth century, social morality was studied following the morality of the Decalogue, and not so much following classical virtue ethics.

The eighteenth century saw the disappearance of the idea of justice as a set of intersubjective relationships that must conform to an objective order known by nature. In most of modern thought, the concept of justice is tied to the development of the constitutionalism of Locke, Kelsen, Bentham, and others, which seeks to guarantee the peaceful coexistence of human beings through the rule of law. What is "just" is that which corresponds to positive law. In light of the crisis of modernity after the two world wars, new approaches to justice were distinguished (such as that of John Rawls with a new contractualism) and developments in individual civil rights that provided partial solutions. The challenges that are generated by the new global society in which we live require us to seek new solutions. I think that it is wisest to seek answers in the tradition we have inherited.

The classical tradition understood justice in conformity with the famous formula of the Roman jurist Ulpian: "*Iustitia est constans et perpetua voluntas suum unicuique tribuendi.*"[15] That is to say: "Justice is the constant and perpetual will to give to each what is his own" (his right).[16] Medieval thought started with this classical concept of law to formulate the object of justice and its distinctive notes of otherness, debt, and equality.[17]

Aristotle formulates the notion of *alteritas* in his Nicomachean Ethics, pointing out that justice implies a recognition of the other: "Justice, alone of the virtues, is thought to be 'another's good,' because it is related to our neighbor; for it does what is advantageous to another, either a ruler or a copartner."[18] From the moral standpoint, it is relevant to determine the damage or abuse of the other's right or the impairment of the common social good in the exercise of the freedom of expression.

As we have seen when dealing with the pragmatic aspect of speech, the contents modify the exercise of the freedom: "informing" is not the same as "telling a story." Likewise, "doing science" (even philosophical) and presenting and defending it—or doing history or journalism—is not the same as advertising. The requirements of each type of text (according to its ends) put different demands on the freedom of the subject who pronounces them and simultaneously "authorizes" the recipient who receives them to raise different demands, which are true limits. In a context in which rights and freedoms are often presented as merely individual, it is important to note otherness (the recognition of the good of others) as an essential feature of justice that, instead, highlights the social dimension of the human being.

The second characteristic of justice is duty. Justice implies a relationship with the other, but with respect to what? With respect to that right that corresponds to everyone, which empowers the holder to demand it. That is why, when we speak of justice generating a duty, we are faced with a giving and a respect that goes beyond mere courtesy or good practices. Justice reminds us that it is about giving what is the other's and respecting what is due. In our object of study, this debt consists of freedom, honor, reputation, and so on. The debt can be taken in two ways: as if it were a right by nature or a good in the sense that it is a right by human convention (positivized).[19] Aristotle referred to the first as natural justice and the second as legal justice. Natural law is the one that "everywhere has the same force and does not exist by people's thinking this or that."[20] One can say that legislation by human beings ratifies and specifies a right that human beings already have by nature.[21]

As we have seen, for Aquinas the object of the virtue of justice was the right, but the right (*ius*) understood as what is just in itself, not the written law (*lex*). That is to say, the ethical demands of justice come from the human being himself, to give him what is his. The law must reflect and enable what is just at the social level. In this way, as Luño says, "the ethical demands of justice constitute a duty in the strictest and most rigorous sense of the word."[22] Thus, acts of injustice are all those in which one seizes, damages, or destroys a good that is due to another person or to the community, which, in the case of freedom of expression would be, for example, injuries to honor or privacy or unjustified restrictions on the expression of ideas, religious convictions, and so on.

On the other hand, those injuries to the right of the other demand restitution, that is, compensation.[23] The state as guarantor of these human rights is obliged to administer a civil or criminal punishment when they are damaged. Just as theft or physical assault damage the rights of the person, the abusive exercise of expression is also capable of causing objective harm to others or to society.[24]

A RIGHT OF THOSE WHO SPEAK AND A RIGHT OF THOSE WHO LISTEN

Freedom of expression is a right of those who speak but also of those who listen in the sense that there is an equality of the possibilities of discourse. As we have seen, equality (*aequalitas*) is the virtue that regulates social relations. This means that justice demands that no voices be unfairly silenced. To ensure pluralism and avoid discrimination, the state must protect what has been expressed (for example, a piece of information) and thus prevent what could lead to selective or arbitrary censorship.

Respect for the personhood and the subjectivity of others is a basic condition for equality in social life. Justice protects what is owed to anyone and is thus a universal kind of protection that does not attend to privileges. Properly understanding justice involves understanding that it is about respecting the rights of others, which introduces a perspective in the debate on freedom of expression that is broader than the mere individualist demand that is often invoked.

As Luño says: "What justice fundamentally demands is the recognition that every person, by virtue of being a person, has a personhood, subjectivity, and dignity that is equal to what I have."[25] For that reason, no link is needed other than that of "being a human person." The trait of the "personal condition," on the one hand, accompanies us all in that duty to give to each his own and, on the other hand, is related to the axiological discourse and foundation of the freedom of expression since it shows again the fact that being a man or a woman constitutes the foundation of justice, not the fact that there is a subsequent legal recognition.

The freedom of expression can be understood from the perspective of those who express themselves or those who listen. It is a right with two extremes, one positive and one negative. On the one hand, the expression is defended and, on the other, the audience is defended. This is a recurring topic of debate in the controversies about the freedom of expression. We are presented with not only a right of those who speak, but also a right of those who listen, because there is a right owed to the other (an individual person, group, or society) in play. The dual face of this right puts freedom of expression in relation with equality, since neither those who express themselves nor those who listen have a position of dominance over the other.

The tradition of freedom of expression can be organized into various schools of thought. Kathleen Sullivan distinguishes two main categories: one linked to freedom and the other to equality.[26] The libertarian category receives the majority of support, and it emphasizes that freedom of expression is a negative precept (not to veto any speech), which protects a system of expression. Speech in itself is protected, whether it is individual or collective, for profit or not, widespread or minority. The libertarian option gives priority to speakers over and above other concerns. The goal of this protection of expression is to invalidate all government interference. The egalitarian school of thought, however, believes that speech restrictions should go in the direction of redistributing the power of speech and discourse, reducing the disproportionate influence of some (for example, when it comes to defending the strengthening of political or cultural minorities).[27]

Once again, the liberal discourse identifies the problem well: freedom and equality must both be maintained because this recognizes that there is a right of those who speak and also a right of those who listen. The problem is that, because of the shortcomings pointed out in Part III, people have not settled on convincing solutions. Some frame the situation as a clash of interests (the libertarian thesis) and others as a balancing of values (the egalitarian thesis).

WHAT WE DO WITH THE NEW NETWORKED PUBLIC SPHERE: SELF-REGULATION AND COMPLIANCE WITH THE LAW

Self-Regulation by the Digital Platforms

The digital platforms[28] organize their self-regulation around two documents: "terms of service" and "community guidelines." The first states the conditions of use in legal terms, establishing certain obligations for the user as well as how to resolve any conflicts or future legal action (litigation). "It addresses not just appropriate content and behavior but also liability, intellectual property, arbitration, and other disclaimers."[29]

The "community guidelines" are written using expressions and turns of phrase to interpellate the user in his or her own language. They express the values that guide the platform and what the platform does or does not consider appropriate. These guidelines declare some principles that are occasionally contradictory. For example, these platforms are identified with the freedom that rules on the web, as a privileged place for self-expression, but at the same time they present themselves as safe communities where moderation is protected. As Tarleton Gillespie says, they are "statements of policy and principle" that are sometimes taken literally and sometimes ignored.[30] It cannot be any other way because the platforms are motivated by principles of private interest (they aim to satisfy users and advertisers) and public service (they are forums for public discourse). A Facebook employee expressed it like this: "If you exist to make the world more 'open and connected' and you're a content-sharing platform, the critical question to answer is why you'd ever delete anything, right?"[31] This dilemma is always surrounded by the fear of intervening too much or not enough.

Sarah Roberts paints a picture of what she calls "commercial content moderators," distinguishing between in-house employees and contractors,[32] who may be in-company or outsourced. She presents the pros and cons of the different models but goes beyond the formulas by putting the underlying question in the mouth of Josh, one of the workers she interviews: these companies play a role "not only in cleaning up abusive content, but in having solicited it in the first place."[33] The companies should ask themselves to what extent they promote the production of so much rubbish.

The content of the different platforms' guidelines is similar, but also different, because they all have different audiences and they want to distinguish themselves. The guidelines are important because, in Gillespie's words, "they work to legitimate the platform's right to impose rules."[34] They are introduction letters to users and advertisers. In any case, they change frequently—at times they are updated daily—at the pace of conflicts that they are having and depending on what the other platforms do. "In this complex tapestry of similarities and differences," he says, there "seems to be a small set of relatively stable orientations, not toward specific rules but toward frameworks of permissiveness and obligation."[35] The notion of truth as *consensual truth* is a negotiated view of the truth in the short term that, as such, is unsustainable in the long term because the reality and nature of how things are does not admit compromises but rather imposes itself.

The platforms are intermediaries of the contents published, but the volume of users, the quantity of information that they handle, the categories of their impact, and the permanence of everything published make them different from traditional mediators (radio, newspaper, and television). As we saw when talking about hate speech laws in Europe, this has led some governments to feel the need to intervene for the sake of the public interest. In the United States, however, complaints of market concentration (anti-trust concerns) weigh on Google and Facebook.

Different media have denounced the system of self-regulation because of its inconsistency and inefficacy. One of them is ProPublica, which asked Facebook to justify its decisions about a sample of forty-nine articles. In twenty-two cases, Facebook said that its reviewers had been incorrect; in nineteen cases, it defended the failures; and in six cases, it said that the content had violated the company's rules, but its reviewers had misjudged it. In the other two cases, it said that it did not have sufficient information to respond.[36]

In the detailed scans of the moderators' work by Gillespie and Roberts, some difficulties that the moderators face, such as cultural and idiomatic diversity, became clear. However, these are not the only challenges. In the testimonies provided by Roberts, the concern is (notoriously) not only legal but a concern that the government and the big partners also wield great influence on whether contents are censored: "So we'll allow anything to be up unless it is becoming a PR or a legal issue," Roberts concludes.[37] These overlapping political and commercial alliances and interests often lead to an "unequal application of policies to material that, content-wise, was very similar."[38]

As in other sensitive commercial sectors (banking, finance, and so on), self-regulation needs to be accompanied by a system of checks and balances in order to guard the common social good. Achieving accountability and better transparency are some of the claims that are on everyone's lips. Self-regulation is unsatisfactory. The facts have shown that good intentions are not enough.

To tackle the serious criticism that was leveled at Facebook's credibility, in 2020 the company created the Oversight Board, an independent body of twenty distinguished experts charged with the mission of helping the platform discern and make recommendations on difficult questions related to content censorship. The Stanford constitutional law professor and former judge Michael McConnell is co-chair of the board. In a March 2022 interview, McConnell explained the first steps taken by the board since it started operating in October 2020 and revealed that during that period of time there had been "well over a million appeals to the board" from current citizens. He said: "Most appeals have to do with people objecting to their own content being taken down. . . . Of those vast number of appeals, the board has decided twenty cases with published opinions."[39] Those cases have been chosen intentionally as instructive cases for dealing with recurring problems.[40] Talking about the authority granted to these experts, McConnell acknowledges: "We have final authority about whether material will be restored to the platform or not. . . . And to make policy recommendations for changes in the way that the company operates its community standards and practices." The company has promised to comply with the former, but it has not promised to adopt all the recommendations made. The company takes sixty days to decide if it will accept or reject a recommendation or say, "We're working on it." Sometimes the answer is "We like the recommendation and plan to implement it, but the engineering tasks are more serious than you might have guessed." In some cases, they believe they've already followed the recommendation. And in others, McConnell says, "they simply say no."[41]

Legal Regulation for Content Moderation

The European countries protect their citizens from the abuses of free expression with hate speech laws, and they require the digital platforms to suppress contents that harm human dignity, in accord with national legislation and the international agreements cited in chapter 15. Beyond belonging to a legal tradition of common law or civil law, the European example of General Data Protection Regulation (GDPR) shows a new way of solving problems that focuses on the person. The creation of this kind of common regulation is proving to be an effective way to resolve new global problems, mainly because those who have the (technological) power to solve it—the large digital platforms—respond to only the reasonable requirements of the law.

The following brief chronology explains the situation in Europe. In December of 2015, Facebook, Google, and Twitter voluntarily agreed to remove hate speech content from their platforms within twenty-four hours of a complaint. In 2016, within the framework of a Council of Europe study group called "Internet Forum of the EU," these three companies accepted a code of conduct that included a commitment to suspend all content considered illegal by hate speech laws in the European zone from its platforms.[42] In early 2017, Heidi Tworek revealed that the good intentions of these companies were not enough: YouTube had eliminated 90 percent of criminal content in the allotted time, but Facebook had removed only 39 percent and Twitter only 1 percent.[43] Consequently, the German government considered legislation the only way to protect democracy from hate speech. That is why, in April of 2017, the German government passed the law Network Enforcement Act, whereby social media companies would be fined for not removing hate speech content in a timely manner.[44] The law fully went into effect on January 1, 2018. In a review performed in February of 2019, the European Commission stated that social media platforms were meeting the requirements in 66 percent of cases.[45] The German legislation is having a domino effect in many different countries, such as Australia, Belarus, France, Honduras, India, Kenya, Malaysia, the Philippines, Singapore, UK, and Vietnam—including those whose guiding ideology is not always democratic, like Venezuela or Russia—which are seeking to restrict online discourse, forcing the platforms to act as censors.[46]

The Internet, by its very nature as high-speed and far-reaching, requires ex ante solutions. Jurisprudential solutions imply a length of time that prevents the two new forms of censorship mentioned in chapter 12 (trolling and flooding) from being addressed. The protection of freedom of expression as a human good and the protection of public order require regulatory measures of positive justice.

I agree with the two aspects of Tim Wu's suggestion for addressing the new forms of censorship: "the introduction of anti-trolling laws designed to better combat the specific problem of 'troll-army'–style attacks on journalists or other public figures" and "regulatory restrictions on the ability of major media and internet speech platforms to knowingly accept money from foreign countries to influence . . . elections."[47] As Wu says, "Without a clear framework as a guide for content moderation regulation, a small number of companies determine what can and cannot be said."[48] That is why it is also essential to protect citizens' right to information by subjecting these companies to a transparency requirement so that the public knows the criteria they use to collect, process, and retain information.

Keeping in mind that the business model of the large technological platforms is based on the collection, processing, and use of private information for commercial and political purposes that affect the public conversation, it would be appropriate to incorporate the concept of "information fiduciaries," a term coined by Jack Balkin,[49] and to apply to these technological platforms the requirement of fiduciary responsibility, that is, the duty to use personal data in such a way that does not betray or harm users. As Balkin and Jonathan Zittrain explain:

> In the law, a *fiduciary* is a person or business with an obligation to act in a trustworthy manner in the interest of another. . . . An information fiduciary is a person or business that deals not in money but in information. Doctors, lawyers, and accountants are examples; they have to keep our secrets and they can't use the information they collect about us against our interests. Because doctors, lawyers, and accountants know so much about us, and because we have to depend on them, the law requires them to act in good faith — on pain of loss of their license to practice, and a lawsuit by their clients. The law even protects them to various degrees from being compelled to release the private information they have learned.[50]

An example of a betrayal of this responsibility on the part of Google occurred on the day of the death of Giovanni Buttarelli, the European data protection supervisor. Google made Buttarelli's cause of death public and accessible in the "snippet in first row" software of quick responses to specific Google searches. This simple tool answers such direct questions as "How old is (actor's name)?" If someone googled "Buttarelli's cause of death," it responded with information that had not been published by any media outlet, blog, or website and that Buttarelli had never made public. This was confirmed by his relatives: "The cause of death is confidential and personal information. They preferred not to talk about it, precisely because he had never mentioned it before."[51]

In Europe, Facebook has been punished for abusive use of the sensitive data of its users.[52] Some researchers at the Charles III University of Madrid were the victims of such abuse. One of them received an advertisement on his Facebook wall that said: "Connect with the gay community & rent affordable places from people like you. Book Now." The person in question had not shared his sexual orientation on Facebook, nor had he given Facebook permission to share it. What happened? An advertising company sought to target potential clients of the gay community with this advertisement. Facebook users are tagged with ad preferences, which represent their potential interests. Facebook labels the users with preferences according to their activity on Facebook and partner websites. The person in question discovered that "homosexuality" was one of the advertising preferences that Facebook had assigned him.[53]

Google and Facebook should not intervene by influencing a referendum, as happened in Ireland,[54] nor should they remind voters of a certain party to go vote, to the detriment of the other party, as occurred in the United States.[55] When providing a best route to a driver, Google maps should not make the driver travel by a business of a partner or Google advertiser. Due to the very dynamics of the Internet, a design (code) and regulation would be necessary to fulfill this fiduciary responsibility.

The legal challenge posed by technology requires that all actors be heard. As Balkin and Zittrain write: "The public wants protection from potential abuses by online businesses that collect, analyze, and manipulate their personal data. But online businesses don't want to be hit with unexpected liability as privacy law takes unexpected turns."[56] In turn, the criteria cannot be arbitrary or unduly burdensome to these platforms:

Companies could take on the responsibilities of information fiduciaries: They would agree to a set of fair information practices, including security and privacy guarantees, and disclosure of breaches. They would promise not to leverage personal data to unfairly discriminate against or abuse the trust of end users. And they would not sell or distribute consumer information except to those who agreed to similar rules. In return, the federal government would preempt a wide range of state and local laws.[57]

EIGHTEEN

Reshaping the Harm Principle

Pragmatics of Language and Natural Ethics

IF THE SPEECH IS AN "ACTION,"
TALKING ABOUT "OBJECTIVE HARM"

With regard to the conceptualization of the human being and society, the fracture of modernity has consequences that are not only theoretical but also affect human rationality (including moral practice). Human action is stripped of its teleological objective, the reference to some hierarchical goods that give an end to human action, separating the connection in human action between being and what ought to be.[1] Nietzsche's critique of rationalist modernity was in this vein: Kantian morality is a mere illusion that appeals to objectivist universalism based on subjective will.[2] This was the beginning of free speech theory's trouble with understanding that there are acts of expression that cause objective damage.

The liberal doctrine of freedom of expression understands damage as emotional or subjective when it is actually linked to an objective good (individual or common). The liberal intuition on this point is incomplete because we derive not a practical indication from it but arbitrariness, when in real life we distinguish between mirth and mockery, between satire and sarcasm. A good example of this difference is embodied by the central character of Victor Hugo's *The Man Who Laughs*. In ancient Greece, the front of theaters was decorated with a jovial bronze face that looked as if it was laughing. It was the symbol of comedy. In Hugo's novel, that mask of permanent hilarity is cruelly applied to a man: "the man who laughs."

Gwynplaine is a performer who was disfigured from birth with a permanent forced smile on his face: "It was Gwynplaine's laugh that so excited the mirth of others; yet he did not laugh himself. His face laughed... The exterior did not depend on the interior. The laugh which he himself had not placed on brow and eyelids and mouth, he was powerless to remove. It had been stamped indelibly on his face; it was automatic, and the more irresistible because it seemed petrified."[3]

The author shows the cruelty of an industry that steals children and makes them grow up with grotesque deformities so that it can dedicate them to the entertainment of the European nobility. Gwynplaine is a symbol of people who suffer inside and smile on the outside. Through the narrative of "the man who laughs," the author strongly criticizes the monarchy, but he also starkly shows the difference between satire and sarcasm.[4]

The first part of Gwynplaine's story is that of a performer who makes people laugh in the daily show of a traveling theater company. When he discovers that he is Lord Clancharlie and presents himself to British royalty, he is the object of sarcasm on the part of the aristocracy, who cruelly reject him, even though he has noble blood.[5] Readers stop seeing the satirical fictional character and start to see the person.

This work emphasizes the difference between laughing with and laughing at. Only the latter constitutes an offence. The difference is not subjective. In the final passage, Hugo shows the destructive power of sarcasm. When the man who laughs (Lord Clancharlie) is speaking to the assembly and they thunderously and vexatiously laugh at him, it is clear that this "mad buffoonery" contains nothing comical but is a death sentence for the person. The effects of sarcasm are destructive: "Having fallen, we can raise ourselves up; but, being pulverized, never. And the insult of their sovereign mockery had reduced him to dust."[6] With the abusive use of freedom of expression, it is not just that feelings are hurt but goods inherent to the human condition (individual and social) are harmed.

Discursive Actions

We experience discursive actions in some hateful expressions that are celebrations of offense more than exercises of speech. Language and information involve not only the locutionary dimension but also the illocutionary dimension because the words are actions, as well as the *perlocutionary* dimension because the possible effects can be anticipated. In the words of Cabú, a cartoonist at the satirical magazine *Charlie Hebdo*: "A vignette is a gunshot." Similarly, as Pope Francis explains:

> Jesus reminds us that words can kill! When we say that a person has the tongue of a snake, what does that mean? That their words kill! Not only is it wrong to take the life of another, but it is also wrong to bestow the poison of anger upon him, strike him with slander, and speak ill of him. This brings us to gossip: gossip can also kill, because it kills the reputation of the person![7]

The deterioration of the content also leads to a mere formalism of the public debate. This is how Ratzinger has said he sees it:

> In many places today, for example, no one bothers any longer to ask what a person thinks. The verdict on someone's thinking is ready at hand as long as you can assign it to its corresponding, formal category: conservative, reactionary, fundamentalist, progressive, revolutionary. Assignment to a formal scheme suffices to render unnecessary coming to terms with the content. The same thing can be seen in more concentrated form, in art. What a work of art says is indifferent. It can glorify God or the devil. The sole standard is that of formal, technical mastery.[8]

The critical point here is that we build society with words and actions. This is how individuals grow and develop as people.

The Issue of Damage

The central theme of freedom of expression in the public sphere has been the damage done by extreme speech with harmful content. Different legal systems set the boundary between tolerable offense and permissible damage at "social peace" and "public order." The substance of the problem is not new, but this legal and moral question has recently been designated using the term "hate speech."

First we should note that both the European and the American models share a starting point that is focused on the problem of hateful discourse. There is a certain unity between the two in identifying the problem and in the defense of some shared human values and contents, contents that involve racism, blasphemy, pornography, and so on. The difference comes in the distinct way of approaching it, from the juridical-legal standpoint but also the philosophical-moral standpoint, which we shall discuss in the following section.

The expression "hate speech" is not easy to properly define, nor does it have a univocal meaning. First, as Waldron points out, the word "hate" can make us think that we are talking about passions and emotions, as when we are dealing with crimes of passion—such as murder or manslaughter—committed with the aggravating factor of a relationship of kinship or friendship between the perpetrator and the victim. "Crimes of passion" refers to the emotions that motivate the crimes, while the hatred that defines hate speech is understood as a possible effect of certain forms of discourse.[9]

According to Robert Post, the word "hate" or "hatred" expresses "an extreme form of dislike,"[10] but it should not be understood as if it were a subjective attitude of a speaker or a listener. Post makes a distinction between hate and mere disgust or ordinary dislike.[11] Most experts limit themselves calling hate speech evil on the basis of the effects that it leads to for certain groups or minorities, not because it is something "bad" in itself, since this ethical-moral category is not admitted in our philosophical context.

The word "speech" mainly leads to confusion in at least two ways: first, because it can refer to written or spoken discourse, and second, because the general term "discourse" can refer to a mere conversation or to a claim made in public, which is very different. This is why it is so useful to distinguish each of the different types of discourse by its purpose: apophantic logos, a text guided by logic that states a truth or falsehood, such as a historical account; poetic logos, a text that creates a world with its own internal meaning, such as a fictional movie; and pragmatic logos, a text that pursues action, such as advertising or political speech. Therefore, what is said is different in each type of discourse, and a different moral evaluation of each one is required.

To tackle the question of the damage caused by speech, I suggest building upon Mill's notion of harm, which assumes a distinction between freedom of expression and its misuse.

A RECONSTRUCTION OF JOHN STUART MILL'S CONCEPT OF HARM

Mill's harm principle states: "The only purpose for which power can be rightfully exercised over any member of a civilized community, against his will, is to prevent harm to others."[12] This is framed by a utilitarian logic that mainly addresses the consequences of an act of expression and not the rationality (practical morality) of the act itself.[13] Thus, Mill makes exceptions to the principle of freedom of expression—public incitement and obscenity—based on their effects. The English author understood incitement as an instigation to physical violence, that is, he understood an expression as a speech act. In the case of public obscenities, he believed that these are insulting actions (or expressions) that, at the level of the individual, would have no legal relevance (e.g., pornography, nudity) but, if committed in public, involve damage at the social level (social decorum, good manners).

Mill assumed that freedom of expression is exercised to protect and claim a right, and, in this sense, some cases would be abuses of freedom of expression (due to their effects): cases of insult (fighting words), incitement, obscenity, defamation, and the dissemination of falsehoods. Thus, it was not part of Mill's mental framework to believe that freedom of expression (and in particular the harm principle) could be invoked, in an opportunistic or cynical sense, not to defend a right but to offend others, based on the protection that is given to freedom of expression.

In this regard, Raphael Cohen-Almagor tries to reconstruct Mill's harm principle, later advanced by twentieth-century American jurisprudence, based on two arguments. First, he suggests a more categorical interpretation of Mill's harm principle, saying: "Any speech, which instigates ... to cause physical harm to certain individuals or groups, ought to be curtailed."[14] Cohen means that for incitement to occur, four requirements must be met: (1) the content of expression must be harmful (its effects, not its intrinsic value); (2) the manner of the expression must be harmful (the way in which it has been expressed); (3) the intention to harm of the speaker must be examined (the motivation of the one who expresses it); (4) the circumstances (in which it takes place) must be such that harm may occur.

Secondly, he suggests adding this to the harm principle: "When the content and/or manner of a certain speech is/are designed to cause a psychological offence to a certain target group, and the objective circumstances are such that make the target group inescapably exposed to that offence, then the speech in question has to be restricted."[15]

Cohen's advancement is especially interesting because of the adaptation of Mill's harm principle to the current circumstances of hate speech. Cohen seems to distance himself from the jurisprudence of Holmes and acknowledges that there are expressions in the public sphere that claim to invoke a "right to offend" that was not included in the "right to expression" theorized by Mill. In this sense, Cohen concludes that when the offense is serious, the intentions of the offender are clear, and the group or minority affected does not have the option to avoid the offense, the democratic system should draw the line and limit that expression.[16]

Cohen's attempt to complete Mill's harm principle with the "offense principle" is inspired by the thesis of Joel Feinberg, who, in turn, bases offense on three standards: the offensive standard (that the intensity and duration of the offense is serious), the reasonable avoidablility standard (that the offense is inescapable), and the Volenti standard (that those affected do not succumb out of their own curiosity or attraction).[17] Cohen recognizes that the notion of harm that Feinberg deals with reduces offense to a psychological issue, like disgust, discomfort, irritation, or other forms of emotional stress. Cohen wants to go further and find a formula that recognizes offenses that meet the criteria mentioned an injury comparable to physical aggression.[18]

Cohen seems to follow in the consequentialist footsteps of Mill, and he refuses to state that there are actions that are evil or wrong "in themselves," focusing on the circumstances and consequences in which those actions are expressed (or performed). On the other hand, as part of his liberal-utilitarian view he distinguishes between expression and action, so that ideas and opinions do not involve harm and therefore are not immediate risks because only actions can cause damage and, therefore, have immediate effects. According to this perspective, the judgment of harm and injustice is reduced to a calculation of probabilities.

A recent case of incitement in the commonwealth of Massachusetts shows plainly the weakness of the liberal distinction between words and actions. At the age of 17, Michelle Carter, through text messages and phone calls, incited her 18-year-old boyfriend to commit suicide by asphyxiation in his car. One of the determining texts during her trial was their last phone conversation, in which Roy (Carter's boyfriend) had been sitting in his car as the fumes were building, then got out and called her, showing that he wanted to live. In this conversation she ordered him to get back in the car. He did so and died. The judge, after evaluating the thousands of texts between them and Roy's final phone call just before his death, decreed that Carter was guilty of involuntary manslaughter.

This decision opens a breach in the liberal discourse about incitement and criminal responsibility in free speech cases. There are two main positions: that of those who align themselves with the judge's decision that Carter had a duty to try to save Roy's life and acted in a reckless and imprudent manner and that of those who, while recognizing that her words were reprehensible, point out that words are not actions, and thus her incitement would have been speech protected by the freedom of expression.[19] In this sense, the ACLU lawyer who defended Carter protested the decision thus: "This is saying that what she did is killing him, that her words literally killed him, that the murder weapon here was her words."[20] This sentence suggests a way that expressions can be related to criminal responsibility for inciting others to commit crimes through social networks and the incitement to violence created by troll mob attacks.

As Tim Wu writes, "The death threat and burning cross serve as archetypical examples. As we have seen, trolls frequently operate by describing horrific acts, and not in a manner suggesting good humor or artistic self-expression."[21] In this sense, the Supreme Court has confirmed the intuition of the intent to create fear: "Intimidation in the constitutionally proscribable sense of the Word is a type of true threat, where a speaker directs a threat to a person or a group of persons with the intent of placing the victim in fear of bodily harm or death."[22] What is the goal of troll mobs? The debate of ideas? It is clear that the objective is not rational discussion but something more pragmatic: to threaten, intimidate, and damage. It would be interesting to rely on studies that analyze the language used by troll armies with the goal of showing the intent to cause objective harm.

Going back to Cohen's proposal to reconstruct the Mill's harm principle based on objective criteria and trying to measure "harm": we should emphasize that it is of great benefit, but its consequentialist a priori assumption limits the scope of his argument on the notion of offense and the resulting conclusions on the limitations of freedom of expression. The absence of objective moral truths and damages, which is typical of contemporary liberalism, prevents Cohen from offering a convincing proposal of the notion of objective damage.

Having said that, Cohen's diagnosis of the damage caused by hate speech and his proposal to reconstruct Mill's harm principle are correct: "We ought not to tolerate every speech, whatever it might be, for then we elevate the value of freedom of expression, and indeed, of tolerance, over other values which we deem to be of no less importance, such as human dignity and equality of concern and respect."[23] What Cohen does not see is that if the motive for prohibiting speech is based on the calculation of probability and not on the harm itself, then we end up with partial solutions and insufficiencies, as in the handling of the Skokie demonstration. Some liberal authors like Bollinger and Cohen believe that judges would think that if the Skokie demonstration were banned, perhaps whites in the South would ban marches for Black civil rights. The utilitarian calculation presents this limitation, among others. Cohen perceives this problem, and he recognizes that it leads to a contradiction: some invoke the offense principle not to "defend against the abuse of rights" but to "cause harm to others."[24] In this sense, as the author maintains, claiming to be offended because Blacks are claiming the same rights as Whites is very different from marching on Skokie to offend the Jewish Holocaust survivors in the neighborhood.

The principle of freedom of expression should be based not solely on the principle of tolerance but also on that of objective harm, which recognizes when fundamental rights related to human dignity are contravened, such as not being discriminated against or violated on the basis of race, origin, religion, or sex. These elements are not feelings or preferences (like political or professional convictions) but objective elements that affect the core dignity of the person. The harm to human dignity is not a damage to private subjectivity. It is a real damage to a personal subject that as such is an end in itself.[25]

Cohen-Almagor's conclusion is categorical: "Tolerance which conceives the right to freedom of expression as a *carte blanche* allowing any speech, in any circumstances, might prove counterproductive, assisting the flourishing of anti-tolerant opinions and hate-movements."[26] Mill never imagined that freedom of expression would be invoked with an anti-humanitarian sentiment as a "right to offend" the respect owed to another.[27] This fact makes it necessary to reconstruct Mill's harm principle to fit the circumstances of our time and based on the actual damage caused, to consider the abuses of expression as matters of justice.

THE ABUSE OF FREEDOM OF EXPRESSION AS AN ISSUE OF JUSTICE

There is a direct connection between the environmental crisis and the degradation of interpersonal relationships in society. In the first, humankind's relationship with nature is compromised by an attitude of dominance; in the second, the degradation is manifested in the interactions between people in the digital ecosystem (hate speech, bullying, the abuse of minors, public shaming, and so on). As Pope Francis argues in his encyclical on the environment: "The present ecological crisis is one small sign of the ethical, cultural and spiritual crisis of modernity."[28] We said this back in Part II when discussing the distinct shortfalls of modernity that prevent the underlying problems generated by the freedom of expression from being resolved. To speak of the "objective damages" of the discourse, it must be accepted that the morality of actions can be objectively judged based on a universal natural ethic.

Many contemporary authors focus on the fact that freedom of expression is an indispensable element for democracy to function and be effective, which is undeniable. What I want to show here, however, in a positive sense, is that freedom of expression must be protected as an individual right precisely because it is a human good that is essential for achieving knowledge and personal development. On the other hand, we have seen that not every expression has this value since some forms of expression contradict their inherent meaning and constitute abusive exercises.

Philosophy and moral theology are concerned with justice as a cardinal virtue that regulates the relation of otherness between people and with society and communication along with it: *Iustitia consistit in communicatione.*[29] On the other hand, the law deals with the relationships of justice within society, which are between individuals and with the state.[30] In the next few paragraphs we shall see how, from the moral standpoint, the exercise of freedom of expression falls within the purview of justice.[31]

The abuses of the freedom of expression are not a new phenomenon because they are linked to the human condition, and they put into play the struggle between good and human evil that will always exist. As we have been seeing though this study, what have changed are the historical circumstances, the political philosophical formulations, and the juridical consideration of what we call political freedoms.

I follow Thomas Aquinas's thesis on justice, which is based on the views of classic pre-Christian authors like Cicero, Aristotle, and the

Roman jurists. I especially agree with Aquinas's development because he understood that rights protect human goods. The notion of common good in the Aristotelian-Thomist tradition has been very relevant to Western political philosophy.[32] The purpose of the law and of every government is not the mere organization of coexistence but the good of the community. In very brief summary, the main conceptions would be those formulated by political and philosophical liberalism, the collectivism of totalitarianism, and communitarianism.[33] For the sake of convenience, I am only mentioning the liberal perspective here, since the concept of freedom of expression has emerged and developed in that tradition.

The classical liberalism of Locke and Mill highlights the preference for individual autonomy over the social dimension of the human being. It does so by distinguishing people from their ends and conceptions.[34] The liberal society would be a mere aggregate of subjects along with their interests in a social contract. In this paradigm, the different conceptions of what is good fall outside of the common project that is governed exclusively by the law. The state occupies the apex of this social contract, adopting an ethically neutral position with the goal of maximizing individuals' happiness. In this sense, individuals and interests are recognized, but not mutual bonds.

From this classical perspective, the main ethical objection is this, from Aquinas: "To govern consists in directing what is governed to its due end."[35] The concept of common good includes a sense of determination (telos) of the human being and society: the perfecting of the individual and the community itself. Adrian Vermule holds that rights as free speech are "determinable" and "intrinsically ordered to the common good."[36] Liberalism rejects this classic normative discourse; however, liberalism developed and still lives in this same cultural and legal ethos.

According to B. J. Diggs, the notion of the "common good" has been displaced from the ethical debate, leading it toward the concept of "public interest,"[37] thus stripping it of any reference to the good of the human being and ignoring its roots, which were established by the Creator who endowed man with reason, and seeking to argue exclusively in a legal arena and in terms of utilitarian calculation. The Christian tradition claims, in the words of Vatican II, that "the beginning, the subject and the goal of all social institutions is and must be the human person."[38] Therefore, the common good is not an institutional or legal goal in which the state equitably distributes freedoms and rights; it is an individual duty of each member of society. Moreover, it is a duty of the state that ensures the structural conditions of life for all members of the community.[39] This personal and collective effort never ends.

As Clifford Christians recalls, the individualism of liberal democracy has reduced the concept of the common good to tattered ribbons.[40] For liberal democracy, the origin of the common good is social and not pre-existing in nature. Christians states that the common good should be the first principle, above individual autonomy.[41]

The classic principle of distributive justice implies that the common good is a collective objective, which reinforces the idea that there are certain common moral goods.[42] For this school of thought, the community is a system of cooperation, and social cooperation is governed by utility and benefit. The choice of the ends and conceptions is arbitrary, a mere expression of preference and with subjective and variable moral implications.[43]

In order to reconcile the relationship between individual good and the common good, there are two antagonistic views: (1) the view of individualist social doctrine, which, out of the three parts of justice,[44] recognizes only commutative justice, which governs the relationships between individuals (individualism does not recognize the existence of "everyone" and therefore does not recognize other relationships), and (2) the view of collectivism, which denies relationships between individuals and holds up legal justice as the basic guideline of public life.[45] The necessary subordination of the particular good to the common good cannot be interpreted as a subordination of the person to society. The state should not replace the individual initiative.

Regarding expressions such as hate speech and pornography, the concept of the common good would provide reasons to condemn such acts of expression, which are celebrations of violence (racist, sexist, or anti-clerical). The notion of the common good goes beyond a civic morality based on social rights granted by the state. It defends individual liberty but appeals to personal and community responsibility. The challenge is that it is not a formula to apply to and impose on citizens but rather a common project in which the human person — not the state — is the beginning, subject, and end. Benedict XVI sets out this argument in *Caritas in veritate*, following in the footsteps of previous popes: "*Integral human development presupposes the responsible freedom* of the individual and of peoples: no structure can guarantee this development over and above human responsibility. The 'types of messianism which give promises but create illusions'

(Paul VI, *Populorum progessio*, 262) always build their case on a denial of the transcendent dimension of development, in the conviction that it lies entirely at their disposal."[46] Political institutions and structures for growth are important, but only to the extent that they are tools of human freedom. "Only when it is free can development be integrally human; only in a climate of responsible freedom can it grow in a satisfactory manner."[47]

Ethics in general, and theology in particular, can shed light on—and sometimes solve—the dilemmas related to the limits of free speech, empowering the discussion with its contribution of valuable knowledge of the human condition and helping to frame it as a matter of justice.

NINETEEN

Repairing the Relationship between the Secular and the Sacred

THREATS TO FREE EXPRESSION: SECULARISM AND RELIGIOUS FANATICISM

Secularism and religious fanaticism are two almost equally intolerant pathologies that threaten freedom of expression. As seen in earlier chapters, they are nearly mirror images, because neither recognizes the freedom of others and both seek to impose their own beliefs. In both cases it has been shown that the violation of freedom of expression is closely linked to the breakdown of religious freedom. Some shed blood in the name of God (Islamic fundamentalism), and others spite and verbally denigrate God with words and images (blasphemy, on the secularist side). We can say that both fundamentalisms instrumentalize the figure of God to impose their ideological ends, whether sharia or secularism. And both are threatening to the pluralism that freedom of expression demands.

Joseph Ratzinger spoke of the pathologies (of reason—secularism—and of religion—fundamentalism) mentioned above. The first, according to Ratzinger, is the bitter fruit of the nuclear bomb, and the second is terrorism in the name of faith.[1] Jürgen Habermas concurs in the diagnosis of both pathologies and their collision in the public arena.[2]

The public sphere is an arena of political discussion in which citizens coexist, discuss, and express all views in a rational way. It is a radically secular, but not secularist, space like an exclusion from God (as an argument in the public sphere).[3] Religion belongs to the public domain just as much as politics does. The religions that inspire the lives of billions of people in the world are another element of the social fabric. In Europe, in the era of the confessional states, religion was mixed with political life. Starting with modernity and with the establishment of liberal Western democracies, religion adopted a distinct place compatible with the secularity of the new secular public sphere.[4] This differentiation between and compatibility of the secular and the sacred have never been accepted by Islamic fundamentalism or European secularism.

Many years ago, Italy and other countries in Europe were discussing the removal of crucifixes from public school classrooms for being potentially discriminatory. It was remarkable that Natalia Ginsburg, an Italian writer of Jewish background, argued to defend the presence of the crucifix, writing at *L'Unità*, the newspaper of the Italian Communist Party: "The crucifix does not generate any discrimination. He is silent. It is the image of the Christian revolution that spread the idea of equality among men, that was lacking until then."[5] She recognized the Christian cultural revolution related to equality with bold words: "The crucifix represents everyone. How come it represents everyone? Because before Christ no one had ever said that all men were equal and brothers: all of them, rich and poor, believers and non-believers, Jews and non-Jews and blacks and whites." And she continued: "The Christian revolution changed the world. Do we want to deny that it has changed the world? We have been saying 'before Christ' and 'after Christ' for almost two thousand years. Or do we want to stop saying so?"[6] Her background, along with the fact that she recognized the social and cultural achievement for the common good that comes from religion, made her statement particularly powerful.

In Part III we saw that there are two traditions in the ways of seeing the relationships between the Christian religion and the modern state: the French way, which wanted to regulate the influence of religion on citizens, and the American way, which had religious pluralism as its starting point.

According to Habermas: "Unlike in France the introduction of the freedom of religion in the United States did not mark a victory of *laicism* over a state authority that had at most tolerated religious minorities according to its own standards which it imposed on the population."[7] Speaking about this contemporary secularism, Michael McConnell adds: "God either does not exist or, if He exists, is irrelevant to affairs of this world. Obviously, some people believe that. But some do not, and the insistence that we all speak as if God were nonexistent or irrelevant is not neutral between the contending positions."[8] He concludes: "A genuine pluralistic liberalism must recognize that secularism is no more neutral than religion. Religious and secular ideas compete in the marketplaces of ideas, and there is no reason to privilege one over another."[9]

On the other hand, looking at the geopolitical landscape of recent years, we find that radical Islam disrupts this balance because a theocracy does not differentiate between political and religious authority. In areas dominated by Hinduism or Buddhism, there are also tensions between Hindu fundamentalism and respect for the religious freedom of Christian or Muslim faithful. In this sense, for Christians the relationship of the Church to political power is informed by these famous words of Jesus: "Render therefore to Caesar the things that are Caesar's, and to God the things that are God's" (Matt. 22:21). This separation between the authority of the state and that of the sacred was a complete novelty to theocracies of ancient history and continues to be so today in the eyes of Islam. This separation of spheres is the deepest guarantee to individual freedoms of the Western world. Modernity built on this dual foundation. Ratzinger wrote that these two societies

[are] related to each other but not identical with each other. . . . The state is no longer itself the bearer of a religious authority that reaches into the ultimate depths of conscience, but for its moral basis refers beyond itself to another community. This community in its turn, the Church, understands itself as a final moral authority which however depends on voluntary adherence and is entitled only to spiritual but not civil penalties.[10]

The Catholic religion recognizes the need for men and women to enjoy full freedom to progress toward their end according to nature,[11] as well as the rightful autonomy of the public sphere. The Vatican II declaration *Dignitatis Humanae* (1965) establishes two foundations of personal freedom: an ontological one that results in a person's occupying the center of public life (and therefore, the state must guarantee and respect the rights that correspond to it by nature); and the ethical-juridical one by which a legal order that protects freedom is postulated.[12] In this way, the Church recognizes political rationality as characteristic of the state, different from the ethical-religious dimension of social existence.[13]

The declaration *Dignitatis Humanae* implies the separation — in practice — of the religious-moral order from the political order, recognizing that the latter has its own entity. We have yet to find the same openness on the part of secular thinking, to admit in rational debate reasons that come from faith and recognizing, without prejudice, the role of religion in the public sphere.

FAITH AND REASON: TWO DIFFERENT LANGUAGES

The public sphere is built and consolidated by rational discourse, and in that universe of meaning and sense there is not only one language, but several. As John Peters puts it: "Reason has many languages in many tongues. I would say, secular reason is only one of these languages."[14] There are many languages of knowledge: the one of the arts and humanities, the language of natural science and technology, and the one that comes from theology and religion. In fact, the liberal arts program, rooted in Greek and Roman culture, developed in Western medieval universities, and carried forth by Renaissance humanism, contained this harmony of languages that expressed humanity's most important ideas.

The love of wisdom raises the human spirit to the truth, and in this process, faith and reason live together in a natural harmony, in which they are different languages that are equally needed. As Peters says: "We enact our beliefs in all that we do."[15] But this complementarity of faith and reason has not always been the case. I cannot narrate here its complete historical journey, but I will underline some aspects of it that have a direct bearing on the philosophy of freedom of expression. Among these origins are the Protestant roots of the liberal notion of freedoms. Protestantism in English-speaking societies was overwhelmingly Calvinist and

Anglican, linking these two denominations to secular liberalism as mutual influences.[16]

For Luther, the guiding principle was *sola fide* (faith alone). When examining the role of reason and its connection to faith, his language becomes particularly harsh: "[Reason] is the Devil's greatest whore."[17] Consequently, Luther's critics accused him of being anti-rational, and certainly, some of his statements on the role of reason are indisputably negative. However, a holistic re-evaluation of his writings shows faith and reason in an endless battle.[18] This underlying subordination of reason has had a decisive influence on the segregation of theology and on its relationship with other areas of knowledge. On the contrary, the method taught by St. Anselm and emphasized by St. Augustine was *fides quaerens intellectum* (faith seeking understanding). Faith is reasonable; it seeks to know and understand. That is why the Church founded universities: to create and spread culture beyond her monasteries and convents. Faith asks questions; it is not a blind assent. This search for the truth finds an example in the "*disputatio* method" used in medieval universities to get a full picture of an argument, showing a fair confidence in reason and providing a space for opposition and discussion. Wisdom is being willing to listen empathetically to the opposing side.

There is an emblematic example that may help to illustrate this. The shield on the Harvard coat of arms contains three open books and the word "*Veritas.*" In the original version, two books were open and the one at the bottom was closed (face down), accompanied by the motto "*Veritas Christo et Ecclesiae*" (Truth for Christ and the Church). The Harvard website explains: "This symbolizes the limits of reason, and the need for God's revelation. With the secularization of the school, the current shield now contains only the word 'Veritas' with three open books."[19] The closed book implied that knowledge has a mysterious part that is never fully revealed, alluding to the sacred sciences. With the Enlightenment came great human progress, and many paths of knowledge were opened. The enthusiasm with which this progress was pursued was accompanied by a certain arrogance, with many wanting to reveal all knowledge, leaving no room for mystery. That which was not empirically demonstrable was considered not true knowledge but superstition or something irrational. Both versions of the Harvard shield currently coexist at Harvard. The original version with a face-down book is a reminder that growth in knowledge is not something that one possesses or masters. It is also a paradox of our times: we believe that we know more than we really do, but those who really know more realize that there is much more that they do not know.

In a short essay, G. K. Chesterton warned that the sixteenth century in Europe was characterized by the bitterness and rage of religious wars. And he related it to the fact that "the seventeenth century might be compared to the second fermentation into vinegar."[20] Chesterton meant that, from the political standpoint, the seventeenth century was a complex and labyrinthine century that gave rise to strong reactive feelings of an anti-Catholic nature in the ranks of those advancing the Reformation.

Contrary to what some may think when reading the works of seventeenth-century political philosophers, many of whom were Puritans, we realize that their view of human freedom was pessimistic and negative: they distrusted natural freedom.[21] This negative presumption of human freedom means that they did not consider the possibility of a responsible communication or exercise of self-censorship. This view undoubtedly contrasts with classical antiquity.[22]

Alongside this negative view of freedom in Protestant thought, Chesterton points out that Calvinism was not republican or democratic; it defended the aristocratic cause. Similarly, Puritanism was not popular but aristocratic.[23] Chesterton expresses the situation clearly with these words: "Calvinism took away a man's liberty in the universe; why then, should it favor his liberty in the State? Puritanism denied free will; why should it be likely to affirm free speech?"[24]

THE ROLE OF RELIGION IN THE PUBLIC SPHERE

Jürgen Habermas used the controversial phrase "post-secular society" in referring to Europe and such countries as Canada, Australia, and New Zealand, where the religious affiliation of the population has been falling steadily since the mid-twentieth century.[25] "In these societies," he wrote, "religion maintains a public influence and relevance, while the secularist certainty that religion will disappear worldwide in the course of modernization is losing ground."[26]

For Habermas, the challenge is to find a "post-secular balance between shared citizenship and cultural difference."[27] In such a balance, aggressive secularism is rejected and a positive role for religion in the public sphere is granted, given that religious doctrines can serve as resources of moral intuitions that are not otherwise accessible to a secular society.[28]

According to Habermas, "Religion is gaining influence not only worldwide but also within national public spheres," and, as a matter of fact, "religious organizations are increasingly assuming the role of 'communities of interpretation' in the public arena of secular societies."[29] This would be one of religion's contributions to the public and to the secular sphere. In the academic dialogue between Ratzinger and Habermas, the first highlighted the mutual disposition to learn and respect the different languages and contributions between reason and religion. Moreover, he highlighted the capacity of religion to be a "positive moral force."[30]

Transcendent faith is a language that provides several valuable things. It presents a legacy of normative values outside of the negotiation of the majorities because its reference is not temporal or local but refers to the common universe of what it means to be human. It also brings a horizon of vital meaning to existence and presents a world of personal development through virtue. Theology could contribute the knowledge it holds about human consciousness and intentionality to the philosophy of freedom of expression, as I shall suggest in the last section of this chapter. According to George Grant, "The greatness of the system is that the tolerance of pluralism is combined with the strength of religion."[31]

Habermas stated: "It is not just a matter of respect. Philosophy also has good reasons to be open to learning from religious traditions."[32] He is alluding to the cognitive discrimination to which believers are subjected because reasons that are part of religious beliefs are not admitted, requiring those who hold arguments from faith to translate their convictions into secular language.[33] This attitude, because it is not very pluralistic, is antiliberal. As Peters says: "The liberal public sphere rests upon a modern vision of the soul and a secular definition of reason."[34] That is to say, public liberal rationality is based on the unproven assumption of being exclusively secular.

To properly address the role of religion in the public sphere we need to face the question of blasphemy in a secular-legal system. The legal recognition of God makes total sense but does not need to turn into legal protection of God's cause. His significance is external to the legal system (giving sense to human dignity, human rights, and so on). As Rafael Domingo explains:

God is a meta-legal concept; though the concept of God is not properly a legal concept like contract or testamentary will, it does have some legal significance. The meta-legal God requires recognition by secular legal systems. This degree of recognition does not demand that the law's recognition of God must be transformed into positive law, since God does not need legal protection. Citizens and legal documents can mention God without falling into discrimination. The existence of God does not have a legal effect in the strictest sense beyond recognition.[35]

The crime of blasphemy in the ancient world existed only in the Jewish religion, which had a law to punish it: "Anyone who blasphemes the name of the Lord is to be put to death. The entire assembly must stone them. Whether foreigner or native-born, when they blaspheme the Name they are to be put to death" (Lev. 24:16). On the other hand, in the ancient Greco-Roman world it was generally assumed that wrongs against the gods were punished by the gods themselves.[36]

The distinction between a sin and a crime was clear in antiquity, and it is worth quoting some words that highlight the difference. Writing about the punishments for a false oath, Cicero said: "*Periurii poena divina exitium, humana dedecus esto; non iudex sed deus vindex constituitur.*"[37] The divine punishment for perjury could be death (*exitium*), whereas the human punishment would be dishonor (*dedecus*). And he concluded by saying that the gods are the ones who punish the crime, not the judge. This makes it clear that legal and divine punishments are totally different. Tacitus writes in the same line: "*Iusiurandum perinde aestimandum quam si Iovem fefellisset: deorum iniurias dis curae.*"[38] The false oath must be seen as deceiving Jupiter: the gods take care of the offenses to the gods. Therefore, there is a clear separation between the human world with its crimes and the divine world, which must defend itself "alone" from offense and insult by human beings.

Daniela Piattelli affirms that in the early period of the Roman Empire, with the constitutional transformation from the republic to the principate (*principatus*), the idea emerged that the person of the prince was an exponent of divine power that exercised authority in God's name. By this logic, any offense against the prince was treated as an offense to the divine power, and vice versa. Blasphemy then became not only a religious crime but also a civil crime.[39] This shift would take on even harsher consequences with the Edict of Milan (313), through which Christianity gained freedom and more space in the social world of the Roman Empire. Over time, the power of the emperor took on the characteristics of religious power. It was the Eastern Roman Emperor Justinian who formulated a law that became the watershed in advancing the new perspective on blasphemy in the Eastern Christian world.[40] The defense of respect for God turned out to be a call to Christians' religious zeal and, consequently, became a law, and blasphemy, apostasy, desecration of sacred images, and so on started to be seriously punished in the new Christian world.[41] However, it must be said that early Christians always distinguished crime from sin and never stoned any Christians for their blasphemy, not even the apostates.[42] They distinguished religious from civil order. St. Augustine, trained in classical pagan culture, took for granted that not every sin was a crime, as we saw when talking about tolerance of evil.

FREEDOM OF EXPRESSION AND RELIGION: BLASPHEMY

Blasphemy can generally be defined as an act (gesture or word) done or said in public to dishonor or deny the dignity that God has as supreme being.[43] As Ireneusz Rogulski observes, the three monotheistic religions (Judaism, Christianity, and Islam) and Buddhism all address this.[44] The interest in facing the question of blasphemy comes from the public dimension of acts of expression. For that reason, John Austin's distinction between constative (enunciative) and performative acts of communication seems especially appropriate.[45]

Austin's distinction helps us to frame the conflict generated by blasphemy because expressions against the sacred can be mere constatations (locutionary acts) or they can be illocutions that express an intention in whoever pronounces them and will have effects on the recipient.[46] Consider, for example, the fact that there are manifestations of religious piety or ways of practicing faith that are routine and formalistic, which might lead one to think that they bear a closer resemblance to superstition than to a personal devotion to God. Criticism of this reality would be a constative act. However, if we approach the same reality using sneering expressions that ridicule these ways of demonstrating piety, that is going beyond the critical constatation. In this case, it is a performative act because the intent to ridicule those who worship in a certain way, to mock their religion, is meant to move them to reject it and thus seeks to separate the public from religious practice. As Rogulski points out, with the word's power of mobilization, human beings can create and preserve values, but they can also destroy them.[47] This is the performative dimension that blasphemy also has.

Some object that religion and its symbols should not be protected in the public space. Stéphane Charbonnier, editor of the weekly *Charlie Hebdo*, thinks that only a believer can blaspheme, since blasphemy applies only to believers: "God is sacred only to those who believe in him."[48] Charbonnier deals with the issue of blasphemy from a position of open rejection of religion, explicitly manifesting his atheism at different times.[49] He equates religions with political ideologies,[50] or rather he considers them a question of preference, like the lifestyle chosen by vegetarians.[51] He thinks that to believe is fundamentally to fear, and he wonders how being afraid can be a right.[52] He thinks that something is *sacred* only for those who consider it so—believers—not for everyone else. Charbonnier launches two types of challenges: he questions religious freedom, and he questions the fact that religion (the sacred) has a rational universal value. The first is an inviolable right of people, and the second is an inheritance of humanity.

It is appropriate to mention the clash between two fundamental human rights: freedom of expression and religious freedom. In summary, one can say that religious freedom gives one the right to profess one's religion and personal convictions as well as the freedom to be an atheist (like Charbonnier). Purporting to exclude religion from the public sphere would be clearly unfair. On the other hand, the defense of the sacred as a universal human value falls within the context of human tradition reflected in many different cultures and laws interruptedly, meaning that the human being is a religious being by nature. History, literature, and archaeology are undeniable testimonies. To get rid of this innate inclination without reasons that prove otherwise makes it an arbitrary decision. In this sense, the denial of the sacred as a value would not operate so much in the field of justice as in that of irrationality and lack of good sense.

However, blasphemy is not a crime invented by religions to protect their status in the public sphere. As I noted earlier, blasphemy is a human act that consists in insulting the sacred, not as a way to "blow off steam" but as a performative act, with intent and purpose, which damages a dimension that is as closely linked to the dignity of a person as his or her convictions.

Charbonnier's criticism is not solely focused on religious leaders; he also denounces the press and politicians as complicit in the system in which blasphemy exists. He rebukes the press for its collusion, which has helped to crystalize the concept of Islamophobia because everything that sounds like radical Islam is associated with terrorism and sells: "Any scandal containing the word 'Islam' in its headline sells copy. . . . Fear sells well."[53] Charbonnier points out that since the incident involving the cartoons of Muhammad, *Charlie Hebdo* has been under media surveillance, and every time something of Muhammad has been published, it has been reported as "another provocation of *Charlie Hebdo*," reinforcing the protection of the sacred in the public sphere.[54] Thus, Charbonnier argues that the press should ignore people's religious convictions and see only "citizens" instead of "Muslims." He offers similar advice to politicians: they should see people not as "believers," but as "citizens."[55]

As Rogulski stresses, the endeavor to eliminate blasphemy from the juridical and sociopolitical landscape[56] stands in contrast with the rise of some new offenses that some consider blasphemy, such as homophobia or transphobia. God is removed as the main point of reference, and other principles are put in his place, such as feminism or gender theory, which are presented as unquestionable absolutes.[57] This is the paradox behind much of the blasphemy debate.

From the legal standpoint, many countries raise the question of how advisable it is to consider blasphemy a criminal offense. This is thoroughly discussed in Rogulski's comparative analysis of different countries,[58] which favors a nonuniform solution: abolishing the crime of blasphemy in the countries where the religious is identified with the political, mainly in Islamic nations, where blasphemy is a political weapon punished as a capital crime. However, in Western countries it is necessary to maintain, and in some cases recover, laws that recognize the crime of blasphemy, considering such laws part of the right of religious freedom and the right to not be violated for professing one's faith.[59] Rogulski suggests the following:

> How to resolve this conflict between the freedom of expression and religious freedom? Perhaps one solution would be to introduce the

defense of the value of religion into the list of goods protected by laws against incitement to hate. If certain categories of people are protected because of their ethnic or racial origin or their sexual orientation, why not also include the faithful of a religion in this group?[60]

Rogulski's suggestion highlights the protection of an inviolable right and responsibility of governments to guard the public order beyond warding off ideological agendas. I believe we must also frame the conflict between freedom of expression and respect for the sacred as an issue of common rationality. Society is built with words and actions. Therefore, either words mean something or everything is arbitrary and rational discourse in the public sphere is not possible. Presented with the two threats to freedom of expression we have identified (relativistic and religious fundamentalism), which do not recognize the freedom of those who think differently and intend to impose their beliefs (sharia or secularism) without rational debate, it is necessary to create some conditions that allow a rational public debate. Although this advances what was set out in the fifth chapter, these sensible conditions for public debate are rational limits to freedom of expression that will sometimes be reinforced by the law and other times will be a matter of socially established common loyalty.

THE CONTRIBUTION OF THEOLOGY: FREEDOM OF EXPRESSION AS A HUMAN ACTION THAT INVOLVES THE CONSCIENCE

From a theological standpoint, freedom of expression lies in the sphere of moral action and justice. I follow certain notions of Thomas Aquinas because he understood rights as goods. The acts of expression are acts of a human being, which involve the contest of will (choice or intention). As we saw earlier, there are some acts of expression that are objectively offensive due to their context and conditions, and these call for justice.

Dealing with human action, Aquinas made an important distinction between choice and intention: "That intention of the will is the act of the will guided by reason directing the means [*ea quae sunt ad finem*] toward the end itself; whereas choice is the act of the will guided by reason deciding between means: and thus, intention and choice differ."[61] This definition helps us to see that expression is a human act, in which the will guided by wisdom intervenes, and thus it has intentionality. It is not a mere impulse or automatism. However, the distinction between intention and choice may be understood for what it is: a nuance of differentiation. But each act (choice or intention) cannot be isolated because there is a strong connection between the two. The fact is that both express what we want in a single and simple act.

According to Aquinas, intention has a reason as its appropriate object: why I do what I do, that is, the *finis operantis* or remote end of the action.[62] "The proper object of choice is the means for the sake of the end,"[63] and this object appears to the will as the particular realization of the *finis proximus* or *finis operis*,[64] not as an impossible thing. Therefore, "The end is the reason for willing the means [*ea quae sunt ad finem*]. Thus, the will does not relate to each in the same way,"[65] and therefore choice (*electio*) and will (here in the sense of *intentio*, that is, the act of wanting) are different acts. However, they belong to the same appetitive power[66]—that of the will.[67]

This distinction can help us to understand that the unity of the act of expression exists in the will. We *want* to act in a concrete way, in accord with all the conditions we know. There is a substantial unity of the different intentional acts of an agent. This point aids opposition to the excuse used in hate speech, which insists on the separation between the action and the intention. Thus, it is in an act of expression, even though the purpose pursued is only self-expression without a desire to harm. However, if one is aware that his or her speech can potentially offend, that preconception forms part of the object of the will. What Aquinas argued helps lead to the conclusion that we cannot separate voluntary human action from its intent.

In expressive acts, we cannot separate the end from intent or the end from the means employed (what we want and what we choose as the means) since they are intrinsically united. *Mutatis mutandis*, form, and content are always united. We distinguish them only in analysis. For example, sexual intercourse is an expressive act, the meaning of which cannot be manipulated by the will. It is a giving of two persons. If it is not, then it will be something else. The interaction between a prostitute and a client is not a loving relationship but a business transaction involving a service.

In order to judge the morality of a specific act of expression, the goodness of the *electio* cannot be considered in isolation since the goodness of all additional terms is also required. According to Duarte Sousa-Lara, in a certain action, "given the substantial unity between the *intentio* and the *electio*, the external act can be called good if both acts of the will are good. If the *intentio* is bad, the external action is bad, because it proceeds from the disordered will, even if nothing bad is externally observable."[68]

A second important distinction needs to be made to properly evaluate specific acts of expression, which is the difference between an "*intentio* of an end desired in itself," toward which the action is ordered, and the ordering of things toward their end. While the second may be an instrumental good or an indifferent good, Aquinas says, "it is not possible for an end toward which a given action was deliberately ordered to be indifferent."[69] This necessarily must have some character of the good, without which the agent will not be moved to action.[70] These nuances in intentionality help us to see that the *intentio operis* is the appropriate criterion for judging acts of expression. Considering the unity between intention and choice, the principle of noncontradiction leads us to affirm that in an act of freedom of expression such as a work of art, a poster, or a book, the author's intent is joined to the very act of expression. That is why it would not make sense for the authors of *Charlie Hebdo*'s racist vignettes to say, "I did not want to offend." It would be an internal contradiction of human behavior. The intervention of reason and will in our free choices renders people responsible for them.

Returning now to the circumstances in which acts are performed, Aquinas says that moral circumstances behave as the accidents of the moral act, whose moral substance is given by the object and the end.[71] This is why the circumstances increase or decrease the goodness or evil of an act, but they never have the power to transform the act into good or evil.[72] However, the circumstances are accidents that are around the substance of the moral act (object and end), which are not far from, but in contact with, the moral act.[73] Thus, these circumstances often help us to understand the real and true intentionality of human action. As we saw in the case of the Skokie demonstration as originally planned, the circumstance of the location was not involuntary or arbitrary.

Sometimes a circumstance functions as a specific difference, and then it defines the moral act. For example, the sexual act within marriage is a good natural action. However, if it is performed in public, that circumstance changes the type of the action, because it is exhibitionism. It is not that this circumstance turns conjugal relations into something "less good" but that it positively transforms this particular act into something bad.

In fact, as Sousa explains: "Saint Thomas also points out that there are as-pects that can at first seem like circumstances, but that are actually part of the substance of the act, and for this reason they are appropriately called conditions of the (moral) object."[74] In the Skokie case, the location was not a mere circumstance outside of the moral act but rather a "primary condi-tion" of it, because in this case "the circumstance [was] desired as an end."[75]

This differentiation between what is a circumstance and a what is a condition, from the standpoint of the moral object, is also very useful for discussing some acts of hate speech. As we have seen when we mentioned certain cases throughout this study, the conditions of the sacred, race, or sex belonged to the object of the action. For example, this is the case with blasphemy. There are authors who demand the abolition of blasphemy laws because they say that the sacred is a category that belongs to the pri-vate sphere. However, at the same time we see that religious symbols or people are attacked or ridiculed precisely because of their religious or sa-cred condition. This theological distinction helps us to differentiate the objective damage that comes from certain acts of expression.

Regarding expression in the public sphere, one often hears the justifi-cation that transgression is an instrument and not an end in itself and that some acts of expression are performed in a strategic and symbolic way. However, beyond strategies and abstractions, what this reflection intends to show is that acts of freedom of expression are free human acts that there-fore involve the responsibility to respond to what is owed. In this regard, invoking the abstract principles of tolerance and ethical suspension to jus-tify acts of hate speech is not enough to resolve the moral dilemma that these acts generate. From an ethical standpoint, expression and harm in the public sphere are not autonomous, abstract, or involuntary. Such acts have a specific purpose: to harm others through expression. Oftentimes, the hesi-tation to accept this view is due not only to the liberal requirement of ethi-cal suspension but also to the imposed neutrality that we mentioned earlier.

TWENTY

Revisiting the Limits of Freedom of Expression

THE LIMITS OF LIBERTY

This final chapter will unfold on the basis of the ideas set out in the earlier chapters. The limits of liberty are not an "obstacle" but a "condition" for freedom to really exist and develop.[1] To accept this premise, it is necessary to dispense with a notion of individualistic freedom as a mere ability to choose, and therefore, it is necessary to understand that the "non-absolute" character of individual liberty is limited by a criterion of justice and by a rationality that the common good imposes.

I examine the limits that freedom of expression requires under these criteria. Freedom of expression, by the very fact of being a right, needs the protection of the law to preserve it and make it effective. However, in addition to the principle of legality, it also requires the moral growth of those who exercise it, because everything cannot and should not be legislated. In this chapter I shall recall and propose limitations in three areas: legal, judicial, and socially institutionalized. These limits (both legal and moral) act as conditions for the exercise of freedom of expression.

If we take a moment to step outside the legal tradition of the last three hundred years and return to the way law and justice were understood for many centuries, we shall find inspiration for overcoming certain bottlenecks to which the liberal tradition of free expression seems to have run out of convincing responses. It is for this reason that I shall follow the concepts postulated by Alasdair MacIntyre in *After Virtue*: the notions of *dikaiosyne* and *sophrosyne*. As we know, Plato linked virtues to political practice, and the virtues of which he spoke include the moderation (*sophrosyne*) that reason imposes on the other powers of the human being, courage (*andreia*), and wisdom (*sophia*). These three virtues are manifested only in conjunction with a fourth: the virtue of justice, understood as *dikaiosyne*.[2]

The limitations on freedom of expression operate in different sectors because there are different kinds of evil, and so the reasons for addressing each one are also different. Some of them must be established by law, whereas others have to be decided by a judge on a case-by-case basis. It also makes sense to have social limits, established and institutionalized civilly, as the natural result of the social and moral dimension of the human being. Finally, we must not forget that good governance also leads us to assume that not all evils should be prohibited.[3] As Campbell Markham, a Presbyterian pastor in Tasmania (Australia), said,

> Free speech is fraught, but the alternative is unthinkable. . . . Jesus taught that human evil arises from the heart. The dull cudgel of hate speech laws can never touch the heart, and so they will never stop the hate, insult, and ridicule. Hearts will only change, and truth and goodness will only rise, in the midst of speech that is vigorous, logical, and at all times free.[4]

LEGAL LIMITS

Public Order and Public Morality

Earlier we saw the advantage of following the differentiation between general justice (*dikaiosne*) and justice in oneself (*dikaios*) for distinguishing between expressions to be dealt with by law and those to be dealt with as specific cases. When mentioning the American model of the First

Amendment and the European model, we already alluded to the fact that the proliferation of laws would easily stifle the principle of freedom of expression. According to this criterion, the limitations on freedom of expression would have to operate within the field of the *dikaiosne*, not in that of a casuistic regulation. The judgment of "particular justice," of the *dikaios*, corresponds to jurisprudence and not to legislation.

From the beginnings of the modern democracies, the problem of the abuse of freedom of expression has been resolved with the limiting criterion of preserving the social and legal good of the public order and public morality.[5] Those principles function as a guarantee of the social common good.

Public order is a commonly accepted principle, but it is hardly clear-cut: offenses to public order range from causing "public alarm" and "disturbing the peace" to outbreaks of violence or the threat of violence against people or property. It protects against disturbance in the exercise of rights, especially those of vulnerable third parties, such as minors. Preserving the security of the state is also a question of public order. This principle protects the public goods of a community's comfort—like social peace—as well as material goods such as public equipment and facilities. Legal measures concerning public order must be reasonable and proportionate, and they can involve incarceration or include arrest with force, if necessary. Lesser measures might lead to the limitation of the itinerary of a rally, a "closure order" or a "removal order." In the context in which we are speaking, indictments are mainly administrative and criminal, and measures are mostly enforced by the police rather than the courts.

According to *The New Oxford Companion to Law*, "Before the development of modern police force, the task of preserving the peace was a function of the Justices of Peace, the Magistrates, who could call where necessary upon the assistance of the military. Since the preservation of public order is now very much the preserve of the police, their powers have been increased considerably in recent years to enable them to undertake this task."[6] The past few decades have seen the rise of a culture of control and a spate of legislation to preserve public order—"the phenomenon which describes how governments seek to use the law to enforce compliance with social norms."[7] Following this trend, there has been a considerable increase in the use of preventive justice measures by courts, the police, and local authorities. Rather than being a principle of general justice, public order "has become, instead, a mechanism of early rather than last resort."[8]

The most recent legal notion of public morality is inherited from eighteenth-century continental Europe for the state's preservation of public order and decorum. William Blackstone defined it in this way in eighteenth-century England: "The individuals of the state, like members of a well-governed family, are bound to conform their general behaviour to the rules of propriety, good neighbourhood, and good manners, and to be decent, industrious, and inoffensive in their respective stations."[9] Nobody doubted that the legitimate purposes of government would include the preservation of public morality.[10] As Louis Henkin goes on say, morality was an assumed legal good: "In truth, the legislation reflected traditional morality, and the preservation of this morality was an unquestionable and unquestioned purpose of government."[11]

The power to regulate public morality was also taken for granted in American law, from its beginnings well into the twentieth century. Along with the prosecution of prostitution as a societal ill, obscenity in the arts was discussed, as was the question of whether drinking or play should be regulated. According to Christopher Wolfe, "Where to draw the line was sometimes unclear, but the power to draw the line was not doubted."[12]

Opposition to the "power to draw the line" and questioning the fundamental principle of the legal regulation of morality are relatively recent. As Santiago Legarre argues, "The modern Court never expressly rejected the validity of moral legislation by way of general principle."[13] Although there has been a change in the American jurisprudence on obscenity since the 1960s,[14] the validity of state legislation regarding social order and morality has remained in force, as has been revealed in recent judgments of the US Supreme Court.[15] The US state governments are still able to regulate public morality in cases in which both of these assumptions occur: immorality is present and it has a relevant impact on the public sphere. It is worthwhile to briefly analyze these two characteristics.

Regarding "morality"—as has been repeated throughout these pages—the criterion by which a behavior is judged immoral is objective. The moral principles that govern human behavior are universal and immutable (human dignity). In this sense, as Valiente Noailles states: "Public morality is not distinct from private morality. Moral sense is one, for the public or for the private. There are public immoralities or private immoralities."[16] The consideration of these objective behaviors on the part of particular individuals or on the part of a social majority constitutes a subjective assessment.[17]

However, as we saw when discussing the tolerance of evil, the public power should prohibit not all vices but only the gravest.[18]

Secondly, the immorality must be "public," as Blackstone explains:

For the end and intent of [human] laws being only to regulate the behaviour of mankind, as they are members of society, and stand in various relations to each other, they have consequently no business or concern with any but social or relative duties. Let a man therefore be ever so abandoned in his principles, or virtuous in his practice, provided he keeps his wickedness to himself, and does not offend against the rules of *public decency*. . . . But if he makes his vices public, though they be such as seem principally to affect himself, (as drunkenness, or the like) they then become, by the bad example they set, of pernicious effects to society; and therefore it is then the business of human laws to correct them. Here the circumstance of publication is what alters the nature of the case.[19]

As Legarre explains, public morality in a positive sense "is a legal good, protected both by the criminalization of certain offensive behaviors and by non-criminal norms that promote their effective validity."[20]

As stated earlier, Aristotle theorized the separation between legality and morality in the law, but in no case did he expel morality from the sphere of the polis. The Aristotelian distinction that I am following makes it possible to differentiate morality, a subjective virtue of the individual of whom just (moral) conduct is required, from objective (legal) justice, which does not regulate the conduct of individuals but defines the principles of general justice, such as public order and public morality. The political space of judgment and the application of those criteria and principles is the terrain of the nation-states: their laws, their political and judicial powers, and so on.

What happened with those two general legal principles? To summarize very briefly, we can say that the principle of public order lent itself to abuse by authority, to the detriment of citizens' freedom of expression. Authoritarian regimes (fascist, communist, totalitarian, and others) took advantage of this principle to control or repress civil liberties. On the other hand, the principle of public morality declined with the advent of legal positivism, which banished morality to the private sphere, and with the imposition of relativism as a doctrine for the public sphere. The concept of freedom as something totally autonomous and independent from any teleology has certainly left a vacuum. As follows from the many cases of the abuse of freedom of expression that have been seen throughout these pages, legalism offers no convincing solutions.

The way we get out of this bottleneck is by recovering the original meaning of those legal principles as a solid basis of law for solving the dilemmas that freedom of expression poses in the public sphere. The legal system already contemplates a large number of the legal limits on freedom of expression: defamation, slander, insult, spread of falsehoods, incitement to violence, obscenity and pornography, intellectual property abuses, and threats to state security.

However, as was said earlier, these limits have been interpreted by jurisprudence without recognizing objective harms. This has led—morally speaking—to a state in which human dignity is not being effectively and fairly protected against *abusive* acts of expression, such as not recognizing an insult, offense, or discrimination against a group based on race, origin, religion, or sexual identity, considering the offense as something impersonal and abstract[21]; reducing the limitations on obscenity to child and hardcore pornography, allowing oppression and abuse on the basis of sex (mainly against women) to accumulate[22]; and understanding incitement to violence only from the physical standpoint, not including psychological violence, therefore protecting discursive acts that involve clear exaltations of discrimination (racial, religious, or sexual).

The Inadequacy of Tech Platforms' Self-Regulation

In this section on legal limits, it is necessary to mention abuse of freedom of expression on the Internet. The abuses of freedom of expression in the public sphere that involved Nazis, Klansmen, and others in the past have moved to the Internet, with new perpetrators: ISIS terrorists displaying their atrocities (beheadings, crucifixions, and so on) or individuals committing hate crimes: torture, murder, or revenge—even live broadcasts of those crimes or their own suicides.[23] As has already been said, the abuses in this medium have particularly serious effects because of the great reach of this technology, but the underlying problem has the same nature as in the face-to-face world. The lack of specific legislation for covering the worldwide web has created a vacuum, but at the same time it is allowing for a debate on the moral foundations for limitations concerning such abuses of online expression.

In the case of online speech, self-regulation is not enough. The regulation of the public conversations of billions of citizens cannot be accomplished by a team of content moderators. These platforms must assume their roles as information fiduciaries, as Jack Balkin and Jonathan Zittrain have stated.[24] It is true that the state must not decide on the ideas or behavior of its citizens, but it must defend the common social good. The social good safeguarded here would be the "democratic debate and deliberation" through the Internet. According to the European Commission, "Disinformation erodes trust in institutions and in digital and traditional media and harms our democracies by hampering the ability of citizens to take informed decisions. It can polarize debates, create or deepen tensions in society and undermine electoral systems, and have a wider impact on European security. It impairs freedom of opinion and expression."[25] The notion of objective harm would help authorities to determine the damage afterward. There is a need to enact a global regulation demanding the subsequent liability of these platforms for their role in spreading disinformation—including misleading or outright false information—as Germany and other European countries are starting to do.

It is important for society and the Internet to be governed by a conception of justice and human dignity that provides security and social peace to all.[26] Christianity has emphasized the concept of the person and his or her human dignity as a creature of God as the ultimate reason for morality. There is also a basic recognition of the person as a member of society. This is the ethical recognition that Hegel calls *sittlichkeit*, which takes place in the community (political society).[27] However, trusting exclusively in government action can easily lead to excesses, as when prime ministers resort to executive decrees as urgent legislative measures of the government, measures that do not go through the prior approval of the chambers. In cases that affect the public order and social peace, governments are entitled to censor content a priori (and restrict some civil liberties), which the judicial order can amend or revoke a posteriori. One example of this type of measure was the one used by the French government after the terrorist attack on *Charlie Hebdo*. A decree was signed whereby websites accused of promoting terrorism and the publication of child pornography could be blocked without a court order.[28] In light of these extraordinary public measures, one can deduce the importance of the separation of powers for the effectiveness of democratic life, since it is the judiciary that determines whether the executive power has been abused.

The spirit that animates the protection of the public good of human dignity (in the face of racism, religious hatred or discrimination based on sexual orientation, human trafficking related to pornography, and so on) is the protection of public order and morality, blocking its manifestations or demanding restitution in the case of a harm already committed. As Jeremy Waldron points out, this position is criticized by some liberal academics, who argue that these laws cause hatred to persist underground.[29] Or, as Kate Coyer suggests, in the case of the German law that requires tech companies to remove hate speech content within twenty-four hours, high fines can lead companies to adopt an attitude of censorship by omission.[30]

The principle of legality provides legal security and reinforces democracy. Moreover, the law has a pedagogical purpose as a model that socially conforms to certain values that, in this case, seek to protect human dignity. However, on the other side of the equation we must consider the danger of legalism and the proliferation of regulations as well as the risk that, due to the dynamic of the democratic process and competing interests, certain ideologies will impose their agendas so that they can be legislated according to their own objectives.

The imperative need to establish a juridical moral and legal framework to moderate content on the Internet offers an opportunity to recover the classic principles of justice and the common good and to take the best of the European and American legal traditions on freedom of expression, joining forces with tech companies to establish and enforce these limits. A system of freedom of expression based on laws that foresee all abuses possible is more sensible for considering the damage caused by expression, but it can also facilitate invasion by the government or ideological interests into individual rights compared with a system that has an absolute protection of freedom, the exceptions to which jurisprudence judges on a case-by-case basis. Weighing the pros and cons of both legal traditions, Madison's intuition that one of the greatest dangers to democracy is the "faction" is better overcome with the American system than with the European.[31]

In addition to recovering the classic principles of public order and public morality, there are two suggestions that would help to resolve some of the legal problems. On one hand, adding the principle of objective harm would help formulate these limits—limits that go along the lines of recognizing the real damage and promoting the respect owed to others— in a framework that is more in line with human dignity. In this respect, pragmatic discourse would help distinguish objectively abusive expressions from the mere disgust and disagreement that result from the diversity of opinions.

In this sense, Waldron points out that perhaps Europe is not entirely wrong in its conviction that we have to safeguard an atmosphere of mutual respect for the law, especially when faced with forms of vicious attacks on dignity (hate speech).[32] In Europe, these protections in the face of racism or xenophobia are considered not violations of individual rights but violations of a law that protects citizens from violence, hostility, and discrimination.[33] Waldron criticizes the abstract defense of the principle of freedom of expression, saying that the issue is not to put the idea in people's heads that "you must defend the speech you hate" but to keep up with the damage caused to individuals and groups.[34] Therefore, it is not about protecting ideas or restricting thoughts of disgust or lack of understanding but about focusing on the damage caused to people and groups when such speech publicly alters the order and social climate.[35]

It is ultimately necessary to consider a common ethos of what is owed to each person.[36] In this sense, it would be important to admit into the juridical-political debate reasons of human ecology that come from the philosophical-theological field. This field's understanding of human action could help determine the intentionality of acts of expression. In this way, we would overcome the vacuum that leads to the dissociation between actions and intentions in which some authors are excused for not responding to acts of expression that in justice demand responsibility. Justice is the central political question, and this would help to foster a paradigm of freedom and responsibility.

JURISPRUDENCE JUDGED CASE BY CASE

Continuing the argument from the previous part and seeking inspiration as to how the law has been understood throughout most of human history, we must recall that the law is not the laws; it is based on jurisprudence.

In this regard, Professor Michel Villey recalls: "In Rome it was the mission of the judge and the jurisconsults to seek legal solutions."[37] These were like priests (ministers) who served justice.[38]

As the Latin root of the word *iuris-prudentia* evokes, it is the science that discerns (act of prudence) what is just and unjust in each case in accordance with the law. The Roman jurist Ulpian defined *iurisprudentia*, the "science of the Law," in these terms: "*Iurisprudentia est divinarum atque humanarum rerum notitia, iusti atque iniusti scientia*" (Jurisprudence is the knowledge of divine and human things, what is just and what is unjust).[39] Some, like Rodolfo Vigo, qualify Villey's position as justicialist reductionism.[40] However, as Robert Post points out, common law peacefully incorporates "norms of citizenship" that are perceived by every reasonable person as an expression of a general level of community morality.[41] The discernment and application of these norms is entrusted to a court of judges or a jury as representatives of the community.[42] The tension between law and custom, between the legal and the socially institutionalized, is a healthy and desirable tension, and jurisprudence is the appropriate context for such a consideration.

Recalling the classical notion of justice — *suum ius cuique tribuendi* (give to each what is his own), and maintaining the distinction between general justice (*dikaiosne*) and particular justice (*dikaios*), we can conclude that jurisprudence (and not an omni-comprehensive list of laws) will be the appropriate path by which justice will be done in the particular case. As one can deduce, the exercise of law proposed in these terms contradicts legal positivism. In this sense, Benedict XVI stressed: "Experience shows that legality often prevails over justice.... When presented purely in terms of legality, rights risk becoming weak propositions divorced from the ethical and rational dimension which is their foundation and their goal."[43]

Modern law equated justice with the law and stripped jurisprudence of its quality as a source of law, making its purpose merely interpretive, as a set of sufficiently concordant decisions. In common law, precedent has a binding authority on subsequent cases issued by inferior jurisdictions about the principles of a judgment.

The distinguishing factor of the administration of justice is precisely that the judges exercise it in judging specific cases in light of what is in accordance with the law. In this way they sanction a posteriori the damages derived from the injurious expression or a priori, in a more restrictive way, they prevent a damage if they believe that such an expression will produce objective harm.

We cannot ignore the fact that in national and international organizations many resources (people and time) are invested in the advancement of legal science for the development of specific regulations. Hannah Arendt attributes this to the fact that modernity shifted the focus from the "what" and the "why" to the "how," so that the process becomes the object and center of the efforts of knowledge.[44] "In the place of the concept of Being we now find the concept of Process," she writes.[45] The insistence on the experimental method extends to all the sciences and to politics and law, making it so that "the means, the production process or development, was more important than the end, the finished product."[46] Ronald Arnett emphasizes Arendt's criticism about efficiency, stressing the need for meaning: "Understanding is more profound that efficiency. . . . We are required to go beyond practices alone and embody them with meaning."[47] The solution of the underlying problems in the processes was sought out, which led to the proliferation of regulations and the bureaucracy. This mechanistic standpoint reversed the meaning of the means and ends. As Arendt writes, "Processes, therefore, and not ideas, the models and shapes of things to be, become the guide for the making and fabricating activities of *homo faber* in the modern age."[48] She concludes: "Fabrication now came to occupy a rank formerly held by political action."[49]

These talent and budgetary resources could be directed toward a more jurisprudential concept of justice, such as the one suggested in these pages. Along with the ordinary jurisdictional system, arbitration or "alternative dispute resolution" has also been implemented to solve extrajudicial conflicts.[50] This "involves an impartial, independent third-party, chosen by the disputants, hearing both sides of a disagreement, then issuing a binding decision to achieve the resolution of the dispute," according to the *Oxford Companion to Law*.[51] Cases in which the prosecutor is required to participate (for example, criminal law cases) cannot be submitted to arbitration because there is a public interest. The "arbitration process is conducted within a legal framework but the process and decision are not as rigidly defined as litigation."[52] The formation of a global arbitration body that overlies the national legal system could eventually integrate and reconcile the different legal systems by playing an important role in conflict resolution. The consensual nature of arbitration and the fact that it is not restricted by borders of territorial sovereignty make it an especially useful tool for legal globalization.[53]

The model of arbitration is found in the history of Rome. In it the parties reach an accord (*compromissum*) and there is an assumption of responsibility on the part of the arbitrator (*receptum arbitri*).[54] In Spain, for example, there is a distinction between arbitration in law and arbitration in equity.[55] The first has a more formal process that is conducted by lawyers and that issues an arbitration award under the law. The second, however, is conducted by experts who are not necessarily lawyers. Arbitration in law would be advisable for conflicts involving freedom of expression because of the dynamics of the matter. As was clear in the case of the *Jyllands-Posten* newspaper, mediation could be effective in certain conflicts, provided that the parties in conflict were willing to submit to the arbitration process (arbitration agreement). In any case, mediation has a limited scope, but it is one suggestion for another way of enforcing the rules of general justice.

CUSTOMARY LIMITS: SELF-LIMITATION AND THE LEGITIMIZATION OF CENSORSHIP IN DIFFERENT FIELDS

Finally, following MacIntyre's notions, we can recall that *diké* basically means the order of the universe, and *dikaios* is the person who respects and does not violate that accepted order.[56] Along with the critical need for the rule of law there are motivations beyond general or particular justice, and these are the reasons that come from the moral nature of the human being, from the principle inscribed in his or her heart: "Do good and avoid evil." The state cannot demand that people demonstrate the moral virtues, but it can encourage them to, and that is why it is relevant to elaborate on them here.

The above-mentioned concept of *sophrosyne* is especially appropriate as a moderation in how objectives are achieved, that is, the quality of knowing how far to go in a specific situation.[57] In order to understand the value of *sophrosyne* as self-limitation, it is useful to draw upon its opposing concept, *pleonexia*, which is the desire for more than one deserves.[58] However, this notion is not protected in modern individualism or utilitarianism, which do not consider greed as a vice, since they do not promote virtue in the public sphere. As MacIntyre explains, *pleonexía* "becomes an instrument of the individual will in grasping after success in satisfying its desires."[59] Thus, moderation in the means employed, as a moral reason, requires the social promotion of a sense of virtue that goes beyond the calculation of interests and utility. It is part of the process of recovering the notion of justice as a virtue, as a human quality.

Ratzinger lamented the disappearance of the category of what is good and evil in itself, as well as the resulting system of weighing advantages and disadvantages. The consequentialist approach leads to the absurdity that certain offenses are protected only if there is a stir. This focus can lead to what Ratzinger calls the "law of the jungle,"[60] because if morality does not deserve the protection of the law because it is considered a subjective preference and is protected only when public and social peace is at risk, then violence and arbitrariness are indirectly promoted.[61]

The message of the speech that Aleksander Solzhenitsyn gave in Liechtenstein in September of 1993 becomes stronger in this context. The Russian author again addressed the issue of morality in politics, resuming the treatment that was in his controversial Harvard Address of 1978.[62] In Liechtenstein he advocated for the moral principle of moderation and self-limitation.[63] Solzhenitsyn strongly affirmed that "self-restraint is the most wise and fundamental step of a man who has obtained his freedom. It is also the safest way to achieve it."[64] At first glance, the idea of limiting oneself in expression goes against, and can even be thought to oppose, the contemporary principle of freedom of speech, which is based on the nearly absolute tolerance of harmful speech. This self-limitation is an attitude that will not easily be accepted by those who hold liberal or libertarian views, who would probably consider this attitude "self-censorship" since they believe that repressing thoughts or expressions is always negative because doing so acts as an inhibitor.

The important thing is to consider the reason behind self-limitation. If the motive is fear or threat, disinterest or inhibition, then it is evident that it is not a positive thing. However, if it is motivated by respect for the other and the subordination of particular interests to universal moral criteria for the sake of the common good, then this moderation does not constitute a threat to freedom of expression but is a virtue and a value — individual and social — that is undoubtedly worth promoting.

Self-limitation operates in the sphere of moral virtues and suggests different areas in which it might be exercised. Robert Post differentiates between "domains" and "boundaries" as limits for preserving social order,[65] and he criticizes the idea that the neutrality of the state based on the individualist approach of the "marketplace of ideas" would also have to extend to the "marketplace of communities,"[66] since there are scandalous speeches that can objectively alter public order at the community level.[67] There are domains or areas in which it is advisable to limit freedom of expression, for example, the educational sphere: the academic field and the family. The limitation of expression (called moderation or censorship) can take on an educational meaning. The goal is to analyze the area in question and review the reasons that support it.

I shall now explore different areas and spaces in which censorship really is exercised as a customary limit to free expression. An example of censorship exercised in the public space took place in a New York City subway train, where some racist and anti-Semitic graffiti appeared one day, quite visible to everyone.[68] Some of the passengers said out loud: "Oh, that is absolutely horrible," and said to a nearby woman, "Do you think there is any way to erase it?" She responded, "Maybe with some hand sanitizer." The initiative of these passengers triggered a generalized collaborative effort to erase the graffiti that filled most of the train cars. In a few minutes, the moral dilemma had been resolved without the use of rules. The reaction of the citizens was eminently moral. In fact, nobody reported the graffiti to the New York Police Department, nor did the Metropolitan Transit Authority have any records in this regard. This type of censorship in the public space can be exercised in view of foreseeable public disturbances, with administrative decisions that may be fallible but necessary for foreseeing damages.

Censorship may also be exercised in familial (natural), religious, and academic communities. Within a family, the main community of life and socialization, censorship is an educational act. Properly justified limitation and privation are noble and necessary resources as long as they are not used arbitrarily and unfairly. Censorship as a private act of educational prudence can be understood as an act of justice when it comes to protecting a good.[69] MacIntyre illustrates this, for example, in the goods of reading that "are only to be achieved through having learned what to read, in what order to read it, and how to read it."[70] Parents and educators exercise this censorship to guide children in the process of human and academic formation in a way that is appropriate for their grades and ages.

Belonging to a religious community is—by its very nature—free association. Thus, the meaning of censorship within a religious group is *eo ipso* "self-censorship" insofar as freely accepting the doctrine includes the acceptance of a doctrinal authority that interprets it.[71] On the other hand, one can always leave a religious group without suffering any harm, unlike a political community, which one cannot leave without prejudice. With this familial (paternal) sense, the old Holy Office (today the Congregation for the Doctrine of the Faith) has censored in the name of the Church for centuries.[72]

The problem of censorship was not that of its legitimacy but that of confusion between the political and religious spheres, which was introduced in the modern era in the confessional nation-states. In this sense, it is important to note that when Paul VI abolished the Index of Forbidden Books,[73] he declared that its mission would endure as a moral force.[74] MacIntyre interprets the Index as a moral guide that helps us to discern the danger posed (to our own thinking and convictions) by reading certain works. This attitude is in stark contrast with the liberal attitude of a freedom with no reference points or restrictions, exercising which, beyond disinhibition, would be irresponsible and to some extent unjust because the criterion for reading is learned from teachers, and the best teachers are parents.[75]

However, MacIntyre distinguishes two types of destructive censorship. The first is that of the "closed mind" that has been programmed or that one has programmed oneself, always responding within a predetermined framework of knowledge and adopting an attitude of resistance and protection toward anything that is not a part of one's mental framework.[76] The author thinks that this mental closure is discovered when there is an "absolute rejection" when one is presented with certain texts or ideas.[77] The other negative effect of censorship is seen in someone who imposes it with outside authority, without further ado. In this case, beliefs that were intended to be protected are often destroyed because those who hold them stop thinking actively or constructively and therefore are unable to deal with any criticism. Thus, "a further effect is to render protected beliefs a desiccated system of thought lacking in liveliness and creativity."[78] So this "good-faith censorship" has worse effects than those it was intended to prevent.

Finally, MacIntyre highlights a pedagogical effect of the Index that sometimes goes unnoticed, which is that of "permission." The necessity of having to formally ask for permission to read these works, according to MacIntyre, made it so that a person intellectually took those authors more seriously and read them critically and carefully. In this sense, the author thinks that "the intellectual life is and ought to be understood as a life of risk-taking and danger."[79] This idea is connected with the position proposed by John Peters, citing St. Paul and Milton, of "courting" the abyss and of the therapeutic and redemptive sense (*felix culpa*) that can be given to evil and transgression.[80] It is understood that the mission of the university has this irreplaceable task: to teach the universality of knowledge in a context of the universality of opinion.

For MacIntyre, the moral force of the Index that must prevail in Catholic believers needs to be framed within this freedom and responsibility that leads to formation: "Read dangerously and be educated through living with that danger, but do not do so before you are well prepared for such dangerous reading."[81] He suggests encouraging the excitement of reading dangerously with this sense of responsibility. This education in reading considers it a necessary part of formation for public discussion.[82]

Finally, there is also de facto censorship in the academic community, and it can be legitimate as long as it is rationally justified. Academic freedom is a fundamental right, linked to the freedom of expression. As Cane and Conaghan write: "Credible universities need institutional autonomy and independence" and must protect the academic freedom and tenure (job security) of academics 'to speak truth to power' for the greater benefit of society."[83] However, since this right is in close relation with rationality and other fundamental rights, it is not unlimited. For example, academic freedom does not include a right to spread falsehoods. In this sense, MacIntyre suggests that someone who publicly demonstrates that he teaches falsehoods should have the privilege of teaching his ideas and his ability to influence students revoked; he should be stripped of the prestige that goes along with teaching, in defense of the common social good.[84] On the other hand, as we saw earlier, the possibility for restoration should be assessed.

Prudential censorship should also be exercised in the media. One example of such censorship was exercised by newspapers in the United States, the United Kingdom, and Canada: despite having more permissive legislation concerning freedom of expression,[85] they did not publish the vignettes of *Jyllands Posten* or *Charlie Hebdo*. Considering that the Anglo-Saxon culture has a long-standing tradition of satire, the refusal to publish these drawings is closely related to the refusal to go beyond satire.[86]

These legal and moral limits on freedom of expression can clash with those who understand freedom as the mere ability to choose, with an unlimited and individualistic meaning. Defending freedom "just because," without accounting for the consequences and abuses that can extend to human dignity and the common good, means, from a theoretical standpoint, abandoning "the full heritage of western liberty."[87] And, from the standpoint of practical morality, it is irresponsible and probably causes an injustice. The unilateral concept of rights, without relation to the human good, worked while there was a common substrate, an ethos with Christian roots that was shared in society. But that is not the case today.

Conclusion

This book is intended to be a recognition of the success of some of the institutions of the classical liberal architects such as Milton, Mill, Locke, and the Founding Fathers of the United States. It is also a criticism of some modern postulates that have proven to be—to continue with the construction metaphor—"defective building material," which jeopardizes the stability of the edifice. Ultimately, I make a proposal for a reconstruction that is based on recovering the legal, philosophical, and moral heritage to which we belong as solid pillars for responding to the challenges that freedom of expression always presents.

This book dares to examine the rational (legal and moral) foundations of freedom of expression from a multidisciplinary perspective. Some readers will understandably think that this leads to more problems than can be solved, but this approach allows us to look at the problem as a whole. Of course, the specialized academic debate about freedom of expression (in the fields of law, history, philosophy, theology, politics, and communication studies) leads to greater precision and erudition, but it also comes with the danger that the discussion will get lost to compartmentalization.

In addition to the fragmentation of knowledge, there is also an abundance of classifications and labels, which are necessarily reductionist.

For example, those who advocate for leaving ample space for freedom of expression and limiting state intervention are opposed to those who emphasize the need to ensure the equality of minorities. In this way, "freedom" is presented as an obstacle to "equality." This causes the proponents of each to be equated with ideological activist groups: the first is the case of white supremacists, and the second is the case of groups making racial or gender claims. In this logic of ideological polarization, it is difficult to maintain a deep and honest discussion of the key issues that affect the philosophy of freedom of expression. This book does not claim to have the final word on this complex debate, but its intention is to open the discussion beyond narrow specialized quarters and direct it toward the underlying roots of manifold discussions.

The tolerance of harmful speech is the key problem of freedom of expression. Classical liberalism holds that authorizing fallible human beings to decide which ideas may be expressed and which are to be suppressed is too risky because, as Madison said, "men are not angels," and they can easily abuse that power. Therefore, it is better not to "delegate" to the government the task of deciding what can and cannot be said, since we all are free.

A sound general legal principle should be applied in this area: each person is free to express himself or herself by any possible means, and no one has to decide for anyone when and how to do it. It is only under exceptional circumstances and with precise legal rules that governments are allowed to prevent something from being said. An example of such an exception is times of war, when the lives and the security of the nation are at stake. Another is whenever public order is at risk, as occurs if fanatics are allowed to fuel public disorder and even put lives at risk through public demonstrations. In the latter case, is it up to the government to decide whether such public demonstrations should be held. The magistrates would need to prove a posteriori if the government's action ultimately constituted an abuse of power.

The general legal limits of public order and public morality have been a shared common boundary. A system based on tolerating a certain degree of evil is uncertain but astute and wise, and it worked well when there was a shared ethical common ground. From the moment that those working for contemporary freedom of speech understood transgression as an end in itself and defended free speech as a "right to offend," as the self-affirmation of the individual, tolerance became a refuge from which to harm others with impunity. Milton, Mill, and the Framers did not consider free speech a weapon to be used to harm others.

EXAMINING THE ORIGIN AND PLANS
OF THE CONSTRUCTION PROJECT

History is a valuable source for refining arguments and putting them into context. The recognition of human rights came from two very different revolutions that wanted to establish political freedoms, which were drawn up in constitutions. As Hannah Arendt notes, the French Revolution was more a liberation from the Old Regime, with sharp anti-clerical tones. The American Revolution, on the other hand, sought to establish freedoms and to create something new. Both traditions diverged not only philosophically but legally. French continental law was based on a broad set of compiled laws of the state that established the rules for the exercise of freedoms, trying not to avoid legal vacuums. The Anglo-American tradition, however, was based on common law and self-government by the citizens, limiting the regulatory power of the state. This has also determined its approach to freedom of expression as a negative right.

The grounding of these political freedoms is an ongoing battle. The shift from an original objective paradigm grounded in natural law to a more subjective paradigm — crafted by Harvard scholars — that is determined by social interests that change with culture and are determined by the state has changed the way Americans think and speak about the First Amendment. This shift has deeply influenced the debate on the foundations of freedom of expression.

When looking at the sources of these foundations and its problems, I have tried to look not only to the historical events such as revolutions or key dates but to the development of the history of ideas. This exercise in analyzing the sources and the evolution of key notions related to freedom of expression helps us to understand further developments. In this sense, the genesis of modern individual liberty is rooted in Protestant thought. Following in the nominalist footsteps of Ockham, Luther separated freedom from its relationship with a natural order and natural ends (telos), and he distrusted the role of human practical reason, which does not discover through its operation the good to be done. Freedom became autonomous and subjective and ultimately a mere choice of the will. This approach to individual freedom is a clue to understanding the journey of individual rights.

The chasms created by distrust in practical reason and the crisis of moral objectivity are filled by a framework of legal and moral positivism. On these grounds, a new authority has granted and continues to grant rights based exclusively in positive law, rejecting natural law as a foundation of rights and duties. The shift to this positivist system of law expanded the list of rights for the sake of granting all desires, thereby becoming a champion of social freedoms. The conflicts between rights were to be solved by a utilitarian calculation. I believe this functional positivist way of reasoning is incomplete and reductive. This is not a parochial argument, and it directly affects the philosophy of freedom of expression and its legal solutions. The Protestant notion of freedom in the public sphere fails to include an important nuance: the distinction between freedom and license, that is, the difference between freedom of expression and the abuse of expression. This is not a moralistic statement but a shift in the idea of political freedoms that is rooted in Ockham and Luther.

In my view, the main pillars of the classical philosophy of free speech are still valid: universal rights grounded in nature, the equal dignity of each human being, the classical notion of tolerance of evil, a secular public sphere with the separation of Church and state, and a society that is governed by laws and is inspired by a realist notion of justice. These pillars are a chain of successful human achievements that belong to different periods of our history, including Greek and Roman philosophy, Roman law, medieval theology, the modern separation of powers, and the universal recognition of human rights, anticipated in the Renaissance by Francisco de Vitoria and formalized with the declarations of rights that came from the liberal revolutions in the United States and France. The Human Rights Project has been a social and cultural accomplishment of the Enlightenment.

The principle of tolerance is key to social life and to the law: for the sake of a greater social good, not all wrongs and evil conduct should be punished. Tolerance has an original link to good (and evil) and to the truth. This solid notion of tolerance is the best guarantee for pluralism and a defense against authoritarian tendencies. This matrix of objective moral bonds allows us to distinguish a legitimate right to satire from its abuse.

At the same time, tolerance means a healthy sense of openness and a willingness to confront evil and error that, as John Peters says, requires "real contact." Transgression in an instrumental sense—as harmful as it may be—can be a catalyst to strengthen life in a democracy. Tolerating evil does not mean being satisfied with evil. However, one cannot pretend to solve this unstable balance by drawing a categorical set of lines or trying to solve all conflicts with rules. This is not a relativistic position but a call to justice (in the realistic sense: give to each what is his own) and to moral growth through prudence (a call to rehabilitate confidence in freedom and practical moral reasoning linked to a natural telos).

The promotion of tolerance advocated by Mill—except for harmful incitement—must be properly presented as it is. Mill's notion of free speech goes together with a claim to fair discussion that is enabled by a strong sense of self-discipline and moderation. Mill did not claim that "anything goes" in the name of free expression. At the same time, his almost absolute openness to discussion does not admit an evaluation that is based on not offending. Again, the unstable liberal equilibrium between tolerance and prudence is sustained by a common cultural ethos (ethical and legal) with Christian roots.

TESTING THE MATERIALS

The main pillars of free expression are still valid. What is shaking up the principle of free speech are the materials with which some of its foundations have been "modernized." The crisis of "truth" that occurred during modernity has had several consequences, including some directly related to speech, such as the merely formal use of words and concepts, as well as the separation of truth, speech, and action from one another.

The notion of freedoms as human goods that must be promoted and protected includes an original harmony between different freedoms. Conflicts between rights are unavoidable, but the need to prioritize rights is different than pitting them against each other, as has been done by setting those who defend free speech in the name of freedom in opposition to those who do it in the name of equality. There was an objective moral foundation of rights that has been removed. When there are no universal foundations, the priorities easily vanish.

Tolerance must not be obscured by permissiveness. This happened in the eighteenth century, when tolerance was reframed as being in opposition to fanaticism—which some people linked to religion and tradition—and was then based on skepticism. This caused a breach with the past because tolerance of evil became like a perpetual carnival in which the rules are permanently suspended.

The anthropological reductionism created by modernity is another important breach that has had significant implications for the whole human condition. The modern promise that autonomous freedom (without internal bonds with truth and goodness) and the assurance of unlimited progress are the keys to a definitive triumph of humanity proved false. The disaster of the two world wars, the perpetuation of social inequalities, and the destruction of the environment are part of the price we are still paying. If the highest value of morality is "achieving the greatest possible happiness for the greatest number of people," how does one ask people to act against their own self-interest? Within a "network of utility" and "personal interest," on what grounds would people be eager to collaborate? This framework of utilitarian subjects who limit each other and are guided by a social contract fosters a third-personal morality—one that comes from the outside—not a morality of virtue, in which the rational morality comes from within (the capacity for objective moral judgement). This scientific morality can only lead to rules of fairness by consensus, which offers no convincing answers to the challenge posed by harmful speech.

The secular public sphere is based on the separation of Church and state and the protection of individual freedoms under the rule of law. This separation must not be confused with antagonism or even hostility. In this sense, I find "pluralism," rather than "neutrality," to be a more accurate term for a liberal public sphere. The former implies appreciation for difference, whereas the latter carries a specific ethical position of intentional indifference and skepticism. The desire to be nondenominational must not be confused with "secularist" because we display our beliefs in all that we do, whether we are practicing Christians or devout atheists. Neutrality is a useful fiction.

A new comprehensive liberalism contradicts the liberal principle of impartiality, imposing a civic moral paradigm. The many anti-discrimination laws promoted by liberal governments are not a simple over-extension of state power; they constitute a true inversion of the liberal paradigm. The growing number of freedoms promised by the social state (to achieve our desires) are secured by law, and in practice this phenomenon leads to an expansion of the law. The state is not only securing freedoms but acting as a liberator. This is part of the risk of solving the problem of hateful speech only with specific laws: the risk that the law will serve the interests of what Madison called "faction."

REBUILDING THE PROJECT WITH THE PROPER MATERIALS

I think that freedom of expression was originally a human good that protected the good of a public, rational, and free debate aimed at achieving knowledge. It was not only about "more speech" but, as Garton Ash says, it was a question of "better speech," and this means working under a set of conditions. It is not enough to have the right to speak; it is also necessary to have the conditions to do it. If not, "freedom of expression" becomes an empty term. Following various authors, I highlight four conditions: access to information, the capacity for criticism, making sure that there is a plurality of voices, and promoting the rationality of the public debate. The current situation, viewed through the lens of these four standards, is not very encouraging. Zeynap Tufecki ironically stated that with the Internet we should be living in the golden age of freedom of expression, but looking at the state of the information on the Internet, it is evident that we are not. The first two conditions are linked to manipulation. At this moment, a huge amount of disinformation impedes many people's basic capacity for judgment. The capacity for criticism depends on a sufficient level of formation to be able follow complex debates — and this is not a given. The plurality of voices is formally granted, but Alexander Meiklejohn's notion that we must ensure that everything important is said does not appear to be the top priority. And finally, our public deliberation should be rational, but the situation here does not look good either. The spread of harmful speech and various kinds of falsehoods calls for a standard that MacIntyre refers to as "intellectual moral integrity." It is about not preventive censorship but liability: if it is proven that someone is spreading false information or hatred through his or her platform, he or she will be punished (sued or fined) a posteriori, according to the degree of damage.

Self-regulation on the part of technological platforms has proven insufficient to safeguard the public conversations of billions of people. The potential of these platforms' technology (artificial intelligence, machine learning) and their role in deciding the public conversation and targeting people require holding them accountable if they jeopardize public deliberation and democracy. The notion of objective harm would help to determine the damage afterward, as well as the resulting crime. We need global regulations to demand subsequent liability from these platforms (as Germany and other European countries are starting to do), for their role in spreading disinformation—including misleading or outright false information.

The protection of freedom of expression as a human good and the protection of public order require regulatory measures of positive justice against troll-army attacks directed at individuals and against information flooding. There also need to be restrictions on the ability of digital platforms to accept money that can influence elections. These platforms are information fiduciaries, and public interest requires them to be transparent and accountable. Some fair information practices should be implemented in the fields of data security or privacy guarantees. In my view, the framework of the General Data Protection Regulation (GDPR) in Europe, now joined by other countries like Japan and more, is a good example of a different way of solving these global problems that focuses on the person and not on state sovereignty. The creation of this kind of common regulation is proving to be an effective way to resolve such issues, mainly because those who have the (technological) power to solve them—the large digital platforms—respond only to legal requirements in the form of large fines.

I suggest that we explore a new paradigm of global law—following Rafael Domingo's proposal—that is inspired by inherited legal traditions: from the Roman *ius gentium*, and the Medieval *ius commune*, and with elements of international law forged in the Enlightenment. The idea of recovering from amnesia regarding our own legal tradition is also echoed by Adrian Vermule. With the Internet, hateful speech is no longer a problem at the level of national governments. The contents of violence, hate, and pornography moderated by digital platforms are inhumane and unfair everywhere. But the public conversation of billions of citizens cannot be decided by nontransparent values and a team of anonymous moderators. The transformation that Domingo proposes is a transition from an international society of nations to a global community that places the person at the center. In this sense, the status of individual rights and their prepolitical foundations could be revisited.

I have emphasized the ideas of Jürgen Habermas and Joseph Ratzinger on the positive role of religion as a moral force: a "community of interpretation" and a source of purpose and meaning in a secular public sphere. In this sense, God is not properly a legal concept but does have legal significance and implications, although the recognition of God does not imply legal protection of his interests. On these grounds I have addressed the question of blasphemy in a secular legal system. For this purpose, history has again been very helpful because it has revealed that—generally speaking—in Greco-Roman antiquity the legal and divine punishments were totally different. There was a clear distinction between sin and crime. The "crime of blasphemy" in the ancient world existed only in the Jewish religion, which had a law to punish it (Lev. 24:16). There was a shift on this view that started in the early period of the Roman Empire, when paganism stopped persecuting Christianity and the protection of human interests began to be mixed with the protection of divine interests. The watershed legal moment came with Justinian (sixth century), who introduced a new law that changed the perspective on blasphemy in the Eastern Christian world. From this moment on, offenses against "respect for God"—blasphemy, apostasy, and the desecration of sacred images—would be criminally punished. Advocating the principle that "the gods will defend themselves alone" is compatible with defending individuals' freedom of religion and effectively tackling the abuse of speech by opportunists.

As for the question of harmful speech (including that against people or groups based on religion, race, or gender), we must rediscover that words—under some circumstances—have the force of actions and can intimidate. The differentiation of the various types of discourse based on purpose is a very useful tool for recognizing some abuses of expression in which speakers or authors are subverting its fair use, as is the case of *The Satanic Verses* or *The Da Vinci Code*, which presented themselves as works of literature when they were actually manipulative pieces of propaganda. This evaluation of the use of expression can enable one to objectively identify fraudulent uses of language (in journalism, politics, cinema, or literature) that can cause objective damage that is not merely emotional. And in that way, insofar as they do real objective damage, they constitute matters of justice. We observe that some hateful expressions are celebrations of offense more than exercises of free speech. Language and information involve not only the locutionary dimension but also the illocutionary dimension,

because the words are really actions, and they also involve the perlocutionary dimension, because some possible effects could be anticipated, as
I have proved in the *Charlie Hebdo* case. French authorities' permissiveness
with the magazine engenders doubt about the government's fulfillment of
its public duty.

Therefore, the principle of freedom of expression should be based not
only on the principle of tolerance (with an objective reference to good and
truth) but also on the principle of objective harm. Throughout these pages
I have proposed a reformulation of Mill's notion of harm based on the development of Raphael Cohen-Almagor that expands on Mill's principle,
better adapting it to the abuses of speech by opportunists who claim a
"right to offend" and extending it to psychological offense when there is an
objective circumstance that makes the damage comparable to an act of
physical aggression. Cohen bases this extension on a set of standards. He
does not, however, see the link between expression and action, which
makes it so that words can constitute incitements and can harm. For
Cohen, the judgment of harm and injustice is reduced to a calculation of
probabilities. Because of the latter, he does not recognize actions as good
or bad "in themselves," and that limits his proposal. To determine objective damage, I suggest using Cohen's extension of the harm principle in
conjunction with the rules of the philosophy of language to identify abusive uses of speech.

Finally, I add the judgment of human action and justice that comes
from moral theology. The acts of expression are actions of the entire human
being, but the distinction made by theology about a choice and its intention is helpful. Both take place in the will because we want to act in the
concrete, in accordance with all the conditions we know. However, in expressive acts we cannot separate voluntary human action from its intent;
we cannot separate the ends from the means since they are united in the
person. To make that objective judgment about the action of harming,
it is also useful to analyze the circumstances, because sometimes they
become — as in the Skokie case — the primary conditions of the actions.
This is very helpful for objectively evaluating hate speech because the condition of race or of being sacred is not mere circumstance but a primary
condition chosen as part of the moral act. Some of these expressive actions, due to their context and conditions, are objectively offensive, and
they demand justice.

This notion of objective harm works as a general principle, like tolerance or justice, and not as a mere rule. Freedom of expression has a complexity that prevents it from being governed by a "system" of rules. It will never be the ultimate solution. But it is not arbitrary either, because it is governed by sound general principles.

Freedom of expression is not incidental to our existence, nor is it only the expression of our thoughts in the public sphere — it is much more. Freedom of expression is what allows us to grow because we are rational beings and our knowledge is limited. To grow we need *disputatio*, confronting all facets that a problem presents, as did medieval theology and as Milton and Mill emphasized. It is from dispute that we learn, we think, and we reflect to see what is true in criticism. And, in the process, we discover what we really think about any issue or question. This is how we grow intellectually and how we become less susceptible to manipulation.

NOTES

INTRODUCTION

1. See Sarah T. Roberts, *Behind the Screen: Content Moderation in the Shadows of Social Media* (New Haven. CT: Yale University Press, 2019), 130.

2. N. F. Johnson, R. Leahy, N. Johnson Restrepo, et al., "Hidden Resilience and Adaptive Dynamics of the Global Online Hate Ecology," *Nature*, August 21, 2019, https://doi.org/10.1038/s41586-019-1494-7.

3. John Durham Peters, preface to *A szakadék szélén: A szólásszabadság és a liberális hagyomány*, Hungarian translation of Peters's *Courting the Abyss: Free Speech and the Liberal Tradition* (Budapest: Wolters Kluwer, 2015).

4. Ibid., 24.

5. Adrian Vermule, *Common Good Constitutionalism* (Cambridge, MA: Polity Press, 2022), 180. Italics added for emphasis.

6. John Durham Peters, "The Liberalism of the Other," *International Journal of Communication* 2 (2008): 703. Peters is responding to a critical review of his book *Courting the Abyss* by Carolyn Marvin. See Marvin's book review at http://ijoc.org/ojs/index.php/ijoc/article/view/304/137.

ONE | I Am Not Charlie Hebdo

1. The full history of the French magazine can be found on its web page. See https://charliehebdo.fr/histoire/. The following is a brief summary of it. In 1960, George Bernier (professor Choron) and François Cavanna started a monthly publication in Paris by the name of *Hara-Kiri*, "journal bête et mechante" [mischievous and silly journal]. In 1961, its publication was forbidden. Publication

resumed in 1964 but was again forbidden in 1966. It reappeared six months later, but half of the staff did not return. In 1969, Cavanna ran the publication and changed it into a weekly (*hebdomadaire*, weekly, hence, *hebdo*), naming it *L'Hébdo Hara-Kiri*. In 1979, because of the cover art of Charles De Gaulle's death, it was forbidden again. Its promoters thought that its release should continue, so they changed the name to *Charlie Hebdo*, using the name of an old publication from 1969, which was called *Charlie Mensuel* [Charlie Monthly]. The name was also a throwback to *Charlie Brown*, the cartoon created by Charles Schultz. In 1981, publication stopped because of a lack of subscriptions, advertising, and sales in kiosks. A new magazine was published in 1982 with the same name and layout, started by Philippe Val and Jean Cabut (Cabu) along with some illustrators of notoriety from the 1970s. It was initially a great success, with 100,000 copies sold of its first edition. The politics of the new magazine were extreme left and antiestablishment. In 2009, Val was dropped from management and Stéphane Charbonier (Charb) took over, continuing the magazine's irreverent editorial tone. Its office was attacked in 2011, resulting in a fire as well as numerous threats and litigation for their offensive material. *Charlie Hebdo* printed 35,000 copies in 2015, at which time its finances were poor due to bad publicity and a reduction in sales.

2. Mike Wendling, "#JeSuisCharlie Creator: Phrase Cannot Be a Trademark," *BBC News*, January 14, 2015, http://www.bbc.com/news/blogs-trending -30797059.

3. See Jessica Guynn, "Twitter: #JeSuisCharlie One of Most Popular Hashtags," *USA Today*, January 9, 2015, https://www.usatoday.com/story/ tech/2015/01/09/jesuischarlie-twitter-hashtag/21511631/.

4. See Fabio Giglietto and Yenn Lee, "A Hashtag Worth a Thousand Words: Discursive Strategies Around #JeNeSuisPasCharlie after the 2015 Charlie Hebdo Shooting," *Social Media + Society* (January–March 2017): 4.

5. Julien Casters, author of the tweet (hashtag) *Je suis Ahmed*, said that the slogan was popular because a good number of Muslims felt stigmatized: "We are Muslims and as such we are also victims of religious fanaticism." The hashtag was used more than 25,000 times. See, for example, BayNews9, "Attack on France Sparks Debate on Free Speech Limits," online editorial, January 10, 2015), https:// www.baynews9.com/fl/tampa/news/2015/1/10/attack_on_france_spa.

6. Giglietto and Lee, "A Hashtag Worth a Thousand Words," 4.

7. See R. Badouard, "Le défi Charlie: Les médias à l'épreuve des attentats," in *Le Défi Charlie: Les médias à l'épreuve des attentats*, ed. P. Lefébure & C. Sécail (Paris: Lemieux éditeur, 2016), 187–220.

8. See Axel Bruns and Stefan Stieglitz, "Towards More Systematic Twitter Analysis: Metrics for Tweeting Activities," *International Journal of Social Research Methodology* 16 (2013): 91–108.

9. Bruns and Stieglitz, "Towards More Systematic Twitter Analysis."

10. See Giglietto and Lee, "A Hashtag Worth a Thousand Words," 4.

11. See Enrique Herrera-Viedma, Juan Bernabé-Moreno, Carlos Porcel Gallego, and María de los Ángeles Martínez Sánchez, "Solidaridad en la redes sociales: Cuando el usuario abandona su zona de confort—El caso de Charlie Hebdo," *ICONO14 Revista Científica de Comunicación y Tecnologías Emergentes* 13, no. 2 (2015): 6.

12. Giglietto and Lee, "A Hashtag Worth a Thousand Words," 11–12.

13. David Brooks, "I Am Not Charlie Hebdo," *New York Times*, January 8, 2015, https://www.nytimes.com/2015/01/09/opinion/david-brooks-i-am-not-charlie-hebdo.html; Roxanne Gay, "If je ne suis pas Charlie, Am I a Bad Person? Nuance Gets Lost in Groupthink," *Guardian*, January 12, 2015, https://www.theguardian.com/commentisfree/2015/jan/12/je-ne-suis-pas-charlie-nuance-groupthink; Robert Shrimsley, "Be Glad Someone Had the Courage to Be Charlie," *Financial Times*, January 8, 2015, https://www.ft.com/content/6ddff0c2-95c4-11e4-a390-00144feabdc0; M. Tarquinio, "Io sono Charlie, eppure non lo sono," *Avvenire*, January 10, 2015, www.avvenire.it; M. Belpietro, "Satira senza limiti: Da Maometto a Benedetto, ce n'è per tutti," *Libero*, January 8, 2015; D. Arasa, "Pardon . . . je ne suis pas Charlie Hebdo," *Forum Libertas*, www.forumlibertas.com.

14. Margaret Sullivan, "A Close Call on Publication of Charlie Hebdo Cartoons," *New York Times*, January 8, 2015, http://publiceditor.blogs.nytimes.com/2015/01/08/charlie-hebdo-cartoon-publication-debate/.

15. For more details, read the article from the *New York Times* editorial page: Sullivan, "A Close Call on Publication of Charlie Hebdo Cartoons."

16. Paul Farhi, "News Organizations Wrestle with Whether to Publish Charlie Hebdo Cartoons after Attack," *Washington Post*, January 7, 2015, https://www.washingtonpost.com.

17. Sullivan, "A Close Call on Publication of Charlie Hebdo Cartoons."

18. Ibid.

19. Farhi, "News Organizations Wrestle with Whether to Publish Charlie Hebdo Cartoons after Attack."

20. Ibid.

21. Roy Greenslade, "Charlie Hebdo Cartoons: Press Strives to Balance Freedom and Responsibility," *Guardian*, January 11, 2015, https://www.theguardian.com.

22. BayNews9, "Attack on France Sparks Debate on Free Speech Limits."

23. Farhi, "News Organizations Wrestle with Whether to Publish Charlie Hebdo Cartoons after Attack."

24. Timothy Garton Ash, "Contra el veto del asesino," January 8, 2015, http://freespeechdebate.com. This appeal was published on January 9, 2015, in ten newspapers, including some important ones, like *El País* (Spain), *La Repubblica*

(Italy), *Gazeta Wyborcza* (Poland), *The Hindu* (India), and in others included in this discussion: *Le Monde* (France) and *The Guardian* (UK).

25. See BayNews9, "Attack on France Sparks Debate on Free Speech Limits."

26. Timothy Garton Ash, "Defying the Assassin's Veto," *New York Review of Books*, February 19, 2015, https://www.nybooks.com/articles/2015/02/19/defying -assassins-veto/.

27. See Aisha Gani, "Charlie Hebdo Attack: Cartoonists Show Solidarity with Paris Victims," *Guardian*, January 7, 2015, https://www.theguardian.com /world/2015/jan/07/charlie-hebdo-attack-cartoonists-show-solidarity-victims.

28. Joe Sacco, "Joe Sacco: On Satire—A Response to the Charlie Hebdo Attacks," *Guardian*, January 9, 2015, https://www.theguardian.com/world/ng -interactive/2015/jan/09/joe-sacco-on-satire-a-response-to-the-attacks.

29. Ibid.

30. Latuff's drawing was composed of two frames. In the first one, a man flying with angels' wings formed by the words *Freedom of speech* held a copy of *Charlie Hebdo* in his hand that read *Mohamed! Mohamed! Mohamed!*, and in the second frame, a concrete weight with a flag and the words "Anti-Semitism" painted on it crushed the man flying with the free speech wings. In the second frame this same man had a "Free Palestine" flag in his hand. See https://twitter. com/LatuffCartoons/status/555707463669149696.

31. Amos Guiora, "To Fear Offense or Reprisals Is to Surrender Our Values," *New York Times*, July 15, 2016, https://www.nytimes.com/roomfor debate/2015/01/10/when-satire-cuts-both-ways/to-fear-offense-or-reprisals-is -to-surrender-our-values.

32. Paul Cliteur, "Terror Has Already Led to Self-Restraint," *New York Times*, January 13, 2015, https://www.nytimes.com/roomfordebate/2015/01/10 /when-satire-cuts-both-ways/terror-has-already-led-to-self-restaint.

33. See Roy Greenslade, "Charlie Hebdo Cartoons: Press Strives to Balance Freedom and Responsibility," *Guardian*, January 11, 2015, https://www .theguardian.com.

34. Chris Boffey, "Charlie Hebdo: Why Won't British Newspapers Publish the Cartoons?," *Drum*, January 9, 2015, https://www.thedrum.com/opinion /2015/01/09/charlie-hebdo-why-wont-british-newspapers-publish-cartoons.

35. Glenn Greenwald, twitter post, January 8, 2015.

36. See Christopher Booker, "What 'Free Speech' Didn't Tell Us about Charlie Hebdo Jokes," *Telegraph*, January 17, 2015, https://www.telegraph.co.uk /comment/11352488/What-free-speech-didnt-tell-usabout-Charlie-Hebdo -jokes.html.

37. In a speech given in Evry, in the north of France, Manuel Valls said: "They're attacking emblems, emblems of France: the freedom to express oneself,

to say your opinion, to characterize." He finished with a call to "love for liberty and tolerance." *La Información*, "Valls llama a ser 'implacables con los enemigos de la libertad,'" January 10, 2015, https://www.lainformacion.com/espana/valls -llama-a-ser-implacables-con-los-enemigos-de-la-libertad_8XQqgHGI8r8U qfa6FNCwQ4/.

38. See Ignacio Aréchaga, "Charlie Hebdo: La solidaridad y la crítica," *Aceprensa service* no. 06/15, January 9, 2015.

39. Álvaro d'Ors, *Derecho y Sentido Común* (Madrid: Civitas, 2001), 29. Translation is mine.

40. G. K. Chesterton, *Illustrated London News*, October 23, 1909. Available at the website of the Society of G. K. Chesterton: https://www.chesterton.org/.

41. A. B. Kernan. "Satire," in *Dictionary of the History of Ideas*, edited by P. P. Weiner, vol. 4. New York: Charles Scribner's Sons, 1973, 212. See http://xtf.lib .virginia.edu/xtf/view?docId=DicHist/uvaGenText/tei/DicHist4.xml&chunk .id=dv4-29&toc.id=dv4-29&brand=default;query=212.

42. Ibid., 214.

TWO The Paradox of Freedom of Expression on Campus

1. Source: Pew Research Center, Spring 2015 Global Attitudes Survey, Q30a–e. To check the details for all countries, see Pew Research Center, "Global Support for Principle of Free Expression, but Opposition to Some Forms of Speech," November 2015, 19, https://www.pewresearch.org/global/2015/11/18 /global-support-for-principle-of-free-expression-but-opposition-to-some-forms -of-speech/.

2. See Jordi Pujol, "The United States Safe Space Campus Controversy and the Paradox of Freedom of Speech," *Church, Communication and Culture*, October 27, 2016, 1–15, https://doi.org/10.1080/23753234.2016.1234124.

3. Knight Foundation-Ipsos, *Free Expression in America Post-2020: A Landmark Survey of Americans' Views on Speech Rights*, January 6, 2022, p. 32, Q7-12, available at https://knightfoundation.org/wp-content/uploads/2022/01/KF _Free_Expression_2022.pdf.

4. Judith Shulevitz, "'Infantilized' College Students Need 'Safe Spaces' to Avoid Scary Free Speech," *New York Times*, March 21, 2015, http://www.nytimes. com/2015/03/22/opinion/sunday/judith-shulevitz-hiding-from-scary-ideas .html.

5. See Erwin Chemerinsky and Howard Gilman, *Free Speech on Campus* (New Haven, CT: Yale University Press, 2017), 1–17.

6. See Shulevitz, "'Infantilized' College Students Need 'Safe Spaces' to Avoid Scary Free Speech."

7. At the same time, these students justify insults to some religions but not others because Christianity is seen as "privileged" in Western culture, which results in a double standard.

8. In the new campus lexicon, a "safe space" is "a room, offering a place of refuge, where students feel they can talk safely without fear of micro-aggression." See Ruth Sherlock, "How Political Correctness Rules in America's Student 'Safe Spaces,'" *Telegraph*, November 28, 2015, http://www.telegraph.co.uk/news/world news/northamerica/usa/12022041/How-political-correctness-rules-in-Americas -student-safe-spaces.html.

9. See Peter Wright, "Problematic: The Battle for Free Speech," *Harvard Political Review*, June 12, 2015, http://harvardpolitics.com/harvard/problematic -battle-free-speech.

10. See Javier Espinoza and Gordon Rayner, "Politically Correct Universities 'Are Killing Free Speech,'" *Telegraph*, December 18, 2015, http://www.telegraph .co.uk/education/educationnews/12059161/Politically-correct-universities -are-killing-free-speech.html; Ruth Sherlock, "How Political Correctness Rules in America's Student 'Safe Spaces,'" *Telegraph*, November 28, 2015, http://www .telegraph.co.uk/news/worldnews/northamerica/usa/12022041/How-political -correctness-rules-in-Americas-student-safe-spaces.html; Sarkis Zeronian, "Aca-demics Warn Politically Correct Universities 'Are Killing Free Speech' with Cen-sorship," *Breitbart News Network*, December 19, 2015, http://www.breitbart.com /london/2015/12/19/academics-warn-politically-correct-universities-killing -free-speech-censorship/.

11. See Espinoza and Rayner, "Politically Correct Universities 'Are Killing Free Speech.'"

12. In the 1980s, a school of critical thinkers came out against absolute free-dom of expression. They put together a series of articles on what they called assaul-tive speech that denounced the use of words as weapons to hurt, humiliate, or de-grade. These thinkers established a direct link between offensive speech and racial exclusion in schools, on college campuses, and in other social structures. In turn, they criticized some of the liberal foundations of free speech, such as the neutrality and objectivity of the state and the distinction between public and private for an offense that supposedly was possible only in the private sphere. They also argued that impersonality in the public domain is a "refuge" for offenders. Mari J. Matsuda, Richard Delgado, Charles R. Lawrence III, and Kimberlè Williams, *Words That Wound: Critical Race Theory, Assaultive Speech, and the First Amendment* (Boulder, CO: Westview Press, 1993). In particular, Matsuda took part in the debate about safe spaces and argued that students in college should not be victims of "violence of the word" because many of them "are away from home for the first time and are in a vulnerable period of psychological development." Shulevitz, "'Infantilized' Col-lege Students Need 'Safe Spaces' to Avoid Scary Free Speech."

13. Public universities are also allowed to impose "reasonable regulations compatible with that mission [education] upon the use of its campus and facilities." *Widmar v. Vincent*, 454 US 263, 268 no. 5 (1981).

14. Robert C. Post, "The Classic First Amendment Tradition under Stress," in *The Free Speech Century*, edited by Lee C. Bollinger and Geoffrey S. Stone (New York: Oxford University Press, 2019), 113.

15. See Post, "The Classic First Amendment Tradition under Stress," 116–17.

16. Ibid.

17. John Henry Newman, *The Idea of a University Defined and Illustrated* (London: Longmans, Green, 1888), xvi.

18. Robert P. George and Cornell West, "Truth Seeking, Democracy, and Freedom of Thought and Expression—A Statement by Robert P. George and Cornel West," James Madison Program, March 14, 2017, https://jmp.princeton.edu/statement.

19. Stanley Kurtz, "A Plan to Restore Free Speech on Campus," *National Review*, December 7, 2015, http://www.nationalreview.com/corner/428122/plan-restore-free-speech-campus-stanley-kurtz.

20. Jonathan R. Cole, a professor at Columbia University, has written two pieces that deal with the reports and explain their context: Jonathan R. Cole, *The Great American University: Its Rise to Preeminence, Its Indispensable National Role, Why It Must be Protected* (New York: Public Affairs, 2009), and Jonathan R. Cole, *Who's Afraid of Academic Freedom?*, edited by Akeel Bilgrami (New York: Columbia University Press, 2015).

21. At the University of Chicago, President Beadle created a faculty committee, of which Harry Kalven was the chairman, to prepare a statement about the university's role in political and social action. The result was the reaffirmation of some principles related to the mission of the university: truth-seeking, critical thinking, freedom of inquiry, and so on, far from political battles and lobbying. Therefore, the university as an institution is neutral and does not have a collective position. See www.uchicago.edu/KalvenRprt.pdf.

22. At Yale University in 1974–75, there were heated debates about race and war that divided students and faculty. The administrators settled on a collection of principles to support protest and counter-protest in a document known as the Woodward Report. See www.yalecollege.yale.edu/report-committee-freedom-expression-yale. For further information on the context, see Edwin Oviatt, *The Beginnings of Yale (1701–1726)* (New Haven, CT: Yale University Press, 1916).

23. Geoffrey R. Stone et al., "Report of the Committee on Freedom of Expression," University of Chicago, January 6, 2015, www.provost.uchicago.edu/FOE CommitteeReport.pdf. At the end of 2014, as a response to the growing climate of censorship by students, the rector of the University of Chicago commissioned a

group of experts to prepare a statement, which was published in January 2015. This document follows the track of the Kalven Report (1967) in favor of freedom of expression. Throughout 2015, other universities joined the Chicago Statement. The FIRE platform (civil rights in education lobby) echoed this view in its 2015 annual report, which evaluates more than four hundred universities.

24. John Palfrey and Urs Gasser, *Born Digital*, rev. ed. (New York: Basic Books, 2016), 245–46.

25. Some works that can help us to properly characterize this generation of students are the following: Christian Smith, "Grasping the Big Sociological Picture Shaping the Moral Lives of College Students Today," *Journal of College & Character* 13, no. 3 (2012): 1–9; Rob Beamish, *The Promise of Sociology: The Classical Tradition and Contemporary Society* (Toronto: University of Toronto Press, 2010); Michael D. Coomes and Robert DeBard, eds., *Serving the Millennial Generation: New Directions for Student Services* (San Francisco: Jossey-Bass, 2004), chaps. 2–3. The Pew Research Center also offers some data about this student generation at http://www.pewsocialtrends.org/2014/03/07/millennials-in-adulthood/.

26. Gallup, Knight Foundation, et al., "Free Expression on Campus: What College Students Think about First Amendment Issues," 2018, 7–8, https://www.knightfoundation.org/reports/free-expression-on-campus-what-college-students-think-about-first-amendment-issues.

27. Gallup et al., "Free Expression on Campus," 10–11.

28. Ibid., 12–14.

29. Ibid., 9.

30. See ibid., 12.

31. Gallup et al., "Free Expression on Campus," 22.

32. See ibid., 21–22.

33. See ibid., 23–27.

34. Voltaire was aware of many of the works about political tolerance that came before him, and they undoubtedly had a deep influence on his *Treatise on Tolerance* (1763). See also Michel de Montaigne, *Essays*, 2nd Book, tract XIX (1580); Baruch Spinoza, *Tractatus Theologico-Politicus* (1670); and John Locke, *Epistola de Tolerantia* (1689), among others.

35. The link between democracy and relativism comes from Hans Kelsen, *On the Essence and Value of Democracy*, originally published as *Vom Wesen und Wert der Demokratie* (Tubingen: Mohr, 1929; reprint Aalen: Scientia, 1963). See also his *General Theory of Law and State* (Cambridge: Harvard University Press, 1945).

36. Aristotle raises the question of the "lesser evil" in the context of justice: "The lesser evil is preferable to a greater evil." See Aristotle, *Nicomachean Ethics*, Book 5, chap. 5. St. Augustine's treaty *On Order* holds the view that it is fitting that those who govern tolerate certain evils that are reasonable so that other goods will be protected or to avoid greater evils. See Augustine, *On Order* (*De ordine*),

Book 2 (South Bend, IN: St. Augustine's Press, 2007), chap. 4, 63. In the same sense, Aquinas speaks about tolerating the rights of nonbelievers: "Accordingly, in human government also, those who are the authority, rightly tolerate certain evils, lest certain goods be lost, or certain greater evils be incurred." Aquinas, *Summa Theologiae* II-II, q. 10, a. 11 c. See also Aquinas, *Summa Theologiae* I-II, q. 101, a. 3 ad 2.

37. The Roman Catholic Church teaches that the duty to prevent evil "is not absolute and unconditional." See Pius XII, *Discourse "Ci riesce,"* December 6, 1953, available in English at https://www.ewtn.com/catholicism/library/ci-riesce-8948; John Paul II, *Veritatis splendor,* encyclical letter, August 6, 1993, no. 52, Vatican website, http://www.vatican.va/content/john-paul-ii/en/encyclicals/documents/hf_jp-ii_enc_06081993_veritatis-splendor.html. Tolerance is based on the relationship between a hierarchy of goods (individual and common goods).

38. John Milton, "Areopagitica and Other Tracts: A Speech for the Liberty of Unlicensed Printing, to the Parliament of England," November 23, 1644, in *J. Milton Complete Poems and Major Prose,* edited by Merritt Y. Hughes (New York: Odyssey Press 1957). Milton also advanced the same idea in the epic poem *Paradise Lost* (1667).

39. For a complete explanation of the meaning and background of this expression, see Willmoore Kendall, "How to Read Milton's Areopagitica," *Journal of Politics* 22 (1960): 462.

40. For a complete explanation of the meaning of this expression on Truth, see Kendall, "How to Read Milton's Areopagitica," 449–53.

41. See Vincent Blasi, "Free Speech and Good Character: From Milton to Brandeis to the Present," in *Eternally Vigilant: Free Speech in the Modern Era,* edited by Lee C. Bollinger and Geoffrey R. Stone (Chicago: University of Chicago Press, 2002).

42. Lee C. Bollinger, *The Tolerant Society: Freedom of Speech and Extremist Speech in America* (New York: Oxford University Press, 1986), 60–62.

43. See Matsuda et al., *Words That Wound.*

44. Matsuda et al., *Words That Wound.*

THREE The Threat of Religious Fanaticism

1. See Flemming Rose, "Muhammeds ansigt," *Jyllands-Posten,* September 29, 2005, https://jyllands-posten.dk/indland/ECE4769352/Muhammeds-ansigt/.

2. The French magazine *Charlie Hebdo* benefited from the crisis by increasing its sales, publishing the drawings and adding new ones. Twelve major cultural players (Bernard-Henri Lévy, Philippe Val, and Salman Rushdie, among others) published a manifesto titled "A Call for Freedom: United Front against the New Totalitarianism."

3. See *El Mundo* (newspaper), "EEUU y Reino Unido arremeten contra la publicación de las 'ofensivas' caricaturas de Mahoma," *El Mundo*, February 8, 2006, http://www.elmundo.es/elmundo/2006/02/03/internacional/1138994425.html.

4. Hjörtur J. Guðmundsson, "Danish Imams Propose to End Cartoon Dispute," *Brussels Journal*, January 22, 2006, https://www.brusselsjournal.com/node/698.

5. Hjörtur J. Guðmundsson, "Danish Paper Apologizes: Dutch Cartoon on Its Way," *Brussels Journal*, January 31, 2006, https://www.brusselsjournal.com/node/736. For more information, see Paul Belien, "The Cartoon Hoax," *Brussels Journal*, July 2, 2006, https://www.brusselsjournal.com/node/775.

6. See Flemming Rose, "Why I Published Those Cartoons," *Washington Post*, February 19, 2006, https://www.washingtonpost.com/archive/opinions/2006/02/19/why-i-published-those-cartoons/f9a67368-4641-4fa7-b71f-843ea44814ef/.

7. See Alasdair MacIntyre, "Intolerance, Censorship, and Other Requirements of Rationality," Philip Quinn Lecture, University of Notre Dame, South Bend, IN, 2009, 12. On the debate in Denmark about integration and preserving national cultural unity, see Kasper Støvring, "The Turn from Cultural Radicalism to National Conservatism: Cultural Policy in Denmark," *Telos* 148 (Fall 2009): 54–72.

8. Elisabeth Eide, Risto Kunelius, and Angela Phillips, *Transnational Media Events: The Mohammed Cartoons and the Imagined Clash of Civilizations* (Gothenburg: Nordicom, 2008); Lene Hansen, "Theorizing the Image for Security Studies: Visual Securitization and the Muhammad Cartoon Crisis," *European Journal of International Relations* 17, no. 1 (2011): 51–74; Signe Kjær Jørgensen, "Not Just Any Order! Revealing Identity Constructions of Muslims in the Mohammad Cartoons," *Journal of Language and Politics* 11, no. 3 (2012): 382–404; Frauke Miera and Valerie Sala Pala, "The Construction of Islam as a Public Issue in Western European Countries through the Prism of the Muhammad Cartoons Controversy: A Comparison between France and Germany," *Ethnicities* 9, no. 3 (2009): 383–408; Marion G. Müller and Esra Özcan, "The Political Iconography of Muhammad Cartoons: Understanding Cultural Conflict and Political Action," *Political Studies* 40 (2007): 287–91. Jesper Strömbäck, Adam Shehata, and Daniela V. Dimitrova, "Framing the Mohammad Cartoons Issue: A Cross-Cultural Comparison of Swedish and US Press," *Global Media and Communication* 4, no. 2 (2008): 117–38.

9. See John K. Locke, "Some Reflexions on the Phenomenon of Fundamentalism," *Vidyajyoti Journal of Theological Reflection* 55 (1991): 243–44; Robert Spaemann, "¿Qué es el fundamentalismo? Miseria y necesidad de la intolerancia," *Atlántida* (June–September 1992): 107; John Coleman, "El fundamentalismo en su globalidad: Perspectivas sociológicas," *Concilium* 3 (1992): 437.

10. See M. Guerra, *Fanatismo*, in *GER* (Madrid: Rialp, 1987), VI, 731.

11. Francis, "In-Flight Press Conference from the Central African Republic to Rome," November 30, 2015, Vatican website, http://w2.vatican.va/content/francesco/en/speeches/2015/november/documents/papa-francesco_20151130_repubblica-centrafricana-conferenza-stampa.html.

12. See John Paul II, *Fides et Ratio*, encyclical letter (Vatican City: Libreria Editrice Vaticana, 1998); Benedict XVI, Regensburg Lecture, September 12, 2006, Vatican website, http://www.vatican.va/content/benedict-xvi/en/speeches/2006/september/documents/hf_ben-xvi_spe_20060912_university-regensburg.html.

13. See Jordi Pujol and Vicenzo Arborea, "La leadership strategica di Papa Francesco nel dialogo interreligioso: Il rapporto con l'Islam dopo le strage terroristiche," in *Actas X Convegno Facoltà Comunicazione* (Rome: Edizioni Santa Croce, 2017).

14. Benedict XVI, "Message for the XLIV World Day of Peace (2011)," January 1, 2011, Vatican website, http://www.vatican.va/content/benedict-xvi/en/messages/peace/documents/hf_ben-xvi_mes_20101208_xliv-world-day-peace.html, no. 7: "Fanaticism, fundamentalism, practices contrary to human dignity, are never justified, and even less so when they take place in the name of religion. Religious profession cannot be the tool of or impose force. It's necessary, then, that countries and human communities don't forget that religious freedom is a condition for seeking truth and that truth doesn't impose itself with violence but by 'the force of that very truth.' (*Dignitatis humanae*, on religious freedom, n. 1). In this vein, religion is a positive force that promotes and constructs civil and political society."

15. These are some of the critical reactions that came from the press: "Ambassador Recalled over Pope Row," *Agence France-Presse*, November 17, 2006; "Pope Urged to Retract Islam Remarks," *Al Jazeera*, November 17, 2006; "Somali Cleric Calls for Pope's Death," *The Age*, November 17, 2006; "Guardian Council Condemns Pope's Anti-Islam Statement," *Islamic Republic News Agency*, November 17, 2006.

16. Jeremy D. Kryn, *The Regensburg Lecture and the November 2006 Papal Visit to Turkey: An Analysis of Major British and American Media Coverage, pro manuscripto*, graduate thesis (Rome: Pontifical University of Santa Croce, 2007).

17. Two British and two American outlets were selected. In each group, one was web-based and the other print-based. The English ones were BBC News Web and the *Guardian*, and the American ones were the CNN website and the *New York Times*.

18. See Haaretz Service, "Rome Tightens Pope's Security after Fury over Islam Remarks," *Haaretz*, September 16, 2006, https://www.haaretz.com/1.4866100.

19. See "Turk Workers Urge Pope's Arrest," *CNN*, September 19, 2006.

20. See "Five Churches Bombed and Attacked," Associated Press, September 16, 2006.

21. See "Al-Qaeda Threatens Jihad over Pope's Remarks," *The Times*, September 17, 2006; "LET Issues Fatwa to Kill the Pope," http://www.saag.org /papers20/paper1974.html; "The Pope Must Die, Says Muslim," *Daily Mail*, September 18, 2006.

22. See Kryn, *The Regensburg Lecture*, 12; "Somalia Islamists Vow to Punish Nun's Killers," *Gulf News*, September 19, 2006, www.gulfnews.com.

23. "Somalia Islamists Vow to Punish Nun's Killers."

24. On October 12, some 38 Muslim clerics and academics published an open letter in response to Pope Benedict's Regensburg Address. The Grand Mufti of Egypt, along with Russia, Bosnia, Croatia, Serbia, Turkey, Uzbekistan, and Oman, as well as clerics and academics from Asia, Africa, Europe, and North America, accepted the Pope's apologies, especially because of his affirmation that the passage at issue did not reflect his personal opinion. In this open letter, these religious and academic authorities also responded to other questions raised by the Regensburg discussion, such as those about forced conversion, "jihad," and the relationship between Christianity and Islam. See "Muslim Clerics Reach Out to Pope," *BBC News*, October 14, 2006.

25. See Ian Fisher, "Pope Calls West Divorced from Faith, Adding a Blunt Footnote on Jihad," *New York Times*, September 13, 2006, https://www.nytimes.com /2006/09/13/world/europe/13pope.html. Fisher suggests in this article that the Regensburg discussion could anger Muslims, but he also quotes Vatican official Marco Politi, who affirmed that the Regensburg Conference was an example of Pope Benedict's open attitude toward dialogue with Muslims. Fisher's second article, two days later, was "Pope Faces Crisis as Muslim Outcry Grows," *New York Times*, September 15, 2006.

26. In an interview with the Vatican's *Sala Stampa*, Father Lombardi said that in handing over the prohibited text on September 12, 2006, the journalists had asked him some questions about the afternoon's discussion and that he had highlighted how the intent of these paragraphs wasn't to criticize Islam, but he did not say anything more. Personal interview of Father Federico Lombardi by the author, January 5, 2007. See Kryn, *The Regensburg Lecture*, 43: "Loro mi hanno fatto alcune domande sul discorso del pomeriggio di Regensburg ed io ho dato la mia interpretazione del senso delle finalità di questo discorso. Questo è quello che è venuto." Benedict XVI definitively cleared any doubt about this in his interview with Seewald for his book when he was asked if it was true that Cardinal Sodano had warned him of the explosive nature of the text. Benedict answered flatly: "No, no one said anything about it." Peter Seewald, Benedict XVI, *Últimas conversaciones* (Bilbao: Mensajero, 2016), 243.

27. Kryn, *The Regensburg Lecture*, 49.

28. Benedict XVI, "Message for the XLIV Word Day of Peace (2011)," no. 8.

29. Boo shows that the figures on victims includes more Muslims than non-Muslims. "The number of 'terrorists' or combatants killed hovers be-

tween 65,000 and 90,000. The problem is that the number of civilians — men, women, children and elderly — killed in their houses by bombs is around a quarter to a half a million, or more, according to other sources. It's not easy to calculate the numbers, but, according to the Iraq Body Count Project, the death of civilians in that country from 2003 to 2012 is between 111,000 and 121,000. For its part, the American agency Associated Press, which covered the conflict thoroughly, estimates a total of 110,000 deaths in six years between 2003 and 2009, inclusive. The number of victims in Afghanistan is even more difficult to calculate, with estimates that run between 11,000 and 240,000. Add to this Somalia, Pakistan. . . . All of this during the first decade of the 21st century." J. V. Boo, *El papa de la alegría* (Barcelona: Espasa Libros, 2016), 227.

30. Francis, "Speech to the Diplomatic Corps," January 15, 2015, Vatican website, www.vatican.va.

31. See Samuel P. Huntington, *The Clash of Civilizations and the Remaking of World Order* (New York: Simon & Schuster, 1996). Spanish edition: *El choque de civilizaciones y la reconfiguración del orden mundia* (Ediciones Paidós, 2005), 10: "My conjecture is that the fundamental source of the conflict in the new world we inhabit is one that will be essentially ideological or economic. The big divisions between humanity and the principal source of conflicts will be related to culture. Nation-states will continue being the principal actors on the global stage, but the most important conflicts will occur between nations and groups from different civilizations. The clash between civilizations will dominate world politics. The fracture lines between civilizations will be tomorrow's battle lines."

32. The Beirut Declaration on religious freedom of June 20, 2015, is an important document for the Islamic world, as much for its content as for the place where it was developed: the University of Makassed. See Fady Noun, "Islamic Makassed Launch Doctrinal Battle against Muslim Extremism," *Asia News*, August 22, 2015, www.asianews.it. There are other articles that examine this: Aceprensa, "Intelectuales suníes publican una declaración sobre la libertad religiosa," January 9, 2015, www.aceprensa.com, and "El terror yihadista y la crisis interna del islam," November 27, 2015, www.aceprensa.com.

33. Noun, "Islamic Makassed Launch Doctrinal Battle against Muslim Extremism."

34. See Fady Noun, "Muftí de Egipto, Líbano y Jordania: Un frente común frente al extremismo religioso y el terrorismo," *Asia News*, December 24, 2015, www.asianews.it.

35. Ibid.

36. Noun, "Islamic Makassed Launch Doctrinal Battle against Muslim Extremism."

FOUR   The Rise of a New Orthodoxy

1. Colorado Court of Appeals, *Charlie Craig and David Mullins v. Masterpiece Cakeshop, Inc., and Jack C. Phillips*, case no. 2014CA1351, date filed August 13, 2015, section "Background," pp. 1–2, https://www.aclu.org/sites/default/files /field_document/craig_v_masterpiece_opinion_81315.pdf.

2. *Masterpiece Cakeshop v. Colorado Civil Rights Commission*, 584 US 4, https://www.supremecourt.gov/opinions/17pdf/16-111_j4el.pdf.

3. *Masterpiece Cakeshop v. Colorado Civil Rights Commission*.

4. Under the Colorado Anti-Discrimination Act, the state places a prohibition on discrimination in places of public accommodation: "It is a discriminatory practice and unlawful for a person, directly or indirectly, to refuse, withhold from, or deny to an individual or a group, because of disability, race, creed, color, sex, sexual orientation, marital status, national origin, or ancestry, the full and equal enjoyment of the goods, services, facilities, privileges, advantages, or accommodations of a place of public accommodation." Colorado Anti-Discrimination Act (CADA), §§ 24-34-601 (2), C.R.S. 2014.

5. See *Masterpiece Cakeshop v. Colorado Civil Rights Commission, Global Freedom of Expression Columbia University*, case no. 16-111, section "Case Analysis: Facts," https://globalfreedomofexpression.columbia.edu/cases/masterpiece -cakeshop-v-craig/.

6. *Masterpiece Cakeshop v. Colorado Civil Rights Commission*, section "Decision Overview."

7. *Masterpiece Cakeshop v. Colorado Civil Rights Commission*, 584 US 12 (2018).

8. Ibid.

9. Ibid., pp. 12–13.

10. Ibid., p. 13.

11. Ibid., p. 12.

12. Ibid., p. 14. Kennedy adds: "This sentiment is inappropriate for a Commission charged with the solemn responsibility of fair and neutral enforcement of Colorado's anti-discrimination law—a law that protects discrimination on the basis of religion as well as sexual orientation." The record shows no objection to these comments from other commissioners, or further reviews, so the Supreme Court ruled that there had been a lack of fairness and impartiality by the Commission in the Phillips case.

13. *Masterpiece Cakeshop v. Colorado Civil Rights Commission*, 584 US 22 (2018).

14. Ibid., 16.

15. Ibid., 17.

16. Ibid., 30.

17. Brief for the Cato Institute et al., *Reason Foundation, and Individual Rights Foundation as Amici Curiae in Support of Petitioners* (Colorado Civil Rights Commission, Charlie Craig, and David Mullins).

18. Ibid., 2.

19. Peter Tatchell, "I've Changed My Mind on the Gay Cake Row: Here's Why," *Guardian*, February 1, 2016, https://www.theguardian.com/commentis free/2016/feb/01/gay-cake-row-i-changed-my-mind-ashers-bakery-freedom-of -conscience-religion.

20. Ibid.

21. Ibid.

22. ECHR, *Lee v. United Kingdom*, Application no. 18860/19, January 6, 2022, n. 36, available at https://hudoc.echr.coe.int/eng#{%22itemid%22:[%22001 -214966%22]}.

23. "Gay Cake Conviction Must Be Overturned," *Telegraph*, February 2, 2016.

24. There were 72 professors out of 3,300 who co-signed the manifesto. See M. Cini, "Se la Sapienza chiama il papa e lascia a casa Mussi: Lettera aperta," *Il Manifesto*, November 14, 2007, http://www.flcgil.it/rassegna-stampa/nazionale /manifesto-se-la-sapienza-chiama-il-papa-e-lascia-a-casa-mussi.flc. See also "Un evento incongruo da annullare"'La lettera dei docenti contro Ratzinger,'" *La Repubblica*, January 14, 2008, http://www.repubblica.it/2007/12/sezioni/esteri/benedet toxvi-18/testo-della-lettera/testo-della-lettera.html.

25. Benedict XVI, *Speech Prepared by Holy Father Benedict XVI for Presentation at the University of Rome La Sapienza, Vatican City*, January 17, 2008, Vatican website, www.vatican.va.

26. Ibid.

27. Ibid.

28. Ibid.

29. See M. de la Torre, *Periodismo y conflicto: El caso de Benedicto XVI y la Universidad la Sapienza, pro manuscripto*, graduate thesis, Pontifical University of Santa Cruz, Rome, 2014.

30. Ibid., 33.

31. Benedict XVI, *Speech for the Angelus Prayer*, January 20, 2008, Vatican website, www.vatican.va.

32. Ibid. In this same speech at St. Peter's Square, after greeting pilgrims in several languages and thanking them for displays of solidarity, Benedict returned to the question, concluding by saying, "Let's continue going forward with this spirit of brotherhood, of love for truth and freedom, in common compromise for a fraternal, tolerant society," highlighting the fundamental role that freedom of

expression plays in democratic life, emphasizing once again the threat that comes from various forms of fundamentalism.

33. See Nigel Warburton, *Free Speech: A Very Short Introduction* (Oxford: Oxford University Press, 2009), 39.

34. See ibid., 40.

35. Ibid.

36. See John Durham Peters, *Courting the Abyss: Free Speech and the Liberal Tradition* (Chicago: University of Chicago Press, 2005), 187–91.

37. See Jürgen Habermas, "Religion in the Public Sphere," the Holberg Prize Seminar, Bergen, Norway, November 29–30, 2005, 10–21, https://es.scribd .com/document/333175446/Religion-in-the-Public-Sphere-The-Holberg -Prize-Seminar-2005, and J. Habermas and J. Ratzinger, *Dialektik der Säkularisierung* (Dialectic of secularization) (Freiburg: Herder, 2008).

38. Jordi Pujol, "Colloquy with John Durham Peters at Yale University on Freedom of Speech," *Church, Communication and Culture* 4, no. 1 (2019): 96–108.

39. Pujol, "Colloquy with John Durham Peters at Yale University on Freedom of Speech."

40. Cf. Fernando Ocáriz, "Delimitación del concepto de tolerancia y su relación con el principio de libertad," *Scripta Theologica* 27, no. 3 (1995): 880.

FIVE   Facebook's Content Moderation Rule

1. Facebook, https://www.facebook.com/pg/facebook/about, accessed March 8, 2019.

2. Mark Zuckerberg, "Live from the Facebook Communities Summit in Chicago," *Facebook*, June 22, 2017, https://www.facebook.com/zuck/videos /10103817960742861.

3. Sheryl Sandberg, COO of Facebook, tried to do some crisis management with her speech at the Digital Life Design innovation conference in Munich on January 20, 2019. She spelled out what seemed to be Facebook's vision for the future: an Internet that is neither out of control nor too tightly controlled. Her speech was highly criticized. The intent to apologize to the world was received more as an admission of having repeatedly failed in privacy issues without taking steps to correct the problem. Her message was over-rehearsed and too polished to be convincing. She "missed a huge chance to regain trust," wrote digital strategist Daniel Fiene. See https://www.youtube.com/watch?v=BbMo6nvlpsE, last visited March 9, 2019. See also Shona Ghosh, "Sheryl Sandberg Gave an Unconvincing Speech about Privacy Just When She Needed to Sound Sincere," *Business Insider*, January 20, 2019, https://www.businessinsider.com/sheryl-sandberg-bland -unconvincing-speech-privacy-2019-1?IR=T.

4. See Robert Faris, et al., "The Role of the Networked Public Sphere in the U.S. Net Neutrality Policy Debate," *International Journal of Communication (19328036)* 10 (January 2016): 5839–64.

5. Jose Antonio Vargas, "Spring Awakening: How an Egyptian Revolution Began on Facebook," *New York Times*, February 17, 2012, https://www.nytimes.com/2012/02/19/books/review/how-an-egyptian-revolution-began-on-facebook.html.

6. Vargas, "Spring Awakening."

7. Zizi Papacharissi and Maria de F. Oliveira, "Affective News and Networked Publics: The Rhythms of News Storytelling on #Egypt," *Journal of Communication* 62, no. 2 (April 2012): 266–82.

8. See https://newsroom.fb.com/company-info/, accessed January 30, 2020. Updated in *Statista*, February 14, 2022, https://www.statista.com/statistics/264810/number-of-monthly-active-facebook-users-worldwide/.

9. Salman Aslam, "Facebook by the Numbers: Stats, Demographics & Fun Facts," Omnicore, https://www.omnicoreagency.com/facebook-statistics/accessed March 16, 2022.

10. See Kate Klonick, "The New Governors: The People, Rules, and Processes Governing Online Speech," *Harvard Law Review* 131, no. 6 (2018): 1598–1670, 1620.

11. Facebook, https://www.facebook.com/communitystandards/, accessed March 9, 2019.

12. Ibid., emphasis added.

13. Ibid., no. 12.

14. Ibid., no. 14, emphasis mine.

15. Ibid., no. 19: "Reducing the spread of false news on Facebook is a responsibility that we take seriously. We also recognize that this is a challenging and sensitive issue. We want to help people stay informed without stifling *productive public discourse*. There is also a fine line between false news and satire or opinion. For these reasons, *we don't remove false news* from Facebook but instead, significantly reduce its distribution by showing it lower in the News Feed." Emphasis mine.

16. *Oxford English Dictionary* (Oxford: Oxford University Press, 2015).

17. Ibid.

18. *The Cleaners*, directed by Moritz Riesewieck and Hans Block (Berlin: Gebrueder-beetz Filmproduktion, 2018), https://gebrueder-beetz.de/wp-content/uploads/2017/06/PressKit-THE-CLEANERS-PDF.pdf.

19. See Klonick, "The New Governors," 1637.

20. Tracy Ith, "Microsoft's PhotoDNA: Protecting Children and Businesses in the Cloud," *Microsoft News Center*, July 15, 2015, https://news.microsoft.com/features/microsofts-photodna-protecting-children-and-businesses-in-the-cloud/.

21. See Katie Collins, "Microsoft Tackles Spread of Child Abuse Imagery with Free Online Tool," *Wired*, July 16, 2015, https://www.wired.co.uk/article/microsoft-free-tool- combats-online-child-sexual-abuse-imagery.

22. Ith, "Microsoft's PhotoDNA."

23. See AFP News, "Google Blocks Singapore Access to Anti-Islam Film," *Yahoo News*, September 20, 2012, https://sg.news.yahoo.com/singapore-asks-google-block- access-islam-film-054710633.html.

24. See Natalie Andrews and Deepa Seetharaman, "Facebook Steps Up Efforts against Terrorism," *Wall Street Journal*, February 11, 2016, https://www.wsj.com/articles/facebook-steps-up-efforts-against-terrorism- 1455237595.

25. Alexei Oreskovic, "Facebook Reporting Guide Shows How Site Is Policed," *Huffington Post*, August 20, 2012, https://www.huffingtonpost.com/2012/06/20/facebook-reporting- guide_n_1610917.html.

26. Sheryl Sandberg, "What Kind of Internet Do We Want?," YouTube, January 20, 2019, https://www.youtube.com/watch?v=BbMo6nvlpsE. Watch minute 13:20 onward.

27. Facebook Newsroom, "Facebook to Establish International Headquarters in Dublin, Ireland," Facebook, October 2, 2008, https://newsroom.fb.com/news/2008/10/facebook-to-establish-international-headquarters-in-dublin-ireland/.

28. See Klonick, "The New Governors," 1634.

29. Adrian Chen, "Inside Facebook's Outsourced Anti-Porn and Gore Brigade, Where 'Camel Toes' Are More Offensive than 'Crushed Heads,'" *Gawker*, February 16, 2012, https://web.archive.org/web/20121014120019/ http://gawker.com/5885714/inside-facebooks-outsourced-anti%2Bporn-and-gore-brigade -where-camel-toes-are- more-offensive-than-crushed-heads.

30. Klonick, "The New Governors," 1642.

31. Thomas Carmichael, "Abuse Standards 6.1," *oDesk Standards*, https://www.scribd.com/doc/81863464/oDeskStandards. These are oDesk's approximation of Facebook's rules.

32. Carmichael, "Abuse Standards 6.1."

33. Ibid., 10.

34. See *Gawker*, "Abuse Standards 6.2," *oDesk Standards*, https://www.scribd.com/doc/81877124/Abuse-Standards-6-2-Operation-Manual.

35. *Gawker*, "Abuse Standards 6.2," 8. My emphasis.

36. See David Ingram, "Facebook Tries to Fix Violent Video Problem with 3,000 New Workers," *Reuters*, May 20, 2017, https://www.reuters.com/article/us-facebook-crime/facebook-tries-to-fix-violent-video-problem-with-3000 -new-workers-idUSKBN17Z1N4.

37. See Sandberg, "What Kind of Internet Do We Want?"

38. See Casey Newton, "The Trauma Floor," *Verge*, February 25, 2019, https://www.theverge.com/2019/2/25/18229714/cognizant-facebook-content-moderator-interviews-trauma-working-conditions-arizona, and "Bodies in Seats," June 19, 2019, https://www.theverge.com/2019/6/19/18681845/facebook-moderator-interviews-video-trauma-ptsd-cognizant-tampa.

39. See Ingram, "Facebook Tries to Fix Violent Video Problem with 3,000 New Workers."

40. Nick Hopkins, "Revealed: Facebook's Internal Rulebook on Sex, Terrorism and Violence," *Guardian*, May 21, 2017, https://www.theguardian.com/news/2017/may/21/revealed-facebook-internal-rulebook-sex-terrorism-violence.

41. According to Facebook Newsroom, "The teams working on safety and security at Facebook are now over 30,000. About half of this team are content reviewers — a mix of full-time employees, contractors and companies we partner with.... This lets us scale globally, covering every time zone and over 50 languages. (Update on March 6, 2018) . . . We now have just over 20 content review sites around the world in such countries as Germany, Ireland, Latvia, Spain, Lisbon, Philippines and the United States.)" See https://newsroom.fb.com/news/2018/07/hard-questions-content-reviewers/.

42. Cf. Paul M. Barrett, "Who Moderates the Social Media Giants?," NYU Stern Center for Business and Human Rights, June 2020, available at https://issuu.com/nyusterncenterforbusinessandhumanri/docs/nyu_content_moderation_report_final_version?fr=sZWZmZjI1NjI1Ng.

43. See Emily Bell, "Facebook's Moderation Is of Public Interest: It Should Be Public Knowledge," May 23, 2017, https://www.cjr.org/tow_center/facebook-moderation-guardian.php.

44. Michael Schudson, *The Rise of the Right to Know* (Cambridge, MA: Harvard University Press, 2015), 14.

45. US Code, Title 47, chapter 5, subchapter II, Part I, § 230, on "Protection for Private Blocking and Screening of Offensive Material," https://www.law.cornell.edu/uscode/text/47/230.

46. Mary Anne Franks, "The Lawless Internet? Myths and Misconceptions about CDA Section 230," *Huffington Post*, February 17, 2014, http://www.huffingtonpost.com/mary-anne-franks/section-230-the-lawless-internet_b_4455090.html.

47. Heidi Tworek, "How Germany Is Tackling Hate Speech: New Legislation Targets U.S. Social Media Companies," *Foreign Affairs*, May 16, 2017, https://www.foreignaffairs.com/articles/germany/2017-05-16/how-germany-tackling-hate-speech.

48. See Mark Sweney, "Google and Facebook 'Will Lose Millions in Ads over Extremism Fears,'" June 22, 2017, https://www.theguardian.com/media/2017/jun/22/google-facebook-ads-extremist-content-advertisers-group-m. See

also Alexi Mostrous, "Top Brands Pull Google Adverts in Protest at Hate Video Links," *The Times*, March 23, 2017, https://www.thetimes.co.uk/edition/news /top-brands-pull-google-adverts-in-protest-at-links-with-hate-videos-5f5sfrcjw.

49. M. Bickert and Brian Fishman, "How We Counter Terrorism," statement, Facebook Newsroom, June 15, 2017. See https://about.fb.com/news/2017/06 /how-we-counter-terrorism/.

50. See Sheera Frenkel, "Facebook Will Use Artificial Intelligence to Find Extremist Posts," *New York Times*, June 15, 2017, https://www.nytimes.com/2017 /06/15/technology/facebook-artificial-intelligence-extremists-terrorism.html ?mcubz=1.

51. Mark Zuckerberg, "Four Ideas to Regulate the Internet," March 30, 2019, https://newsroom.fb.com/ news/2019/03/four-ideas-regulate-internet/.

52. National Assembly Republic of Vietnam, Law on Cybersecurity No. 24/2018/QH14, Hanoi June 12, 2018, available at https://www.economica.vn /Content/files/LAW%20%26%20REG/Law%20on%20Cyber%20Security%20 2018.pdf.

53. James Pearson, "Facebook Agreed to Censor Posts after Vietnam Slowed Traffic — Sources," *Reuters*, April 21, 2020, https://www.reuters.com/article/us -vietnam-facebook-exclusive/exclusive-facebook-agreed-to-censor-posts-after -vietnam-slowed-traffic-sources-idUSKCN2232JX. Cf. Human Rights Watch, "Vietnam: Facebook, Pressured, Censors Dissent. Company Caves to Government after Local Servers Disrupted," April 23, 2020, https://www.hrw.org/news /2020/04/23/vietnam-facebook-pressured-censors-dissent.

54. Pearson, "Facebook Agreed to Censor."

55. Ibid.

SIX   The Sustainability of the Liberal Rationale

1. Cf. William W. Freehling, "The Founding Fathers and Slavery," *American Historical Review* 77, 1 (February, 1972): 81–93; James Farr, "'So Vile and Miserable an Estate': The Problem of Slavery in Locke's Political Thought," *Political Theory* 14, no. 2 (May 1986): 263–89; Anthony Iaccarino, "The Founding Fathers and Slavery," *Encyclopedia Britannica*, July 28, 2016, https://www.britannica .com/topic/The-Founding-Fathers-and-Slavery-1269536.

2. Cf. Thomas G. West, "Free Speech in the American Founding and in Modern Liberalism," *Social Philosophy and Policy* 21, no. 2 (2004): 319.

3. Edwin Baker, *Human Liberty and Freedom of Speech* (New York: Oxford University Press, 1989).

4. See Edwin Baker, "Harm, Liberty and Free Speech," *Southern California Law Review* 70, no. 4 (1997): 992.

5. See ibid., 979–81.

6. Ibid., chap. 4.

7. Cf. Jeremy Waldron, *The Harm in Hate Speech*, (Cambridge, MA: Harvard University Press, 2012), 14, 162.

8. See Timothy Garton Ash, *Free Speech: Ten Principles for a Connected World* (New Haven, CT: Yale University Press, 2016), 77.

9. See Ronald Dworkin, *Justice for Hedgehogs* (Cambridge, MA: Belknap Press of Harvard University Press, 2011).

10. See Ronald Dworkin, *Freedom's Law: The Moral Reading of the American Constitution* (Oxford: Oxford University Press, 1996), 218–19, 230.

11. See Ronald Dworkin, foreword to *Extreme Speech and Democracy*, edited by I. Hare and J. Weinstein (New York: Oxford University Press, 2009), vii–viii.

12. See John Durham Peters, *Courting the Abyss: Free Speech and the Liberal Tradition* (Chicago: University of Chicago Press, 2005), 147ff.

13. See *Whitney v. California*, 274 US 357 (1927), 375.

14. See Raoul Vaneigem, *Niente è più sacro, tutto si può dire. Riflessioni sulla libertà di espressione* (Milan: Ponte alle Grazie, 2004), 18.

15. Ibid., 18, my translation.

16. Ibid., 25, my translation.

17. Ibid.

18. See Ireneusz Marian Rogulski, *Limiti morali della libertà d'espressione letteraria nei confronti della religione. Il caso di blasfemia* (Rome: EDUSC, 2016), 200.

19. Ash, *Free Speech*, 81.

20. Ibid., 3.

21. See S. Heyman, *Free Speech and Human Dignity* (New Haven, CT: Yale University Press), 37–80.

22. Ibid.

23. Ibid. According to Peters, the current ideal of self-actualization, motivated more by art and imagination, replaces that of the Ciceronian self-transcendence, based on abstraction and duty.

24. See Peters, *Courting the Abyss*, 54–58.

25. See Jordi Pujol, "Colloquy with John Durham Peters at Yale University on Freedom of Speech," *Church, Communication and Culture* 4, no. 1 (2019): 96–108.

26. See Jeremy Waldron, "Boutique Faith (*Courting the Abyss: Free Speech and the Liberal Tradition*: Book review)," *London Review of Books* 28, 14 (2006): 20–23.

27. See Owen Fiss, *The Irony of Free Speech* (Cambridge, MA: Harvard University Press, 1996), 83. Fiss argues in favor of accepting the ironic reality that the state is both the friend and the enemy of free expression, as the author demonstrates by comparing various sentences. He concludes that it is desirable for the state not to impose an orthodoxy but to reinforce the principles that favor strong public debate.

28. See Peters, *Courting the Abyss*, 21–22.

29. Ibid., 292–93.

30. Charles Sanders Peirce (1839–1914), scientist, logician, and philosopher, was one of the most relevant figures in North American thought. He is considered the founder of the school of thought called "pragmatism," as well as the father of contemporary semiotics, understood as a philosophical theory of meaning and representation. See Sara Barrena and Jaime Nubiola, *Philosophica: Enciclopedia filosófica online*, edited by F. Fernández Labastida and J. A. Mercado, http://www.philosophica .info/archivo/2007/voces/peirce/Peirce.html, accessed October 2, 2016.

31. See Peters, *Courting the Abyss*, 84. See also Pujol, "Colloquy with John Durham Peters," 104.

32. Pujol, "Colloquy with John Durham Peters," 98.

33. See Peters, *Courting the Abyss*, 293.

34. Pujol, "Colloquy with John Durham Peters," 99.

35. Ibid., 99–100.

36. John D. Peters, *A szakadék szélén: A szólásszabadság és a liberális hagyomány*, Hungarian translation of John D. Peters, *Courting the Abyss: Free Speech and the Liberal Tradition* (Budapest: Wolters Kluwer, 2015), preface.

37. Pujol, "Colloquy with John Durham Peters," 101.

38. Ibid., 101.

39. For a deeper examination, see Victoria Camps, *Introducción a la filosofía política* (Barcelona: Crítica, 2001); M. Walzer, "La crítica comunitarista del liberalismo," in *La Política: Revista de estudios sobre el Estado y la sociedad* (Barcelona: Ed. Paidós, Primer semestre 1996); A. Ferrara, *Comunitarismo e Liberalismo* (Rome: Editori Riuniti 1992).

40. The authors grouped under this denomination come from different traditions and hold nonhomogeneous political-philosophical positions, which results in an inaccurate label. What unites them is their political position concerning liberal individualism and their conception of human good. Some authors classified as communitarians are Charles Taylor, Michael Sandel, Michael Walzer, and Alasdair MacIntyre, although the latter does not like to be classified as such. See A. Da Re, "Lo bueno y lo justo: Un panorama de las propuestas ético-políticas actuales," in *Ética y sociedad*, edited by Robert A. Gahl (Madrid: EIUNSA, 2002), 79.

41. Alasdair MacIntyre, *After Virtue* (Notre Dame, IN: University of Notre Dame Press, 1981), 160–61.

42. Charles Taylor, *Sources of the Self* (Cambridge: Cambridge University Press, 1989), 26–27.

43. Martin Rhonheimer, "The Liberal Image of Man and the Concept of Autonomy: Beyond the Debate between Liberals and Communitarians," in *The Common Good of Constitutional Democracy* (Washington, DC: Catholic University of America Press, 2013), 51.

44. See MacIntyre, *After Virtue*, chap. 14.

45. See ibid., 213.

46. Ibid., emphasis in original.

47. See Rhonheimer, "The Liberal Image of Man and the Concept of Autonomy," 53.

48. See ibid., emphasis in original.

49. See Charles Taylor, "Atomism" in *Communitarianism and Individualism*, edited by Shlomo Avineri and Avner De-Salit (Oxford: Oxford University Press, 1985), 29: "The term 'atomism' is used loosely to characterize the doctrines of social-contract theory which arose in the seventeenth century and also successor doctrines which may not have made use of the notion of social contract but which inherited a vision of society as in some sense constituted by individuals for the fulfilment of ends which were primarily individual. Certain forms of utilitarianism are successor doctrines in this sense. The term is also applied to contemporary doctrines which hark back to social-contract theory, or which try to defend in some sense the priority of the individual and his rights over society, or which present a purely instrumental view of society."

50. See Taylor, *Sources of the Self*, 82.

51. Taylor, "Atomism," 36.

52. Ibid., 47.

53. Ibid.

54. See Mari J. Matsuda, Richard Delgado, Charles R. Lawrence III, and Kimberlè Williams Crenshaw, *Words That Wound: Critical Race Theory, Assaultive Speech, and the First Amendment* (Boulder, CO: Westview Press, 1993), 3–15.

55. See Peters, *Courting the Abyss*, 175.

56. See ibid., 179.

57. Matsuda et al., *Words That Wound*, 95.

58. See ibid., 89ff.

59. See Peters, *Courting the Abyss*, 176–77.

60. See ibid., 95.

61. A twentieth-century scholarship on racism and equality has been developed, first under the name of critical philosophy of race (CPR), then critical legal studies (CLS) and critical race theory (CRT). In an interdisciplinary way, a large group of scholars are exploring the "reach of racist ideas and practices throughout social life and institutions, arguing, for example, that norms of neutrality in legal interpretation or reasoning often concealed structural racism." Linda Alcoff, "Critical Philosophy of Race," in *The Stanford Encyclopedia of Philosophy*, Fall 2021 edition), edited by Edward N. Zalta, https://plato.stanford.edu/archives/fall2021/entries/critical-phil-race/.

62. See Matsuda et al., *Words That Wound*, 136.

63. See Steven G. Gey, "The Case against Postmodern Censorship Theory," *University of Pennsylvania Law Review* 145, no. 2 (1996): 193–297.

64. See Nigel Warburton, *Free Speech: A Very Short Introduction* (Oxford: Oxford University Press, 2009), 68.

65. See Wendy McElroy, *XXX: A Woman's Right to Pornography* (New York: Saint Martin's Press, 1995).

66. See Warburton, *Free Speech*, 64.

67. See Ana Bridges, Robert Wosnitzer, Chyng Sun, and Rachael Liberman, "Aggression and Sexual Behavior in Best-Selling Pornography Videos: A Content Analysis Update," *Violence Against Women* 16 (2010): 1065–85.

68. David Perry, *The Impact of Pornography on Children* (Gainesville, FL: American College of Pediatricians, 2016), 4.

69. See Catharine MacKinnon, *Only Words* (Cambridge, MA: Harvard University Press, 1993).

70. *Shiro v. Clark*, 962, 963, 972 US (February 5, 1993). Cited various times in MacKinnen, *Only Words*, 119, 144.

71. See MacKinnon, *Only Words*, 62.

72. See Perry, *The Impact of Pornography on Children*, 2.

73. See Warburton, *Free Speech*, 67.

74. See James R. Stoner and Donna M. Hughes, eds., *Los costes sociales de la pornografía* (Madrid: Rialp, 2014); Warburton, *Free Speech*, 68–69.

75. See Ronald Dworkin, "Liberty and Pornography," *New York Review of Books* 38, no. 4 (August 15, 1991); Dworkin, "Women and Pornography," *New York Review of Books* 40, no. 17 (October 21, 1993); Gey, "The Case against Postmodern Censorship Theory," 193–297.

SEVEN A Fabricated Notion of Tolerance

1. Aristotle raises the question of "lesser evil" in the context of justice: "The lesser evil is preferable to the greater one." Aristotle, *Nicomachean Ethics*, Book 5, chap. 5. In his treatise *De ordine*, Saint Augustine writes that it is desirable that those who govern tolerate certain evils that are reasonable so as to prevent other evils or avoid greater evils. See St. Augustine, *De ordine*, Book 2 (South Bend, IN: Saint Augustine's Press, 2007), chap. 4, 63.

2. "An Ordinance for the Regulating of Printing," in *Acts and Ordinances of the Interregnum, 1642–1660*, edited by C. H. Firth and R. S. Rait (London, 1911), 184–86, in *British History Online*, http://www.british-history.ac.uk/no-series/acts -ordinances-interregnum/pp184-186.

3. See John Milton, *Areopagitica: Discorso per la libertà di stamp* (Milan: RCS quotidiani, 2010), 7.

4. Albert C. Labriola, *Encyclopædia Britannica*, https://www.britannica.com /biography/John-Milton. Accessed October 19, 2019.

5. John Milton, *Areopagitica and Other Tracts* (London: J. M. Dent, 1900), 7.

6. See Vincent Blasi, "Free Speech and Good Character: From Milton to Brandeis to the Present," in *Eternally Vigilant: Free Speech in the Modern Era*, edited by L. C. Bollinger and G. R. Stone (Chicago: University of Chicago Press, 2002), 65.

7. Milton, *Areopagitica*, 21.

8. Ibid., 61. This idea is also advanced in *Paradise Lost*.

9. See John D. Peters, "'The Marketplace of Ideas': A History of the Concept," in *Toward a Political Economy of Culture: Capitalism and Communication in the Twenty-First Century*, edited by Andrew Calabrese and Colin Sparks (Boulder: Rowman and Littlefield, 2004), 66.

10. See ibid., 67.

11. See Milton, *Areopagitica*, 36, 38–42. Milton believes that virtue lies in the "maturity" of a person—alone—to choose between good and evil. He considers it "against nature" to impose a greater rigor than what things take on by nature or greater than that used by God in Scripture, implying the spontaneous exercise of virtue and revealing the truth. In the latter case, he refers to freely circulating books. Thus, in advocating for absolute naturalism, he and other later liberal and Protestant authors have forgotten that human beings do not enjoy the righteousness they suppose; human nature and the capacity to choose have been encumbered by the internal disorder caused by original sin.

12. Ibid., 26–27.

13. Ibid., 22.

14. See ibid., 22. Here he refers to the conception of Scotus and Aquinas.

15. Ibid., 23.

16. See Blasi, "Free Speech and Good Character," 69.

17. Ibid., 71.

18. See Milton, *Areopagitica*, 29.

19. See John Durham Peters, *Courting the Abyss: Free Speech and the Liberal Tradition* (Chicago: University of Chicago Press, 2005), 69.

20. See Peters, "The Marketplace of Ideas," 68.

21. See Peters, "The Marketplace of Ideas."

22. Saint Paul follows Jesus's teaching on purity: "Everything that goes into a person from outside cannot defile." . . . "But what comes out of a person, that is what defiles" (Mark 7: 18 and 20).

23. See Peters, *Courting the Abyss*, 87ff.

24. John Henry Newman, "Protestant View of the Catholic Church," in *Lectures on the Present Position of Catholics in England* (London: Longmans, Green, 1908), 9.

25. K. C. O'Rourke argues that Mill's defense of free thought and discussion is influenced not so much by Milton as by James Mill and Bentham. In this sense, O'Rourke emphasizes the fact that *Areopagitica* is cited only once in Mill's essay on freedom. However, he acknowledges that Mill and Milton are part of the same

tradition. See K. C. O'Rourke, *John Stuart Mill and Freedom of Expression: The Genesis of a Theory* (New York: Routledge, 2013), 161.

26. See Peters, "The Marketplace of Ideas," 69.

27. See Peters, "The Marketplace of Ideas."

28. John Stuart Mill, *On Liberty* (1859) (London: Penguin, 2006), 35.

29. Peters, "The Marketplace of Ideas," 69.

30. Mill, *On Liberty*, 16.

31. Ibid., 17.

32. Ibid., 24.

33. Ibid., 42.

34. Ibid., 61.

35. Ibid., 23.

36. Robert P. George and Cornel West, "Truth Seeking, Democracy, and Freedom of Thought and Expression: A Statement by Robert P. George and Cornel West," James Madison Program, Princeton University, Princeton, NJ, March 14, 2017, available at https://jmp.princeton.edu/statement.

37. Cf. K. C. O'Rourke, *John Stuart Mill and Freedom of Expression: The Genesis of a Theory* (New York: Routledge, 2013), 161ff.

38. Mill, *On Liberty*, 61.

39. Ibid.

40. Ibid.

41. Peters, *Courting the Abyss*, 133.

42. As John Paul II said in 1990: "This tolerance is not a passive virtue, but is rooted in active love and is meant to be transformed into a positive commitment to ensuring freedom and peace for all." John Paul II, *Message for the XXIV World Day of Peace*, December 8, 1990, Vatican website, https://w2.vatican.va/content /john-paul-ii/en/messages/peace/documents/hf_jp-ii_mes_08121990_xxiv-world -day-for-peace.html, no. IV.

43. Thomas Aquinas, *Summa Theologiae* I-II, q. 101, a. 3 ad 2, in Thomas Aquinas, *Summa Theologiae*, translated by Fr. Laurence Shapcote, vol. 16 (Lander, WY: Aquinas Institute for the Study of Sacred Doctrine, 2012), 314; see also Aquinas, *Summa Theologiae*, II-II, q. 10, a. 11 c.

44. Augustine, *Confessions*, 7.7.11 (Peabody, MA: Hendrickson, 2004), 124.

45. Cf. Hannah Arendt, *Eichmann in Jerusalem: A Report on the Banality of Evil* (1963) (New York: Penguin, 2006).

46. See Cornelio Fabro, *Introduzione all'ateismo moderno* (Rome: Studium, 1969); Carlos Cardona, *Metafísica de la opción intelectual* (Madrid: Rialp, 1973); Fernando Ocáriz, *Voltaire: Tratado sobre la tolerancia* (Madrid: EMESA, 1979).

47. There are many works of political philosophy that inspired this Enlightenment concept of tolerance, such as Michel de Montaigne, *Essays*, Book 2,

tract XIX (1580); Baruch Spinoza, *Tractatus Theologico-Politicus* (1670); John Locke, *Epistola de Tolerantia* (1689); and Voltaire, *Treatise on Tolerance* (1763).

48. Ocáriz, *Voltaire*, 69.

49. The relationship between Democracy and relativism comes from Hans Kelsen, *On the Essence and Value of Democracy*, originally published as *Vom Wesen und Wert der Demokratie* (Tubingen: Mohr, 1929; reprint, Aalen: Scientia, 1963), and *General Theory of Law and State* (Cambridge, MA: Harvard University Press, 1945).

50. To view a complete explanation of the meaning of Milton's expression about the truth, see Kendall Willmoore, "How to Read Milton's *Areopagitica*," *Journal of Politics* 22, no. 3 (August 1960): 449–53.

51. See Ronald Corthell and Thomas N. Corns, eds., *Milton and Catholicism* (South Bend, IN: University of Notre Dame Press, 2017); Andrew Hadfield, "Milton and Catholicism," in *Milton and Toleration*, edited by Sharon Achinstein and Elizabeth Sauer (Oxford: Oxford Scholarship Online, 2007).

52. See Kendall, "How to Read Milton's *Areopagitica*," 462.

53. See Lee C. Bollinger, *The Tolerant Society* (Oxford: Oxford University Press, 1988), 61.

54. Ibid., 261.

55. Ocáriz, *Voltaire*, 89, my translation.

56. John Locke, "A Letter Concerning Toleration," in *Locke on Toleration*, edited by Richard Vernon (Cambridge: Cambridge University Press, 2010) 35.

57. George Parkin Grant, *English-Speaking Justice* (South Bend, IN: University of Notre Dame Press, 1985), 63.

58. See Michael Novak and Brian C. Anderson, *On Cultivating Liberty: Reflections on Moral Ecology* (New York: Rowman & Littlefield, 1999), 12–13, 27.

59. Cf. Michel Villey, *Filosofía del Derecho* (Barcelona: Scire Universitaria, 2003), 97.

60. Ibid., 98, emphasis and translation mine.

61. Francisco L. Mateo Seco, "Ley y libertad según Lutero," *Persona y Derecho* 7 (1980): 140, my translation.

62. "Free choice is a plainly divine term, and can be properly applied to none but the Divine Majesty alone; for he alone can do and does (as the psalmist says) whatever he pleases in heaven and on earth. If this is attributed to men, it is no more rightly attributed than if divinity itself were attributed to them, which would be the greatest possible sacrilege." Martin Luther, *The Bondage of the Will*, translated by Philip S. Watson, in *Luther's Works*, vol. 33 (Philadelphia: Fortress, 1972), 35.

63. "God could be presented at the same time as the highest justice and the highest iniquity, He could be called merciful while claiming that He 'delights in the torments of the damned.'" Mateo Seco, "Ley y libertad según Lutero," 177, my translation.

64. "For the expression 'free choice' is too imposing, too wide and full, and the people think it signifies—as the force and nature of the term requires—a power that can turn itself freely in either direction, without being under anyone's influence or control." Luther, *The Bondage of the Will*, 68–69.

65. Luther, *The Bondage of the Will*, 73.

66. Francisco L. Mateo Seco, *Martin Lutero sobre la libertad esclava*, edited by Magisterio Español (Madrid: Col. Crítica Filosófica, 1978), 63, my translation.

67. Benedict XVI, *Meeting with Representatives of the World of Culture*, September 12, 2008, Vatican website, http://www.vatican.va/content/benedict-xvi/en/speeches/2008/september/documents/hf_ben-xvi_spe_20080912_parigi-cultura.html, 5.

68. Ibid.

69. See John Rawls, *Political Liberalism* (New York: Columbia University Press, 1993), 11, 29–35, 62. I will elaborate on Rawls's account of human good in chapter 9.

70. Andrew Denton, "The Damage Done—The Price Our Community Pays without a Law for Assisted Dying," National Press Club, August 10, 2016, https://www.abc.net.au/tv/programs/national-press-club-address/.

71. John J. Dilulio (moderator), "Religious Freedom: A Conversation with Rick Warren and Robert P. George," *Review of Faith & International Affairs* 11, no. 4 (2013): 66, doi 10.1080/15570274.2013.857113.

72. J. Dyson Heydon, "The Inaugural PM Glynn Lecture by the Honourable Dyson Heydon, AC QC," PM Glynn Institute (Australia), October 17, 2017, https://www.pmglynn.acu.edu.au/news/the-inaugural-pm-glynn-lecture-by-the-honourable-dyson-heydon-ac-qc#_edn02.

73. Milton Friedman, "Free to Choose," part 5, in *Created Equal: Featuring Milton Friedman*, PBS Television, 1980, https://www.youtube.com/watch?v=YRLAKD-Vuvk.

74. Peter Kurti, *The Tyranny of Tolerance* (Brisbane: Connor Court Publishing, 2017), 12.

75. Ibid., 6.

76. "The Threat from the Illiberal Left," *Economist*, September 4, 2021, https://www.economist.com/leaders/2021/09/04/the-threat-from-the-illiberal-left. See also "Left-Wing Activists Are Using Old Tactics in a New Assault on Liberalism," *Economist*, September 4, 2021, https://www.economist.com/briefing/2021/09/04/left-wing-activists-are-using-old-tactics-in-a-new-assault-on-liberalism.

77. M. W. McConnell, "Why Is Religious Liberty the 'First Freedom'?" *Cardozo Law Review* 21 (2000): 1260.

78. See Martha C. Nussbaum, *Hiding from Humanity: Disgust, Shame and the Law* (Princeton, NJ: Princeton University Press, 2004).

79. See John Durham Peters, "Preludes to a Theory of Obscenity," in *Obscenity and the Limits of Liberalism*, edited by Loren Glass and Charles Francis Williams (Columbus: Ohio State University Press, 2011), 152–53.

80. See ibid., 152.

81. See ibid., 150–51.

82. Peters, "Preludes to a Theory of Obscenity," 155.

83. See Peters, "Preludes to a Theory of Obscenity."

84. See ibid., 156.

EIGHT The Epistemological Shortfall

1. Cf. Zechariah Chafee Jr., *Free Speech in the United States* (Cambridge, MA: Harvard University Press), 560ff.

2. Luis Amiguet, "La Contra: Entrevista a Teun van Dijk," *La Vanguardia*, August 1, 2019, https://www.lavanguardia.com/lacontra/20190801/463803450485/si-hablas-de-una-ola-de-inmigracion-ya-eres-racista.html, my translation and emphasis.

3. See Antonio Vilarnovo and José F. Sánchez, *Discurso, tipos de texto y comunicación* (Pamplona: EUNSA, 1994), 22–23.

4. These three types of language are advanced by Aristotle in the following: in *On Interpretation*, apophantic logos is described as the art of logical deliberation; in *De Poetica*, poetic logos is referred to as the art of creating a discourse of imitation or representation through tragedy, comedy, or epic poetry; and in *Rhetoric*, pragmatic logos is set out as the art of persuasion with words. Cf. *The Complete Works of Aristotle: The Revised Oxford Translation*, edited by Jonathan Barnes (Princeton NJ: Princeton University Press, 1991).

5. This idea is discussed extensively in Vilarnovo and Sánchez, *Discurso, tipos de texto y comunicación*, 24–39.

6. Aristotle, *Rhetoric*, 1358a, 36–39: "The one who speaks, that about which he speaks, and the one to whom he speaks."

7. See Vilarnovo and Sánchez, *Discurso, tipos de texto y comunicación*, 30.

8. See ibid., 41ff.

9. Cf. *National Socialist Party of America v. Village of Skokie*, 432 US 43 (1977).

10. Vilarnovo and Sánchez, *Discurso, tipos de texto y comunicación*, 41–45.

11. This expression will be explained in more detail in the following section when we speak of John Austin and speech acts.

12. An elaboration on this article can be seen in Ireneusz M. Rogulski, *Limiti morali della libertà d'espressione letteraria nei confronti della religione. Il caso di blasfemia* (Rome: EDUSC, 2016).

13. See Vilarnovo and Sánchez, *Discurso, tipos de texto y comunicación*, 101–2, 129ff.

14. See ibid., 104.

15. Catharine A. MacKinnon, *Only Words* (Cambridge MA: Harvard University Press, 1993), 21.

16. On the doctrine of "intentional infliction of emotional distress" (IIED), see *Snyder v. Phelps*, 562 US 443 (2010); on the doctrine of "symbolic speech," see *Cohen v. California*, 403 US 15 (1971); on "expressive conduct," see *Stromberg v. California*, 283 US 15 (1931); on "symbolic expression," see *West Virginia Board of Education v. Barnette*, 319 US 624 (1943), and *Wooley v. Maynard*, 430 US 705 (1977); and on "artistic expression," see *Masterpiece Cakeshop v. Colorado Civil Rights Commission*, 584 US 16 (2018).

17. Amiguet, "La Contra."

18. MacKinnon, *Only Words*, 40.

19. Ibid., 60.

20. See ibid., 46.

21. See Paolo G. Carozza, "Human Rights, Human Dignity, and Human Experience," in *Understanding Human Dignity*, edited by Cristopher McCrudden (Oxford: Oxford University Press, 2013), 615–30.

22. Paolo G. Carozza and Clemens Sedmak, *The Practice of Human Development and Dignity* (Notre Dame, IN: University of Notre Dame Press, 2020), 7.

23. A list of the main philosophers of language and bibliography can be found in Sergio Tapia Velasco, *Filosofía de la conversación: Claves para una teoría contemporánea sobre las relaciones interpersonales y el conocimiento humano a través de la interacción verbal* (Valencia: Edicep, 2014), 153–266.

24. Two of his works are Herbert P. Grice, "Meaning," *Philosophical Review* 66, no. 3 (July 1957): 377–88 and *Intention and Uncertainty*, Annual Philosophical Lecture, British Academy (London: Oxford University Press, 1971). See A. Menassé, *Significado* (Mexico: Universidad Nacional Autónoma de México, Instituto de Investigaciones Filosóficas, 1977).

25. Tapia Velasco, *Filosofía de la conversación*, 156, my translation.

26. Tapia explains: "Implicatures designate both the meaning that the speaker wants to imply with a phrase — the intentional meaning of the issuer, based on what has been said or has stopped being said — as well as the ability of the listener to infer new knowledge from that rational ability to relate in order to interpret the phrase heard in relation to the context and how it was said." Ibid., 189.

27. See Tapia Velasco, *Filosofía de la conversación*, 197.

28. See John L. Austin, "Other Minds," in *J. L. Austin Philosophical Papers*, edited by J. O. Urmson and G. J. Warnock (Oxford: Oxford University Press, 1970), 99ff. The original article was published in J. Wisdom, J. L. Austen, J. L. Austin, and A. J. Ayer, eds. "Symposium: Other Minds," Proceedings of the Aristo-

telian Society, Supplementary Volume 20 (1946): 122–97, www.jstor.org/stable /4106432.

29. See John L. Austin, *How to Do Things with Words: The William James Lectures Delivered at Harvard University in 1955*, 2nd ed., edited by J. O. Urmson and M. Sbisà (Cambridge, MA: Harvard University Press, 1975. Austin subsequently dedicated another talk, broadcast by the BBC in 1956, to performative utterances. See also John L. Austin, "Performative Utterances," in *J. L. Austin Philosophical Papers*, edited by J. O. Urmson and G. J. Warnock (Oxford: Oxford University Press, 1970), 233–52.

30. See Tapia Velasco, *Filosofía de la conversación*, 156.

31. See ibid., 144, 144, and 145ff.

32. See ibid., 95, my translation.

33. See Jaime Nubiola, "J. L. Austin: Análisis y Verdad," *Anuario Filosófico* 10, no. 2 (1977): 218ff.

34. See Tapia Velasco, *Filosofía de la conversación*, 168.

35. See Austin, *How to Do Things with Words*, 17.

36. Cf. Aristotle, *Poetics* (Cambridge, MA: Harvard University Press, 1995), 1447a, 15.

37. See Vilarnovo and Sánchez, *Discurso, tipos de texto y comunicación*, 72.

38. Aristotle expresses this idea with the term *kata to eikós*, which can be understood as the "according to what is expected" or "according to what is plausible" of the work itself. For a closer look, see Vilarnovo and Sánchez, *Discurso, tipos de texto y comunicación*, 107–9.

39. See Norberto González Gaitano, *La interpretación y la narración periodísticas* (Pamplona: EUNSA, 1997), 57.

40. Aristotle, *Poetics*, 1451b, 1–2.

41. Ibid., 5–7.

42. See Hannah Arendt, *The Human Condition* (Chicago: University of Chicago Press, 1998), 121–22.

43. González Gaitano, *La interpretación y la narración periodísticas*, my translation and emphasis.

44. Vilarnovo offers a grouping of texts to justify the uniqueness of action in Aristotle, which happens because the parts have a coherence that gives meaning to the whole. See Vilarnovo and Sánchez, *Discurso, tipos de texto y comunicación*, 73.

45. Aristotle distinguishes three characteristics of action: integrity (completeness), unity (wholeness), and magnitude. See Aristotle, *Poetics*, 1450b, 24–25. Vilarnovo develops this idea in Vilarnovo and Sánchez, *Discurso, tipos de texto y comunicación*, 73–80.

46. Norberto González Gaitano, "Comunicación e información: Clarificaciones conceptuales," in *Introducción a la información y a la comunicación*, edited by Gabriel Galdón López (Barcelona: Ariel, 2001), 23, my translation

47. González Gaitano, "Comunicación e información," my translation.

48. See González Gaitano, *La interpretación y la narración periodísticas*, 52, my emphasis.

49. Cf. Aristotle, *Poetics*, 1448a, 22–23.

50. The functional elements of mimesis according to Aristotle are fable, character, thought, and diction. In the case of representation, Aristotle adds melody and spectacle. Vilarnovo believes that, in view of the reality of current audiovisual discourses, the elements of spectacle and melody must also be included for the narrative. For a closer look, see Vilarnovo and Sánchez, *Discurso, tipos de texto y comunicación*, 81–93.

51. See Teun A. Van Dijk, "Philosophy of Action and Theory of Narrative," *Poetics* 6 (1976): 306.

52. Vilarnovo and Sánchez, *Discurso, tipos de texto y comunicación*, 93, my translation.

53. See ibid., 101.

54. See Vilarnovo and Sánchez, *Discurso, tipos de texto y comunicación*.

55. See ibid.

56. "1. Concealment, on the part of the sender, of the type of communicative project offered to the recipient; 2. Proposal to the recipient of a type of unequal exchange; 3. Concealment of part of the information; 4. Approaching of one type of communicative relationship with little to know possibilities for intervention and dialogue on the part of the recipient; 5. The offering of a text that seduced the recipient through his or her lack of intellectual, moral, and operational resources."

57. For greater detail on the analysis of these two works, consult chapter 1 of Rogulski's study, *Limiti morali della libertà d'espressione letteraria nei confronti della religione*, 14–61.

58. See González Gaitano, *La interpretación y la narración periodísticas*, 58.

59. Ibid., my translation.

60. Ibid.

61. See ibid.

62. Ibid.

63. The forgery was published for the first time in Russia in 1903 and was then translated into multiple languages and spread internationally during the first half of the twentieth century. See John S. Curtiss, *An Appraisal of the Protocols of Zion* (New York: Columbia University Press, 1942). The Nazis used the Protocols as propaganda against the Jews. See Norman Cohn, *Warrant for Genocide: The Myth of the Jewish World-Conspiracy and the Protocols of the Elder of Zion* (New York: Harper & Row, 1966), 32–36.

64. Opus Dei (Work of God) is a Catholic organization that operates worldwide, composed 98 percent of laypersons and 2 percent of priests, founded in 1928 by Saint Josemaría Escrivá in Spain. Its mission is to spread the Christian message of holiness through ordinary life and work, serving God, others, and the world.

The main activity of Opus Dei is to provide permanent formation to its members and friends from all sorts of backgrounds. See https://opusdei.org/en-us/.

65. See Alasdair MacIntyre, "Intolerance, Censorship, and Other Requirements of Rationality," Philip Quinn Lecture, University of Notre Dame, South Bend, IN, 2009), 13. This lecture has never been published. The author gave me a copy of his manuscript and permission to quote it in February 2017.

66. Vilarnovo and Sánchez, *Discurso, tipos de texto y comunicación*, 104, my translation and emphasis.

67. See Vilarnovo and Sánchez, *Discurso, tipos de texto y comunicación*, 106.

68. Ibid., 108. One of the texts in which Aristotle's unity of action is most clearly seen is Aristotle, *Poetics*, cit. 1451a 23ss.: "But, just as Homer is superior in other respects, it seems that he saw this clearly as well (whether by art or by nature). In composing the Odyssey, he did not put into his poem everything that happened to Odysseus, e.g., that he was wounded on Parnassus and pretended to be insane during recruitment, whether one of these things happened did not make it possible that the other would happen. But he constructed the Odyssey around a single action of the kind we are discussing, and the *Iliad* similarly," translated by Richard Janko (Indianapolis, IN: Hackett, 1987), 11.

69. Vilarnovo and Sánchez, *Discurso, tipos de texto y comunicación*, 110.

70. Cf. Gianfranco Bettetini and Armando Fumagalli, *Lo que queda de los medios* (Pamplona: EUNSA, 2001), 61.

71. This does not mean that "reality" does not matter for artistic creation or that art is disconnected from reality. In Aristotle's thesis, which we have been unpacking, the starting point of mimesis is reality. That is to say, film and literature can tell stories because their authors live and have seen things, and as a result they can imitate and represent worlds and characters.

72. See Vilarnovo and Sánchez, *Discurso, tipos de texto y comunicación*, 112–13. This is expressed very well in Aristotle, *Poetics*, 1454b, 20: "Since tragedy is a representation of people who are better than we are, (the poet) should emulate the good portrait-painters. In rendering people's particular shape, while making them (life)like, they paint them as finer (than they are). So too the poet, as he represents people who are angry, lazy, or have other such traits, should make them such in their characters, (but) decent (too). E.g., Homer (made) Achilles good as well as an example of stubbornness."

73. Vilarnovo and Sánchez, *Discurso, tipos de texto y comunicación*, 114, my translation. See Aristotle *Poetics*, 1460b, 37: "(If) impossibilities have been produced, there is an error; but it is correct, if it attains the end of the art itself . . . , if in this way it makes that part (of the poem) more astonishing."

74. González Gaitano, *La interpretación y la narración periodísticas*, 51, my translation and emphasis.

75. See Vilarnovo and Sánchez, *Discurso, tipos de texto y comunicación*, 116.

76. González Gaitano, *La interpretación y la narración periodísticas*, 48.

77. Bettetini and Fumagalli, *Lo que queda de los medios*, 40, my translation.

78. See Bettetini and Fumagalli, *Lo que queda de los medios*, 60. This argument is also advanced in Gianfranco Bettetini, *L'occhio in vendita* (Venice: Marsilio, 1985).

NINE The Anthropological Shortfall

1. See Charles Taylor, *Sources of the Self: The Making of the Modern Identity* (Cambridge MA: Harvard University Press, 1989), 26–27, and Charles Taylor, "Atomism," in *Philosophy and the Human Sciences* (London: Cambridge University Press, 1985), 185–337.

2. Mary Ann Glendon, *Rights Talk: The Impoverishment of Political Discourse* (New York: Free Press, 1991).

3. See Joseph Ratzinger, "Truth and Freedom," *Communio* 23 (Spring 1996): 16–26.

4. Some who advocate compelling the baker's speech view this as fighting discrimination in the public sphere, similar to racial discrimination at public accommodations.

5. Mariano Fazio, *Historia de las ideas contemporáneas* (Madrid: Rialp, 2006), 308.

6. Pera considered Hobbes and Locke two of the authors of this change. See Marcello Pera, *Diritti umani e cristianesimo: La Chiesa alla prova della modernità* (Venice: Marsilio, 2015), 127–28.

7. Jean Grondin, *A la escucha del sentido* (Barcelona: Herder, 2014), 59, my translation.

8. Ibid.

9. Ibid.

10. The author argues that "values" as a universal normative concept did not appear in the declarations of rights of the Enlightenment man. See Grondin, *A la escucha del sentido*, 60–61.

11. This refers to Levi-Strauss, Foucault, or Derridà, who, influenced by Nietzsche and the structuralists, advocated for the deconstruction of the classical image of the human being, which they deem too metaphysical. See Grondin, *A la escucha del sentido*, 67–68.

12. Grondin, *A la escucha del sentido*, 67, my translation.

13. At its base, atheist humanism rebels against the deep origin of human dignity: "If human beings deserve special care, it is because God Himself dedi-

cated special attention in creating them in His image." Grondin, *A la escucha del sentido*, 71, my translation.

14. See John Stuart Mill, *On Liberty* (1859), edited by Alan Ryan (New York: Penguin, 2006), 16.

15. See Ángel Rodríguez Luño and Arturo Bellocq, *Ética general* (Pamplona: EUNSA, 2015), 31ff.

16. See Maria A. Ferrari, *A liberdade política em John Stuart Mill* (Rome: Pontifical University Sancta Croce, Faculty of Philosophy, 2001), 361.

17. See Giuseppe Abbà, *Quale impostazione per la filosofía morale? Ricerche di filosofía morale* (Rome: LAS, 1995), 265.

18. See Ferrari, *A liberdade política em John Stuart Mill*, 348.

19. See J. C. Smart and Bernard Williams, *Utilitarianism: For & Against* (Cambridge: Cambridge University Press, 1973).

20. See Ferrari, *A liberdade política em John Stuart Mill*, 348.

21. See ibid., 349.

22. See Abbà, *Quale impostazione per la filosofía morale?*, 264–65.

23. Ibid., 265. This is what pre-modern ethics held—Platonic, Aristotelian, Stoic, and Neoplatonic, as well as Augustinian and Thomist Christian ethics. They conceived of ethics as a path toward virtue or personal excellence (*areté, virtus*).

24. See Ferrari, *A liberdade política em John Stuart Mill*, 371.

25. This "First Rawls" conceives of the choice of a conception of the good on the part of the human being in a Kantian sense of autonomous freedom, that is, as if the human being were totally independent, as in an original state, without any connection or purpose. This autonomous or independent freedom is what allows one to be subordinated to the rules of fairness. See Martin Rhonheimer, "La imagen del hombre en el liberalismo y el concepto de autonomía: Más allá del debate entre liberales y comunitaristas," in *Más allá del liberalismo*, edited by Robert A. Gahl (Madrid: EIUNSA, 2002), 4.

26. See John Rawls, *A Theory of Justice* (Oxford: Oxford University Press, 1973), 561.

27. See Rhonheimer, "La imagen del hombre en el liberalismo y el concepto de autonomía," 48.

28. Ibid., my translation.

29. Professor Da Re emphasizes the difference between the utilitarian position of *subordinating* the good (useful) to what is just and Rawls's deontological position that puts the just before the good. Utility has the primacy in the first, and justice has the primacy in the second. See A. Da Re, "Lo bueno y lo justo: Un panorama de las propuestas ético-políticas actuales," in *Más allá del liberalismo*, edited by Robert A. Gahl (Madrid: EIUNSA, 2002), 77–78.

30. John Rawls, *Political Liberalism* (New York: Columbia University Press, 1993), xix.

31. See Rawls, *A Theory of Justice*, 523.

32. Da Re, "Lo bueno y lo justo," 79.

33. Robert P. George, "Pluralismo morale, ragione pubblica e legge naturale," in *Etica e Politica nella Società del Duemila*, edited by R. A. Gahl (Rome: Armando editore, 1998), 84. This speech was originally given in English, but it was never published in English. The text quoted here is a translation of the first published version, which was in Italian.

34. John J. Dilulio (moderator), "Religious Freedom: A Conversation with Rick Warren and Robert P. George, *Review of Faith & International Affairs* 11, no. 4 (2013): 60, doi: 10.1080/15570274.2013.857113.

35. Sandel and Taylor—among other authors—caution against this contradiction. See Michael J. Sandel, *Liberalismus und Republikanismus* (Vienna: Passagen, 1995), and Charles Taylor, *Sources of the Self*, and "Atomism."

36. Rhonheimer, "La imagen del hombre en el liberalismo y el concepto de autonomía," 57, note 55.

37. See Sandel, *Liberalismus und Republikanismus*, 45–54.

38. See Luño and Bellocq, *Ética general*, 110.

39. Ibid.

40. The consensual theory of truth is postulated by Habermas, among others. A good critical exposition can be found in Sergio Belardinelli, "La teoría consensual de la verdad de Jürgen Habermas," *Anuario Filosófico* 24 (1991): 115–23, and bibliographical references in José María Carabante Muntada, "Jürgen Habermas," in *Philosophica: Enciclopedia filosófica online*, edited by Francisco Fernández Labastida and Juan Andrés Mercado, consulted February 2, 2017, http://www.philosophic a.info/archivo/2011/voces/habermas/Habermas.html.

41. See Rodríguez Luño and Bellocq, *Ética general*, 111.

42. Freedom is certainly autonomous, but it also needs to be cultivated in close connection with its nature and the reality of what things are, that is to say, according to the truth of the human being. This idea of a moral law comes from God and at the same time is a law that is proper to human beings as the principal actors of the moral experience. It is present in John Paul II, *Veritatis Splendor*, encyclical letter, August 6, 1993, Vatican website, http://www.vatican.va/content/john-paul -ii/en/encyclicals/documents/hf_jp-ii_enc_06081993_veritatis-splendor.html. Aquinas expressed this same thought when speaking of natural law: "It is nothing other than the light of understanding infused in us by God, whereby we understand what must be done and what must be avoided. God gave this light and this law to man at creation." Thomas Aquinas, *In dúo praecepta caritatis et in praecepta legis diciem, Prologus: Opuscula Theologica*, II, n. 1129, edited by Taurinens (1954), 245, cited in *Veritatis Splendor*, no. 40. See also Martin Rhonheimer, *La perspectiva de la moral* (Madrid: Rialp, 2000), 334ff.

43. See Joseph Ratzinger, "Conscience and Truth" (Original title: *Gewissen und Wahrheit: Stark Verkürzter Abdruck in Poln*), EWTN library, February 1991, https://www.ewtn.com/catholicism/library/conscience-and-truth-2468.

44. Ibid.

45. Ibid.

46. Ibid.

47. Joseph Ratzinger, "Truth and Freedom," *Communio* 23 (Spring 1996): 28.

48. See ibid., 34.

49. Cf. Aquinas, *In duo praecepta caritatis et in decem legis praecepta exposition*, c. I, in *Opuscola Theologica*, vol. 2: *De re spirituali* (Turin: Marietti, 1954), 245.

50. If this autonomy denied its origin, which is God, or depended completely on historical or cultural contingencies, it would contravene the truth of the human being: "Except the tree of knowledge of good and evil. From that tree you shall not eat; when you eat from it you shall die" (Gen. 2: 16–17).

51. John Henry Newman, "Certain Difficulties Felt by Anglicans in Catholic Teaching," in *A Letter Addressed to the Duke of Norfolk, on Occasion of Mr. Gladstone's Expostulation of 1874* (London: Longmans Green, 1900), 261.

52. Ratzinger, "Conscience and Truth."

53. See Taylor, "Atomism."

54. Ratzinger, "Conscience and Truth."

55. James W. Carey, *Communication as Culture: Essays on Media and Society* (New York: Routledge, 2009), 64.

56. Ibid.

57. Ibid.

TEN   The Neutrality of the Public Space

1. John Locke, *Two Treatises of Government* [1690], vol. 2, 123 (London: Dent, 1975) 180.

2. For Locke—writing at the end of the seventeenth century—the protection of religious freedom was not an individual right, but it derived from the Protestant tradition of "the Two Kings": religious freedom "was not a deduction from the personal autonomy of the individual, but an inference from the sovereignty of God," according to Michael W. McConnell in "Why Is Religious Freedom the First Freedom?," *Cardozo Law Review* 21 (2000), 1247. McConnell affirms: "In Lockean theory, there was no tension between liberalism and religious freedom: they were essentially the same" (ibid., 1248).

3. Quotation from Thomas Jefferson, *Letter to the Baptists of Danbury, Connecticut, 01-01-1802*, in *Jefferson's Writings*, edited by M. D. Peterson, (New York: Library of America, 1984), 510.

4. John Locke, *A Letter Concerning Toleration*, in *Locke on Toleration*, edited by Richard Vernon (Cambridge: Cambridge University Press, 2010) 6.

5. Ibid., 124.

6. Hobbes believed that the sovereign must be "Supreme Pastor" as well as "Civil Ruler." Rousseau thought these two obediences were contradictory and destroyed social unity. See McConnell, "Why Is Religious Freedom the First Freedom?," 1248–49.

7. See *McCollum v. Board of Education*, 333 US 203 (1948).

8. See Leonard Levy, *The Establishment Clause* (New York: Macmillan, 1986), chap. 2.

9. See *Everson v. Board of Education of Ewing Township*, 330 US 203, 226 (1947), Justice Jackson dissenting; *Abington Township School District v. Schempp*, 374 US 221 (1963); *Walz v. Tax Commission of the City of New York*, 397 US, 664, 669 (1970); and *Wallace v. Jaffree*, 472 US 38, 60 (1985).

10. See Michael J. Sandel, *Democracy's Discontent* (Cambridge, MA: Harvard University Press, 1996), 59.

11. See *Wallace v. Jaffree*, 472 US 60, 85 (1985).

12. See Sandel, *Democracy's Discontent*, 61ff.

13. Ibid., 64.

14. Ibid., 65.

15. See Hannah Arendt, *The Human Condition* (Chicago: University of Chicago Press, 1998), 28.

16. Ibid.

17. See ibid., 40.

18. Arendt, *The Human Condition*, 41.

19. See Arendt, *The Human Condition*, 52–54. This "common world" consists of the same object, in which everyone is interested, regardless of the differences in their positions and their variety of perspectives. If the identity of the object disappears and stops being discerned, that is when this common world is inexorably destroyed.

20. See ibid., 175.

21. Arendt, *The Human Condition*, 58.

22. Ibid., 26.

23. Ibid., 175–76.

24. McConnell, "Why Is Religious Liberty the 'First Freedom'?," 1259.

25. Some classic authors of this "civic public sphere" are Locke, Mill, Smith, and Franklin.

26. Some authors of the transgressive romantic-stoic position are Voltaire, Holmes, and Brandeis.

27. The concept of "truth" that underlies this approach is that of Enlightenment relativism based exclusively on rationality. There is no pre-existing transcen-

dent truth. Truth and falsehood compete, as Milton argued. As we saw earlier, Mill criticized the Miltonian optimism about the triumph of truth over falsehood, but he still believed in the educating power of fighting wrong ideas. See John Stuart Mill, *On Liberty*, edited by Alan Ryan (London: Penguin, 2006), 35.

28. The term "free market of ideas" is a widely used metaphor in various spheres: the political and religious, as well as that of communication and university life, and so on. Applied to communication, it was not widely used until the jurisprudence of the twentieth century, as John Peters argues in "'The Marketplace of Ideas': A History of a Concept," in *Toward a Political Economy of Culture: Capitalism and Communication in the Twenty-First Century*, edited by Andrew Calabrese and Colin Sparks (Boulder, CO: Rowman and Littlefield, 2004), 66, 72. Peters believed there are reasons to call Milton, Mill, and Holmes "friends of the concept marketplace of ideas," although he does so reluctantly. In *On Liberty* (1859), Mill refers to the open debate, where no opinion should be silenced, however harmful. In this "discursive war" nobody can sit with his or her truth in an infallible position. According to Holmes's skeptical and relativistic view, the truth would also be the product of the free debate of ideas, as if it were an automatic mechanism. Cf. Mathew D. Bunker, *Critiquing Free Speech* (Mahwah, NJ: Lawrence Erlbaum Associates, 2001), 2–8.

29. What I mean by "absolute" is that they believe in a marketplace of ideas with no regulation or restriction of any kind, one in which there is no privileged or protected speech.

30. From the case *Abrams v. United States*, 250 US 630 (1919), Justice Holmes dissenting.

31. Martin Rhonheimer, "La imagen del hombre en el liberalismo y el concepto de autonomía: Más allá del *debate entre liberales y comunitaristas*," in *Más allá del liberalismo*, edited by Robert A. Gahl (Madrid: EIUNSA, 2002), 45.

32. Ángel Rodríguez Luño, "Laicità e pluralismo," *L'Osservatore Romano*, January 24, 2003, 9, my translation.

33. See Joseph H. H. Weiler, *Una Europa Cristiana: Ensayo exploratorio* (Madrid: Encuentro, 2003), 105.

34. See John Paul II, *Centesimus annus*, encyclical letter, May 1, 1991, Vatican website, http://www.vatican.va/content/john-paul-ii/en/encyclicals/documents/hf_jp-ii_enc_01051991_centesimus-annus.html, no. 46.

35. Alexis de Tocqueville, *Democracy in America*, translated by James T. Schleifer, vol. 1 (Indianapolis, IN: Liberty Fund, 2010), 24.

36. Congregation for the Doctrine of the Faith, *Doctrinal Note on Some Questions Regarding the Participation of Catholics in Political Life*, November 24, 2001, Vatican website, http://www.vatican.va/roman_curia/congregations/cfaith/documents/rc_con_cfaith_doc_20021124_politica_en.html, no. 2: "A kind of cultural relativism

exists today, evident in the conceptualization and defense of an ethical pluralism, which sanctions the decadence and disintegration of reason and the principles of the natural moral law."

37. See Tocqueville, *Democracy in America*, 1:25.

38. See Thomas L. Tedford, *Freedom of Speech in the United States*, 5th ed. (State College, PA: Strata, 2005), 446.

39. See Pera, *Diritti umani e cristianesimo*, 16.

40. See Hannah Arendt, *On Revolution* (New York: Viking Press, 1963), 186.

41. Ibid., 186.

42. See Michel Villey, *Filosofía del Derecho* (Barcelona: Scire Universitaria, 2003), 64.

43. See ibid., 64–65.

44. Arendt, *On Revolution*, 190.

45. Ibid., 191.

46. See ibid.

47. See ibid., 192.

48. Martin Kriele, *Liberación e Ilustración* (Barcelona: Herder, 1982), 54, my translation.

49. See Kriele, *Liberación e Ilustración*, 54–55.

50. Thomas Jefferson, "The Virginia Declaration," in *The Complete Jefferson* (New York: Saul Padover, 1973), 295.

51. See Thomas Jefferson, *The Complete Jefferson*, 295ff.

52. See Jean Grondin, *A la escucha del sentido* (Barcelona: Herder, 2014), 81–89. The idea of the person who constructs himself or herself is also captured by Hannah Arendt in her treatise on violence, where she emphasizes that this is an attitude of rebellion against the human condition. See Hannah Arendt, *On Violence* (London: Allen Lane, Penguin Press, 1970, 12ff.

53. Benedict XVI, *Address at the Reichstag Building*, September 22, 2011, Vatican website, http://www.vatican.va/content/benedict-xvi/en/speeches/2011/september/documents/hf_ben-xvi_spe_20110922_reichstag-berlin.html.

54. See ibid., 4.

55. Ibid.

56. Ibid.

57. "We must listen to the language of nature and we must answer accordingly . . . there is also an ecology of man. Man too has a nature that he must respect and that he cannot manipulate at will. Man is not merely self-creating freedom. Man does not create himself. He is intellect and will, but he is also nature, and his will is rightly ordered if he respects his nature, listens to it and accepts himself for who he is, as one who did not create himself. In this way, and in no other, is true human freedom fulfilled." Ibid.

58. See McConnell, "Why Is Religious Liberty the 'First Freedom'?," 1260.

59. Ibid., 1264, emphasis added.

60. Ronald C. Arnett, *Communication Ethics in Dark Times: Hanna Arendt's Rhetoric of Warning and Hope* (Carbondale and Edwardsville: Southern Illinois University Press, 2013), 87.

61. See Arendt, *The Human Condition*, 95, 176.

62. Pierpaolo Donati, *Oltre il multiculturalismo: La ragione relazionale per un mondo comune* (Bari: Editori Laterza, 2008), 125.

63. The burka is the garment that women wear in public, which completely covers the head and body, with mesh over the eyes. The niqab is a garment that covers the whole body and hides just the head and face, leaving the eyes exposed.

64. Loi n° 2010–1192: *Loi interdisant la dissimulation du visage dans l'espace public* (Law of 2010–1192: Act Prohibiting Concealment of the Face in Public Space), October 11, 2010, https://www.legifrance.gouv.fr/affichTexte.do?cid Texte=JORFTEXT000022911670&categorieLien=id.

65. This decision was not exempt from controversy among sectors that saw in this concession an "insult to Australian values." For greater detail, see Peter Kurti, *The Tyranny of Tolerance: Threats to Religious Freedom in Australia* (Redland Bay, Australia: Connor Court, 2017), 12–13.

ELEVEN   The Origins of Freedom of Expression

1. See Pierre Albert, *Historia de la prensa* (Madrid: Rialp, 1990), 15.

2. Ibid., 16, my translation.

3. Some of Redondo's considerations regarding equality seem very correct to me: "In spite of all the legal pronouncements, the differences between people can never be erased. . . . However, it is understood that there must be legal equality and equal opportunity, so that, in principle, nobody is discriminated against." Gonzalo Redondo, *La Iglesia en el Mundo Contemporáneo: De Pío VI a Pío IX (1775–1878)* (Pamplona: EUNSA, 1979), 136–37, my translation.

4. Redondo, *La Iglesia en el Mundo Contemporáneo*, 41, my translation.

5. Ibid., 25, my translation.

6. Albert, *Historia de la prensa*, 28, my translation.

7. Ibid., 23–24.

8. "Declaration of the Rights of Man—1789," August 26, 1789, at the Lillian Goldman Law Library, Yale Law School, New Haven, CT, https://avalon .law.yale.edu/18th_century/rightsof.asp, no. 11.

9. See Antonio Acerbi, *Chiesa cultura società: Momenti e figure dal Vaticano I a Paolo VI* (Milan: Vita e Pensiero, 1998), 54–57.

10. See *ibid.*, 57ff.

11. The revolutionary period gave a great boost to the press: more than 1,500 new periodicals appeared in France between 1789 and 1800. See Albert, *Historia de la prensa*, 36ff. Taking advantage of the curiosity that political and social events aroused in the citizens, the press joined the forefront of the political scene. However, in France the press was also the victim of terror, as freedom of the press was suspended, and many newspapers had to dissolve. "Control of the press became increasingly overwhelming. . . . In 1805, the censors were integrated into the newsroom" (ibid., my translation).

12. See Redondo, *La Iglesia en el Mundo Contemporáneo*, 51.

13. Pius VI, brief *Quod aliquamtum*, March 10, 1791, in U. Bellocchi, *Tutte le encicliche e i principali documenti pontifici emanati dal 1740*, vol. 2 (Vatican City: LEV, 1994), 150–82.

14. Ibid., my translation.

15. Redondo, *La Iglesia en el Mundo Contemporáneo*, 63, my translation.

16. See ibid., 90.

17. See Mariano Fazio, *Historia de las ideas contemporáneas* (Madrid: Rialp, 2006), 360.

18. Francis, *Evangelii gaudium*, apostolic exhortation, November 24, 2013, Vatican website, http://www.vatican.va/content/francesco/en/apost_exhortations /documents/papa-francesco_esortazione-ap_20131124_evangelii-gaudium.html, no. 116.

19. See Antonio Acerbi, *Due ecclesiologie: Ecclesiologia giuridica ed ecclesiologia di comunione nella Lumen Gentium* (Bologna: EDB, 1975), 22ff.

20. See ibid.

21. See Pius XII, *Mystici corporis Christi*, encyclical letter, June 29, 1943, Vatican website, http://www.vatican.va/content/pius-xii/en/encyclicals/documents /hf_p-xii_enc_29061943_mystici-corporis-christi.html, 193ff.

22. See Acerbi, *Due ecclesiologie*, 55ff.

23. See ibid., 105.

24. Fazio, *Historia de las ideas contemporáneas*, 384, my translation.

25. See Benjamin Constant, "De la liberté des Anciens comparée à celle des Modernes: Discours prononcé a l'Athénée Royal de Paris (1819)," in *Collection complète des ouvrages publies sur le government representatif et la constitution actuelle, au Cours de politique constitutionelle* (Paris: Béchet, 1820), 238–74.

26. Cf. Hannah Arendt, *On Revolution* (New York: Viking Press, 1963), 21ff. Arendt summarizes the revolution in three concepts: novelty, origin, and violence.

27. Arendt explains the separation between the public and private spheres. See Hannah Arendt, *The Human Condition* (Chicago: University of Chicago Press, 1998), 28–37. The author distinguishes between the familial sphere, where

needs are satisfied, and the political grounds of public matters, where civil liberty unfolds. N. González Gaitano has clarified the distinction between intimacy, privacy, and public life, showing that the first, intimacy, is a condition of possibility in private life and public life without being dissolved into them. Unlike in the case of "moral liberalism" or relativism, this distinction does not exclude the morality of the public or the private sphere. See N. González Gaitano, *El deber de respeto a la intimidad* (Pamplona: EUNSA, 1990), 31–35.

28. Arendt, *On Revolution*, 121.

29. This refers to the polis, to the government of the *res publica*. In Greece and Rome, membership in the political body was given by the status of the citizen. See Arendt, *The Human Condition*, 23ff.

30. See Arendt, *On Revolution*, 121.

31. Ibid., 123. In the Declaration of Independence, Jefferson speaks of the "pursuit of Happiness," and this expression introduces an equivalence between two concepts: private well-being and public happiness. It would take us too far off course to get into this debate here.

32. Arendt, *On Revolution*, 122.

33. Cf. ibid., 129. However, the revolution in France, with Robespierre, was ultimately dedicated to the liberation from necessity (and from suffering, rage, and helplessness) by violence.

34. Cf. ibid., 135. It should be said that in the United States the question remains as to whether the purpose of the government is to guarantee prosperity (happiness) or to promote freedom. I refer the reader to the book referenced for a closer examination of this argument.

35. Ibid., 136.

36. The author discusses the two traditions that affect how constituent power is formed and how individual rights are enforced. See ibid., 146–48, 202–8.

37. Cf. ibid., 146–47.

38. Ibid., 147.

39. Tocqueville makes his point on virtue using a comparison regarding human ambition. He distinguishes how in America those who work hard try to thrive through commerce or industry, while in some European countries, such as France, ambition pushes many people to ask for a "public post" as a more comfortable path. Once inside a public office, "the search for positions becomes the most popular of all industries." Cf. Alexis de Tocqueville, *Democracy in America*, edited by Eduardo Nolla, translated by James T. Schleifer, vol. 2 (Indianapolis, IN: Liberty Fund, 2010), 1129–30.

40. See ibid., 707.

41. See ibid., 708.

42. Ibid., 707.

43. Arendt, *On Revolution*, 160.

TWELVE Old-School and New-School Censorship

1. M. del Pozo, *s.v. "Censura,"* in *Gran Enciclopedia Rialp*, vol. 5 (Madrid: Rialp, 1984), 494, my translation.

2. Ibid.," 495, my translation.

3. Milton asked the English Parliament in 1643 to retract the law that introduced censorship. See ibid."

4. That is to say, the ecclesiastical authorization to publish books relating to faith and Catholic doctrine. We must keep in mind that religious and political power had not yet been separated in the Christian kingdoms, which were all still Catholic at that time, as the Peace of Westphalia was still nearly two centuries away.

5. "So that you may bring to fruition what you have started so well, through these means, with Apostolic authority, we grant you license and authority to repress with ecclesiastical censorship, and with other appropriate remedies, the printers, merchants, and readers of such books." Gratius Ortwin, *Lamentationes Obscurorum Virorum* (Cologne: Cet ouvrage, 1518), 612. Quoted in Antonio Legname, *Il diritto d'informazione nella dottrina del Magistero e nell'ordinamento canonico*, Pontifical University Lateranense, 1995, 25, my translation.

6. This document is found not in the various editions of the *Bullaria* nor in the *Annales ecclesiastici* but was reproduced by a scholar who worked on the version kept at the Vatican Pontifical Archive. See Joseph Hilgers, *Der Index der verbotenen Bücher in seiner neuen Fassung dargelegt und rechtlich-historisch gewürdigt, Herdersche Verlagsbuchhandlung* (Freiburg im Breisgau, 1904), 480–82, available at https://archive.org/details/derindexderverb03hilggoog/page/480/mode/1up ?view=theater.

7. Pius IV, *De indice librorum*, decree, December 4, 1536, in Cebollada, *Del Génesis a Internet*, 5ff, which Pius IV put into effect through the bull *Dominici gregis* on March 24, 1564, with the list of books that were banned for the Catholic faithful. On June 14, 1966, the Holy Office would eliminate the institution of the Index.

8. Leticia Soberón, *"Historia de los documentos sobre comunicación social,"* in Actas Congreso UCAM, *Iglesia y medios de comunicación social: El Magisterio de la Iglesia católica* (Murcia: UCAM, 2000), my translation.

9. "But lying opinions, than which no mental plague is greater, and vices which corrupt the heart and moral life should be diligently repressed by public authority, lest they insidiously work the ruin of the State. The excesses of an unbridled intellect, which unfailingly end in the oppression of the untutored multitude, are no less rightly controlled by the authority of the law than are the injuries inflicted by violence upon the weak. And this all the more surely, because by far the greater part of the community is either absolutely unable, or able only with great difficulty, to escape from illusions and deceitful subtleties, especially such as flatter

the passions." Leo XIII, *Libertas praestatissimum*, encyclical, June 20, 1888, Vatican website, http://www.vatican.va/content/leo-xiii/en/encyclicals/documents /hf_l-xiii_enc_20061888_libertas.html, no. 23.

10. Leo XIII, *Officiorum ac numerum*, constitution, January 1, 1897, January 1, 1897, Vatican website, http://www.vatican.va/content/leo-xiii/la/apost_constitutions /documents/hf_l-xiii_apc_18970125_officiorum-ac-munerum.html. The magisterial document reiterated the condemnation and prohibition of all those newspapers, writings, and magazines that deliberately fought the Catholic religion and morality, and it forbade Catholics (especially clergy) to write without reasonable cause in that type of press. See Leo XIII, *Officiorum ac numerum*, nos. 21–22. Ordinaries were also urged to prohibit and eliminate from the attention of the faithful prejudicial books and other writings published or distributed in their dioceses. See Leo XIII, *Officiorum ac munerum*, no. 29.

11. Leo XIII approved the new *Index librorum prohibitorum* in the apostolic constitution *Officiorum ac munerum*, January 25, 1897, https://www.vatican.va /content/leo-xiii/it/apost_constitutions/documents/hf_l-xiii_apc_18970125 _officiorum-ac-munerum.html

12. The decrees on the prohibition and censorship of books were published along with the document repealing the regulations of the Council of Trent. See Benedict XIV, *Sollicita ac provida*, apostolic constitution, July 9, 1753, in Cebollada, *Del Génesis a Internet*, 5ff.

13. This is the same Pope who, in the 1907 encyclical *Pascendi*, gives the name "modernism" to the doctrinal challenge of what we call modernity, which could be summarized as follows: "an intent to make faith into a science, to submit Revelation to human reason." See http://www.vatican.va/content/pius-x/en /encyclicals/documents/hf_p-x_enc_19070908_pascendi-dominici-gregis.html.

14. See Emmanuel Cabello, *San Pío X y la renovación de la vida cristiana*, in Josep-Ignasi Saranyana, *Cien años de pontificado romano* (Pamplona: EUNSA, 1997), 51.

15. See Federico M. Requena, *Benedicto XV, un Papa entre dos mundos*, in Saranyana, *Cien años de pontificado romano*, 71.

16. "It is also the duty of the bishops to prevent writings infected with Modernism or favourable to it from being read when they have been published, and to hinder their publication when they have not." Pius X, *Pascendi*, no. 50.

17. "It is forbidden to secular priests, without the previous consent of the Ordinary, to undertake the direction of papers or periodicals. This permission shall be withdrawn from any priest who makes a wrong use of it after having been admonished. With regard to priests who are correspondents or collaborators of periodicals, as it happens not unfrequently that they write matter infected with Modernism for their papers or periodicals, let the Bishops see to it that this is not permitted

to happen, and, should they fail in this duty, let the Bishops make due provision with authority delegated by the Supreme Pontiff." Pius X, *Pascendi*, no. 53.

18. And he prescribed "a special Censor for newspapers and periodicals written by Catholics. It shall be his office to read in due time each number after it has been published, and if he find anything dangerous in it let him order that it be corrected." Pius X, *Pascendi*.

19. Gonzalo Redondo, *La Iglesia en el Mundo Contemporáneo: De León XIII a Pío XI (1878–1939)* (Pamplona: EUNSA, 1979), 108–9, my translation.

20. Benedict XV, *Alloquentes proxime*, motu proprio, March 25, 1917, Vatican website, http://www.vatican.va/content/benedict-xv/it/motu_proprio/documents /hf_ben-xv_motu-proprio_19170325_alloquentes-proxime.html.

21. Paul VI, *Integrae servandae*, apostolic letter, December 7, 1965, Vatican website, http://w2.vatican.va/content/paul-vi/en/motu_proprio/documents /hf_p-vi_motu-proprio_19651207_integrae-servandae.html.

22. Congregation for the Doctrine of the Faith, *Notification Regarding the Abolition of the Index of Books*, June 14, 1966, Vatican website, http://www.vatican .va/roman_curia/congregations/cfaith/documents/rc_con_cfaith_doc_19660614 _de-indicis-libr-prohib_en.html, emphasis mine.

23. See Thomas Patrick Doherty, *Pre-Code Hollywood: Sex, Immorality, and Insurrection in American Cinema, 1930–1934* (New York: Columbia University Press, 1999), 6.

24. See Henry E. Scott, *Shocking True Story, The Rise and Fall of "Confidential," America's Most Scandalous Magazine* (New York: Pantheon Books), 2010.

25. The Production Code specified: "1. No picture should lower the moral standards of those who see it. 2. Law, natural or divine, must not be belittled, ridiculed, nor must a sentiment be created against it. 3. As far as possible, life should not be misrepresented, at least not in such a way as to place in the mind of youth false values on life." Quoted in E. Michael Jones, *John Cardinal Krol and the Cultural Revolution* (South Bend, IN: Fidelity Press, 1995), 308.

26. See Doherty, *Pre-Code Hollywood*, 9.

27. He uses a famous passage from Dante's Divine Comedy in which Dante is in hell talking to a couple, finding out the reason for their sin. The woman tells Dante that reading a certain book—"*Galeotto fu il libro e chi lo scrisse*"—was the catalyst for their sin: (*Inferno*, Canto 5, verse 137). Talking about the moral rule for arts, Alessandro Manzoni, said: "Never betray or utter a word that applauds vice or belittles virtue." Quoted in J. Iribarren, *El derecho a la verdad: Doctrina de la Iglesia sobre prensa, radio y televisión* (Madrid: BAC, 1968), 63.

28. Pius XI, *Vigilanti cura*, encyclical, July 7, 1936, Vatican website, http:// www.vatican.va/content/pius-xi/en/encyclicals/documents/hf_p-xi_enc_29061936 _vigilanti-cura.html.

29. "The motion picture should not be simply a means of diversion, a light relaxation to occupy an idle hour; with its magnificent power, it can and must be a bearer of light and a positive guide to what is good." Pius XI, *Vigilanti cura*.

30. Cf. Dario Edoardo Viganò, *Pío XII e il cinema* (Rome: Ente dello Spettacolo, 2005), 9.

31. To understand the context of the era, see Jones, *John Cardinal Krol and the Cultural Revolution*, 301–53. Other works include Gregory Black, *Hollywood Censored: Morality Codes, Catholics and Movies* (Cambridge: Cambridge University Press, 1994); Gregory Black, *Catholic Crusade against the Movies: 1940–1975* (Cambridge: Cambridge University Press, 1998); Paul Facey, *The Legion of Decency: A Sociological Analysis of the Emergence and Development of a Pressure Group* (New York: Arno Press, 1974); L. Wittern-Keller and R. Haberski, *The Miracle Case: Film Censorship and the Supreme Court* (Kansas: University Press of Kansas, 2008); James Skinner, *The Cross and the Cinema: The Legion of Decency and the National Catholic Office for Motion Pictures, 1933–1970* (Westport, CT: Praegar, 1993); Frank Walsh, *Sin and Censorship: The Catholic Church and the Motion Picture Industry* (New Haven, CT: Yale University Press, 1996).

32. The Catholic Church's position on immoral content in motion pictures was intended to encourage self-regulation on the part of the film industry. On the other hand, the Pope considered that film, by its nature, has two dimensions: a cultural-artistic one in which a growing number of people work, some of them Christians, and another dimension as a means of entertainment and recreation. That is why he wanted to clarify that the objectivity of morality is not cast aside in the name of art. The artistic dimension does not change the moral qualification of sexual perversion as a disordered attitude. Pius XII, *Apostolic Exhortations of His Holiness Pius XII to Representatives of the Cinema World*, June 21, 1955, Vatican website, http://www.vatican.va/content/pius-xii/en/apost_exhortations/documents/hf_p-xii_exh_25101955_ideal-film.html.

33. In the 1965 report, Msgr. Thomas Little, executive director of the Legion of Decency, reported that Hollywood was breaking the codes: "In the last two years 34 films, of which 20 were major American productions, would have been released with scenes employing nudity had not the producers realized that they would then have been condemned." Jones, *John Cardinal Krol and the Cultural Revolution*, 303.

34. See ibid., 302.

35. Quoted in ibid., 305.

36. See *Ginsberg v. New York*, 390 US 629.

37. See https://www.mpaa.org/film-ratings/.

38. See *Miller v. California*, 13 US 15.

39. "The fulfilment of this pledge supposes that the people be told plainly which films are permitted to all, which are permitted with reservations, and which

are harmful or positively bad. This requires the prompt, regular, and frequent publication of classified lists of motion picture plays so as to make the information readily accessible to all. Special bulletins or other timely publications, such as the daily Catholic Press, may be used for this purpose." Pius XI, *Vigilanti cura*.

40. See https://ncac.scdn6.secure.raxcdn.com/wp-content/uploads/import /FilmCensorshipInfographic.png.

41. Legname, *Il diritto d'informazione nella dottrina del Magistero e nell'ordinamento canonico*, 39.

42. "It is therefore one of the supreme necessities of our times to watch and to labour to the end that the motion picture be no longer a school of corruption but that it be transformed into an effectual instrument for the education and the elevation of mankind." Pius XI, *Vigilanti cura*.

43. The Holy See, "Text of Letter from Rome on the Legion of Decency," *Catholic Advocate* 8, no. 20 (May 15, 1959): 5.

44. For example, in the United States the statute of decency was challenged on the ground of free speech: cf. D. A. Downs, *The New Politics of Pornography* (Chicago: University of Chicago Press, 1989). However, there is still doctrine that hard-core pornography is not protected by the US Constitution.

45. Gerard V. Bradley, "The Moral Basis for Legal Regulation of Pornography," J. R. Stoner Jr., "Freedom, Virtue and the Politics of Regulating Pornography," and H. Arkes, "Pornography: Settling the Question in Principle," in *The Social Costs of Pornography: A Collection of Papers* (Princeton, NJ: Witherspoon Institute, 2010). See also R. Scruton, "Pornography and the Courts," *Public Discourse: Ethics, Law and the Common Good*, February 9, 2009, available at http:// www.thepublicdiscourse.com/2009/02/90.

46. Cf. Mary Eberstadt and Mary Anne Layden, *The Social Costs of Pornography: A Statement of Findings and Recommendations*, the Withersopoon Institute and The Social Trends Institute, Princeton, NJ, 2010.

47. See Zeynep Tufekci, "It's the (Democracy-Poisoning) Golden Age of Free Speech," *Wired*, January 16, 2018, https://www.wired.com/story/free-speech -issue-tech-turmoil-new-censorship/.

48. Zeynep Tufekci, *Twitter and Tear Gas: The Power and Fragility of Networked Protest* (New Haven, CT: Yale University Press, 2017), 226.

49. Richard R. John, "Freedom of Expression in the Digital Age: A Historian's Perspective," *Church, Communication and Culture* 4, no. 1 (2019): 34, doi 10.1080/23753234.2019.1565918.

50. For more information, see Peter Pomerantsev, "The Menace of Unreality: How the Kremlin Weaponizes Information, Culture and Money," *Interpreter*, November 22, 2014, http://www.interpretermag.com/the-menace-of-unreality-how -the-kremlin-weaponizes-information-culture-and-money/, and Tim Wu, *The Attention Merchants* (New York: Knopf, 2016).

51. Pomerantsev, "The Menace of Unreality."

52. Jack M. Balkin, "Old-School/New-School Speech Regulation," *Harvard Law Review* 127 (2014): 2297.

53. See Tim Wu, "Is the First Amendment Obsolete?," in Lee C. Bollinger and Geoffrey R. Stone, *The Free Speech Century* (New York: Oxford University Press, 2019), 281.

54. See Jordi Pujol and Rolando Montes, *Trasparenza e Segreto nella Chiesa Cattolica* (Venice: Marcianum Press, 2022), 103.

55. Nathaniel Hawthorne, *The Scarlet Letter* (Boston: Ticknor, Reed & Fields, 1850; New York: Barnes & Noble Classics, 2003), 177. Citations refer to the Barnes and Noble edition. Also in Julian Hawthorne, "'The Scarlet Letter' by Nathaniel Hawthorne Reviewed," *Atlantic*, April 1886, 17.

56. See John Witte Jr. and Joel A. Nichols, *Religion and the American Constitutional Experiment* (New York: Oxford University Press, 2016), 26ff.

57. Ibid., 90.

58. This type of flooding finds its the roots in "Astroturfing." The use of so-called Astroturf groups is widespread across all nations and walks of life, from China to Britain, from book reviews to online surveys, and from big business to local politics. See Adam Bienkov, "Astroturfing: What Is It and Why Does It Matter?," *Guardian*, February 8, 2012, https://www.theguardian.com/commentisfree /2012/feb/08/what-is-astroturfing.

59. See Jack Goldsmith and Tim Wu, *Who Controls the Internet? Illusions of a Borderless World* (New York: Oxford University Press, 2006).

60. Gary King, Jennifer Pan, and Margaret E. Roberts, "How Censorship in China Allows Government Criticism but Silences Collective Expression," *American Political Science Review* 107 (2017): 484.

61. Wu, "Is the First Amendment Obsolete?," 283.

THIRTEEN The Classical Tradition of the Founding Fathers of the United States

1. Those seven figures were Benjamin Franklin, George Washington, Thomas Jefferson, John Adams, Alexander Hamilton, James Madison, and John Jay. See Richard B. Morris, *Seven Who Shaped Our Destiny: The Founding Fathers as Revolutionaries* (New York: Harper & Row, 1973).

2. See Thomas G. West, "Free Speech in the American Founding and in Modern Liberalism," *Social Philosophy and Policy* 21, no. 2 (2004): 311.

3. US Declaration of Independence (1776).

4. See Jack N. Rakove, ed., *The Annotated U.S. Constitution and Declaration of Independence* (Cambridge, MA: Harvard University Press, 2009), 73ff.

5. Henry Kalven Jr., *A Worthy Tradition: Freedom of Speech in America*, edited by Jamie Kalven (New York: Harper & Row, 1988), xviii.

6. Henry Kalven, "Tradition in Law," in *The Great Ideas Today*, edited by R. Hutchins & M. Adler (Chicago: Encyclopedia Britannica, 1974), p. 33, quoting Karl Llewellyn, *The Common Law Tradition* (Boston: Little, Brown & Co., 1960).

7. Henry J. Kalven Jr., *A Worthy Tradition*, xviii.

8. Alasdair MacIntyre, *After Virtue* (Notre Dame, IN: University of Notre Dame Press, 1981), 222.

9. See Michael P. Zuckert, *The Natural Rights Republic: Studies in the Foundation of the American Political Tradition* (South Bend, IN: University of Notre Dame Press, 1996), 40.

10. Michael P. Zuckert, *Natural Rights and the New Republicanism* (Princeton, NJ: Princeton University Press, 1994); Zuckert, *The Natural Rights Republic*.

11. For a deeper treatment of this argument, see Michael P. Zuckert, *Launching Liberalism: On Lockean Political Philosophy* (Kansas: University Press of Kansas, 2002); Jeremy Waldron, *God, Locke, and Equality: The Christian Foundations of John Locke's Political Thought* (Cambridge: Cambridge University Press, 2002).

12. It is a long debate that includes many legal philosophers, starting on the side of legal positivism with Hans Kelsen, *Pure Theory of Law* (Berkeley: University of California Press, 1967), and some critiques within positivism: Herbert L. A. Hart, *The Concept of Law* (Oxford: Clarendon Press, 1961); Lon L. Fuller, *The Morality of Law* (New Haven, CT: Yale University Press, 1964); Joseph Raz, *The Morality of Freedom* (Oxford: Clarendon Press, 1986). Other criticisms outside positivism are from John Rawls, *Theory of Justice* (Cambridge, MA: Harvard University Press, 1971); Ronald Dworkin, *Taking Rights Seriously* (Cambridge, MA: Harvard University Press, 1977); Michael Sandel, *Liberalism and the Limits of Justice* (Cambridge: Cambridge University Press, 1981). The criticisms from contemporary legal iusnaturalism come mostly from Germain Grisez and John Finnis, among others: John Finnis, *Natural Law and Natural Rights* (Oxford: Oxford University Press, 1980); Germain Grisez, *The Way of the Lord Jesus*, vol. 1: *Christian Moral Principles* (Chicago: Franciscan Herald Press, 1983); Robert P. George, ed., *Natural Law Theory: Contemporary Essays* (Oxford: Clarendon Press, 1992), and a critique of this new natural law theory from Russell Hittinger, *A Critique of the New Natural Law Theory* (Notre Dame, IN: University of Notre Dame Press, 1989).

13. See Charles J. Chaput, *Render unto Caesar* (New York: Image-Random House, 2012), 81.

14. For more details, see Chaput, *Render unto Caesar*, 81ff.

15. The Founders embraced different understandings of the formula for the separation between Church and state and of how the right to religious liberty should be exercised. See Vincent Phillip Muñoz, *God and the Founders* (New York: Cambridge University Press, 2009).

16. As we saw in chapter 10, the existence of "religious establishments" made this reality more complex. See several authors: Michael J. Sandel, *Democracy's Discontent* (Cambridge, MA: Harvard University Press, 1996), 59ff.; Leonard Levy, *The Establishment Clause* (New York: Macmillan, 1986), chap. 2; Michael W. McConnell, "Why Is Religious Freedom the First Freedom?," *Cardozo Law Review* 21 (2000): 1247ff.

17. Rakove, ed., *The Annotated U.S. Constitution and Declaration of Independence*, 77.

18. See ibid., 220.

19. See Steven Heyman, *Free Speech and Human Dignity* (New Haven, CT: Yale University Press, 2008), 12.

20. Alexander Hamilton, James Madison, and John Jay, *Federalist Papers* (Oxford: Oxford University Press, 2008), 257.

21. See West, "Free Speech in the American Founding," 319.

22. Eugene Volokh, "Freedom of Speech and of the Press," in *The Heritage Guide to the Constitution*, consulted December 13, 2019, https://www.heritage.org /constitution/#!/amendments/1/essays/140/freedom-of-speech-and-of-the-press.

23. See Jeffrey Langan, "God, Nietzsche and the Contemporary Political Philosophy," in *Ethics without God?*, edited by Fulvio Di Blasi, Joshua P. Hochschild, and Jeffrey Langan (South Bend, IN: St. Augustine's Press, 2008), 4.

24. By his own admission, Schauer borrows these terms from the pluralist tradition of Rawls and Berlin, with reference to the Coherence Theory elucidated by later scholars, including Ronald Dworkin. See Frederick Schauer, *Free Speech: A Philosophical Enquiry* (Cambridge: Cambridge University Press, 1982), 207.

25. Ibid., 5.

26. Ibid., 15.

27. Ibid., 34.

28. See Zuckert, *The Natural Rights Republic*, 95. The term "Whig" refers to the old name of the British liberal party.

29. Rakove, ed., *The Annotated U.S. Constitution and Declaration of Independence*, 223.

30. See Heyman, *Free Speech and Human Dignity*, 14–15.

31. See ibid., 15.

32. See ibid., 20.

33. This was an act that appeared on July 14, 1798, "for the punishment of certain crimes against the United States." Internal security was increased by limiting some individual rights, especially immigration, freedom of expression, and criticism of the government by the press. This transitory measure expired in 1801. As we shall see later, the Founding Fathers' original idea of free expression did not protect defamatory speech aimed at authority, obscenity, pornography, or incitement to

violence. In *New York Times Co. v. Sullivan*, 376 US 254 (1964), the Supreme Court determined that the First Amendment's protection of the freedom of expression affects all levels of government (federal, state, and local) but not private citizens or private businesses. There is a vast bibliography on the controversy surrounding the Sedition Act and the concept of freedom of expression. See Geoffrey R. Stone, *Perilous Times: Free Speech in Wartime; From the Sedition Act of 1798 to the War on Terrorism* (New York: W. W. Norton, 2004); Wendell R. Bird, *Press and Speech under Assault: The Early Supreme Court Justices and the Sedition Act of 1798*, and the *Campaign against Dissent* (New York: Oxford University Press, 2016); John Chester Miller, *Crisis in Freedom: The Alien and Sedition Acts* (Boston: Little Brown, 1951); Charles Slack, *Liberty's First Crisis: Adams, Jefferson, and the Misfits Who Saved Free Speech* (New York: Atlantic Monthly Press, 2015); Thomas G. West, *Vindicating the Founders: Race, Sex, Class, and Justice in the Origins of America* (Lanham, MD: Rowan & Littlefield, 1997).

34. See Heyman, *Free Speech and Human Dignity*, 9.

35. See Hamilton et al., *Federalist Papers*, 49.

36. See ibid.

37. See ibid.

38. See ibid., 51.

39. See ibid., 257.

40. See ibid. Madison uses the expression "subordinate distributions of power."

41. See Volokh, "Freedom of Speech and of the Press."

42. Heyman, *Free Speech and Human Dignity*, 221, no. 31.

43. Blackstone was part of the Church of England. When we study Milton, we shall devote a section to the conception of freedom that derives from the authors who identified with the Protestant Reformation. The ideas expressed there can be used to understand Blackstone's approach to natural rights and freedoms.

44. Heyman, *Free Speech and Human Dignity*, 10.

45. Ibid., 12.

46. West warns that the modern liberal tradition of freedom of expression has modified the original limits that the Founding Fathers set on defamation, obscenity, pornography, and incitement to violence. See West, "Free Speech in the American Founding," 313ff.

47. West, "Free Speech in the American Founding."

48. See ibid., 312–13.

49. See ibid., 314.

50. Rakove, ed., *The Annotated U.S. Constitution and Declaration of Independence*, 77.

51. John Locke, *Two Treatises of Government* (1690), edited by Peter Laslett (Cambridge: Cambridge University Press, 1960), Second Treatise, sec. 123–31,

350–53. On Locke's influence on the political philosophy of the Founding Fathers, see Thomas G. West, "The Political Theory of the Declaration of Independence," in *The American Founding and the Social Compact*, edited by Ronald J. Pestritto and Thomas G. West (Lanham, MD: Lexington Books, 2003).

52. James Wilson (1742–1798) is known as one of the "forgotten Founders." He played an important role in drafting the preamble to the Constitution and, as one of the first Supreme Court justices, helped establish the foundations of the legal principles of the new constitutional project. For further reading, cf. Charles P. Smith, *James Wilson, Founding Father: 1742–1798* (Chapel Hill: University of North Carolina Press, 1956); Ian C. Bartrum, "James Wilson in the State House Yard: Ratifying the Structures of Popular Sovereignty" (2016), in *Scholarly Works*, Scholarly Commons@UNLV Boyd Law, https://scholars.law.unlv.edu/facpub/1195.

53. See West, "Free Speech in the American Founding," 320.

54. See James Madison, "Notes for Speech in Congress" (June 8, 1789), in *Papers of James Madison*, vol. 12, edited by Charles F. Hobson and Ronald A. Rutland (Charlottesville: University Press of Virginia, 1979), 194.

55. See Thomas Paine, "Candid and Critical Remarks on a Letter Signed Ludlow," in *The Roots of the Bill of Rights* (Schwartz, 1777), 315–16, quoted in West, "Free Speech in the American Founding," 321.

56. West, "Free Speech in the American Founding," 321.

57. See Hamilton et al., *Federalist Papers*, 50 no. 10.

58. See West, "Free Speech in the American Founding," 321–22.

FOURTEEN The Contemporary Redefinition of the Free Speech
Tradition in the United States

1. See Steven Heyman, *Free Speech and Human Dignity* (New Haven, CT: Yale University Press, 2008), 23–24.

2. See ibid., 14.

3. "Oliver Wendell Holmes, Jr.," *Encyclopædia Britannica Online*, 2016, https://www.britannica.com/biography/Oliver-Wendell-Holmes-Jr.

4. This expression is cited in John Durhan Peters, *Courting the Abyss: Free Speech and the Liberal Tradition* (Chicago: Chicago University Press, 2005), 150.

5. See *Abrams v. United States*, 250 US 616 (1919), 630. This case contains the famous phrase "The Constitution is a fighting faith," with which Holmes defined truth and discourse in the public sphere as a competition or battle.

6. See Peters, *Courting the Abyss*, 146ff.

7. *Schenck v. United States*, 249 US 47 (1919), 52.

8. See David A. Strauss, "Freedom of Speech and the Common-Law Constitution," in *Eternally Vigilant: Free Speech in the Modern Era*, edited by Lee C. Bollinger and Geoffrey R. Stone (Chicago: University of Chicago Press, 2002), 50.

9. *Schenck v. United States*, 249 US 47 (1919): "The question in every case is whether the words used are used in such circumstances and are of such a nature as to create a clear and present danger that they will bring about the substantive evils that Congress has the right to prevent."

10. Strauss, "Freedom of Speech and the Common-Law Constitution," 49.

11. See Kent Greenawalt, "Clear and Present Danger and Criminal Speech," in *Eternally Vigilant: Free Speech in the Modern Era*, edited by Lee C. Bollinger and Geoffrey R. Stone (Chicago: University of Chicago Press, 2002), 119.

12. Ibid., 102–4, 119.

13. See Strauss, "Freedom of Speech and the Common-Law Constitution," 47–48, and *Abrams v. United States*, 250 US 616 (1919).

14. *Abrams v. United States*, 250 US 630 (1919).

15. See Strauss, "Freedom of Speech and the Common-Law Constitution," 50.

16. Lee C. Bollinger, *The Tolerant Society: Freedom of Speech and Extremist Speech in America* (New York: Oxford University Press, 1986), 87.

17. See Nigel Warburton, *Free Speech: A Very Short Introduction* (Oxford: Oxford University Press, 2009), 62–70.

18. Bollinger, *The Tolerant Society*, 34.

19. See ibid., 37–38.

20. Heyman, *Free Speech and Human Dignity*, 25.

21. See ibid., 24.

22. Roscoe Pound, "Interests of Personality," *Harvard Law Review* 28 (1915): 344. On Pound's sociological doctrine, see Mark A. Graber, *Transforming Free Speech: The Ambiguous Legacy of Civil Libertarianism* (Berkeley: University of California Press, 1991), 69–74.

23. Cf. Z. Chafee Jr., *Free Speech in the United States* (Cambridge, MA: Harvard University Press, 1941), 31–34.

24. Zechariah Chafee Jr., *Freedom of Speech* (New York: Harcourt, Brace and Howe, 1920), 34.

25. Cf. Chafee, *Free Speech in the United States*, 35.

26. See *Chaplinski v. New Hampshire*, 315 US 568–72 (1942), quoted in Thomas L. Tedford, *Freedom of Speech in the United States*, 5th ed. (State College, PA: Strata, 2005), 436.

27. See ibid., 435.

28. Ibid., 436.

29. See Heyman, *Free Speech and Human Dignity*, 27.

30. See ibid., 28.

31. Ibid., 29.

32. See Alexander Meiklejohn, *Free Speech and Its Relation to Self-Government* (New York: Harper and Brothers, 1948), 26ff.

33. "There are, in the theory of the Constitution, two radically different kinds of utterances. The constitutional status of the merchant advertising his wares, of a paid lobbyist fighting for the advantage of his client, is utterly different from that of a citizen who is planning for the general welfare." Meiklejohn, *Free Speech and Its Relation to Self-Government*, 37.

34. The text of the Fifth Amendment (emphasis added): "No person shall be held to answer for a capital, or otherwise infamous crime, unless on a presentment or indictment of a Grand Jury . . . ; nor shall any person be subject for the same offence to be twice put in jeopardy of life or limb; nor shall be compelled in any criminal case to be a witness against himself, *nor be deprived of life, liberty, or property, without due process of law*; nor shall private property be taken for public use, without just compensation." Jack N. Rakove, ed., *The Annotated U.S. Constitution and Declaration of Independence* (Cambridge, MA: Harvard University Press, 2009), 233.

35. See Mark A. Graber, *Transforming Free Speech: The Ambiguous Legacy of Civil Libertarianism* (Berkeley, CA: University of California Press, 1991).

36. Meiklejohn, *Free Speech and Its Relation to Self-Government*, 39.

37. See Bollinger, *The Tolerant Society*, 156.

38. His thought is laid out in two works: Thomas I. Emerson, *Toward a General Theory of the First Amendment* (New York: Random House, 1966), and, a few years later, Thomas I. Emerson, *The System of Freedom of Expression* (New York: Random House, 1970).

39. See Emerson, *The System of Freedom of Expression*, 16–18.

40. See ibid., 495–503.

41. See ibid., 537–43.

42. See Heyman, *Free Speech and Human Dignity*, 29.

43. Thomas G. West, "Free Speech in the American Founding and in Modern Liberalism," *Social Philosophy and Policy* 21, no. 2 (2004): 321.

44. *Dennis v. US*, 341 US 494 (1951).

45. See the majority decision in *Dennis*: "The words cannot mean that, before the Government may act, it must wait until the putsch is about to be executed, the plans have been laid and the signal is awaited. If Government is aware that a group aiming at its overthrow is attempting to indoctrinate its members and to commit them to a course whereby they will strike when the leaders feel the circumstances permit, action by the Government is required."

46. *Dennis v. US*, 341 US 494 (1951), per Justice Black (dissenting).

47. *Yates v. US*, 354 US 298 (1957).

48. Henry Kalven Jr., *A Worthy Tradition: Freedom of Speech in America* (New York: Harper & Row, 1988), 228.

49. Ibid.

50. *Brandenburg v. Ohio*, 395 US 444 (1969).

51. Ibid.

52. Kalven, *A Worthy Tradition*, 227.

53. *O'Brien v. US*, 391 US 367 (1968).

54. Ibid.

55. Ibid.

56. Ibid., per Justice Kennedy.

57. *US v. Eichman*, 496 US 310 (1990).

58. *R.A.V. v. City of St. Paul*, 505 US 377 (1992).

59. Ibid.

60. Ibid.

61. *Rosen v. United States* (1896) and *Roth v. United States*, 354 US 476 (1957).

62. Although the US Supreme Court, in *Miller v. California*, 413 US 15, 23 (1973), resolved this question to an extent by linking it to "patently offensive hard core sexual conduct."

63. *Joseph Burstyn, Inc., v. Wilson*, 343 US 495 (1952).

64. *Roth v. United States*, 354 US 476 (1957).

65. *Miller v. California*, 413 US 15, 23 (1973).

66. *Beauharnais v. Illinois*, 343 US 250 (1952).

67. *New York Times v. Sullivan*, 376 US 254 (1964).

68. Ibid.

69. *Curtis Publishing Co. v. Butts*, 388 US 130 (1967).

70. *Hustler Magazine, Inc., v. Falwell*, 485 US 46 (1988).

71. See *Gertz v. Robert Welch, Inc.*, 418 US 323 (1974).

72. *New York Times v. Sullivan*, 376 US 270 (1964).

73. Ibid. at 273.

74. Kalven, *A Worthy Tradition*, 228.

75. *Bantam Books, Inc., v. Sullivan*, 372 US 58, 70 (1963) and *Near v. Minnesota*, 283 US 697 (1931).

76. *New York Times v. US*, 403 US 713 (1971).

77. *Better Austin v. Keefe* (1971), in ibid.

78. *New York Times v. US*, 403 US 713 (1971).

79. *Branzburg v. Hayes*, 408 US 665 (1972).

80. *Turner Broadcasting System v. FCC*, 512 US 662 (1994).

81. Kalven, *A Worthy Tradition*, 235, emphasis added.

82. Ibid., xxi.

83. Ibid., xxi–xxii.

84. Ibid., xxii.

FIFTEEN   The European Tradition

1. See Eugene Volokh, "Freedom of Speech and of the Press," *The Heritage Guide to the Constitution*, consulted December 13, 2019, https://www.heritage.org /constitution/#!/amendments/1/essays/140/freedom-of-speech-and-of-the-press.

2. See Jeremy Waldron, *The Harm in Hate Speech* (Cambridge, MA: Harvard University Press, 2012), 102.

3. See rapport A/PV.180, December 9, 1948, 54, quoted in Paul Coleman, *Censored: How European "Hate Speech" Laws Are Threatening Freedom of Speech* (Vienna: Kairos, 2016), 21.

4. United Nations General Assembly, *Universal Declaration of Human Rights* (UDHR), December 10, 1948, art. 19.

5. Ibid., art. 7.

6. Rapport E/CN.4/AC.2/SR/9, December 10, 1947, 6–7, quoted in Coleman, *Censored*, 23–24.

7. Eleanor Roosevelt, Commission on Human Rights, 6th Session, E/ CN.4/SR.174, 06.05.1950, 6, quoted in Coleman, *Censored*, 28.

8. Cf. Coleman, *Censored*, 33–34. On the other end was the Soviet delegate Alexander Bogomolov, who argued: "It could not be said that to forbid the advocacy of racial, national or religious hatred constituted a violation to the freedom of the press or of free speech. . . . Freedom of the press and free speech could not serve as a pretext for propagating views which poisoned public opinion." Paul Coleman, "Europe's Free Speech Problem: A Cautionary Tale," *Public Discourse: The Journal of The Witherspoon Institute*, July 5, 2016, https://www.thepublic discourse.com/2016/07/17113/.

9. See Coleman, *Censored*, 31–34.

10. UN Human Rights Office of the High Commissioner, *International Covenant on Civil and Political Rights*, December 16, 1966, art. 20.2, https://www .ohchr.org/en/professionalinterest/pages/ccpr.aspx.

11. "[The European Parliament] welcomes the adoption of Council framework Decision 2008/913/JHA of 28 November 2008 on combating certain forms and expressions of racism and xenophobia by means of criminal law further to the political agreement of December 2007; points to its position of 29 November 2007 (11), which endorsed the proposal; calls on the Commission, after consulting the Agency, to propose similar legislation to combat homophobia." European Parliament resolution on the situation of human rights in the EU 2004–2008, January 14, 2009, 2007/2145(INI), quoted in Coleman, *Censored*, 225.

12. Coleman, *Censored*, 38–39.

13. ECRI (Council of Europe), *General Policy Recommendation No. 15*, December 8, 2015, https://www.coe.int/en/web/european-commission-against -racism-and-intolerance/recommendation-no.15.

14. Quoted in Nadine Strossen, *Hate: Why We Should Resist It with Free Speech, Not Censorship* (New York: Oxford University Press, 2018), 26.

15. Strossen, *Hate*, 27.

16. Ibid., 20.

17. Johannes Morsink, *The Universal Declaration of Human Rights: Origins, Drafting, and Intent* (Philadelphia: University of Pennsylvania Press, 1999), 72.

18. See ibid., 35.

19. Robert C. Post, "Hate Speech," in *Extreme Speech and Democracy*, edited by Ivan Hare and Steven J. Weinstein (Oxford: Oxford University Press, 2009), 123.

20. See ibid., 123–25.

21. See Waldron, *The Harm in Hate Speech*, 37.

22. Susan Benesch, Cathy Buerger, Tonei Glavinic, and Sean Manion, *Dangerous Speech: A Practical Guide*, in *The Dangerous Speech Project*, December 31, 2018, https://dangerousspeech.org/guide/, 1.

23. Ibid., 3.

24. Ibid., 4.

25. *Prosecutor v. Nahimana et al.* (trial judgment), case no. ICTR 99-52-T, para. 436, http://www.unictr.org/Portals/0/Case/English/Ngeze/judgement/Judg&sent.pdf.

26. International Criminal Tribunal for Rwanda (ICTR) transcript, June 4, 2001, para. 33, http://www.unictr.org/Portals/0/Case/English/Ngeze/judgement/Judg&sent.pdf.

27. See Andrew F. Sellars, "Defining Hate Speech," *Berkman Klein Center*, December 8, 2016, https://papers.ssrn.com/sol3/papers.cfm?abstract_id=2882244.

28. The cases listed below can be found in John Durham Peters, *Courting the Abyss: Free Speech and the Liberal Tradition* (Chicago: University of Chicago Press, 2005), 166ff.

29. See Volokh, "Freedom of Speech and of the Press."

30. See Waldron, *The Harm in Hate Speech*, 30.

31. For greater detail, see ibid., chap. 4.

32. *Sunday Times v. The United Kingdom*, 2 EHRR 245 (1979–80), 49, emphasis added.

33. Quoted in Strossen, *Hate*, 105.

34. Coleman, *Censored*, 104.

35. See Strossen, *Hate*, 27–29, 77–103.

36. Ibid., 134–38.

37. See Alexander Hamilton, James Madison, and John Jay, *Federalist Papers* (Oxford: Oxford University Press, 2008), 49.

38. See Jordi Pujol, "The Threat of Faction," *Church, Communication and Culture* 3, no. 2 (2018): 192–94, doi 10.1080/23753234.2018.1474718.

39. See Coleman, *Censored*, 47–59.

40. Cf. Gerard Alexander, "Illiberal Europe," *American Enterprise Institute for Public Policy Research*, 2006, 3, https://www.aei.org/articles/illiberal-europe/.

41. Coleman, *Censored*, 59.

42. Ibid., 117. See also EU Fundamental Rights Agency, "Homophobia, Transphobia and Discrimination on Grounds of Sexual Orientation and Gender Identity," Report 2010, 18 and 37, https://fra.europa.eu/sites/default/files/fra_uploads/1659-FRA-homophobia-synthesis-report-2011_EN.pdf.

43. On June 6–7, 2020, J. K. Rowling came under fire on Twitter because her remarks about biological sex were understood as targeting trans people: "If sex isn't real, there's no same-sex attraction. If sex isn't real, the lived reality of women globally is erased. I know and love trans people, but erasing the concept of sex removes the ability of many to meaningfully discuss their lives. It isn't hate to speak the truth." J. K. Rowling tweet, 12:02 a.m., June 7, 2020.

44. In March 2020, the feminist journalist Suzanne Moore wrote a piece in her column criticizing the disinvitation of an Oxford professor, Selina Todd, because Todd was gender critical. Moore denounced the fact that women and never men are the ones losing jobs, income, and their public platforms over this issue: "I wrote that I believed biological sex to be real and that it's not transphobic to understand basic science." This was met with death threats in social media and a letter at her workplace that was signed by 338 people expressing dismay about the column's being "hostile to trans rights and trans employees." It is an odd case in that a renowned feminist and Orwell Prize winner was being censored and targeted for her views. "My concern with this issue is only to do with the rights of women and the welfare of children," Moore said. Cf. Suzanne Moore, "Why I Had to Leave The Guardian," November 25, 2020, https://unherd.com/2020/11/why-i-had-to-leave-the-guardian/.

45. Timothy Garton Ash, *Free Speech: Ten Principles for a Connected World* (New Haven, CT: Yale University Press, 2016), 3–4.

SIXTEEN   Reframing Freedom of Expression as a Human Good

1. See John H. Garvey, *What Are Freedoms For?* (Cambridge, MA: Harvard University Press, 2000), 5–77.

2. See ibid., 76–77.

3. Ibid., 40.

4. Ibid., 66.

5. See John Durham Peters, afterword to *Transnational Media Events: The Mohammed Cartoons and the Imagined Clash of Civilization*, edited by Elisabeth Eide, Risto Kunelius, and Angela Phillips (Gothenborg, Sweden: Nordicom, 2008), 279–80.

6. Garvey, *What Are Freedoms For?*, 65.

7. Frederick F. Schauer, *Free Speech: A Philosophical Enquiry* (Cambridge: Cambridge University Press, 1982), 16.

8. See Garvey, *What Are Freedoms For?*, 73.

9. Michael W. McConnell, "Old Liberalism, New Liberalism, and People of Faith," in *Christian Perspectives on Legal Thought*, edited by Michael W. McConnell, Robert F. Cochran Jr., and Angela C. Carmella (New Haven, CT: Yale University Press, 2001), 14.

10. Ibid.

11. Ibid.

12. Cf. T. I. Emerson, *The System of Freedom of Expression* (New York: Random House, 1970), chap. 17.

13. Human Rights Watch, *World Report 2020: Shutting Down the Internet to Shut Up Critics*, https://www.hrw.org/world-report/2020/country-chapters /global-5.

14. Kenneth Cmiel and John Durham Peters, *Promiscuous Knowledge: Information, Image and Other Truth Games in History* (Chicago: Chicago University Press, 2020), 252.

15. Ibid., 255, emphasis mine.

16. See Emerson T. Brooking and P. W. Singer, "War Goes Viral: How Social Media Is Being Weaponized across the World," *Atlantic*, November 11, 2016, https://www.theatlantic.com/magazine/archive/2016/11/war-goes-viral/501125/.

17. Jon Ronson, *So You've Been Publicly Shamed* (New York: Riverhead Books, 2015), 244.

18. See Max Read, "How Much of the Internet Is Fake? Turns Out a Lot of It, Actually," *Intelligencer*, December 26, 2018, http://nymag.com/intelligencer /2018/12/how-much-of-the-internet-is-fake.html.

19. See T. K. Nvidia et al., "A Style-Based Generator Architecture for Generative Adversarial Networks," March 29, 2019, https://arxiv.org/abs/1812.04948.

20. See Nicholas Confessore, Gabriel Dance, Richard Harris, and Mark Hansen, "The Follower Factory: Everyone Wants to Be Popular Online: Some Even Pay for It; Inside Social Media's Black Market," *New York Times*, January 27, 2018, https://www.nytimes.com/interactive/2018/01/27/technology/social-media -bots.html.

21. The term "bot" comes from "robot," an automated nonhuman actor in the digital landscape. Bots are "programs," software applications designed to interact autonomously within a network of users on the Internet doing certain tasks such as periodically providing information, monitoring a site, or amplifying a message. A "bot farm" is a system (or farm) of bots used to generate Internet traffic and activity through clicks. A "deepfake" is a video or an image that has been ed-

ited with the assistance of artificial intelligence to transpose someone's face or voice into a clip or picture that already exists, creating an image or voice with great verisimilitude to the original.

22. Cf. Cmiel and Peters, *Promiscuous Knowledge*, 253–55.

23. See Emerson, *The System of Freedom of Expression*, 628.

24. See ibid., 629–73. In the "system of freedom of expression," Emerson distinguishes between the right of expression (647ff.), the right to listen as a means of access to information (650ff.), and the right to know certain information about institutions (672ff.).

25. Emerson believes that freedom of expression is a system formed by rights, principles, practices, and inter-related institutions. See Emerson, *The System of Freedom of Expression*, 4–7.

26. See Jonathan Zittrain, *The Future of the Internet—And How to Stop It* (New Haven, CT: Yale University Press, 2009); Frank Pasquale, *The Black Box Society: The Secret Algorithms That Control Money and Information* (Cambridge, MA: Harvard University Press, 2015); Luciano Floridi, *The Fourth Revolution: How the Infosphere Is Reshaping Human Reality* (Oxford: Oxford University Press, 2016); Zeynep Tufekci, *Twitter and Tear Gas: The Power and Fragility of Networked Protest* (New Haven, CT: Yale University Press, 2017).

27. The master lesson was titled "Intolerance, Censorship, and Other Requirements of Rationality," but it was never published. The author kindly authorized me to cite the manuscript (in February of 2017). The references made correspond to the numbering of the author's manuscript.

28. Ibid., 3–4.

29. Ibid., 3.

30. MacIntyre, "Intolerance, Censorship, and Other Requirements of Rationality," 6.

31. See ibid., 11.

32. "In our opinion the 12 cartoons were moderate and not intended to be insulting. They did not go against Danish laws, but have evidently offended many Muslims, for which we apologize. Meanwhile a couple of offending cartoons have circulated in the Muslim world which were never published in *Jyllands-Posten* and which we would never have published if they had been offered to us. We would have dismissed them on the grounds that they breached our ethical limits." Hjörtur J. Guðmundsson, "Danish Paper Apologizes: Dutch Cartoon on Its Way," *Brussels Journal*, January 31, 2006, https://www.brusselsjournal.com/node/736. For further information, see Paul Belien, "The Cartoon Hoax," *Brussels Journal*, February 7, 2006, https://www.brusselsjournal.com/node/775.

33. See Flemming Rose, "Why I Published Those Cartoons," *Washington Post*, February 19, 2006, https://www.washingtonpost.com/archive/opinions

/2006/02/19/why-i-published-those-cartoons/f9a67368-4641-4fa7-b71f-843
ea44814ef/.

34. See MacIntyre, "Intolerance, Censorship, and Other Requirements of
Rationality," 12. On the debate in Denmark about integration and preserving
national cultural unity, see Kasper Støvring, "The Turn from Cultural Radicalism to National Conservatism: Cultural Policy in Denmark," *Telos* 148 (Fall
2009): 54–72.

35. See Aristotle, *Nicomachean Ethics* II; Thomas Aquinas, *S. Th* II-II, q. 58, a. 10.

36. For Aristotle all virtues and all moral values such as truth, rights, temper-
ance, and so on are part of the "golden mean" (between extremes) of eternal reality
(not of the subject). That golden mean is not mediocrity but requires doing something in its just measure. See Michel Villey, *Filosofía del Derecho* (Barcelona: Scire
Universitaria, 2003), 54–55.

37. See MacIntyre, *After Virtue*, 125–27.

38. Villey, *Filosofía del Derecho*, 54, my translation.

39. Ibid., 56, my translation.

40. Ibid., 57, my translation and emphasis.

41. Gaius, *Institutes*, I, 1, http://thelatinlibrary.com/law/gaius1.html.

42. Javier Hervada, *Lecciones propedéuticas de filosofía del Derecho* (Pamplona: EUNSA, 1992), 496ff. Roman law distinguished between *ius civile*, *ius
gentium*, and *ius commune* and between *ius proprium* and *ius commune*. Thus, positive law was partially in *ius civile*, as well as in *ius gentium*. To see the evolution
of this law in the Middle Ages, see Hervada, *Lecciones propedéuticas de filosofía
del Derecho*, 499ff.

43. William of Ockham, *Opus nonaginta dierum* (Lyon: Treschell, 1965),
quoted in Hervada, *Lecciones propedéuticas de filosofía del Derecho*, 240ff.

44. See Hervada, *Lecciones propedéuticas de filosofía del Derecho*, 240–41.

45. Hannah Arendt, *The Human Condition* (Chicago: University of Chicago
Press, 1998), 63.

46. See Villey, *Filosofía del Derecho*, 94.

47. Ibid., 95, my translation.

48. See MacIntyre, *After Virtue*, 127.

49. This argument is discussed by several contemporary philosophers, who
oppose each other. See John Rawls, *A Theory of Justice* (Oxford: Oxford University
Press, 1973), and MacIntyre, *After Virtue*.

50. Villey, *Filosofía del Derecho*, 97, my translation.

51. Immanuel Kant, *Metaphysische Anfangsgründe der Rechtslehre* (1796),
quoted in Villey, *Filosofía del Derecho*, 99.

52. See Marcello Pera, *Diritti umani e cristianesimo* (Padua: Marsilio, 2015)
31ff. Are we looking at a tension or a contradiction? The issue is complicated be-

cause it requires an examination of historical, philosophical, and theological reasons. The cited book by Pera contains a vast bibliography on the issue.

53. See Pera, *Diritti umani e cristianesimo*, 20ff.

54. See MacIntyre, *After Virtue*, 58.

55. Patrick J. Deneen, *Why Liberalism Failed* (New Haven, CT: Yale University Press, 2018), 49.

56. Benedict XVI, *Address to the Members of the General Assembly of the United Nations Organization*, April 18, 2008, Vatican website, http://www.vatican .va/content/benedict-xvi/en/speeches/2008/april/documents/hf_ben-xvi _spe_20080418_un-visit.html.

57. From the start of his 20 years of exile in the United States (1974–1994) until he could return to his homeland, Aleksandr Solzhenitsyn gave different speeches, mainly to European and American audiences. A few of those speeches, specifically that of his reception of the Nobel Prize for Literature, his master class at Harvard, and the speeches in Templeton and Liechtenstein, are some of his main texts. In them, the author expresses his view of the twentieth century, extending his criticism, not only to the Soviet system but to the West. The political and academic elites did not welcome those speeches. Solzhenitsyn's reflections express a criticism that resembles that of Tocqueville, "as a friend, not as an adversary." His critical intuitions are soaked in a certain innocence, typical of those who come from a less cynical culture, but they have the value of having come from a writer who spoke very freely. See Edward E. Ericson; and Daniel J. Mahoney, eds., *The Solzhenitsyn Reader: New and Essential Writings 1947–2005* (Wilmington, DE: ISI Books, 2006), 561ff.

58. Aleksandr Solzhenitsyn, "A World Split Apart" (cited as Harvard Address), in *The Solzhenitsyn Reader: New and Essential Writings, 1947–2005*, edited by Edward E. Ericson and Daniel J. Mahoney (Wilmington DE: ISI Books, 2006), 565.

59. Ronald C. Arnett, *Communication in Dark Times: Hannah Arendt's Rhetoric of Warning and Hope* (Carbondale: Southern Illinois University Press, 2012), 90.

60. Hannah Arendt, *Eichmann in Jerusalem: A Report on the Banality of Evil* (1963) (New York: Penguin Books, 2006), 135.

61. Arnett, *Communication in Dark Times*, 103.

62. Solzhenitsyn, Harvard Address, 566.

63. Ibid., 568.

64. Ibid., 570.

65. Benedict XVI, "Address at the Reichstag Building," September 22, 2011, Vatican website, http://www.vatican.va/content/benedict-xvi/en/speeches/2011 /september/documents/hf_ben-xvi_spe_20110922_reichstag-berlin.html.

66. Solzhenitsyn, Harvard Address, 570.

SEVENTEEN Reconsidering the Legal Grounds

1. See Rafael Domingo, *The New Global Law* (New York: Cambridge University Press, 2010).

2. See Sandra Braman, *Change of State: Information, Policy, and Power* (Cambridge, MA: MIT Press, 2006).

3. Jean Monnet, a founding father of Europe, said in a speech in Washington, DC (April 30, 1952): "We are not forming coalitions of states, we are uniting people" (original: *"Nous ne coalisons pas des États, nous unissons des hommes."*) Jean Monnet, *Memoires* (Paris: Fayard, 1976), vol. 9, 617.

4. Jürgen Habermas, "Does the Constitutionalization of International Law Still Have a Chance?," in *The Divided West*, edited by Ciaran Cronin (Cambridge: Polity, 2006).

5. See Domingo, *The New Global Law*; David J. Bederman, *Globalization and International Law* (New York: Palgrave MacMillan, 2008); Martin Shaw, *Theory of the Global State* (New York: Cambridge University Press, 2000); Jeremy A. Rabkin, *Law without Nations? Why Constitutional Government Requires Sovereign States* (Princeton, NJ: Princeton University Press, 2005); Daniele Archibugi, *The Global Commonwealth of Citizens: Toward Cosmopolitan Democracy* (Princeton, NJ: Princeton University Press, 2008).

6. Cf. Domingo, *The New Global Law*, 4.

7. Domingo, *The New Global Law*, 122.

8. See John Finnis, "The Priority of Persons," *Oxford Essays of Jurisprudence*, Fourth Series, edited by Jeremy Horder (Oxford: Oxford University Press, 1997), 79–99.

9. See Domingo, *The New Global Law*, chap. 5.

10. Ibid., 4.

11. Roscoe Pound, "The Idea of Universal Ius," *UCLA Law Review* 1 (1953–54): 17.

12. Adrian Vermule, *Common Good Constitutionalism* (Cambridge, MA: Polity Press, 2022), 24.

13. Ibid., 180–81.

14. Ibid., 19.

15. Ulpian, *Digest*, 1, 10, *Institutes* 2, translated by Alan Watson (Philadelphia: University of Pennsylvania Press, 2009).

16. For a deeper examination of the concept of justice in Roman law, see Javier Hervada, *Introduzione critica al diritto naturale* (Rome: Giuffrè Editore, 1990), chap. 1.

17. See Aquinas, *S. Th* II-II, qq. 57ff.

18. Aristotle, *Nicomachean Ethics*, translated by W. D. Ross, in *The Internet Classics Archive* (Cambridge, MA: MIT Press, 1994), http://classics.mit.edu/Aristotle/nicomachaen.html.

19. See Aquinas, *S. Th* II-II, q. 57, a. 2.

20. Aristotle, *Nicomachean Ethics*, V, 7.

21. See Martin Rhonheimer, *The Perspective of Morality* (Washington, DC: Catholic University of America Press, 2011), 234–35.

22. Ángel Rodríguez Luño and Arturo Bellocq, *Ética general* (Pamplona: EUNSA, 2015), 228, my translation.

23. See Aquinas, *S. Th* II-II, q. 62, a. 1

24. It is interesting to see how the declarations of rights of different nations, such as the Massachusetts Bill of Rights, article II, speak of damages not only to a person or property but also to one's personality, such as a rumor or defamation. See Thomas G. West, "Free Speech in the American Founding and in Modern Liberalism," *Social Philosophy and Policy* 21, no. 2 (2004): 323–24.

25. Rodríguez Luño and Bellocq, *Ética general*, 227–28, my translation.

26. See Kathleen M. Sullivan, "Two Concepts of Freedom of Speech," *Harvard Law Review* 124, no. 143 (2010): 176.

27. See ibid.

28. I believe that the digital platforms are "online sites and services that (a) host, organize, and circulate users' shared content or social interactions for them; (b) do so without having produced or commissioned (the bulk of) that content; (c) are built on infrastructure, beneath that circulation of information, for processing data for customer service, advertising, and profit; and (d) do, and must, moderate the content and activity of users using some logistics of detection, review, and enforcement." See Tarleton Gillespie, *Custodians of the Internet* (New Haven, CT: Yale University Press, 2018), 18–21.

29. Gillespie, *Custodians of the Internet*, 46.

30. Ibid., 46–47.

31. Ibid., 49.

32. See Sarah T. Roberts, *Behind the Screen: Content Moderation in the Shadows of Social Media* (New Haven, CT: Yale University Press, 2019).

33. Ibid., 111.

34. Gillespie, *Custodians of the Internet*, 71.

35. Ibid., 72.

36. See Ariana Tobin, Madeleine Varner, and Julia Angwin, "Facebook's Uneven Enforcement of Hate Speech Rules Allows Vile Posts to Stay Up," *ProPublica*, December 28, 2017, https://www.propublica.org/article/facebook -enforcement-hate-speech-rules-mistakes.

37. See Roberts, *Behind the Screen*, 104.

38. Ibid., 105.

39. "Facebook's Oversight Board's Work—and Other Free Speech Challenges," interview with Michael McConnell by Lindsay Lloyd of the Human Freedom Initiative at the George W. Bush Institute, March 22, 2022, https://www.bushcenter.org /publications/articles/2022/03/democracy-talks-mcconnell-facebook-oversight.html.

40. The decisions are published and can be read at the website of the Oversight Board: https://www.oversightboard.com/decision/.

41. "Facebook's Oversight Board's Work."

42. European Commission, "Code of Conduct on Countering Illegal Hate Speech Online," https://ec.europa.eu/info/sites/info/files/code_of_conduct_on _countering_illegal_hate_speech_online_en.pdf.

43. Heidi Tworek, "How Germany Is Tackling Hate Speech: New Legislation Targets U.S. Social Media Companies," *Foreign Affairs*, May 16, 2017, https:// www.foreignaffairs.com/articles/germany/2017-05-16/how-germany-tackling -hate-speech.

44. German Bundestag, Network Enforcement Act, July 12, 2017, https:// www.bmjv.de/SharedDocs/Gesetzgebungsverfahren/Dokumente/NetzDG_engl .pdf?__blob=publicationFile&v=2.

45. Mehreen Khan, "More 'Hate Speech' Being Removed from Social Media," *Financial Times*, February 4, 2019, https://www.ft.com/content/868f9d96 -27bc-11e9-a5ab-ff8ef2b976c7.

46. See a report published by Justitia: Jacob Mchangama and Joelle Fiss, "The Digital Berlin Wall: How Germany (Accidentally) Created a Prototype for Global Online Censorship," November 2019, www.justitia-int.org.

47. Tim Wu, "Is the First Amendment Obsolete?," in *The Free Speech Century*, edited by Lee C. Bollinger and Geoffrey R. Stone (New York: Oxford University Press, 2019), 287.

48. Ibid., 237, 241.

49. Jack M. Balkin, "Information Fiduciaries and the First Amendment," *UC Davis Law Review* 49, no. 4 (2016): 1183–1234.

50. Jack M. Balkin and Jonathan Zittrain, "A Grand Bargain to Make Tech Companies Trustworthy," *Atlantic*, October 3, 2016, https://www.theatlantic. com/technology/archive/2016/10/information-fiduciary/502346/.

51. Martina Pennisi, "Google dice di sapere di cosa è morto Buttarelli (anche se l'informazione non è pubblica)," *Corriere della Sera*, August 21, 2019, https:// www.corriere.it/tecnologia/19_agosto_21/google-dice-sapere-cosa-morto -buttarelli-anche-se-l-informazione-non-pubblica-73e34c8c-c42a-11e9-b4f3 -f200f033f7a0.shtml.

52. José González, Ángel Cuevas, and Rubén Cuevas, "Facebook Use of Sensitive Data for Advertising in Europe," *Cornell University*, February 14, 2018, https://arxiv.org/abs/1802.05030v1.

53. Ibid., 1–2.

54. See Gog Magog, "Le vere 'interferenze' sulla democrazia: Google e FB hanno oscurato profili e inserzioni pro-vita al referendum in Irlanda," *Medium*, June 27, 2019, https://medium.com/@gogmagog/irlanda-interferenze-pro-aborto -google-facebook-youtube-censura-64abb159f9c2.

55. See Robert Epstein, "How Google Shifts Votes: A 'Go Vote' Reminder Is Not Always What You Think It Is," *Epoch Times*, January 2, 2019, https://www .theepochtimes.com/another-way-google-manipulates-votes-without-us-know ing-a-go-vote-reminder-is-not-what-you-think-it-is_2754073.html; Robert Epstein, "How Google Could Rig the 2016 Election," *Politico Magazine*, August 19, 2015, https://www.politico.com/magazine/story/2015/08/how-google-could-rig -the-2016-election-121548.

56. Balkin and Zittrain, "A Grand Bargain to Make Tech Companies Trustworthy."

57. Ibid.

EIGHTEEN Reshaping the Harm Principle

1. See Alasdair MacIntyre, *After Virtue* (Notre Dame, IN: University of Notre Dame Press, 1981), 58, 80–81.

2. Based on modernity's contradiction of the autonomous self, Nietzsche radicalizes the argument of the will as the center of his moral project: "If there is nothing to morality but expressions of the will, my morality can only be what my will creates. There can be no place for such fictions as natural rights, utility, the greatest happiness of the greatest number. I myself must now bring into existence 'new tables of what is good.'" Ibid., 107.

3. Victor Hugo, *The Man Who Laughs* (Boston: University Press Company, 1869), 297.

4. During the climax of a speech to the assembly, it is clear that the man who laughs embodies the desolation of humanity. It is a forced laugh that hides torment: "Mankind is mutilated. That which has been done to me has been done to it. In it have been deformed right, justice, truth, reason, intelligence, as eyes, nostrils, and ears have been deformed in me; its heart has been made a sink of passion and pain, like mine, and, like mine, its features have been hidden in a mask of joy. Where God had placed his finger, the king set his sign-manual. Monstrous superposition!" Ibid.

5. "Of all the lava which that crater, the human mouth, ejects, the most corrosive is joy. To inflict evil gaily is a contagion which no crowd can resist. All executions do not take place on the scaffold; and men, from the moment they are in a body, whether in mobs or in senates, have always a ready executioner amongst them, called sarcasm. There is no torture to be compared to that of the wretch condemned to execution by ridicule. This was Gwynplaine's fate. He was stoned with their jokes, and riddled by the scoffs shot at him. He stood there a mark for all." Ibid.

6. Ibid.

7. Frances, "Ángelus," February 16, 2015, Vatican website, http://www.vatican .va/ content/francesco/en/angelus/2014/documents/papa-francesco_angelus _20140216.html.

8. Joseph Ratzinger, "Conscience and Truth" (original title: *Gewissen und Wahrheit: Stark Verkürzter Abdruck in Poln*), speech presented at the 10th Workshop for Bishops in Dallas, Texas, February 1991, EWTN library, https://www.ewtn.com/catholicism/library/conscience-and-truth-2468.

9. See Jeremy Waldron, *The Harm in Hate Speech* (Cambridge, MA: Harvard University Press, Cambridge, 2012), 35.

10. Robert C. Post, "Hate Speech," in *Extreme Speech and Democracy*, edited by Ivan Hare and Steven J. Weinstein (Oxford: Oxford University Press, 2009), 123.

11. See ibid., 123–25.

12. John Stuart Mill, *On Liberty*, edited by Alan Ryan (London: Penguin, 2006), 16.

13. See ibid., chap. 2. Mill tries to reconcile (limit) individualism with the harm principle, according to which everyone must be allowed to do what they believe is right while not harming others. Governments and nations act as the guarantors of these individual rights. In the context of "expression," any scientific, philosophical, or theological doctrine must be allowed, dangerous as it may seem, with only the limitation that it does not harm others.

14. Raphael Cohen-Almagor, *Speech, Media and Ethics: The Limits of Free Expression* (New York: Palgrave, 2001), 7.

15. Ibid., 22.

16. See ibid., 15.

17. See Joel Feinberg, *Offence to Others* (New York: Oxford University Press, 1985), 1–2, quoted in ibid., 9–12.

18. See Cohen-Almagor, *Speech, Media and Ethics*, 18.

19. See Robby Soave, "Michelle Carter Didn't Kill with a Text," *New York Times*, June 16, 2017, https://www.nytimes.com/2017/06/16/opinion/michelle-carter-didnt-kill-with-a-text.html?mcubz=1.

20. Katharine Q. Seelye and Jess Bidgood, "Guilty Verdict for Young Woman Who Urged Friend to Kill Himself," *New York Times*, June 16, 2017, https://www.nytimes.com/2017/06/16/us/suicide-texting-trial-michelle-carter-conrad-roy.html?hp&action=click&pgtype=Homepage&clickSource=story-heading&module=first-column-region&region=top-news&WT.nav=top-news.

21. Tim Wu, "Is the First Amendment Obsolete?," in *The Free Speech Century*, edited by Lee C. Bollinger and Geoffrey R. Stone (New York: Oxford University Press, 2019), 288. See also references of the author to the following cases: *Watts v. United States*, 394 US 705 (1969), and *Elonis v. United States*, 135 US 2001 (2015).

22. See Black v. Clarke, 538 US at 360, https://globalfreedomofexpression.columbia.edu/cases/black-v-clarke/.

23. Cohen-Almagor, *Speech, Media and Ethics*, 23.

24. Ibid., 21.

25. Karol Wojtyla thoroughly develops these ideas in various essays on ethics and personalism, especially, "Subjectivity and the Irreducible in the Human Being." See Karol Wojtyla, *Person and Community: Selected Essays*, vol. 4 (New York: Lang, 1993), 209–18.

26. Cohen-Almagor, *Speech, Media and Ethics*, 23.

27. For a closer look, see the footnote on page 68 of Mill's *On Liberty*, quoted in Cohen-Almagor, *Speech, Media and Ethics*, 21.

28. Francis, *Laudato Sí: On Care for Our Common Home*, encyclical, May 24, 2015, Vatican website, http://www.vatican.va/content/francesco/en/encyclicals /documents/papa-francesco_20150524_enciclica-laudato-si.html, no. 119.

29. Thomas Aquinas, *In VIII Ethic.*, lect. 9, no. 1658.

30. See Martin Rhonheimer, *The Perspective of Morality* (Washington, DC: Catholic University of America Press, 2011), 247ff., and Ángel Rodríguez Luño and Arturo Bellocq, *Ética general* (Rome: EUNSA, 2014), 227.

31. A close relationship can also be found between freedom of expression and classical rhetoric as an "art of persuasion" that, according to Plato, Aristotle, or Quintilian, was to be used for "honorable purposes." See Aristotle, *La retórica* (Madrid: Gredos, 1990); Plato, *Diálogos*, vol. IV, *República* (Madrid: Gredos, 1986), 210ff.; Quintilian, *The Institution Oratoria*, ed. Charles E. Little (Nashville, TN: George Peabody College for Teachers, 1951).

32. See Aristotle, *Política: Un tratado sobre la governancia*, Book III, chaps. 6–7; Cicero, *De Re Publica*, chap. 1, art 25; Aquinas, *S. Th* I-II, q. 92, art. 1; J. Locke, *Second Treatise of Government* (New York: Liberal Press, 1954), 73, 91.

33. For further detail, see Antonio Argandoña, who offers a summary of the classical conception of the common good (Aristotelian-Thomist) and of other conceptions, mainly collectivist, liberal, and communitarian. Antonio Argandoña, "The Common Good," in *Handbook of the Economics of Philanthropy, Reciprocity and Social Enterprise*, edited by Luigino Bruni and Stefano Zamagni (Cheltenham, UK: Edward Elgar, 2013), 364.

34. For a deeper examination of this debate between liberals and communitarians, see John Rawls, *A Theory of Justice* (Oxford: Oxford University Press, 1973); Charles Taylor, *Sources of the Self* (Cambridge: Cambridge University Press, 1989); Michael Sandel, *Liberalism and the Limits of Justice* (Cambridge: Cambridge University Press, 1982).

35. Thomas Aquinas, *De regimine principum*, Lib. II, c. 3. See also *Summa Theologiae*, I-II, q. 90. Jacques Maritain expanded on the Thomist doctrine on the common good in the twentieth century, emphasizing that it is an abstract concept.

It is not something quantitative or material but is formed by a network of goods of different scopes and levels—from goods and services of public utility, such as public and social infrastructures, to other civic and political goods, such as the law and institutions, but also the cultural and spiritual treasure that freedom and the exercise of the moral virtues, justice, friendship, and the pursuit of happiness entail. Jacques J. Maritain, *The Person and the Common Good* (South Bend, IN: University of Notre Dame Press, 1966), 52–54.

36. Adrian Vermule, *Common Good Constitutionalism* (Cambridge, MA: Polity Press, 2022), 168.

37. See B. J. Diggs, "The Common Good as Reason for Political Action," *Ethics* 83, no. 4 (1973): 283–84.

38. Vatican Council II, *Gaudium et Spes*, pastoral constitution, December 7, 1965, Vatican website, http://www.vatican.va/archive/hist_councils/ii_vatican_council/documents/vat-ii_const_19651207_gaudium-et-spes_en.html, no. 25.

39. See Argandoña, "The Common Good," 367ff.

40. See C. G. Christians, "The Common Good as First Principle," in *The Idea of Public Journalism*, edited by T. L. Glasser (New York: Guilford, 1999), 68.

41. See ibid., 79–80, and also, by the same author, "The Common Good and Universal Values," in *Mixed News*, edited by Jay Black (Mahwah, NJ: Erlbaum, 1997), 18–33.

42. See Robert Merrihew Adams, "Religious Ethics in a Pluralistic Society," in *Prospects for a Common Morality*, edited by Gene Outka and John P. Reeder Jr. (Princeton, NJ: Princeton University Press, 1993), 93–103.

43. See Christians, "The Common Good as First Principle," 69ff.

44. Commutative justice orders the relationships of the members among themselves; distributive justice orders the relationship of all members; legal justice orders the relationships of the isolated members to the whole. See Josef Pieper, *Las virtudes fundamentales* (Madrid: Rialp, 1976), 18.

45. St. Thomas Aquinas says that, certainly, the whole moral life of the human being is subordinated to the common good. Thus, legal justice really is a very special category and has a special position. However, St. Thomas's thesis has two facets: one expresses that there is a true obligation of the individual with respect to the common good (and this obligation refers to the whole person), and another emphasizes that the entire virtue of the individual is necessary for everyone's well-being, meaning that the common well-being requires the virtue of isolated individuals. See Pieper, *Las virtudes fundamentales*, 18–20.

46. Benedict XVI, *Caritas in veritate*, encyclical letter, June 29, 2009, Vatican website, http://www.vatican.va/content/benedict-xvi/en/encyclicals/documents/hf_ben-xvi_enc_20090629_caritas-in-veritate.html, no. 17.

47. Ibid.

NINETEEN Repairing the Relationship between the Secular and the Sacred

1. See Joseph Ratzinger, "Ragione e Fede: Scambio reciproco per un'etica comune," in *Ragione e Fede in dialogo*, edited by M. Rosati (Milan: Marsilio, 2005), 71–72, 79–80.

2. See Jürgen Habermas, *Between Naturalism and Religion* (Cambridge: Polity Press, 2008), 144.

3. See Charles Taylor, *A Secular Age* (Cambridge, MA: Harvard University Press, 2007).

4. See Charles Taylor, *Modern Social Imaginaries* (Durham, NC: Duke University Press, 2004), 183ff.

5. Natalia Ginzburg, "Non togliete quel crocifisso è il segno del dolore umano," *l'Unità*, March 25, 1988, 2, https://archivio.unita.news/assets/main /1988/03/25/page_002.pdf.

6. Ibid.

7. Habermas, *Between Naturalism and Religion*, 118, my emphasis.

8. Michael W. McConnell, "Old Liberalism, New Liberalism, and People of Faith," in *Christian Perspectives on Legal Thought*, edited by Michael W. McConnell and John Garvey (New Haven, CT: Yale University Press, 2001), 22.

9. McConnell, "Old Liberalism, New Liberalism, and People of Faith," 23.

10. Joseph Ratzinger, *Church, Ecumenism and Politics* (New York: Crossroad, 1988), 161.

11. Unlike the modern constitutions of 1917, Ratzinger points out that the Code of Canon Law does not mention the right to the *personal freedom* of the Christian; it mentions only the freedom of the Church (canons 2333, 2334, 2336). See ibid., 201.

12. Starting with the declaration *Dignitatis Humanae*, the Church has recognized not only a "regime of tolerance" but also a "regime of (religious) liberty," as a consequence of natural law itself. See José Orlandis, *La Iglesia católica en la segunda mitad del s. XX* (Madrid: Palabra, 1998), 56–57.

13. See Acerbi, *Chiesa e Democrazia: Da Leone XIII al Vaticano II* (Milan: Vita e Pensiero, 1991), 277. In turn, the Church demands the civil recognition of the religious dimension of the human being as part of the other individual rights, and she does not accept a mere indifference on the part of the state toward the transcendent dimension of the human being.

14. Jordi Pujol, "Colloquy with John Durham Peters at Yale University on Freedom of Speech," *Church, Communication and Culture* 4, no. 1 (2019): 100.

15. Ibid., 99.

16. George Parkin Grant, *English-Speaking Justice* (South Bend, IN: University of Notre Dame Press, 1985), 59–65.

17. Martin Luther, *D. Martin Luthers Werke: Kritische Gesamtsusgabe* (Weimar: Hermann Boehlaus Nachfolger, 1914), band 51:126, ll. 7ff. See Last Sermon in Wittenberg, Second Sunday in Epiphany, January 17, 1546. The original German of the emphasized phraseis *"Vernunft . . . ist die höchste Hur, die der Teufel hat."*

18. Cf. David Andersen, *Martin Luther—The Problem of Faith and Reason* (Bonn: Verlag für Kultur und Wissenschaft, 2019), 159–67.

19. https://hgscf.org/harvard-shield/.

20. G. K. Chesterton, "Milton: Man and Poet," *Catholic World* 104 (1917): 466.

21. See Michael P. Zuckert, *The Natural Rights Republic: Studies in the Foundation of the American Political Tradition* (South Bend, IN: University of Notre Dame Press, 1996), 145.

22. See E. J. Watts, "Freedom of Speech and Self-Censorship in the Roman Empire," *Revue belge de philologie et d'histoire (Belgisch tijdschrift voor filologie en geschiedenis)* 92, no. 1 (2004).

23. See Chesterton, "Milton: Man and Poet," 467–68.

24. Ibid., 467.

25. See Jürgen Habermas, "Notes on a Post-secular Society," *New Perspectives Quarterly* 25, no. 4 (2008): 27.

26. See Jürgen Habermas, "Religion in the Public Sphere," *European Journal of Philosophy* 14, no. 1 (2006): 15.

27. See Habermas, "Notes on a Post-Secular Society," 27.

28. Habermas, "Religion in the Public Sphere," 1–25.

29. Habermas, "Notes on Post-Secular Society," 20.

30. See Joseph Ratzinger and Jürgen Habermas, *The Dialectics of Secularization: On Reason and Religion* (San Francisco: Ignatius Press, 2007).

31. George Parkin Grant, *English-Speaking Justice* (South Bend, IN: University of Notre Dame Press, 1985), 81.

32. Jürgen Habermas, *Between Naturalism and Religion* (Cambridge: Polity Press, 2008), 109.

33. See Jürgen Habermas, "Religion in the Public Sphere," Holberg Prize address, Bergen, Norway, http://www.holberg.uib.no/downloads/diverse/hp/hp_2005/2005_hp_jurgenhabermas_reli-gioninthepublicsphere.pdf, and Jürgen Habermas and Joseph Ratzinger, *Dialektik der Säkularisierung (Dialectic of Secularization)* (Freiburg: Herder, 2008).

34. John Durham Peters, "In Quest of Ever Better Heresies," afterword to *Transnational Media Events: The Mohammed Cartoons and the Imagined Clash of Civilizations*, edited by Elisabeth Eide, Risto Kunelius, and Angela Phillips (Gothenburg, Sweden: Nordicom, 2008), 285.

35. Rafael Domingo, "God and the Law in the Age of Secularization," published in *The Canopy Forum*, Emory University, Atlanta, April 14, 2020, available

at https://www.academia.edu/42766094/God_and_the_Law_in_the_Age_of _Secularization.

36. See Ireneuzs Rogulski, *Limiti morali della libertà d'espressione letteraria nei confronti della religione* (Rome: Edizioni Santa Croce, 2016), 111.

37. Cicero, *De Legibus*, 2, 10, 25.

38. Tacitus, *Annales*, 1, 73.

39. Cf. Daniela Piattelli, *Libertà individuali e sistemi giuridici: Profili storico-giuridici (Mondo antico ed Israele)* (Turin: G. Giappichelli Editore, 1997), 39.

40. In 538–539 Justinian, in accordance with the Acts of the Council of Constantinople, established an entirely new principle by which any behavior aimed at disturbing the ecclesiastical order also affects civil law: "*Si enim contra homine factae blasphemiae impunitae non reliquuntur, multo magis qui ipsum Deum blasphemat dignus est supplicia sustinere*" (If the blasphemies uttered against men do not go unpunished, all the more the man who blasphemes against God, is himself worthy of torture), translation mine. Cf. Rogulski, *Limiti morali della libertà d'espressione letteraria*, 113.

41. Cf. Giovanni Greco, *La bestemmia come rivolta: Una riflessione metodologica* (Salerno: Edisud, 1994), 62.

42. Cf. David A. Lawton, *Blasphemy* (New York: Harvester Wheatsheaf, 1993), 28.

43. Rogulski discusses this concept fully from the semantic, philosophical, and theological standpoints. See Rogulski, *Limiti morali della libertà d'espressione letteraria nei confronti della religion*, chap. 2.

44. See ibid., 94–97.

45. See John L. Austin, *Cómo hacer cosas con palabras* (Barcelona: Paidós, 1996), 12ff.

46. The author distinguishes between locutions (acts of saying something), illocutions (the intentions contained in what is said that have an effect on the recipient), and perlocutions (the effects of what has been said produced in the recipient). See Austin, *Cómo hacer cosas con palabras*, 94–99.

47. See Rogulski, *Limiti morali della libertà d'espressione letteraria nei confronti della religione*, 102.

48. Stéphane Charbonnier, *Open Letter: On Blasphemy, Islamophobia, and the True Enemies of Free Expression* (New York: Little Brown, 2016), 17.

49. See ibid., 18–19, 26, 79–80.

50. See ibid., 16.

51. See ibid., 50–51.

52. See ibid., 11–13.

53. Ibid., 21.

54. Charbonnier is also inconsistent when he comments on the media's interpretation of the main vignette of the *Jyllands-Posten* controversy, published on

September 30, 2005, in which Muhammad was depicted wearing a turban in the form of a bomb. The French editor says that the media univocally interpreted it as suggesting that all of Muhammad's followers were terrorists. And Charbonnier suggested that there was another possible interpretation but that the media was not interested in it because it was less inflammatory and would not sell as much: "Showing Muhammad in a bomb-hat could have been a way of condemning the exploitation of religion by terrorists." Charbonnier, *Open Letter*, 24. The contrast between his words in his earlier work and this last consideration speaks for itself.

55. Charbonnier, *Open Letter*, 29.

56. On June 29, 2007, the European Parliament approved Recommendation no. 1805 on blasphemy, religious insults, and expressions against people based on their religion, calling on the member states to adapt their legislation. In this case, it believes that blasphemy should not constitute a crime. In the same sense, the Council of Europe stated in a 2008 report: "It is neither necessary nor desirable to create an offence of religious insult" and "The offence of blasphemy should be abolished." See Rogulski, *Limiti morali della libertà d'espressione letteraria nei confronti della religione*, 155–56.

57. See ibid., 185.

58. See ibid., 141–83.

59. See ibid., 180–82.

60. Ibid., 182.

61. Aquinas, *De veritate*, q. 22, a. 13, ad 16: "Quod intentio est actus voluntatis in ordine ad rationem ordinantem ea quae sunt ad finem, in finem ipsum; sed electio est actus voluntatis in ordine ad rationem comparantem ea quae sunt in finem ad invicem: et propter hoc intentio et electio different," my translation.

62. See Aquinas, *Super Sent.*, tomo 2, d. 38, q. 1, a. 1, arg. 4.

63. Aquinas, *Summa Theologiae*, I, q. 83, a. 3, c.

64. See Aquinas, *Super Sent.*, tomo 2, d. 40, q. 1, a. 2, c.

65. Aquinas, *De Malo*, q. 6, ad 8: "Quod finis est ratio volendi ea quae sunt ad finem. Unde non similiter se habet voluntas ad utrumque," my translation.

66. See Aquinas, *Summa Theologiae*, I, q. 83, a. 4, ad 2.

67. See Duerte Sousa-Lara, "'Intentio' and 'Electio' in Aquinas," *Etica e Politica*, www.eticaepolitica.net, 2. (This essay was originally chapter 7 of his dissertation, *Un especificação moral de los Actos Humanos Segundo San Tomás de Aquino* [Rome: Edizioni Università della Santa Croce, 2008].

68. Duarte Sousa-Lara, "'Intentio' and 'Electio' in Aquinas." See also Duerte Sousa-Lara, "Aquinas on Interior and Exterior Acts: Clarifying a Key Aspect of His Action Theory," *Josephinum Journal of Theology* 15 (2008): 277–316.

69. Aquinas, *Super Sent.*, libro. 2, d. 40, q. 1, a. 5, ad 5: "Impossibile est quod finis ad quem ordinatur actio ex deliberatione, sit indifferens," my translation.

70. See Sousa-Lara, "'Intentio' and 'Electio' in Aquinas," 3.

71. See Aquinas, *Summa Theologiae*, I-II, q. 7, a. 1, c. Not all "accidents" that occur around a moral action are automatically "circumstances." In this sense, the circumstances have a direct relationship with moral action in the sense that they morally qualify the action without putting it in a different category of moral action.

72. See Aquinas, *De Malo*, q. 2, a. 6, c.

73. See Aquinas, *Summa Theologiae*, I-II, q. 7, a. 3, c, my emphasis.

74. D. Sousa-Lara, "'Circumstantia' and 'Conditiones' in Aquinas," *Etica e Politica*, www.eticaepolitica.net, 12, my translation. (This essay was originally in chapter 9 of his dissertation, cited above).

75. Aquinas, *Summa Theologiae*, I-II, q. 7, a. 3, ad 3.

TWENTY   Revisiting the Limits of Freedom of Expression

1. See Alfonso Aguiló, *Libertad y tolerancia en una sociedad plural: El arte de convivir* (Madrid: Palabra, 2011), 111.

2. See Alasdair MacIntyre, *After Virtue* (Notre Dame, IN: University of Notre Dame Press, 1981), 125–28.

3. This idea is developed in the chapter dedicated to tolerance.

4. Campbell Markham, "Areopagitica in Tasmania," *Mercatornet*, September 29, 2016, https://www.mercatornet.com/features/view/ areopagitica-tasmania /18746.

5. The term "public order" is the set of established legal and regulatory conditions that, respecting constitutional principles and fundamental rights, determine the minimum rules for coexistence in the public space. In Anglo-Saxon culture there is the notion of a "breach of the peace," that it is not just a concern for preserving tranquility but an act or a threat to be carried out that harms a person or his property. "The concept involves a fairly immediate (imminent) outbreak of violence directed at persons or property." See Peter Cane and Joanne Conaghan, eds., *The New Oxford Companion to Law* (Oxford: Oxford University Press, 2008), 278.

There is no single and specific definition of "public morality," but its doctrine can be found in Christopher Wolfe, "Public Morality and the Modern Supreme Court," *American Journal of Jurisprudence* 45, no. 1 (2000): 65, and Robert P. George, "The Concept of Public Morality," *American Journal of Jurisprudence* 45, no. 1 (2000): 17. And, from a different perspective: Peter M. Cicchino, "Reason and the Rule of Law: Should Bare Assertions of 'Public Morality' Qualify as Legitimate Government Interests for the Purposes of Equal Protection Review?," *Georgetown Law Journal* 87, no. 1 (1998): 139.

6. Cane and Conaghan, *The New Oxford Companion to Law*, 279.

7. Ibid.

8. Ibid.

9. William Blackstone, *Commentaries on the Laws of England, 1765–1769* (Chicago: University of Chicago Press, 1979), vol. IV, 162.

10. Louis Henkin, "Morals and the Constitution: The Sin of Obscenity," *Columbia Law Review* 63, no. 391 (1963): 403.

11. Ibid., 404.

12. Wolfe, "Public Morality and the Modern Supreme Court," 71.

13. Santiago Legarre, "Ensayo de delimitación del concepto de Moral Pública," *Revista Chilena de Derecho* 1, no. 3 (2004): 174, my translation.

14. For a deeper examination of the argument, see these cases: *Griswold v. Connecticut*, 381 US 479 (1965) and *Stanley v. Georgia*, 394 US 557 (1969). In these the Supreme Court declared state legislation of public obscenity unconstitutional.

15. In the case *Barnes v. Glen Theatre*, 501 US 568, 569 (1991), the Court said: "It is clear from the statute's text and history that the law's purpose is to protect 'societal order and morality.'... [This law was designed for] protecting societal order and morality."

16. Carlos L. Valiente Noailles, *La moral pública y las garantías constitucionales* (Buenos Aires: La Ley, 1966), 52, my translation.

17. See Santiago Legarre, "Ensayo de delimitación del concepto de Moral Pública," *Revista Chilena de Derecho* 1, no. 3 (2004): 177.

18. The immorality of the prohibited act is a necessary but not sufficient condition of the legitimacy of its prohibition. "Wherefore human laws do not forbid all vices, from which the virtuous abstain, but only the more grievous vices, from which it is possible for the majority to abstain." See Thomas Aquinas, *Summa Theologiae* I-II, q. 96, a. 2c, in *Summa Theologiae*, trans. Fr. Laurence Shapcote, vol. 16 (Lander, WY: Aquinas Institute for the Study of Sacred Doctrine, 2012), 399.

19. Blackstone, *Commentaries on the Laws of England, 1765–1769*, vol. I, 119–20, my emphasis.

20. Legarre, "Ensayo de delimitación del concepto de Moral Pública," 181, my translation.

21. See the case of the Nazi demonstration in Skokie, a Chicago neighborhood inhabited primarily by Jewish Holocaust survivors, or the burning of a cross in front of the house of a Christian African American family by the Ku Klux Klan.

22. Catharine MacKinnon and Ronald Dworkin have abundant literature on the causal relation between pornography and inequality. The woman is characterized in pornographic terms by her feminine condition. This debate has posed an important question for the individualist approach, especially since the 1930s, which inspired the first free speech theory in the United States. The First Amend-

ment does not permit the prevention of insults to groups (group libel, as it is thought of in Europe). The following share this position: Jeremy Waldron, *The Harm in Hate Speech* (Cambridge, MA: Harvard University Press, 2012); Robert C. Post, *Constitutional Domains: Democracy, Community, Management* (Cambridge, MA: Harvard University Press, 1995), 89–116. And see the works of Catharine A. MacKinnon, *Only Words* (1993) and *Feminism Unmodified: Discourses on Life and Law* (1987), and Ronald Dworkin, *Sovereign Virtue: The Theory and Practice of Equality* (2000); *Pornography: Men Possessing Women* (1981); and "Against the Male Flood: Censorship, Pornography, and Equality" (1985).

23. See, for example: Holly Yan, Sheena Jones, and Steve Almasy, "Chicago Torture Video: 4 Charged with Hate Crimes, Kidnapping," CNN, January 5, 2017, http://www.cnn.com/2017/01/05/us/chicago-facebook-live-beating/.

24. See Jack M. Balkin and Jonathan Zittrain, "A Grand Bargain to Make Tech Companies Trustworthy," *Atlantic*, October 3, 2016, https://www.theatlantic .com/technology/archive/2016/10/information-fiduciary/502346/.

25. European Commission, "Tackling Online Disinformation," September 13, 2019, https://ec.europa.eu/digital-single-market/en/tackling-online-disinformation.

26. See Waldron, *The Harm in Hate Speech*, 101, 103–4.

27. See Charles Taylor, *Hegel and Modern Society* (Cambridge, MA: Cambridge University Press, 1979), 82–85. Other authors identify human dignity as a basic element. See Steven J. Heyman, *Free Speech and Human Dignity* (New Haven, CT: Yale University Press, 2008), chaps. 3 and 6; Waldron, *The Harm in Hate Speech*, 105ff.

28. President of France, et al., Decree n° 2015–125, February 6, 2015, https:// www.legifrance.gouv.fr/affichTexte.do?cidTexte=JORFTEXT000030195477& dateTexte=&categorieLien=id.

29. See Waldron, *The Harm in Hate Speech*, 95.

30. According to Kate Coyer, a member of the Berkman Center for Internet and Society at Harvard University: "The high fines for not taking down illegal content quickly enough give companies an incentive to rather remove content than not—since there are no fines if they wrongly determine to remove content." See Davey Alba, "Germany's Flawed Plan to Fight Hate Speech by Fining Tech Giants Millions," *Wired*, March 18, 2017, https://www.wired.com/2017/03/tech-giants -cant-bear-weight-battling-online-hate/.

31. Madison, in *Federalist Papers* no. 10, uses "faction" to refer to a group of citizens motivated by passion and by a particular interest against other citizens. See Alexander Hamilton, et al., *Federalist Papers*, 49. This topic is discussed in the second section of chapter 2.

32. See Waldron, *The Harm in Hate Speech*, 8–9, 30.

33. In many EU countries (including Denmark, Norway, Germany, and France), defamation and public insult against groups and minorities on the basis

of race, ethnicity, color, origin, religion, or sexual orientation is prohibited. See Waldron, *The Harm in Hate Speech*, 29, 39–40.

34. See ibid., 33.

35. See ibid., 38–39.

36. It is important to proceed to these two levels. On the first, one must recognize a common sense of justice (*diké*), that is, a universal accepted order that does not change and is valid for all times and peoples. This is the basis for later asserting, on a second level, the rights and duties that originate from interpersonal relationships. As Benedict XVI recalled, "This intuition was expressed as early as the fifth century by Augustine of Hippo, one of the masters of our intellectual heritage. He taught that the saying: Do not do to others what you would not want done to you 'cannot in any way vary according to the different understandings that have arisen in the world' (*De Doctrina Christiana*, III, 14). Human rights, then, must be respected as an expression of justice, and not merely because they are enforceable through the will of the legislators." Benedict XVI, "Address to the Members of the General Assembly of the United Nations Organization," New York, April 18, 2008, Vatican website, https://www.vatican.va/content/benedict-xvi/en/speeches/2008/april/documents/hf_ben-xvi_spe_20080418_un-visit.html.

37. Michel Villey, *Filosofía del Derecho* (Barcelona: Scire Universitaria, 2003), 96, my translation.

38. See ibid., 66.

39. See Juan Iglesias, *Derecho Romano, Instituciones de Derecho Privado* (Barcelona: Ariel, 1965), 75–76.

40. See Rodolfo Vigo, *El iusnaturalismo actual: De M. Villey a Finnis* (Mexico DF: Biblioteca de ética, filosofía del derecho y política, 2003), 46.

41. See Post, *Constitutional Domains*, 64–65.

42. The author clarifies that these norms of citizenship must be few, must be institutionalized in a dual sense (socially but also in being compatible with the functioning of the legal system), and must assume a heterogeneity (geographic and temporal) that makes them changeable. See Post, *Constitutional Domains*, 65–67.

43. Various authors, of whom we have been providing references, have expressed it in this sense. See Post, *Constitutional Domains*, 89–116; Villey, *Filosofía del Derecho*; Martin Kriele, *Liberación e Ilustración* (Barcelona: Herder, 1982); John Finnis, *Human Rights and Common Good* (Oxford: Oxford University Press, 2011); Benedict XVI, "Address to the Members of the General Assembly of the United Nations Organization."

44. See Hannah Arendt, *The Human Condition* (Chicago: University of Chicago Press, 1958), 296.

45. Ibid.

46. Ibid., 297.

47. Ronald C. Arnett, *Communication in Dark Times: Hanna Arendt's Rhetoric of Warning and Hope* (Carbondale: Southern Illinois University Press, 2013), 169.

48. Hannah Arendt, *The Human Condition* (Chicago: University of Chicago Press, 1998), 300, emphasis in original.

49. Ibid., 301.

50. Cane and Conaghan, *Oxford Companion to Law*, 26–28.

51. Ibid., 27.

52. Ibid.

53. See Rafael Domingo, *The New Global Law* (New York: Cambridge University Press, 2010), 111–12.

54. See Álvaro D'Ors, "El arbitraje jurídico," in *Parerga Historica* (Pamplona: EUNSA, 1991), 271–91.

55. The Arbitration Laws in Spain are Ley 361/1988 of December 5, 1988 and Ley 60/2003 of December 23, 2003.

56. See MacIntyre, *After Virtue*, 179–80.

57. See ibid., 128–29.

58. See ibid., 128.

59. See ibid., 129.

60. See Joseph Ratzinger, *Church, Ecumenism and Politics* (New York: Crossroad, 1988), 210.

61. This argument of Ratzinger is connected to the Protestant conception of freedom advanced earlier in Part II.

62. Aleksandr Solzhenitsyn, "A World Split Apart" (cited as "Harvard Address"), in *The Solzhenitsyn Reader: New and Essential Writings, 1947–2005* (Wilmington, DE: ISI Books, 2006), 565ff.

63. Alexander Solzhenitsyn, "We Have Ceased to See the Purpose: Address to the International Academy of Philosophy," in *The Solzhenitsyn Reader: New and Essential Writings, 1947–2005*, edited by Edward E. Ericson and Daniel J. Mahoney (Wilmington, DE: ISI Books, 2006), 598–99.

64. Ibid., 599.

65. See Post, *Constitutional Domains*, 2, 15–16, 180–96, 234–67, 269–89, 329–30.

66. This concept is advanced by the author in ibid., 138–39, 151.

67. According to the First Amendment, the criterion that speech is scandalous or outrageous cannot be used to limit it, based on the principle of the neutrality of ideas in the public sphere, but this distinction does not take into account the structures of community life and the norms that define its identity. See Post, *Constitutional Domains*, 139, 151. The reader should see the description of communitarianism's contribution to FST in chapter 3.

68. See Jonah E. Bromwich, "Subway Riders Scrub Anti-Semitic Graffiti, as 'Decent Human Beings,'" *New York Times*, February 5, 2017, https://www.ny times.com/2017/02/05/nyregion/swastika-nyc-subways.html?smid=tw-share. In social networks, some libertarian groups criticized this citizen reaction, calling it intolerant.

69. See MacIntyre, "Intolerance, Censorship, and Other Requirements of Rationality," University of Notre Dame, 2009, 14. The lecture was never published. The author kindly authorized me to cite the manuscript (February of 2017). The references made correspond to the numbering in the author's manuscript.

70. Ibid.

71. In a letter to the S episcopate in March of 1958, Pius XII wrote: "The word 'censorship' sounds like a provocation today, and it often lends itself to error and engenders controversy by provoking those who reject any legal or moral break to freedom of expression. It lends itself to error because the problems that it poses are hardly treated with objectivity." He went on to say: "On the moral level, the Church can and does exercise what is called 'censorship' because it is a right that belongs to her by virtue of the mandate she received to teach morality and preserve the divine truth. The consequences that can affect the faithful are only spiritual and moral." Pascual Cebollada, *Del Genesis a Internet: Documentos del Magisterio sobre las comunicaciones sociales* (Madrid: BAC, 2005), 298–99, my translation.

72. See MacIntyre, "Intolerance, Censorship, and Other Requirements of Rationality," 15. To MacIntyre, it seems like a superficial generalization to describe the censorship exercised with the Index as a "tragedy." The negative effects of this censorship were, as will be noted below, the consequence of a system that arose with a righteous sense and would become, in the last decades of its operation, a bad solution to the problems that it was intended to address. See MacIntyre, "Intolerance, Censorship, and Other Requirements of Rationality," 17.

73. See Paul VI, *Integrae servandae*, apostolic letter, December 7, 1965, Vatican website, http://w2.vatican.va/content/paul-vi/en/motu_proprio/documents/hf_p-vi_motu-proprio_19651207_integrae-servandae.html.

74. The Congregation for the Doctrine of the Faith commissioned by Pope Paul VI published a document in which the Pope declared that "the Index remains morally binding, in light of the demands of natural law, in so far as it admonishes the conscience of Christians to be on guard for those writings that can endanger faith and morals. But, at the same time, it no longer has the force of ecclesiastical law with the attached censure." Congregation for the Doctrine of the Faith, *Notification Regarding the Abolition of the Index of Books*, June 14, 1966, Vatican website, http://www.vatican.va/roman_curia/congregations/cfaith/documents/rc_con_cfaith_doc_19660614_de-indicis-libr-prohib_en.html.

75. A good teacher knows to say, "Read this" or "Do not read that," "Read this now," but "Don't read that yet." Giving such advice is an act of prevention (and censorship) that serves the good of acquiring the criteria for "reading well" because the books that subjects read must be consistent with their abilities and levels of spiritual growth. See MacIntyre, "Intolerance, Censorship, and Other Requirements of Rationality," 14.

76. See ibid., 15.

77. See ibid., 16.

78. According to MacIntyre, this occurred with Catholic philosophy and theology between 1700 and 1850.

79. MacIntyre, "Intolerance, Censorship, and Other Requirements of Rationality," 18.

80. See John Durham Peters, *Courting the Abyss: Free Speech and the Liberal Tradition* (Chicago: University of Chicago Press, 2005), 14, 54–58.

81. MacIntyre, "Intolerance, Censorship, and Other Requirements of Rationality," 18.

82. See ibid., 20.

83. Cane and Conaghan, *Oxford Companion to Law*, 1214.

84. See MacIntyre, "Intolerance, Censorship, and Other Requirements of Rationality," 5, 7.

85. In 2006, the laws in Canada were very similar to those in the United States, but in 2017 several laws against hate speech had been passed, following a more European trend.

86. The director of *Guardian* considered it a very abusive act: "Freedom of expression as it has developed in the democratic west is a value to be cherished, but not abused." See "Insults and Injuries," *Guardian*, February 4, 2006, http://www.guardian.co.uk/ leaders/story/0,1701921,00.html. The director of the *Boston Globe* described publishing the cartoons as an act of intolerance: "Depicting Mohammed wearing a turban in the form of a bomb with a sputtering fuse is no less hurtful to most Muslims than Nazi caricatures of Jews or Ku Klux Klan caricatures of blacks are to those victims of intolerance. That is why the Danish cartoons will not be reproduced on these pages." See "Forms of Intolerance," *Boston Globe*, February 4, 2006, http://www.boston.com/news/globe/editorial_opinion/editorials /articles/2006/02/04/forms_of_intolerance/.

87. "Father Raymond J. de Souza: What Is Free Speech For?," *National Post*, January 27, 2015, https://nationalpost.com/opinion/father-raymond-j-de-souza -what-is-free-speech-for.

INDEX

JORDI PUJOL

is an associate professor of media ethics and media law

at the School of Church Communications in

the Pontifical University of Santa Croce in Rome.

JOHN DURHAM PETERS

is the Maria Rosa Menocal Professor of English and

of Film and Media Studies at Yale University.